CLEAN POWER POLITICS

The United States has been experiencing an energy transition for over four decades, and now as a result of various economic and political events discussed in this book, a clean energy future is moving closer to reality. In *Clean Power Politics*, Joseph Tomain describes how clean energy policies have been developed and, more importantly, what's necessary for a successful transition to a clean energy future, including technological innovation, new business models, and regulatory reforms. The energy system of the future will minimize the environmental costs of traditional energy production and consumption, and emphasize expanded use of natural resources and energy efficiency. Because many new energy technologies can be produced and consumed at smaller scales, they will shift decision-making power away from traditional utilities and empower consumers to make energy choices about consumption and price. In this way, a clean energy future embodies a democratization of energy.

Joseph P. Tomain has been teaching and writing in the field of energy law since 1977. He has published numerous articles, essays, casebooks, treatises, and monographs on energy law and has delivered papers at conferences throughout the US and Europe. Tomain is actively involved with energy organizations, including the Center for Progressive Reform and the PUC Collaborative.

Clean Power Politics

THE DEMOCRATIZATION OF ENERGY

JOSEPH P. TOMAIN

CAMBRIDGE
UNIVERSITY PRESS

CAMBRIDGE
UNIVERSITY PRESS

University Printing House, Cambridge CB2 8BS, United Kingdom

One Liberty Plaza, 20th Floor, New York, NY 10006, USA

477 Williamstown Road, Port Melbourne, VIC 3207, Australia

4843/24, 2nd Floor, Ansari Road, Daryaganj, Delhi – 110002, India

79 Anson Road, #06–04/06, Singapore 079906

Cambridge University Press is part of the University of Cambridge.

It furthers the University's mission by disseminating knowledge in the pursuit of education, learning, and research at the highest international levels of excellence.

www.cambridge.org
Information on this title: www.cambridge.org/9781107039179
DOI: 10.1017/9781139856539

First published 2017

Printed in the United States of America by Sheridan Books, Inc.

A catalogue record for this publication is available from the British Library.

ISBN 978-1-107-03917-9 Hardback
ISBN 978-1-316-64213-9 Paperback

Jessi and John
Susie and Joe

Contents

Abbreviations

AR5	United Nation's Intergovernmental Panel on Climate Change Fifth Assessment Report entitled *Climate Change 2014: Impacts, Adaptation and Vulnerability*
ARPA-E	Advanced Research Projects Agency-Energy
ARRA	American Recovery and Reinvestment Act of 2009
BAU	Business as usual
BSER	Best system of emissions reduction
CAA	Clean Air Act, 42 U.S.C. §7401 et seq.
CAP	Climate Action Plan
CCPI	Clean Coal Power Initiative
CCS	Carbon capture and storage
CEIP	Clean energy incentive program
CES	Clean energy standards
CMI	Critical Materials Institute
COS	Cost of service
CPP	Clean Power Plan
DARPA	Defense Advanced Research Projects Agency
DER	Distributed energy resources
DG	Distributed generation
DOE	US Department of Energy
DSM	Demand-side management
DSP	Distributed Service Provider
EES	Energy efficiency standards
EFC	Energy Future Coalition
EFRC	Energy Frontier Research Center
EGUs	Electric generating units
EIA	Energy Information Administration

EISA	Energy Independence and Security Act of 2007 Pub. L. No. 110–140 (2007)
EPA	US Environmental Protection Agency
EPAct 1992	Energy Policy Act of 1992 (EPAct 1992) Pub. L. No.102–486 (1992)
EPAct 2005	Energy Policy Act of 2005 Pub. L. No. 109–58 (2005)
ERCs	Emission rate credits
ERO	Electric reliability organization
ESA	Energy Security Act, Pub. L. No. 96–294 (1980)
EVs	Electric vehicles
FERC	Federal Energy Regulatory Commission
GW	Gigawatt (1 billion watts or 100 megawatts)
ICT	Information and communications technologies
IEA	International Energy Agency
IOUs	Investor-owned utilities
IPCC	International Panel on Climate Change
IRA	Integrated Resource Analysis
IRP	Integrated Resource Plan
ISO	Independent system operator
IT	Information and technology
JCAP	Joint Center for Artificial Photosynthesis
JCESR	Joint Center for Energy Storage Research
LCOE	Levelized cost of electricity or energy
Mbd	Millions of barrels per day
NERC	North American Electric Reliability Council
NGCC	Natural gas combined cycle
NIMBY	Not-in-my-backyard
NRC	Nuclear Regulatory Commission
PCAST	President's Council of Advisors on Science and Technology
PE	Private equity
PPPL	Princeton Plasma Physics Laboratory
PSC	New York Public Service Commission
PUCs	State public utility commissions
PURPA	Public Utilities Regulatory Policy Act, 16 U.S.C. §2601 et seq.
QFs	Qualifying facilities
R&D	Research and development
RE	Renewable electricity
RFS	Renewable fuel standard
RIA	Regulatory impact analysis
RPS	Renewable portfolio standards

RTO	Regional transmission organization
SCC	Social cost of carbon
Tcf	Trillion cubic feet
T&D	Transmission and distribution
VC	Venture capital
VOCs	Volatile organic compounds

Introduction

On December 12, 2015, meeting in Paris under the auspices of the UN Framework Convention on Climate Change, 195 nations signed what has been hailed as an historic climate agreement.[1] The agreement was recognized as a "turning point, that this is the moment we finally determined we would save our planet" and that the assembled nations "share a sense of urgency about this challenge and a growing realization that it is within our power to do something about it."[2] The signatories pledged to reduce carbon emissions with the intent of keeping global warming below 2°C while pursuing the more ambitious target of limiting temperature increases to 1.5°C from preindustrial levels. Although the short 11-page agreement does not set legally binding emissions limits, the parties committed themselves to a regime that requires them to report on the progress of their commitments every five years beginning in 2020.[3]

The technical, economic, and political complexities of climate change meant that the conference would not, by itself, solve climate change problems and the agreement was not cheered by everyone.[4] Of most concern was the fact that even if every country's pledge to reduce greenhouse emissions is honored and implemented, they would not be sufficient to reach the climate goals set by the convention.[5] There are, though, significant upsides to the agreement even if it fails to solve the problems of a warming Earth.

First, the United States is taking a leadership role on the global climate stage.[6] We are now in the international arena as a country committed to addressing the challenges posed by climate change. Although the United States has stepped forward in the past, its voice has been notably absent in recent years. Next, US leadership on the international front is supported by its domestic energy initiatives directed at climate challenges. US energy policy can no longer operate independently of and unconnected to climate change. Finally, while it is true that there are large pockets of skepticism about global warming, particularly in US party politics,[7] it is also true that the majority of people both in the United States and in the world recognize the need for action as the Paris climate talks bring attention to this increasingly serious global problem. There is, then, coalescence and awareness of the international dimensions of climate change, the need for domestic commitments to address it, and a growing public concern about the importance of acting now.

Most relevant to this book, the Paris conference emphasized the need for continued investment in energy/environmental innovations. Indeed, of central concern to the success of the Paris talks was the necessity for financial commitments to address both adaptation and mitigation measures. Those financial commitments were based on the recognition that industry participation and further public–private investments were necessary.[8] Significantly, a group of more than 20 billionaires announced the formation of a multibillion dollar fund named the Breakthrough Energy Coalition[9] to create a new, clean energy mix for the future. The Breakthrough Coalition will work together with a group of countries through a project known as the Mission Initiative to accelerate the clean energy revolution.[10] More importantly, the need for investments in clean power is now being recognized in the marketplace as financial institutions such as Goldman Sachs, Citi, and Bank of America also announce multibillion dollar investment commitments[11] in a clean energy market that is currently estimated to be worth more than one-half trillion dollars.[12] The value and necessity of innovation and investment is the central theme of this book. More particularly, innovation and investment must take place along three dimensions – in technologies and new markets, in business practices, and in the regulations that monitor both the energy and the environmental sectors of our economy.

Clean Power Politics is a book about political ideas as much is it is a book about energy policy. The politics of clean power is three-dimensional. At the ground level, partisan politics occupies the contemporary discussion of clean power initiatives and that partisanship has given rise to the current litigation fighting the president's energy agenda. Next, politics moves from the local and partisan level to an examination of the political economy of clean power and energy more generally. Finally, and most broadly, the book discusses the politics of clean power and the direction of US energy policy in terms of democratic theory.

Given the magnitude and complexity of climate change and the interactions of that phenomenon with a century-old energy paradigm, the matter of politics is inescapable. It is also inescapable that our country, as well as the world, is experiencing an energy transition away from a dirty fossil fuel economy to a cleaner economy utilizing increasing amounts of renewable resources and energy efficiency. The shift away from fossil fuels to cleaner ones has been under way for decades now. Until recently, the transition has been moving slowly because of barriers erected by incumbent energy firms and their regulators for over a century. Nevertheless, those barriers and resistance to change must be traduced to make the clean power transition occur more swiftly and more efficiently. In order to accomplish a more aggressive approach to clean power, a new political narrative is necessary. *Clean Power Politics* describes and contributes to that new narrative in terms of the democratization of energy.

The core political idea that our energy politics and policy must become more democratic is also an idea that is central to our political economy – our energy economy must become more competitive. More competition, in turn, means a greater variety of energy resources, producers, and markets as well as expanded choices for consumers. For too long, US energy policy has been narrowly focused and limited to a handful of energy resources, and shaped by a narrow corporate and industrial structure once called the "hard path" by Amory Lovins. This narrow structure contributed to a fossil fuel economy dominated by a limited number of producers and by passive consumers.

For the sake of argument, it can be conceded that the traditional hard path energy policy contributed to US power and its economy for most of the twentieth century. It must also be conceded that most energy policies focus on short-term economic gains while ignoring long-term environmental and social costs. The recently announced investigation of Exxon Mobil's years-long concealment of information about the damaging effects of carbon emissions underscores the short-term nature of energy policy.[13] Generating short-term private gain and imposing long-term social costs is not a new phenomenon; however, it is a dispiriting one.

In a prior book, *Ending Dirty Energy Policy*, I argued that a clean energy transition is a good policy option, at least in part, because traditional dirty energy policy is no longer consistent with the energy policy principles that have been developing for decades. I also argued that since the energy crises of the 1970s, energy policy studies have been moving toward a clean power transition and eventually began supporting it through specific policy recommendations. Importantly, those energy studies increasingly recognized the environmental consequences of the energy fuel cycle.

There is a natural physical connection between the exploration, processing, transportation, consumption, and disposal of the natural resources that we use to produce energy and the environment. At every stage of the energy fuel cycle negative environmental consequences follow. The energy studies supporting a clean power future recognize the inextricable link between energy and the environment. This book, then, is a broad and sustained argument that the United States is and should make the transition to a clean power economy. And, more importantly, energy and the environment should be conceived of and treated as a whole. They should not be considered and regulated independently of each other. Suffice it to say here that neither our environmental nor energy futures will progress much if that separation is maintained.

In the late 1960s and early 1970s, the environmental movement became part of our social consciousness. At that time, concerns about the environment were not perceived as being related to energy policy in any sharply defined way. Then, the 1970s energy crises focused the country on its growing need for energy independence particularly from Middle Eastern oil. Also during that period, the country experienced dislocations in energy markets. The natural gas market was destabilized and shortages resulted; the electric industry hit a technological plateau as electricity prices begin to rise even to the point of consumers worrying about "rate shock"; and the expansion of commercial nuclear power came to a standstill. The reverberations from all of these energy events continued through the last decades of the twentieth century as energy policymakers and regulators concentrated on energy independence while deemphasizing the environmental consequences of energy production and consumption.

By the first decade of the twenty-first century, it was clear that our energy policy was more complex than we once assumed. At one time, the hardcore belief was that more energy production and consumption would result in greater economic growth. That assumption began to be questioned as policymakers started to concentrate on environmental needs, economic gains from energy efficiency, and the availability of renewable energy resources as ways of decreasing oil imports and increasing energy independence. Where nineteenth- and twentieth-century energy policy was grounded in the assumption of a direct and positive correlation between energy and economic growth, twenty-first-century energy policy became grounded in need for energy and economic security together with the need for environmental sensitivity.

Evolving energy policy principles have contributed to a major energy transition from a fossil fuel economy to a clean energy future. Although states have been involved with the clean transition for decades now, the Obama administration's energy and environmental regulations put the federal government at the front and center of this transition. More importantly, it does so by aligning energy and environmental regulation in ways that have not occurred before and in ways that are necessary for the transition to be successful. While the coordination of energy and the environment is a necessary element of the transition, it brings with it political and policy complications to the evolving energy/environmental policy landscape. Still, the clean energy transition has only become more important as markets for clean energy products and services expand with the help of a new regulatory apparatus. *Clean Power Politics* explains these developments in three parts.

Part I discusses the preconditions needed for a successful clean power transition. For too long, the federal government has largely been absent from climate change initiatives. In the past, clean air regulations did address greenhouse gas emissions but did not do so comprehensively. In June 2014, the Obama administration issued a proposed rule directed specifically at fossil fuel, most notable coal, generating power plants. Known as the Clean Power Plan (CPP), the rule was finalized in 2015 and is now being implemented as well as challenged. With the election of Donald Trump to the U. S presidency, it is likely that the CPP will not survive. Nevertheless, the regulation is instructive about a sound future energy policy. The objective of the rule is to reduce greenhouse gas emissions, particularly carbon dioxide, by 32 percent below 2005 levels. As explained in Chapter 1, the CPP can be a significant advance for federal leadership both domestically and globally. Importantly, the CPP has been issued by the Environmental Protection Agency rather than from a federal energy agency, thus emphasizing the need to merge energy and environmental policies and regulations.

The second precondition for a transition to a clean power economy is to more precisely identify those energy resources that can assist the transition and distinguish them from those resources that perpetuate the traditional energy policy that relies on large-scale, capital-intensive centralized energy producers and relies upon dirty fossil fuels. Traditional energy policy is no longer consistent with current environmental needs; nor is it any longer consistent with the contemporary energy policy. In Chapter 2, clean power resources are defined and metrics for assessing progress on an energy transition are discussed.

The third precondition for the clean power transition is to understand the economic and political contexts in which the transition is being conducted. At its core, because of its significance as an economic input, energy is a crucial element of any nation's political economy. Today, in the United States, as well as other developed nations including China, clean energy resources are becoming an increasingly important part of an energy portfolio. Chapter 3 explains how a clean power future is shaped by and will continue to shape our political economy.

Once the preconditions for an energy transition have been specified, Part II explains how the transition will occur by first focusing on the necessity of innovation. Innovation is discussed in three contexts. First, Chapter 4 describes the energy innovation process, the necessity of government financial and other support, and the central importance that markets will play in adopting clean energy technologies. Next, Chapter 5 discusses the business innovations that traditional electric utilities must adopt in order to contribute to that transition. Finally, Chapter 6 explains the necessary role for innovative government regulation in the energy sector to complement new technologies and new business practices.

Historically, energy industries and regulators worked from the same script. Both operated with a single goal in mind. Most simply, energy businesses and their regulators promoted the production and consumption of energy. Because of gains to be made from energy conservation and energy efficiency, the direct and positive correlation between energy and the economy no longer holds. All consumers can continue to rely on the availability of energy, continue to live and operate their businesses as before, and, at the same time, pay less for that energy. Our previous belief in the need for continued expansion of energy production must give way to a smarter and more efficient use of energy. Energy firms and their regulators must recognize that the traditional energy paradigm has shifted away from dirty fuels to cleaner fuels and to increased efficiencies and reduced energy consumption.

The book closes with Part III, which explains the transition to a clean power future. Together with innovations in technology, business practices, and regulations, a new political narrative about energy and the environment is revealed. In brief, that new politics is more democratic in two ways. First, energy markets are becoming more competitive. Incumbent energy firms that have long grown accustomed to government regulatory financial support now recognize and accept the fact that they must participate in a more competitive sector with a variety of new entrants. These new entrants provide a greater array of energy services and products at a smaller scale, at more localized sites, and will sell efficiency as well as energy.

Second, not only decision-making power over the energy future will shift away from large-scale incumbents to smaller new entrants but also decision-making power will shift to consumers themselves. Consumers of the future will enjoy more energy choices than they have had in the past and they will have greater control about their energy budgets and they will play a more significant role in energy planning and in the administration of energy regulations. Increasing energy market competition, the expansion of choices available to consumers, and the development of new energy resources and products are all part of the democratization of energy.

PART I

PRECONDITIONS FOR A CLEAN POWER TRANSITION

1

The Clean Power Plan and Clean Power Politics

The most dramatic event in US energy policy, or, as President Obama has called it, "the biggest, most important step we've ever taken to combat climate change,"[1] has begun to unfold. Curiously, perhaps, the event has been initiated not by the Department of Energy but by the Environmental Protection Agency (EPA). On June 14, 2014, the EPA publicized proposed rules under the Clean Power Plan (CPP). A little over a year later, on October 23, 2015, final rules were published in the Federal Register.[2] The rules are complex; they are directed to reducing emissions from existing electric power plants, particularly coal-fired facilities; and they cover the entire country. The scope of the CPP is broad, its provisions are many, and the legal challenges are substantial.[3]

Of most immediate concern is that the CPP is now in legal limbo and political jeopardy with the election of Donald Trump who vowed during the campaign to repeal it. And, with Republican majorities in both houses of Congress and a likely Republican Supreme Court, the CPP is unlikely to survive even if it does prevail in courts. On February 9, 2016, the US Supreme Court issued an order to the EPA that its CPP rules could not go forward; in legalese, those regulations were "stayed." The order was a 5–4 decision that included Justice Scalia in the majority one week before he passed away, leaving his seat on the Court vacant. Most notably, the order staying a government agency from doing its job was unprecedented. At no time in its history had the Court stopped an agency from carrying out its constitutional obligations while litigation was pending.

To be sure the CPP has its defenders as well as its detractors and the plan is subject to ongoing litigation as arguments about its legality were heard on September 27, 2016, in the US Court of Appeals for the District of Columbia Circuit. Those arguments took place; however as we wait for a decision in the case, this highly unusual action by the Supreme Court signals their view of the merits of the case before the Justices have the benefit of the lower court's ruling and before they either grant or deny a petition for the case to be heard in their own Court.

The Scalia vacancy and the Trump election now make predictions about what the Court will do regarding the CPP uncertain since the Court now seems to be divided on the merits of the case 4–4. Such a tie vote ordinarily means that any lower court opinion will be the law. However, the Court's stay order was unusual in another respect because the last line read: "If a writ of certiorari is sought and the Court denies the petition, this order shall terminate automatically. If the Court grants the petition for a writ of certiorari, this order shall terminate when the Court enters its judgment."[4] In other words, if this order remains in effect, then regardless of what the lower court rules, the CPP remains stayed until the Supreme Court itself decides to accept or reject any appeal.

Regardless of the legal or political outcome, the significance of these rules for a successful transition to a clean power economy must be underscored. Even with the expected demise of the CPP, a discussion of the regulations is important for understanding the possible role of the federal government in shaping a clean energy future. Simply from the fact that the EPA rather than the Department of Energy (DOE) issued the CPP, federal energy policy is now directly connected to environmental goals in unprecedented ways. Going forward, future energy policy must recognize the environmental consequences of the fuel cycle, especially the harmful pollutants emitted during their burning and then disposal. Future energy policy must also recognize that renewable resources and energy efficiency will be essential elements in the country's energy mix.

The linkage between energy and the environment may well be the most lasting legacy of the CPP. Yet, the significance of these rules goes beyond connecting energy and the environment. The CPP can change the US energy paradigm and, with it, the US energy economy in two notable ways. First, the CPP signals a transition away from the traditional fossil fuel energy economy in the United States to a clean power economy. Second, the CPP recognizes that the basic assumption of traditional energy policy – that there is a direct and positive correlation between energy production and consumption and economic growth – is no longer operative for a developed country like the United States. The United States' energy economy, the industries that sustain it and the consumers that use it, can prosper with less energy consumption per capita rather than with ever-increasing energy production. In fact, the United States has been experiencing increases in energy efficiency for decades now as we consume less energy for each dollar of gross domestic product that is spent.[5]

The most significant aspect of the CPP is the federal recognition that not only has the country been experiencing a transition to a clean power economy but that transition must be accelerated and can be done economically with cleaner energy resources. The energy transition can increase productivity by adopting efficiency measures, financing renewable energy, developing alternative fuels and vehicles, and encouraging utilities and their regulators to adapt to new business realities.[6] This book is a study of how technological innovations, emerging energy markets, and complementary regulations can encourage and support the transition to a clean power future. Even if, as is most likely, the CPP is a noble, but failed, experiment, its lessons for the energy future remain true.

To start, this chapter discusses the structure and operations of the CPP and addresses the primary criticisms of the CPP and the responses to it, to understand the potential benefits and pitfalls of clean power regulations. The CPP becomes the vehicle to explore the associated and complementary issues that will be developed throughout the book. *Clean Power Politics* argues that we must transition away from the old energy paradigm of fossil fuels and nuclear power to a cleaner energy economy. We must aggressively pursue a clean future rather than fall back and rely on traditional fossil resources, even as the country increases its domestic development of oil and natural gas, for two reasons. First, if we continue to subsidize fossil fuels and nuclear power, then the clean power transition will occur more slowly than is economically desirable. Second, and complementarily, continuing to support a traditional fossil fuel policy is environmentally costly and is not in our economic best interests.[7] The book also argues that with or without federal leadership, the U.S. is developing and will continue to develop a clean energy economy. While federal leadership could hasten and advance such an economy, its failure to do so will not alter the course of clean power investments in the private sector nor of regulatory innovations by states, regions and local governments.

THE EPA'S CLEAN POWER PLAN

Most simply, the CPP directed electricity generators to reduce greenhouse gas emissions, especially carbon dioxide. Although its legal authority has been questioned,[8] the EPA issued the rules under Clean Air Act §111(d) (CAA). Similar to other CAA operations, the CPP set individual state emissions goals based on each state's individual energy resources and particular needs. The CPP allowed states to satisfy those goals through a set of flexible standards. Pursuant to that flexibility, any individual state can draw on a variety of resources, including renewable resources, natural gas, clean coal technologies, energy efficiency and conservation, and nuclear power to name a few. The CPP explicitly engaged states together with the federal government, through the practice of cooperative federalism,[9] to address climate change directly.

In June 2014, the EPA announced proposed rules for its CPP to regulate and limit the pollution caused by existing fossil fuel electric generating units (EGUs)[10] and the final rule was enacted a year later. During the time between the proposed and final rules, the agency received in excess of four million comments, and the final rule incorporated those comments. In order to satisfy the emissions goals set under the CPP, states could respond in one of three ways: (1) A state could impose limits on each power plant, (2) a state could set a statewide limit for carbon emissions, or (3) a state could enter into multistate or regional agreements to achieve targeted levels.

The EPA engaged in aggressive outreach efforts and consulted with government energy and environmental officials, utilities, environmental organizations, Native American tribes, and other various stakeholders with over 600 meetings and then drafted the final rule accordingly.[11] The EPA's state targets were not created in a vacuum. Instead, they were adopted after studied consideration by the agency, which concluded that the CPP should "follow the lead of numerous states and not only identify improvements in the efficiency of fossil fuel-fired EGUs ... [b]ut also include ... EGU-emissions-reduction opportunities that states have already demonstrated to be successful"[12] in decreasing electric demand and in generating cleaner, more efficient electricity. The more specific goal is to achieve a 32 percent CO_2 reduction below 2005 levels by 2030.[13]

In establishing emissions goals, the EPA considered a range of existing state policies and programs, including

- market-based initiatives such as the Regional Greenhouse Gas Initiative (RGGI) operating in nine Northeastern states and California's Global Warming Solutions program;
- greenhouse gas performance standards as adopted by states such as California, New York, Oregon, and Washington;
- planning programs in which states and investor-owned utilities develop multi-pollutant reduction plans over multiyear periods;
- renewable portfolio standards (RPSs) that have been adopted by 41 states and the District of Columbia[14] of which 25 set mandatory standards and which have stimulated the growth of renewable resources markets;
- demand-side energy efficiency programs such as integrated resource plans that reduce pollution emitted by existing generating units (EGUs)
- while increasing energy efficiency; and
- energy efficiency standards as adopted by more than 20 states that require utilities to save a certain amount of energy each year or achieve a cumulative target over a set period of time.[15]

Accompanying the proposed rule, the EPA published an extensive regulatory impact analysis (RIA) examining the costs, benefits, and economic impacts of the proposed regulations setting individual state emissions goals.[16] The RIA recognized that greenhouse gas pollution threatens the health and welfare of the country by causing long-lasting climate changes that have a range of negative consequences on human health and the environment. Carbon dioxide is the primary concern because it accounts for nearly three-quarters of all global greenhouse gas emissions and 84 percent of US greenhouse gas emissions. Further, fossil fuel EGUs are the largest source of those emissions. The RIA, then, proposed state-specific goals for emissions and provided guidelines for states to use in developing their attainment plans.

The EPA intended the CPP to be flexible and to allow states leeway to craft their own responses. Different states have different energy resource mixes and different states are engaged in a variety of emissions reduction and energy efficiency activities. Each state was required to submit its final plan by September 6, 2016, unless it was granted an extension until September 6, 2018. The Supreme Court's stay effectively canceled these dates. Affected EGUs, in turn, must achieve final emission performance rates by 2030 and maintain that level going forward. Either a state plan can satisfy the rule through a "rate-based" method of reducing carbon emissions (i.e., measured in pounds of CO_2 per megawatt hour of generation) or the state can set a "mass-based" goal of an equivalent amount of pollution (i.e., measured by the number of tons of carbon emitted).

The EPA estimates that the net monetized climate and health benefits range from $1.0 billion to $6.3 billion in 2020 and from $26 billion to $45 billion in 2030, depending upon assumed discount rates and a state's choice of either a rate-based or a mass-based measurement of carbon reduction.[17] In determining these benefits, the EPA considered health risks from heat stroke, heat-related deaths, and reduced particulate pollution, as well as the cost savings incident to a decrease in the intensity of extreme weather events. The agency also calculated lower electricity costs as a benefit of its CPP.[18] Further, the EPA estimated that the health and climate benefits will outweigh the estimated total compliance costs of meeting the standards, costs that are projected to run from $1.4 billion to $8.4 billion in 2030.[19]

These cost-benefit calculations are of central importance for the legal survival of EPA's final rule. In *Michigan v. EPA*,[20] the US Supreme Court ruled that when acting under CAA §112, the EPA must consider costs and benefits. In that case, the EPA had issued final rules directed at reducing "hazardous air pollutants," more specifically mercury emissions, from existing power plants. In a 5–4 ruling, the Court held that the EPA "must consider costs – including, most importantly, cost of compliance – before deciding whether regulation is appropriate and necessary."[21] While the EPA has compared costs and benefits of the CPP, concluding that the "monetized benefits of this rule are substantial and far outweigh the costs,"[22] because of the Supreme Court's recent interest in overly stringent cost-benefit analyses, it is an open question as to whether the CPP's cost-benefit analysis will satisfy reviewing courts.

As noted, the CPP established state-by-state emissions reduction targets and offers states a flexible framework known as the "best system of emissions reduction" (BSER), with which they may meet those goals. A state's BSER would be calculated based upon the mix of the power sources in each state and the application of three "Building Blocks" to achieve an individual state's emissions reduction target. The Building Blocks were as follows: (1) improving the heat rate at affected EGUs, (2) substituting increased generation from lower-emitting existing natural gas combined cycle (NGCC) units for generation from higher-emitting EGUs, and (3) substituting increased generation from new zero-emitting renewable energy generating capacity for the purpose of reducing electricity generation from fossil-fired units.[23] Although the proposed rule had a fourth Building Block addressing demand reduction and energy efficiency, which was eliminated in the final rule, the final rule does allow states to satisfy their targets by using demand reduction, energy efficiency, or any other low or no carbon strategy.

Building Block 1 was aimed at heat rate improvements by EGUs. By increasing the efficiency with which an EGU converts fuel to electricity, carbon intensity can be reduced. Increasing the heat rate reduces the amount of fuel needed to produce the same amount of electricity and therefore lowers carbon dioxide emissions. These improvements can be realized through a variety of measures such as equipment upgrades and adopting more efficient operations.

Building Block 2 was directed at changing dispatch practices. The intent was to encourage EGUs that are carbon intensive to switch to less carbon-intensive generation. Under this Building Block, rather than dispatch high carbon-emitting electricity first, dispatch to the grid should be accomplished through less carbon-intense resources such as a greater utilization of NGCC units in place of coal.

The method of changing dispatch practices is not free from controversy. Critics have argued that, historically, state public utility commissions (PUCs) have employed a least-cost dispatch approach, referred to as economic dispatch, which generally means that coal-fired electricity will be put onto the grid before more expensive resources such as wind or solar power. The criticism continues that Building Block 2, as a low-carbon or environmental dispatch practice instead of economic dispatch, is unlikely to succeed because PUCs have been reluctant to adopt them for two reasons. First, PUCs and the utilities that they regulate are both familiar with least-cost practices and prefer to minimize the costs of doing business. Second, and relatedly, PUCs prefer not to raise rates to consumers for environmental goals.[24] Under this Building Block, then, it may be the case that higher-priced, but lower-carbon, units are brought online instead of coal units, with the potential of raising the cost of electricity to consumers.

The criticism of this Building Block, however, is misplaced for the simple reason that natural gas prices have been one of the major factors for utilities switching from coal to natural gas since at least 2000. More notably, "generation from NGCC EGUs in 2012 reached over four times the level of NGCC generation in 2000, while generation from coal and oil/gas steam EGUs decreased by about one third."[25] In other words, power plants have been reducing their reliance on coal and using natural gas to generate electricity. Building Block 2 encourages a trend that has been ongoing and supports a reduction in carbon intensity rather than maintaining reliance on least-cost, carbon-heavy resources.

Building Block 3 encouraged affected EGUs to expand the amount of new zero-emitting renewable electricity (RE) generating capacity to produce replacement generation. In particular, this Building Block is intended to stimulate increased electricity generation from solar and wind power. The EPA points to the fact that RE has been developing since the 1970s and has been encouraged by federal legislation such as the Public Utilities Regulatory Policies Act (PURPA) and the Energy Security Act of 1980. Additionally, states have been promoting RE through a number of regulations, most notably RPSs, which require local electric utilities to sell a certain amount of electricity from renewable resources. The adoption of RE is expanding significantly. In 2013, for example, electricity from RE technologies comprised 13 percent of total US electricity production, up from 9 percent in 2005. Further, since 2009, US wind generation has tripled and solar generation has increased 20-fold, while the global market for RE is projected to grow to $460 billion per year by 2030.[26]

The market for non-hydropower renewable resources has been expanding noticeably as the cost of generating electricity from wind and solar energy has been declining appreciably. It has been estimated that the levelized costs of electricity from utility-scale wind and solar electricity, on unsubsidized bases, have been decreasing annually in ranges from 58 percent to 78 percent, respectively.[27] The EPA takes the position that current trends in RE adoption are strong enough to ensure that the projected 2030 levels of RE deployment can be achieved.[28]

While Building Block 4, directed at demand-side energy efficiency, was dropped from the final rule, energy efficiency and reduced demand remain viable and important compliance options.[29] By reducing the demand for high carbon generation at affected EGUs, emissions reductions will occur. Every state has established a demand-side energy efficiency policy and the CPP encouraged their use and development. The CPP recognized that significant gains have been made in states such as California and Minnesota, which have realized reduced electricity demands of 12.5 percent and 13.1 percent, respectively, through such programming.[30] Further, the CPP recognized that multiple studies[31] have demonstrated that significant improvements in end-use energy efficiency can be achieved at less cost than the savings that can be realized from avoided power purchases.[32] Moreover, demand-side policies also provide health benefits as a result of reduced carbon emissions.[33] Increased investment in demand-side energy efficiency is being supported at every governmental level as well as by private sector actors and should be encouraged and expanded. Indeed, bipartisan legislation has been introduced in Congress to promote energy efficiency[34] by such measures as promoting efficiency in buildings, which is projected to produce $4.6 billion in savings by 2030 while significantly reducing greenhouse gas emissions.[35]

The EPA envisioned that states will adopt a variety of measures to achieve the stated goals. In addition to the examples listed immediately above, states may choose to install carbon capture and sequestration technologies, improve energy storage technologies and facilities, adopt energy conservation programs, or use biomass, as well as other zero- or low-carbon strategies such as geothermal power to generate electricity. In addition to the goal of reducing carbon emissions, state plans could be designed to pursue other policies, including the following: (1) utilizing a diversity of energy resources; (2) maintaining electric reliability; (3) providing affordable electricity; (4) recognizing low carbon investments made by states and power companies; and (5) meeting a state's specific energy environmental and economic needs. States could proceed individually or in collaboration with other states on multistate or regional plans, and emissions trading through such programs has proven to be economically efficient.[36]

As noted, final plans were to be submitted by September 6, 2016, unless a state requests extra time, in which case an optional two-phase extension process is available. Regardless, should the CPP survive judicial and political scrutiny, the adoption of state plans could be accomplished in phases. Under this process, a state can make an initial submission that addresses how it will address each of the Building Blocks by a specific date and when it will submit a final plan. Affected EGUs will be required to begin making carbon reductions no earlier than 2022, and they are scheduled to meet final CO_2 emission performance rates no later than 2030. In order to encourage as well as assist EGUs in meeting those targets, the EPA provided an eight-year interim period divided into three stages (2022–2024, 2025–2027, and 2028–2029), each with their own emissions reduction targets. In this way, the EPA envisions that EGUs will have sufficient guidance for necessary investments and sufficient time to meet the established goals along a reasonable trajectory. Again, it must be noted that the CPP is under judicial review. However, its architecture is instructive.

The CPP is a national attempt to address climate change as part of President Obama's Climate Action Plan[37] and to do so by recognizing the interdependence between energy and the environment. The CPP sets ambitious goals, encourages state flexibility and participation, and is an attempt by the federal government to take a leadership role in this area. Because the CPP is such a broad rule, it will continue to be subject to numerous legal challenges, policy disagreements, and political debates. Regardless, the CPP is significant precisely because it acknowledges that energy and the environment are of a whole and should be regulated as such.

CRITICISMS AND RESPONSES

Given the range and the magnitude of the CPP, particularly the imposition of a new set of environmental regulations on a trillion-dollar, century-old electric industry, resistance and criticism is unsurprising, and there is a range of challenges that have been made on behalf of the utility industry and interest groups generally opposed to regulation. Some of the challenges are motivated by political partisanship. Indeed, an antienvironmental industry coalition was formed to fight the CPP even before the draft rules were announced.[38] There are also serious challenges from states and regulators that must be considered.

The following presents an overview of the initial and the ongoing criticisms of the CPP. In most instances, the supporting documentation for the CPP, as well as studies by advocates for a clean energy economy, offers solid responses to those criticisms. Most significantly, it is important to note that during the comment period between the proposed rule in June 2014 and the final rule in October 2015, the EPA responded to those criticisms and changed the proposed rule in important ways. Still, concerns, particularly about reliability and governance, may well be warranted. The significance of those challenges, as well as the responses to them, demand consideration as well as continued attention. The challenges range from the legal to the political and from the economic to the technical.

Legal and Political Challenges: The Issue of Partisanship

Legal. The CPP is a novel regulation to the extent that it so widely imposes environmental requirements on an energy industry that historically has been regulated separately and independently from the environment. While this is not the first environmental regulation imposed on the energy sector, it is the first federal regulation written so broadly and written to address climate change. Moreover, it is a regulation written by an environmental agency rather than an energy agency, and it is written in the context of a regulatory regime that itself has multiple regulators at the state, federal, and regional levels. The regulatory environment for the electric industry is complex and growing, and the CPP adds another layer of regulatory complexity as well as financial challenges.

The legal challenges to the CPP include both traditional challenges to regulation and specific and unusual challenges to the rule. The traditional challenge asserts that the EPA lacks the legal authority to issue certain regulations. The unusual challenge can be traced to a clerical error in the official posting of the CAA's statutory provisions under which the EPA exercised its CPP authority.

The Clean Air Act requires the EPA to regulate air pollutants that endanger public health and welfare.[39] This environmental goal had been affirmed by the US Supreme Court.[40] Nevertheless, there have been, and will continue to be, legal challenges to the exercise of that authority as well as challenges regarding the scope of the EPA's jurisdiction over power plant emissions. Recently, for example, the US Supreme Court has been critical of the EPA's broad reading of the CAA and has denied the EPA a certain degree of deference when it attempted to broadly regulate "a significant portion of the American Economy." Instead, the Court noted that it expects Congress to speak clearly if it wishes to assign decision-making authority to an agency that may have vast "economic and political significance" and when it intends to "regulate millions of small sources."[41] The CPP affects "significant portions" of the economy and has the potential for affecting "millions of small sources." Simply, the critics argue that the EPA has gone a step too far. In response, supporters assert that the EPA is on solid legal ground given its statutory mandate under the CAA as supported by Supreme Court interpretations to promulgate clean-air regulations, including the mandate to address air pollutants that affect climate change.

More notably, critics argue that since the EPA has already regulated power plants under CAA §112, it cannot also regulate that *source* of pollution under CAA §111(d). However, the EPA is regulating *different pollutants* under those two provisions. Mercury is regulated under §112 and carbon is targeted for regulation under §111. Nevertheless – and here is the unusual legal assertion – there has been a drafting era in the promulgation of §111(d). More specifically, it is possible that both the House and Senate versions, followed by President George H.W. Bush's signature, contain two inconsistent legislative provisions that have mistakenly been put into law.

According to the legislative history, during the 1990 amendments to the CAA, two different versions of §111(d) were passed, one of which, the House version, *arguably* prevents the EPA from issuing the CPP. Critics of the CPP assert the legal argument that the EPA lacks jurisdiction while supporters refute that assertion. Under a broad reading of the House version, critics argue that the EPA cannot regulate the same *source* of pollution under both §112 and §111. Under the Senate version, CPP supporters argue that §111(d) only precludes the EPA from regulating *pollutants* that have been regulated under §112; therefore, the EPA can regulate another *pollutant* under §111(d) even if it has regulated a specific *source* under §112.

The Senate reading appears to be the more reasonable reading and it is consistent with EPA practice. In the past, the EPA has regulated the same *source* while regulating *different pollutants* under each section. The EPA is regulating mercury from power plants and other pollutants under §112 and is regulating carbon under §111(d) from those same plants. The EPA interpretation of these provisions, that it may regulate different pollutants under different sections of the statute even from the same source, makes sense and effectuates the purpose of the CAA to reduce air pollution.

In addition to this issue of statutory interpretation, critics have argued that the regulation constitutes a taking of private utility property in contravention of the Constitution; that EPA lacks authority to regulate in this area because such regulation is better left to the states; that such an extensive exercise of regulatory authority violates the principle of nondelegation from the legislature to an administrative agency; and that the EPA cannot impose a federal implementation plan if states fail to act.

Under regulatory law, these legal arguments are standard and they are also difficult to sustain. Government has not only the authority but the duty to prevent harm to its citizens. More specifically, government has the Congressional mandate and authority under the CAA to regulate air pollution. Consequently, requiring utilities to reduce harmful pollution is not a taking of private property. Instead, it is a protection from harm and, therefore, is a usual and required exercise of governmental authority that has no constitutional-takings implications.

The idea that pollution regulation is a province of the states and not the federal government goes against the grain of the history of environmental regulation and the reality of environmental harms. More specifically, federal-state cooperation, also known as "cooperative federalism," particularly through the administration of the CAA, has been the norm.[42] State participation with the federal government regarding air pollution control is standard practice. Further, not since the New Deal has the Supreme Court found that Congress has delegated too much authority to an agency. More to the point, Congress lacks the time, expertise, and focus to administer a set of regulations as complex as those embodied in environmental legislation, and the delegation of clean air regulation to the EPA has been sustained by the US Supreme Court.[43] The EPA argument that it will implement its own plan if a state fails to act is a legitimate and statutorily authorized exercise of its backstop authority, as well as a legitimate exercise of an agency's constitutional authority to preempt state laws.[44] All in all, although there are multiple legal challenges to EPA authority, most similar challenges have generally not succeeded.[45]

Political. There are several arguments that can be called "political" regarding the CPP. Some arguments, as described next, are purely partisan while others are political in the sense that different states' interests may be adversely affected. Research, though, indicates that even though greenhouse gas regulations are fairly consistent among regions and that the benefits of regulation notably exceed the costs, political partisanship among the states is significant.[46]

There is evidence that resistance to the CPP is infected with political partisanship.[47] As noted above, after the 2016 election, Republicans enjoy a unitary government with control the White House, the House of Representatives, the U.S. Senate, and, most likely, United States Supreme Court. The demise of the CPP clearly appears imminent. Regardless, partisanship on this issue has been strong. States with Republican governors and coal states with Democratic governors, for example, have shown resistance to the CPP on political grounds. This is true even though a coal state, such as Kentucky, is well on its way to satisfying CPP requirements. Such partisanship was manifest once the final rule was published. The Senate voted to block the CPP by a vote of 57–43 with all Republicans and three Democrats from coal states (Indiana, North Dakota, and West Virginia) voting to block the CPP and all remaining Democrats voting in support of it.[48] Such partisanship is also manifest in the 2016 presidential campaign as Republican candidates either ignore climate change altogether or question whether or not it is affected by human activity[49] as well as Republican opposition to the Paris climate talks.[50]

Such political partisanship, however, does not comport with the reality that CPP compliance may be less of an obstacle than the critics maintain. Significantly, 14 states are on track to surpass their benchmarks; 31 states are more than halfway toward meeting the 2020 goal; and through regional collaboration, states can reliably and cost-effectively meet their targets.[51] Tellingly, the president of the National Association of Regulatory Utility Commissioners and a member of the Montana Public Service Commission expressed opposition to the CPP even while acknowledging that given Montana's heavy reliance on hydroelectric power and natural gas, compliance is easily achieved and reliability is not threatened.[52]

Some states, though, have a legitimate and not purely partisan reason for opposing the CPP. An example of a state interest that may be adversely affected by the CPP is the argument made by those states that have been front-runners in terms of addressing climate change by encouraging use of renewable resources and energy efficiency in their states. Such states are concerned that they may not receive sufficient credit for already engaging in emissions reductions and clean power activities.

The CPP uses 2012 as the baseline year for calculating each state's emissions reduction goals. Several states, however, have been involved in carbon emissions reductions many years prior to 2012. In its proposed form, the CPP did not provide credits to those early performing states. Such front-runners argued not only that they should be credited for early performance but also that by using a 2012 baseline, compliance costs for them will be higher than laggard states. In other words, states that have refused to engage in carbon reductions prior to 2012 are effectively rewarded for their recalcitrance and comments on the proposed rule addressed this issue.

The final rule provides four responses to this equity argument. First, the EPA amended the proposed rule by establishing uniform CO_2 emissions rates for fossil fuel EGUs. The idea behind the requirement of uniformity is to avoid the unintended outcome of putting greater reduction burdens on lower-emitting states while exempting higher-emitting states.[53] Second, in response to equity concerns, the EPA also emphasized and encouraged interstate emissions trading programs to smooth out differences among higher- and lower-emitting states.[54] Third, the final rule provides incentives for investments in carbon emissions reduction activities such as investments in renewable energy and demand-side energy efficiency that deliver results in either 2020 or 2021, which are prior to 2022, the time that compliance is to begin. In this regard, the final rule provides provisions to reward early adopters through a clean energy incentive program (CEIP), which allows a state to set aside allowances for such emissions reduction gains in their compliance plans.[55] Fourth, the CEIP will facilitate interstate trading through a program that creates a market for the trading of emission rate credits.

A final example of a serious political criticism of the CPP is that several states oppose it arguing that they should have opportunities for relief from the particularly harsh terms of the CPP and that they need a longer compliance period. The EPA responded to these concerns by revising the proposed rule, extending the time for compliance, and adopting a safety valve mechanism as discussed in a later section. Indeed, there are several legitimate political issues involved with the CPP such as apportioning regulatory responsibilities between states and the federal government; apportioning such responsibilities among and within various federal and state agencies; the creation and maintenance of new energy markets; and the intricacies of aligning environmental and energy regulation.[56] Several of these issues are addressed in the economic and technical criticisms discussed next.

Economic and Technical Challenges: The Issue of Reliability

Because of the importance of readily available electricity, as well as the structural characteristics of the industry that require supply and demand be kept in balance, reliability can be considered the most important dimension of the industry. Reliability must be maintained in the face of disruptive events such as outages or blackouts, fuel price volatility, unexpected increases in demand, and severe weather events, or as a result of changes in technologies such as the increased use of variable electricity from wind and solar power.[57] The CPP presented a different sort of reliability challenge: Can the industry satisfy the regulatory requirements of the CPP and maintain reliability? While the industry has experienced, and has successfully weathered, a history of market, as well as regulatory changes, over the last few decades, the CPP is a regulatory change that warrants specific attention.

The issue of reliability has become a central focus and a primary concern of clean power regulations. In assessing reliability, generation and transmission facilities must be considered; interconnections among power systems must likewise be taken into account; and the impact of demand-side and variable resources must also be assessed. Fortunately, these practical concerns are being addressed. Reliability studies are being undertaken by a wide variety of actors including regulators, trade associations, research centers,[58] interest groups, and the industry itself. To the extent that the CPP encourages the expanded use of variable resources, CPP opponents claim that grid reliability is threatened. Contrary to these claims, evidence is mounting that variable resources can contribute to grid reliability.[59]

Further, the industry has developed a set of probability models for assessing demand and reliability and has been conducting such reliability studies for decades. By way of example, the regional transmission organization (RTO) PJM Interconnection conducted a study that concluded that with adequate transmission expansion, PJM would have no significant problem operating with up to 30 percent of its energy provided by wind and solar generation.[60]

In addition to reliability models, the industry, as well as its state and federal regulators, has planning practices and procedures that are already in place and are currently used to assess reliability. Further, the Federal Energy Regulation Commission (FERC) can play a dominant role in helping increase coordination among states, RTOs, and other regional planning entities through enhanced, as well as existing, planning processes. These processes, in turn, can further assist states to satisfy CPP targets by creating and supporting more competitive electric and emissions trading markets.[61]

Even though reliability issues are receiving serious attention, some industry actors and other opponents claim that meeting the CPP's carbon reduction targets will compromise the reliability of the US electricity sector. The North American Electric Reliability Corporation (NERC), an entity designated by the FERC to provide congressionally required reliability assessments, has conducted a study assessing the reliability issues posed by the CPP.[62] In its initial study, published in November 2014, NERC identified several reliability issues including: (1) the adequacy of clean energy replacements for fossil fuel plant retirements; (2) whether EPA's assessment of potential heat rate improvements under Building Block 1 is achievable; (3) the need for transportation investments in natural gas pipelines and electricity transmission lines (particularly to connect variable resources to the grid); (4) the adequacy of the EPA's assessment of the penetration of renewable resources for electricity generation; (5) the effects of the increased use of distributed energy resources (DER) on reliability; (6) whether EPA's estimates of the increased use of energy efficiency will meet the growth in electricity demand; (7) the effect of the CPP on reliability services such as load balancing and voltage and frequency support; and (8) whether the CPP allows enough time for states to comply.[63] The initial comments of the Electric Power Research Institute, the research arm of the electric industry, made similar criticisms.[64] Each issue is significant and will be addressed in turn.

Fossil Plant Retirements. Utilities have been retiring coal plants prior to the CPP for three key reasons: the aging of the coal fleet; environmental regulations such as mercury air toxics standards; and lower natural gas prices, which make electricity generation from natural gas cheaper than from coal.[65] The environmental regulations under the CPP were likely to contribute to retirements because states can achieve their emission-rate targets most easily by retiring high-emitting coal-fired power plants. However, plant retirements should not affect reliability. According to the US Energy Information Administration (EIA), in 2015 approximately 16 gigawatts (GW) of generation will be lost of which 12.9 GW are from retiring coal plants. The EIA reports that lost generation will be more than replaced by 20 GW of new generation including wind (9.8 GW), natural gas (6.3 GW), and solar power (2.2 GW).[66] While coal plants are being retired and retirements will continue under the CPP, new generation from renewable resources and natural gas, plus improved efficiency, is likely to allay reliability concerns.

Heat Rate Improvements. The proposed CPP suggested that heat rate improvements, that is, efficiency improvements in plants, can be improved by 6 percent nationwide. NERC noted that a 6 percent heat rate improvement may be difficult to achieve. However, the NERC criticism addressed individual plant-level heat rate improvements rather than fleet-level heat rate improvements, which are likely to improve due to retirements of the least efficient plants and increased dispatch of lower carbon plants. The CPP was flexible and does not require upgrades at each plant. Thus, as utilities retire less efficient coal plants and rely on more efficient coal plants or NGCC, fleet-wide heat rate improvements are likely. Additionally, increased cogeneration and waste heat recovery can contribute to heat rate improvements at existing coal plants because of greater operational efficiencies.[67] Nevertheless, in response to such comments, EPA adjusted its calculations and its requirements for determining heat rate improvements. Additionally, instead of imposing a heat rate requirement on a national basis, EPA assesses the potential heat rate improvements on a regional basis within the Eastern, Western, and Texas interconnections.

Transmission Planning and Investment. As old generation plants retire and new ones are constructed and brought online, new and/or upgraded transmission facilities will be needed to interconnect new generation, particularly variable generation from solar and wind. Additionally, as natural gas plays a larger role in electricity generation, gas pipelines will be needed. The criticism, then, is that the CPP paid inadequate attention to the need for new electric transmission lines and new natural gas pipelines.

Electric transmission lines present a significant challenge because transmission line siting authority has been divided between state and federal governments, which presents two problems. First, acquiring the necessary approval and construction can take years, and, second, not-in-my-backyard (NIMBY) resistance to transmission line siting is a familiar obstacle.[68] There are promising signs that sufficient electricity and natural gas transportation systems will be available to satisfy CPP requirements. First, increased penetration of renewable generation from variable resources has already created a strong impetus for new transmission lines. Because of the increase in RE, independent transmission companies, known as merchant transmission firms, are entering the transmission market to connect renewable energy to the grid. As costs decline and as renewables penetration increases, some regions of the country already exceed variable penetration levels assumed by EPA without having negatively affected transmission or operational reliability.

Second, the electric industry and its state regulators are engaged in ongoing transmission planning processes that will continue without regard to the CPP. Third, because natural gas, unlike electricity, can be stored, utilities can store natural gas in advance to reduce reliability risks during periods of high use. Finally, multistate or regional cooperation can lower compliance costs, address reliability concerns, and more easily satisfy CPP requirements.[69]

Penetration of Renewable Resources. NERC notes that RPS programs may not achieve the goal that the EPA suggests. It is true that the states have uneven records in setting and achieving RPS goals. However, that potential deficit can be offset by states whose RPS targets already exceed EPA estimates as well as by states that adopt best practices.[70] Further, as costs for renewable resources decline, penetration levels of renewable resources increase. Significantly, in its most recent report, the EIA notes that RE will meet much of the growth in electricity demand. It is projected that RE generation will increase by 72 percent from 2013 to 2040 and will account for more than one-third of new generation.[71]

Increased Use of Distributed Energy Resources. Consumers are beginning to enjoy greater control over their energy consumption, an issue that will be discussed in more detail in Chapter 7. Distributed resources such as rooftop solar, heat pumps, micro-grids, and even programmable thermostats and appliances provide consumers with information with which they can shape consumption choices. While some utilities have expressed concern about the expansion of DER because increased DER penetration may reduce their retail sales, forward-thinking electricity organizations, such as the Electric Power Research Institute and General Electric, are proactively engaged in incorporating DER into their studies and estimates of generation mixes.[72] Further, state utility regulators can mitigate and have been mitigating concerns about lost revenue through adjustments in state rate regulations. Reduced sales, moreover, must not be confused with reliability. Rather, DER must be seen as a reliability asset rather than as a threat because DER reduces stress on the grid and, therefore, increases reliability.[73]

Energy Efficiency and Demand Growth. NERC points out that EPA estimates of the growth in energy efficiency may not keep up with demand for electricity. However, the EIA projects that energy consumption will be at the near-zero growth rate of 0.3 percent per year from 2013 through 2040.[74] Further, states are experimenting with and are realizing savings through their energy efficiency programs.

Moreover, new technologies reduce energy costs to consumers, and some states are developing best practices to reduce demand that can be adopted by other states. In addition, through the use of building codes, appliance standards, and fuel economy standards, energy efficiency gains are being continually made.[75] Finally, energy efficiency programs that rely on tradable energy credits can be improved through multistate and regional programs, which create more sustainable and fluid energy efficiency markets. Thus, energy efficiency measures are keeping up with demand without raising reliability concerns.

Reliability Services. Because electricity cannot be stored at the necessary scale, supply and demand must be managed through a process known as load balancing. Although there are no large-scale commercial electricity storage solutions to help maintain and balance load, storage options are starting to enter the market.[76] In addition to load balancing, voltage levels must be maintained; otherwise, grid disruption results. Reliability services are used to achieve load balancing and maintain voltage levels. Adding variable resources to the electricity mix does pose challenges to both load balancing and voltage stability. Nevertheless, increased energy production from multiple sources, including variable resources, has so far not imposed reliability problems.

Many states, for example, have RPS mandates that exceed those suggested by the CPP and have not encountered reliability problems. As noted earlier, the industry and its regulators have been engaged in ongoing reliability planning for decades.[77] Further, in the last four decades, the industry has experienced multiple financial challenges (that are discussed in more detail in Chapter 5) including the rapid increase of electricity prices, the collapse of nuclear power, and failed restructuring efforts. In each case, the industry and its regulators weathered each of those challenges while adequately managing load balancing, maintaining voltage stability, and sustaining reliability.

The EPA has been responsive to comments about reliability concerns and the final rule has made several adjustments. First, the start date for compliance was pushed back from 2020 to 2022. Additionally, the EPA adjusted the interim targets with the intent of providing a smooth guide path for state and EGU compliance. Both of these measures provide more time for states and EGUs to plan to satisfy the final rule. The final rule also requires each state to demonstrate that it can satisfy reliability demands. Further, after a state submits its final plan, if unanticipated reliability issues arise, then it can seek amendments to the plan. Additionally, if an individual EGU encounters a conflict between requirements of the plan and reliability, it can seek relief from the plan through a "safety valve." The safety valve, however, will only be available "in the face of an extraordinary and unanticipated event that presents substantial reliability concerns."[78] Finally, in order to assure that reliability issues are addressed, the final rule requires coordination among EPA, DOE, and FERC. In short, the final CPP addresses multiple reliability concerns as raised in the comments.

Timing for Compliance. In response to the proposed rule, NERC, as well as other industry commentators such as the Edison Electric Institute,[79] suggested that the compliance window was too short and that states should have more time to comply to ensure reliability. EPA was sensitive to this criticism and took three steps to ameliorate concerns about timing. First, it extended the time for mandatory reductions from 2020 to 2022. Second, the EPA said the scheduled emissions reduction targets would be phased in more gradually during the interim period than originally proposed. Third, the EPA introduced the reliability safety valve mentioned earlier so that system reliability will be maintained if there is a conflict between a state plan and an individual EGU's ability to satisfy it.[80]

While the EPA was responsive to the timing criticism, an earlier study by the Brattle Group noted that efforts to transition to a clean energy economy are occurring regardless of the CPP and, therefore, timing does not present a material issue. The study states:

> [W]e find that the combination of the ongoing transformation of the power sector, the steps already taken by system operators, the large and expanding set of technological and operational tools available, and the flexibility under the CPP are likely sufficient to ensure that compliance with the CPP can be planned by states in ways that will not materially affect reliability.[81]

Another study similarly concluded that "[t]he evidence does not support the argument that the proposed CPP will result in a general and unavoidable decline in reliability. . . . [W]e believe resource planners and markets will have sufficient time and resources to respond to a realistic projection of system redispatch and facility retirements."[82]

As noted, many commentators argued for relief through a safety valve and the EPA provided one. However, the necessity of such a mechanism is questionable. At least one study indicates that "[m]any of these mechanisms to address 'reliability' are either too lenient, constituting an escape clause from compliance, or are investment cost avoidance measures masquerading as reliability protections."[83] The study argues that should some safety valve or mechanism be implemented that it should not delay compliance planning and that it should satisfy certain principles including that such a mechanism should be demonstrated to work through standard industry tools, be transparent, be equitable among asset owners of state, and be cost effective.[84] While the CPP provided a safety valve, the requirements to obtain relief under it are stringent and the mechanism should not be used to deter the schedule for emissions reductions.

A number of factors further undercut the criticism that the states cannot meet the scheduled timetable. First, many organizations are putting together toolkits to help facilitate planning.[85] Second, the industry has regularly and successfully addressed reliability issues through ongoing planning processes, particularly through regional organizations for decades. Third, the flexibility of the CPP allowed for a variety of responses and resource mixes to allow time to adequately manage plant retirements as well as manage the integration of variable resources and energy efficiency while maintaining reliability.[86]

Reliability is absolutely essential for the functioning of the electric system. Electricity, as we all know, must be available at the flip of a switch. The CPP was cognizant of reliability issues, and through EPA's communications with states and utilities and its study of existing technologies and regulations, the CPP's flexibility in terms of satisfying emissions reduction targets, and its encouragement of multistate planning, reliability is fully addressed. Over the last decades, reliability issues have been addressed through voluntarily and statutorily authorized regional arrangements known as power pools, RTOs, or independent system operators, and the CPP drew on those experiences. Because different states in different regions of the country have different resource mixes and different generation fleets, regional arrangements can enhance reliability, create competitive wholesale energy markets, and improve transmission while reducing carbon emissions.[87] Regardless, new gas-fired plants, renewable resources, energy storage, and efficiency and demand response resources are all available to meet the CPP targets without threatening reliability.[88]

As a number of commentators have stated: (1) reliability assessments and processes are largely in place, (2) reliability assessments are favorable for higher penetrations of renewable energy and more coal plant retirements, (3) transmission improvements have been highly effective in bringing renewable energy to market, and, (4) improved use of new and existing infrastructure is a valuable way to lower consumer costs while complying with the CPP.[89] Simply, industry and its regulators have a long history of successfully planning and assessing reliability. Such activities will continue with or without the CPP because of the importance of electricity to the economy and to citizens. Reliability is a critical concern, but history demonstrates that industry and its regulators closely and successfully monitor reliability and the CPP does not present reliability obstacles.[90]

Moving beyond reliability, the CPP could be a valuable contribution to a clean power transition. Indeed, a more aggressive pursuit of a clean future is likely due to "market forces, policy trends, and technology advancements [that] are converging to produce a key result: reducing electric-sector emissions lowers electricity costs."[91] This promise of a complete cleaner and cheaper energy future is likely decades off. Yet, the possibility is a real one and, as the remaining chapters of this book demonstrate, that future is within reach; more importantly, it is a future the benefits of which we are already enjoying.[92] Indeed, DOE's EIA finds that, at modest cost, CPP goals could (1) reduce power sector carbon emissions significantly; (2) enable renewable resources to play an increasingly significant, then dominant, role from the mid-2020s and beyond even though natural gas generation will be a dominant compliance strategy in the early years of the plan; (3) promote increasing use of demand-side energy efficiency in satisfying energy needs; and (4) have a significant effect on coal plant retirements and on coal production all to the end of facilitating a clean transition.[93]

A NEW POLITICS OF ENERGY AND THE ENVIRONMENT

The importance of the CPP for the transition to a clean power economy lies in the fact that it demonstrates the essential significance of aligning energy and environmental regulation. Historically, energy and the environment have been separately regulated with the consequence that each sector has been treated independently of the other. By keeping energy and the environment in silos, energy industry actors and their regulators paid too little attention to the environmental consequences of their actions. Likewise, environmental actors and their regulators paid too little attention to the energy mix and the needs of energy in our society. Energy production, transportation, consumption, and disposal must account for the environmental harms generated throughout the process. The CPP did exactly that as it defines a new energy future. That future will require a new regulatory regime and a new energy politics to sustain it.

Politics is an essential element of the energy transition. Indeed, politics pervades all public policy. In the United States, until recently, the politics of energy was largely nonpartisan and noncontroversial. The same cannot be said about politics of the environment. Indeed, both energy and environmental politics have become more contentious especially now that energy and the environment were linked together through the CPP. As we contemplate a clean power future, there has been a ramping up of partisan politics that must be overcome. Additionally, a clean power future must encounter the politics of federalism and the politics of public opinion on the way to creating a new narrative. Each of those forms of politics will be discussed in turn.

Partisan Politics

As essential as politics is, however, it remains a many-layered and challenging topic. At times, the concept is elusive as well as plastic and susceptible to several definitions. "Politics" can be used to describe the partisan battles between liberals and conservatives, red states and blue states, Republicans and

Democrats over such issues as the Keystone Pipeline, ANWR, and, not so long ago – "Drill Baby Drill." Today, politics rears its head as utilities assert that they are in a "death spiral" because of increasing competition and declining sales;[94] as lobbying dollars seek to stall needed climate regulations;[95] as state legislators attempt to repeal renewable energy portfolio standards;[96] and, most dramatically, as a variety of actors push back against the CPP.[97]

Throughout the twentieth century, and into the twenty-first century, US energy policy was largely noncontroversial. The overwhelming consensus was that large-scale energy production and consumption were integrally related to economic growth and, therefore, that the traditional energy paradigm should be financially and legally supported. And it was. Partisan debates, aside from an election year skirmish or two, rarely occurred regarding energy policy. Instead, to the extent that partisan debates occurred, they focused on environmental regulations that affected energy firms, which, to their critics, inhibited economic growth and were "job killers."[98]

Even though energy regulation has been largely nonpartisan, environmental regulation has become increasingly partisan. Recall that major environmental legislation such as the National Environmental Policy Act and significant Clean Water Act amendments together with other associated environmental legislation was signed into law by President Richard Nixon and President George H.W. Bush. If it cannot be said that environmental law was a Republican idea, it can be said that it had Republican endorsement and support. Since that time, however, largely due to a growing anti-regulatory sentiment in the country, environmental laws have been increasingly subject to criticism by the Republican Party.

Because the CPP was the first major federal effort linking energy and the environment, the partisan divide between those who favor environmental regulations and those who oppose them is now part of the discussion about our energy future. The energy future has now become infected with the partisanship that has brought political gridlock to Washington and that now dominates discussion of the CPP.

Partisanship over energy/environmental matters has been prominent within the 114th Congress. In its first hundred days, for example, energy and environmental issues were voted upon four times as much as the next most significant congressional item – homeland security. Most of those votes demonstrated a strong anti-environmental agenda with emphasis on blocking efforts to address climate change. Votes were taken on measures to weaken environmental protections for public lands, wildlife, and clean water. Other votes were taken to remove safeguards from wilderness areas and new national parks while also proposing to sell public lands. And, unsurprisingly, many votes were taken for the purpose of approving the Keystone pipeline. Partisan voting is predominant as 49 senators, all Republican, voted to deny that "climate change is real" and that "human activity significantly contributes to climate change" while over $700 million has been spent lobbying Congress by coal, oil, and natural gas companies.[99] To the same point, in their 2016 budget proposals, the Republican House and Senate threaten to shut down government or substantially reduce funding for environmental protection with specific antipathy to the CPP.[100]

It will come as no surprise that the positions taken by the Union of Concerned Scientists[101] and the Center for American Progress[102] regarding the CPP differ markedly from the position taken by the US Chamber of Commerce[103] as an example of the increased partisanship surrounding the country's developing energy policy. This growing partisanship, ironically, comes at a time when public opinion regarding climate change is growing increasingly bipartisan[104] as more Americans believe that global warming is happening.[105]

Federal-State Politics

In addition to partisan energy/environmental politics, a significant group of scholars assesses "politics" in terms of energy federalism that is the federal, state, and local conflicts that occur over the production, consumption, and disposal of our energy resources.[106] As desirable as a national energy policy might be for a transition to a clean power economy, existing institutions, case law, legislation, and regulations have created a web of energy governance at all levels of government that remains on the books and presents challenges as well as opportunities. A persistent energy federalism challenge, for example, is the siting of electricity transmission lines.[107] The need for a smart grid is acute; however, authority for siting is left largely to the states, thus complicating (and slowing down) smart grid development. Further, even recent decisional law has tamped down the federal reach into transmission siting.[108] On the other side of the equation, opportunities are plentiful as states and local governments experiment with various ways to increase the use of renewable resources and energy efficiency and can do so using the cooperative federalism mechanisms embedded in the CPP.[109] In short, the politics of energy federalism is alive, well, and vigorous.[110]

Public Opinion Politics

"Politics" can also refer to shifting public opinions about any variety of energy and environmental topics including fossil fuels, nuclear power,[111] clean energy,[112] and climate change.[113] Each of these uses of the term "politics" are part of a national conversation on energy and the environment that continues the fallacy of perceiving them as separate issues. It is necessary, though, to put politics into a broader, more normative context in order to more fully address the current energy transition. More pointedly, future energy policy cannot be built by separately assessing energy and environmental regulation. Instead, we must consider developing a new energy/environmental politics particularly along the lines of the CPP. A new politics will emerge from an energy/environmental narrative that demonstrates that energy policy can attend to environmental challenges while also contributing to economic growth and development without significant changes in lifestyle.

A CLEAN POWER POLITICS

The CPP, precisely because it intended to bring energy and environmental regulation closer together, takes a more nuanced and sophisticated approach to the energy/environmental complex. And in doing so, it rejects the narrow approaches made by those that concentrate on either energy or on the environment. By way of example, consider and compare how energy advocates such as Daniel Yergin and environmentalists such as Gus Speth address the energy/environmental future and notice that they talk past each other. First, consider a quotation from energy advocate Daniel Yergin:

> America needs a new political discourse on energy. This would recognize the emerging reality that the United States has turned around as an energy producer and is on a major upswing. And the impact will be measured not just in energy security and the balance of payments. Energy development also turns out to be an engine for job creation and economic growth – something that would hardly have been considered the last time we were electing a president.[114]

Next, consider a quotation from Gus Speth, former dean of the Yale School of Forestry and Environmental Studies and cofounder of the Natural Resources Defense Council: "Many environmental scientists and economists, including many in ecological economics, advocate for a study-state economy, with continuous technological change, broadly conceived, applied to reduce the environmental burden of the non-growing GDP."[115]

The distinctions between the two quotations should be clear. Yergin addresses energy and Speth addresses the environment, and it is this separate treatment of these two realms of natural physical behavior that must be rejected. Instead, it is better and more accurate to consider the energy/environmental complex rather than to treat them independently of each other.

Consequently, the political assessment of the energy/environmental paradigm and the laws and policies attendant to that assessment must be considered as a whole.

The more significant distinction between the positions of Yergin and Speth is that these two quotations are speaking not only about different core topics; they are speaking in different languages, using different vocabularies. Speth speaks in the language of the environment and Yergin in the language of energy. These separate languages create different and separate narratives, which, in turn, have the effect of creating different and separate policy programs as well as different political agendas. This separation need not be the case. Indeed, pitting energy against the environment is a false binary that must be avoided.[116]

The language of the environment is about conservation, species protection, ecological sensitivity, and precaution. The language of energy is about production, consumption, jobs, and, most importantly, economic growth. Both languages, though, are too narrow; each misses important aspects of the other. The language of the environment is too insensitive to economic growth, technological advances, and general consumer lifestyles. The language of energy is too insensitive to the commons, too reliant on "free markets," and too defensive about incumbent fossil fuel and nuclear energy firms while less attentive to new clean energy entrants. This is not to say that these issues are ignored altogether by one language or the other; rather, it is to say, though, that one language often downplays and, at times, obscures the other as a result of a path-dependent politics that has divided energy and the environment into separate spheres.

These two languages simply pay inadequate attention to the reality of the energy fuel cycle. From the environmental side, the energy narrative tends to downplay, if not ignore, the environmental effects that occur from exploration through disposal. Simply, the natural resources we use to produce, process, and consume energy impose identifiable and often serious social and economic costs. From the energy side, the environmental narrative tends to downplay, if not ignore, the costs of doing business such as the sunk costs of past investments, the transition costs of moving from one energy paradigm to another, and the possibility of lost opportunity costs available under current business practices.

Consider further that the two languages do not appear to merge well – a circumstance that must be overcome. The fears and frustrations of environmentalists of free market rhetoric, the anguished application of cost-benefit analyses,[117] the distortion of science,[118] and the skepticism that technological advances can be relied upon to solve climate challenges may overstate fears about the future and sound apocalyptic. The fears and frustrations from the energy sector about low or no economic growth, the need for reliability, wariness about soft variables such as fairness and environmentalism, and the loss of the incumbents' positions in the energy economy may overstate their fears about the future, sound recalcitrant, and appear unwilling to tackle change and experiment with and adopt new business models and regulatory strategies.[119]

Such fears, on both sides, are not irrational because those fears tap into the deepest commitments of both narratives. In brief, the energy narrative is about efficiency and our immediate and near-term economic well-being. The environmental narrative is about the inevitable interconnectedness of humans and the natural environments. The energy narrative also expresses a deep concern about our political and economic status in the world. The environmental narrative also expresses a deep concern about the future of the planet.[120] And, finally, the energy narrative is explicitly instrumental because energy is simply a means to the end of economic productivity. In turn, the environmental narrative is often explicitly intrinsic as protection of the environment is discussed as a good in and of itself. The concerns, then, of energy advocates and environmental advocates do have distinct dimensions. Nevertheless, it is incumbent upon us to adopt a new approach to energy and the environment and one that merges the hopes and promises, as well as the concerns and fears, of both narratives into a consistent whole.

To that end, we might consider adopting an energy/environmental politics along the lines set out by Sir Anthony Giddens in his book, *The Politics of Climate Change*, in which he writes that "we have no politics of climate change. In other words, we do not have a developed analysis of the political innovations that have to be made if our aspirations to limit global warming are to become real."[121] So too, and in the same sense, we have no "energy/environmental politics." In other words, while partisan approaches to energy and the environment and the several political strategies regarding them appear to be in abundance, we lack an overarching political theory or normative structure for our energy/environmental future.

Giddens provides guidance in this regard from the environmental side of the energy/environmental complex. He argues that challenges of the magnitude of climate change, which directly affect both energy and the environment, must be addressed through a political and economic convergence. It is through this political and economic convergence that governments play a central role in establishing workable markets, contribute to technological advances, and engage in thoughtful planning as well as manage risk and uncertainty in a changing world.[122] For Giddens, political convergence involves innovative policy and regulatory changes that have wide public support.[123] Economic convergence, in turn, involves technological innovations and the creation of new markets that can address climate challenges and generate competitive advantages for smart actors.[124] Successful political and economic convergence means that the public and private sectors must engage in innovative and collaborative activities.

From the energy side, William Boyd's discussion of "public utility" offers fertile ground. Boyd argues that public utility is a historically rich and important concept that has been underdeveloped. More importantly, today, precisely in order to face climate change challenges and aggressively pursue carbon emissions reduction strategies, we must revive the historic vision of public utility and adapt it for contemporary electricity markets and firms. In this conception, a public utility is simply not an entity that sells electricity. Rather, the Progressive idea of public utility is that it is driven by the idea of service; not electricity or energy sales, but by public service more broadly.[125] Given today's climate challenges, public utility means a clean future. As described in Chapter 7, this broader vision of public utility captures the concept of the democratization of energy and becomes a richer source of normative value rather than a narrow focus on efficiency or economic growth and/or profit. Aligning energy and the environment is necessary to achieve that vision.

As the two often conflicting narratives uncomfortably reveal, there are inevitable trade-offs[126] between energy and the environment that must be addressed and, more importantly, overcome. Our energy future must adequately and responsibly account for both efficiency and equity interests. Most importantly, however, our energy future must adequately and responsibly account for climate change, and climate change is a problem of a different order requiring different regulatory and political responses.

Climate change has structural characteristics such that it has been described as a "super wicked problem."[127] Climate change is of a magnitude and structure unlike the types of social and economic problems that we have addressed in the past through government regulation. In the past, a problem such as tainted meat was identified and a government response was initiated through legislation such as the Federal Meat Inspection Act.[128] Then a government bureau, in this case the Department of Agriculture, was directed to address the problem and monitor progress.

The challenges associated with climate change are structured in radically different ways and, therefore, require dramatically different responses. We can no longer rely on our ability to implement *ex post* regulations that address and fix a problem that has occurred in the past. Instead, forward-thinking *ex ante* regulations are necessary.[129] To adequately address super wicked problems, the focus must be more on the future than on the past. Further, we must realize that the energy/environmental future presents complex problems that are multidisciplinary, intergenerational, and multi-jurisdictional, and imbued with scientific, technological, economic, and social uncertainties. Additionally, the super wicked or "hot"[130] nature of climate change means that the problem is nonlinear; that "time is running out" for a solution; that no central authority can solve the problem; and that by not addressing the problem now, the cost of doing so in the future will only increase.[131] Nevertheless, it is a future we must address today because waiting will be costly both financially and in terms of human health and lives.[132] To successfully respond to this new type of problem, we need a new frame of reference, a new language, and a new political narrative.

The Clean power regulations can lead to a new energy/environmental politics that is forward-looking, anticipates rather than reacts to problems, plans with a wide variety of stakeholders, and engages the type of convergence discussed earlier. Energy and the environment will be regulated together within the context of a new political economy that is described in more detail in Chapter 3.

CONCLUSION

As other scholars have recognized, the division between energy and the environment and the languages used to describe, analyze, and regulate them has lasted too long.[133] The division is unproductive and unsuited to the times. The CPP demonstrated the folly of maintaining a division between energy and the environment by perpetuating the languages and institutions that have supported energy and the environment as separate regulatory regimes throughout the twentieth century.[134] Reframing the discussion of future energy and environmental policy has a direct implication for assessing Clean power regulations. The proper assessment is not limited to the cost of energy with and without the Clean power regulations; instead, the proper assessment considers the short-term costs of implementation balanced against the long-term benefits to health and the environment. In this way, then, the Clean power regulations is a particularly important driver for the energy future. While it is true that for decades states have been actively involved in mediating our need for energy with the desire to protect the environment, federal leadership is a significant precondition for that transition, one that until now has been unrealized.

Assume, for the moment, that a merger of energy and environmental policy is a wise step. Assume further that not only a clean power future is promising as a practical matter, but also it is desirable as a normative one. Those assumptions then raise two significant questions. First, what political strategies should be engaged to achieve this promising future? While the strategic political question is a necessary one, a second political question precedes it: What new narrative does the merger between energy and the environment need to receive acceptance from the public, politicians, and policymakers? If we can begin to describe that narrative, then it should lead us to the appropriate political strategies.

The remainder of this book addresses those strategies and specific aspects of a clean power future including defining the parameters of clean energy and the necessity for technological, business, and regulatory innovations. The book concludes with a discussion of a new political narrative emphasizing the democratization of energy. By way of preview, a more democratic focus on the energy future moves away from concentrating on large-scale central power production and on protecting incumbent energy firms that provide it to a focus on decentralized energy production and consumption and to a greater role for consumers in their energy choices.

2

Defining and Measuring Clean Power

A clean power future is neither a fantasy nor a pipe dream as cities such as San Diego plan to use 100 percent renewable energy within the next two decades.[1] In a widely recognized study, the National Renewable Energy Laboratory reports that renewable electricity can supply 80 percent of all US demand in 2050 with commercially available technologies.[2] In another important study by a group of energy and environmental scholars, it is reported that by 2050, 100 percent of our energy needs for electricity, transportation, heating and cooling, and industrial uses can be supplied by clean renewable resources in all 50 states.[3] Obstacles, of course, remain, the most significant of which is the existing energy infrastructure comprising incumbent industries with their supporting regulatory structure of laws and regulations. Nevertheless, the potential for a clean future is real, and that future can be advanced by first defining clean power and then by presenting more specific steps that need to be taken by industry and regulators to achieve it. In this chapter, the first step, defining clean power, is taken and the remaining steps are discussed in the following chapters.

The Clean Power Plan (CPP) did not prohibit the use of any resource for producing energy including oil, natural gas, coal, and nuclear power. The plan does, however, encourage the further development of some of those resources such as natural gas and also encourages the further development of renewable resources and energy efficiency. Although clean power is generally understood to encompass a greater use of renewable resources and to capture increased gains from energy efficiency,[4] it is necessary to more precisely identify those resources that constitute a clean power portfolio for several reasons. First, simply as a matter of interest group politics, the correct naming and framing of policy issues is necessary for a sound clean power politics.[5] Second, it must be noted and emphasized that clean power politics is not inimical to economic growth;

instead, clean power is necessary for a vibrant economic future.[6] This point will be more fully developed in Chapter 3. Third, and correlatively, a clear definition will enable policymakers and analysts to more accurately define the metrics and set the goals needed to measure the gains in the emerging clean power economy.

Currently, the definition of "clean power" differs according to particular applications.[7] As states move forward and promote clean power initiatives, the resources that qualify under those programs differ from state to state. Some states include nuclear power and clean coal, while others exclude them. Indeed, some electricity advocates favor clean energy standards (CES) that explicitly include clean coal and nuclear power in their definitions of clean energy.[8] Lester and Hart,[9] for example, include nuclear, natural gas, and clean coal in their definition. The definitional problem is complex because the availability and use of energy resources differ from region to region. Therefore, one unresolved issue is whether or not a definition of clean power can be uniform or rationalized across the country or whether states should be free to use distinct definitions in order to take advantage of regional differences.[10]

Although clean power plays a small role in today's US fossil fuel economy, it is making notable gains. Renewable resources, particularly wind power, are outstripping the installation of new fossil fuel electricity generation.[11] As noted in the White House's first Quadrennial Energy Review: "In 2014, renewable energy sources accounted for half of newly installed electric-generation capacity, and natural gas units made up most of the remainder. Electricity generation from wind grew 3.3-fold between 2008 and 2014, and electricity generation from solar energy grew more than 20-fold."[12] As importantly, the costs of solar and wind resources continue to decrease and the use of energy efficiency is increasing notably.[13] While it is the case that clean power is not currently cost competitive in every region, and it continues to enjoy government subsidies, it is also the case that no energy resource operates in an unfettered competitive market. Rather, all energy resources have some form of government assistance.

Although the definition of "clean power" is fluid, I argue that clean coal, natural gas, nuclear power, and some biofuels should not be included in the definition for reasons set out next. I realize, of course, that these resources are embedded in our energy portfolio and enjoy significant political support. Still, the approach to clean power taken here is one that promotes renewable resources and energy efficiency through policies and financial supports and, simultaneously, argues in favor of removing similar supports for traditional fossil fuels and nuclear power.

RENEWABLE PORTFOLIO STANDARDS AND FEED-IN-TARIFFS

For years now, at the state level, regulations have been adopted that promote renewable resources and energy efficiency over fossil fuels. Renewable portfolio standards (RPSs) (or alternative energy portfolio standards)[14] have been adopted by 41 states and the District of Columbia[15] and cover over 50 percent of total US electric demand.[16] The intended purposes of both programs include increasing the amount of clean power that is used to generate electricity, thus reducing greenhouse gas emissions; promoting technological energy innovations; and creating new and more competitive energy markets. Both standards can be defined as "a regulatory mandate to increase production of energy from renewable sources such as wind, solar, biomass and other alternatives to fossil fuels and nuclear electric generation."[17] This general definition does not convey the complexity and variety of RPS programs. The first difficulty is that of the various state programs; 29 have mandatory programs while the others are voluntary. With voluntary programs, the states set specific goals; however, there is no penalty for failure to achieve them.

In general, there are two requirements behind a typical RPS program. First, the state regulator will require identified utilities (usually local IOUs) to generate a certain percentage of electricity from specific natural resources. The utility, then, will be required to purchase that percentage from qualifying providers or the regulated utility can purchase renewable energy credits to satisfy its RPS obligations.[18]

The second general requirement is that the percentage goal will be set according to a published schedule. By way of example, a state may require that a utility purchase 3 percent renewable energy beginning in 2012 and increasing to 20 percent by 2020. Some RPS programs also allow utilities to satisfy their clean energy obligations through the adoption of conservation or energy efficiency programs.[19]

Because energy resources are unevenly distributed across the country, different states will emphasize different resources in their RPS programs. States in the Pacific Northwest and states in New England, as examples, have more access to relatively inexpensive hydroelectric power than other states in the country. The state of Maine, as another example, adopted a very aggressive 30 percent RPS goal. However, eligible resources included existing hydroelectric and biomass power plants. Therefore, Maine utilities were able to satisfy the 30 percent requirement on the effective date that the RPS program was launched. As a consequence, the Maine program did not require any new renewable generation facility to satisfy the mandate. Later, Maine adjusted its RPS program to require electricity suppliers to show that at least

1 percent of their total of electricity sales came from new renewable resources. Additionally, the new RPS program required an additional 1 percent contribution by new renewables each year until 10 percent of such sales from renewable resources were satisfied.[20] Similarly, states in the Southwest have more access to wind and solar power than northern states and Southeastern states have stronger potential for the development of biomass and less so for solar and wind power.[21]

Moreover, the various states differ on what constitutes an eligible resource. Some states, for example, include clean coal which is defined as coal-fired plants that capture and store carbon dioxide emissions. Further, some state RPS requirements attempt to achieve other goals such as promote in-state renewable resources. Such favoritism, however, is subject to constitutional challenges under the "dormant" commerce clause.[22] The significant lesson is that RPS programs must be flexible and over time new goals must be set.

Because states differ in their goals and in their RPS program designs, there is discussion of a national RPS program. The arguments in favor of such a program include: (1) a clear understanding of what constitutes clean power; (2) an increase in the amount of clean power that is required to be provided; (3) the creation of a national market for renewable energy credits; (4) increased efficiency by electricity suppliers; (5) rationalization of utility practices, that is, utilities satisfy the national standard rather than individual state standards; (6) more uniform and reliable enforcement; and (7) an alignment of energy and environmental regulations.[23] A national RPS should smooth out markets and bring consistency to eligible resources as well as consistency in monitoring and enforcement.

Regardless of such benefits, a national RPS comes with political costs. Renewable power is often more expensive than traditional energy sources; therefore, there is a political reluctance to impose higher costs on consumers. Second, as noted earlier, the uneven distribution of energy resources and the varied mix of power plants within each state make regional application of RPS programs attractive.[24] Further, because of the uneven distribution of resources, questions arise as to the distribution of the cost burdens associated with such programs.[25] In the latter regard, a national RPS could serve as "a form of wealth transfer from residents and states that lack natural resources to states that have resources that are rich for development and export for renewable development."[26] Still, RPS programs have proliferated and have opened clean power markets with the effect of reducing carbon emissions.

A feed-in-tariff (FIT) has the same goal as an RPS program, which is to increase the percentage of electricity generated from low-carbon resources.

A FIT, though, operates differently from an RPS program. Specifically, with a FIT there is a contract between a utility and a renewable energy developer. The contract sets a certain rate for the electricity purchased from the developer for a specific period of time. Through long-term contracts, new energy providers can rely on an income stream and utilities can use those contracts to satisfy state requirements.

FITs have been developed in Europe, particularly Germany, for a number of years and FIT policies have been adopted in six US states.[27] FITs can be used for the purpose of expanding renewable technologies ranging from wind and solar to geothermal and biomass to fuel cells and tidal power. There are several benefits associated with FIT programs. First, clean energy resources displace fossil fuels, thus reducing carbon emissions. Second, the fixed prices can stabilize electricity rates. Third, because clean energy developers can rely on an income stream, economic development and job creation can occur. Fourth, clean power initiatives can contribute to economic growth.

FITs do not come without serious challenges. Although Germany is notable for widespread adoption of FIT programs for the purpose of eliminating nuclear power and replacing it with renewable resources, particularly solar power, the German experience was not problem free. More specifically, electricity rates as a result of the FIT program were higher than anticipated, leading some critics to argue that the program failed in its essential purpose. Admitting that rates were higher than anticipated does not necessarily constitute a programmatic failure. Instead, corrections can be made to pricing, and the German goal of increasing solar penetration can be and is being met as solar penetration exceeded expectations. Originally, the program was expected to represent about 7 percent of total German wholesale generation. In 2014, however, solar power was close to 20 percent of installed capacity and close to 50 percent of peak demand.[28] FIT programs do face specific challenges. Most specifically, setting a contract rate that allows suppliers to rely on an income stream while not imposing high costs on retail customers is difficult. Experience with FIT programs reveals that flexibility and adjustments are necessary to accomplish both goals. In Spain, for example, a solar FIT program was designed to provide guaranteed income to power suppliers but it also put a ceiling on retail rates. As a consequence of constraining prices, Spain's FIT program failed.[29] Again, the challenge lies in program design.[30]

In the United States, FIT programs may include a variety of renewable technologies but generally include solar photovoltaic. In Virginia, for example, the FIT applies only to residential consumers who have installed solar photovoltaic while Hawaii's and California's FIT regulations apply to all investor-owned utilities. In each case, the FIT specifies a rate and a contract period, usually 10–20 years.[31]

States can adopt either RPS or FIT programs or both and the programs can be seen as complementary to each other.[32] RPS programs, for example, are intended to achieve a certain quantity of electricity that is generated by renewable resources (or efficiency). FITs, by contrast, focus on cost and creating clean power markets. Both programs, however, can be seen as promoting technological innovation in order to satisfy CES. According to Professor Lincoln Davies, there is a "potential regulatory symbiosis" between RPS and FIT standards. "Broadly, the renewable portfolio standard might be seen as a planning procedure and the feed-in tariff as its implementing device."[33] In short, the RPS sets the goal and the FIT is the primary method for achieving it. By combining both regulatory tools, a larger clean power market is created, simultaneously interacting with utilities and emerging clean power providers. Second, energy planning should be more comprehensive. Third, both programs should reinforce each other, thus making the attainment of clean power goals more likely. Finally, the use of these tools provides public support for a clean power transition.[34]

CLEAN ENERGY STANDARDS AND ENERGY EFFICIENCY STANDARDS

For most of its history, the United States has engaged in resource conservation. Building on American Romantic notions of authors such as Henry David Thoreau and Ralph Waldo Emerson and later John Muir, the preservation movement developed and was transformed into law.[35] As an example, Yellowstone National Park, considered the first national park in the world, was created in 1872 with the express intent that lands be "withdrawn from settlement, occupancy or sale" and dedicated for the benefit of the public.[36] Through the establishment of national parks and wilderness areas, millions of acres of government-owned land have been off-limits to resource development.[37]

More recently, legislation at the state and federal levels has focused on energy efficiency as another type of resource conservation. It is important to distinguish between the two. In a real sense, only resource conservation is truly carbon zero while energy efficiency will have some carbon effects through the manufacturing processes needed for energy-efficient appliances, buildings, and other technologies. More significantly, conservation and efficiency laws can act at cross purposes. To the extent that both reduce consumption, they are consistent. However, efficiency laws also have the intent of promoting certain technologies, which can have the effect of increasing consumption.[38]

To the extent that efficiency laws may reduce the cost of energy, there can be a rebound effect, which means that as the cost declines there is an incentive to consume more energy.[39] It must be noted that the rebound effect is subject to the laws of the price elasticity of demand, which is to say that even with price reductions, there is not a one-to-one increase in demand. Still, in some situations known as "backfire,"[40] rebound can result in increasing energy demand and may increase demand beyond the point at which the efficiency standards were implemented to achieve.

In response to the energy crises of 1973, a wide range of energy legislation was passed to increase US energy independence. In 1975, for example, the Energy Policy and Conservation Act[41] was passed and directed the Department of Transportation to establish corporate average fuel efficiency (CAFE) standards for automobiles and required the adoption of energy performance standards for household appliances. The act delegated to the Department of Energy (DOE) responsibility for establishing test procedures for appliances and delegated to the Federal Trade Commission responsibility for labeling requirements regarding energy efficiency.[42] Then, in 1976, Congress passed the Energy Conservation and Production Act[43] that required states to set energy efficiency standards (EES) for new commercial and residential buildings. And, in 1978, the National Energy Conservation Policy Act[44] required state planning processes for saving energy in buildings and establishing energy efficiency labeling for certain industrial equipment.[45] As Dernbach and Tyrrell note, President Reagan cut back on some of this legislation by repealing mandatory requirements for buildings and making those requirements voluntary. Nevertheless, conservation legislation continues and the National Appliance Energy Conservation Policy Act of 1987[46] has set performance standards for appliances.[47]

From the 1950s into the 1990s, US dependence on foreign oil increased even though energy independence remained a priority. In an effort to respond to the continuing need for independence, Congress passed the Energy Policy Act of 1992 (EPAct 1992),[48] the Energy Policy Act of 2005 (EPAct 2005),[49] and the Energy Independence and Security Act of 2007 (EISA 2007).[50] Each of the statutes contained energy efficiency provisions. The 1992 legislation, for example, revised the energy efficiency requirements for residential and commercial buildings and required states to consider the adoption of energy-efficient building codes. The act also sets standards for some appliances.

The 2005 legislation imposed standards on a variety of products including commercial and industrial equipment. EPAct 2005 also established tax credits for energy efficiency investments in new homes, commercial buildings, appliances, and hybrid vehicles.[51] EISA 2007, in turn, raised the CAFE standards for automobiles and set EES for electric lights.[52] The Obama administration also contributed to energy efficiency by authorizing several billion dollars through the American Recovery and Reinvestment Act of 2009[53] for such activities as home weatherization grants and energy efficiency upgrades in public housing.[54] The administration also raised the CAFE standards.

In addition to a history of conservation and preservation legislation, CES and EES are regularly considered and they operate differently from RPS and FIT programs. While all of those programs share the common objective of reducing carbon emissions, CES and EES programs reduce energy demand and RPS and FIT programs are intended to stimulate technological innovation, encourage new entrants in the power production sector, and create new energy markets.

Further, although CES and EES are both tools to promote the use of clean energy resources, they are distinguishable. A CES is a requirement imposed upon a utility, similar to an RPS program, which requires utilities to reduce electricity (and/or natural gas) usage by a certain percentage by a certain date. An EES, by contrast, is a standard imposed upon appliances and buildings to increase their energy efficiency.

CES programs can be used to require utilities to invest in energy efficiency programs to reduce energy usage by consumers. The utility, in turn, would recover that investment from ratepayers. Together with either an RPS or a FIT program, the CES can have two direct effects. First, investment decisions should be driven to clean energy technologies. Second, to the extent that renewable electricity generation made available through RPS or FIT programs may be more costly, efficiency goals should lower total energy costs to the consumer. Indeed, it has been reported that states that have adopted CES programs find that utilities "can change consumer investment behavior with rebates for efficient investments at a cost of 3–4 cents per kWh – one-third to one-half the cost of power from new plants."[55] CES energy is not costless, but it is cheaper than locally provided power.

In 2012, the Clean Energy Standard Act was introduced in Congress although not adopted.[56] The bill operated similarly to an RPS plan in that it identified eligible resources that electric utility retailers would be required to supply in specified amounts. The purpose of the act was to adopt a market-oriented regulation to stimulate clean energy innovation and promote low- and zero-carbon electricity generation. The goals of the act were ambitious. Starting in 2015, for example, the minimum percentage of electricity generated from qualifying facilities was 24 percent, rising to 84 percent by 2035.

In order to achieve the goal of clean power innovation, certain resources would be designated that could satisfy the goals. All generation from existing and new wind, solar, geothermal, biomass, municipal solid waste, and landfill gas plants earned full credits under the proposal. Hydroelectric and nuclear generation capacity placed in service after 1991 would also receive full credits. Partial credits would be awarded for generation that was using specific natural gas and clean coal technologies based upon the carbon intensity of each source. The standard was to apply to large electric utilities while small retailers were exempt from compliance.

According to an Energy Information Administration report, a national CES would have the effect of "significantly reducing the role of coal-fired generation, while increasing the role of nuclear, natural gas, and non-hydropower renewable technologies."[57] Further, the proposal was projected to result in a 25 percent decrease in coal-fired generation by 2025 and a 54 percent decrease by 2035. Concomitantly, the EIA projected that non-hydroelectric renewable generation would increase significantly by 42 percent in 2025 and 34 percent in 2035 with wind and biomass exhibiting largest increases. Further, carbon dioxide emissions were estimated to fall 20 percent by 2025 and 44 percent by 2035.[58]

The argument in favor of a national CES is similar to that made for national RPS. A national CES can rationalize clean power markets and more efficaciously achieve the goals of increasing the use of clean power technologies while reducing carbon emissions. In short, under the proposal, clean power was defined to include nuclear, natural gas, and clean coal technologies but did not expressly include energy efficiency.

A comprehensive CES should include energy efficiency for two reasons. First, "improving energy productivity is by far the lowest-cost, largest, quickest, and cleanest way to meet clean energy goals."[59] Second, efficiency gains reduce carbon emissions. For decades now, even though consumers are receiving more energy per dollar spent and, therefore, are getting more energy per dollar,[60] energy efficiency remains an important clean energy resource that needs to be further developed to play a larger role in the nation's energy portfolio. Indeed, reports by the National Academy of Sciences, McKinsey and Company, and the American Council for an Energy-Efficient Economy all demonstrate that efficiency gains not only remain to be made but also can promote economic growth by reducing waste.[61]

The advantages of including energy efficiency in a CES are manifest. Efficiency improvements are widely available and can be implemented with existing technologies. Expanding efficiency, particularly through appliances and buildings, is labor-intensive, thus creating new jobs. Further, as energy demand decreases so do energy prices. To the extent that CES may have a tendency to push up prices initially due to installation costs, including efficiency in such a standard will push energy bills downward as consumption declines.[62]

The CAFE standards that were established for cars and light-duty trucks in legislation passed in 1975, 1987, 2007, and during the Obama administration operate as efficiency standards by requiring that the average fuel economy for a fleet of vehicles attain a certain mileage per gallon by a specific date. In 1975, manufacturers were required to achieve 18.0 mpg by 1978 and 27.5 mpg by 1990. Later, the standards were increased to 17.2 mpg in 1979 and then to 20.7 mpg for the model years 1996–2004. Additionally, manufacturers were required to put labels on cars indicating their fuel efficiencies. Pursuant to the EISA 2007, fuel efficiency requirements must rise to 35 mpg by the year 2020. Then, through negotiations with the automobile industry, the Obama administration raised the CAFE standards to 54.5 for cars and light-duty trucks by model year 2025.[63]

Appliance standards work similarly in that, through the 1975 and 2007 legislation, the DOE established procedures for determining standards of energy efficiency, energy use, and estimated cost for identified products. And, the Federal Trade Commission was required to adopt labeling rules based upon that information. Labeling provides consumers with information about energy savings.

Programs such as Energy Star and Leadership in Energy and Environmental Design (LEED) labels have been popular as well as successful. In 2009, Energy Star prevented 45 million metric tons of greenhouse gas emissions, the equivalent of emissions from 30 million vehicles, and saved consumers $17 billion in their utility bills.[64] Indeed, energy consumption by such appliances as refrigerators, air-conditioners, and electric lighting has been reduced dramatically. Such product requirements are said to reduce operating costs after the initial payback period, reduce energy consumption, and improve energy planning and can attract investor capital.[65]

Automobiles and power plants are obvious sources of greenhouse gas emissions. Buildings, however, account for 40 percent of total US energy consumption and, correspondingly, 40 percent of carbon dioxide emissions. Consequently, improved energy efficiency in buildings can have a significant impact on emissions reductions.[66] The green building movement is intended to create "high performance buildings" that more efficiently use resources through improved siting, design construction, operation, and maintenance.[67] Today, the most popular effort to promote the development of green buildings is the U.S. Green Building Council's LEED program.

The Green Building Council is a nonprofit organization that evaluates the green features of new construction through a point system and awards certifications at silver, gold, and platinum levels. Several states and municipalities require that all state government buildings meet LEED criteria. "Overall, forty-five states and numerous school districts and universities have adopted various LEED initiatives in the form of legislation, executive orders, resolutions, ordinances, policies, and incentives."[68] It has been estimated that if these practices are applied to all new buildings in the United States, then projected CO_2 emissions could be reduced by over 10 percent by 2030.

It must be noted that while state and federal governments require energy efficiency in their own buildings, there are few legal requirements that private construction satisfy such standards. Instead, LEED certification remains voluntary.[69] The public sector, though, has adopted efficiency measures. In 2009, for example, by Executive Order, President Obama established a set of requirements for federal agencies to increase their energy efficiency and reduce greenhouse gas emissions. Pursuant to the order, agencies are required to set a percentage target for an absolute reduction in greenhouse gas emissions by reducing energy intensity in their buildings as well as by reducing the agency's vehicle fleet consumption by at least 2 percent annually until 2020. Additionally, the order requires that new contracts for products and services meet Energy Star standards.[70]

The Energy Star program, which applies to appliances and buildings, has a slightly different genesis. As part of EPAct 1992, the program is a voluntary labeling one intended to identify and promote energy-efficient products. The program certifies and labels products ranging from computers, major appliances, and office equipment to new homes and commercial and industrial buildings. Several states and municipalities have enacted ordinances to either encourage or require government buildings to satisfy Energy Star standards.

Additionally, at least 40 states have enacted building codes that require new and existing buildings that are undergoing major renovations to meet minimum EES.

It has been estimated by the EPA that Energy Star and similar programs have resulted in $19 billion in cost savings to consumers in 2009 alone.[71] Similarly, according to the Environmental Protection Agency (EPA), from 1992 through 2013, Energy Star participants through investments in energy-efficient technologies and practices have reduced utility bills by $30 billion and have prevented more than 277 million metric tons of greenhouse gas emissions in 2013, thus providing over $10 billion in social benefits by reducing damages from climate change.[72] The agency also reports that Energy Star has certified over 4.8 billion products, and more than 1.5 million households have earned the Energy Star label since the program began.[73]

Each of these regulatory approaches identifies specific energy resources that can qualify for preferred treatment. The argument against preferring resources is sometimes stated by saying that the government "should not pick winners." This argument appears attractive. After all, government should not prefer certain industries or firms over others. However, the argument ultimately fails on two counts. First, since the late nineteenth century through to the present, the government has always picked energy winners. In the late nineteenth century and the early twentieth centuries, municipalities and then states "picked winners" by granting monopolies to specific public utility companies that were providing electricity and natural gas. Early in the twentieth century and later in the 1930s, the federal government granted licenses to interstate oil pipelines,[74] interstate electric transmission lines,[75] and interstate natural gas pipelines.[76] These licenses constituted monopolies that had the intended effect of protecting license holders from competition. Further, during both world wars, the federal government established administrative agencies specifically for the purpose of promoting the use of coal and oil for war mobilization.[77] And, in the 1950s, legislation was passed that specifically created and protected the commercial nuclear power industry.[78] Later in the twentieth century, through a series of subsidies and tax credits clean power resources also received protection[79] and those subsidies have continued with the passage of the 2016 US budget.[80] There is no time in modern energy history in which the government did not pick winners and, correspondingly, there is no time in modern energy history in which energy resources engaged in full and open competitive markets.

Second, clean power is not likely to be provided for by the private sector alone because it has aspects of a public good that requires government assistance to open and sustain clean energy markets. Today clean power must be seen as a public good[81] that avails itself of regulatory and other public support mechanisms designed to transform our energy economy regardless of the barriers erected by incumbent companies. Indeed, the argument that the government "should not pick winners" is often made by incumbents seeking to protect their market share and erect costly barriers for new entrants. A clear example of incumbents trying to protect their market position is the "death spiral" argument made by utilities claiming that competition from nonutility electricity providers, more specifically rooftop solar installations, threatens their financial existence. The reality, however, is that rooftop solar barely scratches the surface of electricity production and the utilities' arguments about a death spiral are rhetorical and simply an argument for more government protectionism.[82]

TRANSITION CHALLENGES

"[I]t is probably safe to say that any such [an electricity] future will include a mix of utility-scale generation based on renewables, nuclear, and fossil fuels with carbon capture and storage, together with increasing penetration of distributed generation, demand response, and storage."[83] As safe and as realistic as that prediction may be, the problems associated with several of those forms of power production must be noted. More specifically, several of those resources should not be considered clean power resources at all.

The programs described earlier defined clean energy resources in a variety of ways. While the general consensus is that renewable resources and energy efficiency should form the core of the definition, for various political and geographical reasons, other resources such as clean coal, nuclear power, biofuels, and natural gas have been contained in some definitions of clean power. Each of these resources, however, presents problems that must be addressed. Biofuels and natural gas, for example, may be less environmentally friendly and carbon reducing than might be desirable. And, in the cases of clean coal and nuclear power, the cost of electricity generated from those resources may be more costly than might be hoped.

Clean Coal

Clean coal can also be referred to as carbon capture and sequestration (CCS), which involves three steps. First, CO_2 is captured either before or after burning the coal (or other fossil fuels) at a point source such as an electric power plant or at a large industrial plant. Then, the CO_2 is transported through pipelines for processing into useful products such as calcium or magnesium or injected into wells for enhanced oil and gas recovery. Finally, the unused CO_2 must be stored in underground geologic formations such as depleted oil and natural gas fields, off-shore, or in deep coal beds.[84] According to a report published by the Massachusetts Institute of Technology, the United States has a sufficient number of safe geological deposits available for sequestration.[85]

On the surface, the idea of clean coal is attractive because carbon can be extracted from the coal-burning process, thus reducing emissions while electricity is produced and the captured carbon may be put to other beneficial uses. The idea has proven so attractive that the federal government has been actively involved, until fairly recently, with pursuing and funding clean coal technologies. As early as 1985, Congress created a clean coal technology program to provide financial assistance for demonstration projects. The program, through the DOE, funded several demonstration projects around the country, most often in partnership with private industry.[86] Government support and funding was continued under §1303 of EPAct 1992 which required DOE to undertake clean coal research, development, and demonstration with the intent of commercialization. DOE responsibilities for clean coal projects were expanded by §401 of EPAct 2005 through the establishment of the Clean Coal Power Initiative (CCPI) that provided funding and loan guarantees for clean coal technologies.[87]

DOE continues funding under CCPI and reports several initiatives. However, there has been little to no progress toward the goal of cost-effective CCS let alone any significant commercialization of clean coal technologies. Of the eight projects initiated in 2003, only three were completed; of the two projects initiated in 2004, only one was completed and another is expected to enter commercial operation in mid-2015; and, of the six projects selected in 2009–2010, three are still active due to an infusion of funds from the American Recovery and Reinvestment Act of 2009 (ARRA).[88]

The DOE Office of Fossil Energy has received $3.4 billion from the ARRA for clean coal research and development. The office has funded three large-scale demonstration projects that were expected to capture and store a total of 6.5 million tons of CO_2 per year and the demonstration phase was expected to be completed in 2015. However, one project was completed, one is still under construction, and one was discontinued.[89] The office has also funded 7 projects for the purpose of converting captured CO_2 into useful products and 22 small-scale projects to accelerate CCS research and development. Again, completion of all of these projects is yet to occur.[90]

In addition to CCPI, the DOE has also continued the FutureGen project that was begun under President George W. Bush. In 2010, the DOE awarded $1 billion under ARRA to build a clean coal power project with carbon dioxide storage in Illinois under the title FutureGen 2.0. The CCS industry suffered a substantial blow in February 2015 as the DOE terminated funding of the Illinois project after determining that the project could not be completed even with the $1 billion allocated. And without federal funding, the entire project was terminated.[91] As of this writing, one CCS plant is in commercial operation in Edwardsport, Indiana, and another is expected to operate in 2016 in Kemper County, Mississippi. It should be further noted that both plants cost about as much as a nuclear plant and will generate about half as much electricity.

Thus, despite over $6 billion of federal funds available for CCS projects since 2008, as of May 2014, only two industrial projects are in operation, only one commercial-scale CCS project is in advanced construction, and only five CCS projects are under development.[92]

With decades of government support and with the wide availability of coal, the country's most abundant and inexpensive energy resource, CCS technology seemed promising yet remains noncommercial. Further, according to a federal interagency task force, CCS technologies also face economic challenges due to climate policy uncertainty and first-in-kind technology risks in addition to their already high costs.[93] As another study describes: "[a]ll the necessary components of a CCS system are in commercial use today. However ... [they] do not currently function together in a manner required for large-scale CO_2 mitigation."[94] Nevertheless, the technology has been endorsed by such groups as the Union of Concerned Scientists, the Environmental Defense Fund, and the Natural Resources Defense Council.[95] Clean coal, though, comes with four significant and interrelated impediments – "cost and cost recovery, lack of a price signal or financial incentives for CCS use, liability, and lack of comprehensive CCS regulation."[96]

Even though clean coal technologies are fairly well understood, they are not yet "off-the-shelf," which is to say that they are not commercially viable. Reducing those costs requires technological advances and technological progress that remain to be made. Most CO_2 is captured after combustion and doing so requires high degrees of heat, which means that the heat used to operate CCS processes is not used to produce electricity, thus contributing to the high cost of CCS projects. Once captured, CO_2 must be safely stored, and while the MIT report indicates an adequate number of safe storage sites exist, in order for carbon capture to make a significant impact on climate change, questions about the environmental consequences of storage remain to be addressed.[97]

Environmentally, CCS projects require anywhere from 3200 percent more water than non-CCS plants.[98] Also, the technological issues regarding long-term storage involve carbon seepage at storage facilities that may prove more porous than expected. Additionally, carbon emissions will result both from the construction and the operation of CCS projects. The environmental risks from CCS storage include CO_2 venting, aquifer contamination, increased earthquakes, and unknown impacts on biological communities.[99]

While environmental risks of clean coal are significant, the main culprit for the paucity of commercial viability of CCS projects is their cost. It has been estimated, for example, that the cost of a power plant with CCS is multiples higher than those for a conventional plant. Further, there is a cost premium of over 75 percent for operating a plant with CCS as opposed to without it. Additionally, even existing subsidies are insufficient to bring projects online.[100] CCS projects also require a transportation infrastructure. Pipelines are needed to move the CO_2 to either site for enhanced oil recovery or for long-term storage. CCS projects are unlikely to attract investors as they become more expensive as clean power regulations rules are adopted and as natural gas prices stay low. Finally, another form of costs associated with CCS projects is the fact that such processes can consume between 15 and 30 percent of the power generated by a plant, thus constituting a significant, and costly, "energy penalty."[101] As a result of these additional costs, it is estimated that electricity from CCS power plants would be expected to cost 75 percent more than electricity from conventional plants.[102] In short, CCS is a very expensive proposition, and, at this time, too expensive to be considered an attractive clean power option.

Biofuels

Biomass, of which biofuels are a subset, has been statutorily defined as "any organic matter which is available on the renewable basis, including agricultural crops and agricultural wastes and residues, wood and wood wastes and residues, animal wastes, invisible wastes, and aquatic plants."[103] Biofuels, in turn, can be defined as "transportation fuels made from biological materials, including ethanol made from corn or sugar and biodiesel made from vegetable oil waste fats"[104] and seem to offer considerable promise as a clean energy resource. Indeed, "[b]ioenergy is one of several elements in a comprehensive climate strategy that could cut projected oil use in half by 2030 and phase out coal in the electricity sector."[105] Biofuels are renewable, low in carbon emissions, can serve as a substitute for fossil fuels in the transportation sector, and are extensively available. However, all biofuels are not created equal and must be distinguished from each other. Further, biofuels come with specific problems including carbon intensity, market side effects, and cost.

Although renewable fuels policies have been part of US energy programming for decades, the significant push to develop alternative fuels first came with EPAct 2005 that mandated the use of at least 4 billion gallons of renewable fuels in the US gasoline supply by 2006 and then that mandate was increased to 7.5 billion gallons in 2012. This program was known as renewable fuel standard 1 (RFS1).

Pursuant to the EISA 2007, the second program, RFS2, increased the minimum quantity of biofuels to 9 billion gallons in 2008, rising to 36 billion gallons in 2022. Of that total, 21 billion gallons is to consist of advanced biofuels. Advanced biofuels are produced from nonfuel sources such as cellulosic materials. Thus, it has been estimated that domestic biofuels can be produced cheaper than gasoline and can be produced at nearly 8 billion barrels of oil equivalent by 2050, thus replacing over one-half of the oil used for transportation. Biomass and biofuels can be deployed to generate electricity that will be central to moving the transportation sector away from oil.

It is important to distinguish among biofuel stocks so that the most efficient and least damaging stocks are used. Corn ethanol, for example, can be and is being used as a biofuel although corn ethanol is only about 12 percent efficient. In other words, 78 percent of the potential energy in corn ethanol is wasted. Next, extensive use of corn-based biofuels raises food prices and has the potential of disrupting food markets. Further, corn ethanol production requires significant amounts of water and thus imposes a burden on that resource.[106] Finally, corn-based ethanol also releases carbon dioxide in significant quantities.[107] Again, all biofuels are not created equal and all cannot be considered clean power resources. Instead, decarbonized advanced biofuels that have marginal emissions should be preferred over biofuels, especially over food-based corn ethanol.[108]

In contrast to corn products, cellulosic ethanol is a more promising biofuel. Feedstocks for cellulosic ethanol include certain forestry and agriculture residues and grasses. These stocks are nonedible, easily and inexpensively grown, and lower in greenhouse gas emissions, and do not compete with food crops. Still, even nonfood biofuels require fertile land, thus competing with agricultural production.[109] Currently, cellulosic ethanol production is moving from the demonstration to the commercial stage, and it is estimated that the United States can produce 75 billion gallons of cellulosic ethanol per year by 2030.[110]

The first generation of renewable fuels depended upon food crops as fuel stocks and they were expensive, were disruptive to food markets, and had only modest greenhouse gas improvements over fossil fuels. So far, second-generation advanced biofuels, which depend less on food crops, have turned out to be expensive and have not met statutory goals because of technical and regulatory hurdles. Technically, many cars on the road are limited to gasoline that can be blended at most with 10 percent ethanol (E10) thus hitting a "blend wall" short of reaching the stated goals.[111] From a regulatory perspective, the EPA has the authority to grant waivers in one or more of the four fuel categories. However, the waiver process has not been evenly administered, and as a direct consequence, uncertainty regarding end goals was created, thus confusing alternative fuels markets. Even though the EPA must regularly revisit goals and objectives, it must administer the program with clarity so that markets function effectively.[112] In order to meet RFS program goals of reducing dependence on oil, protecting the environment and avoiding damaging food markets, second-generation, advanced, nonfood biofuels can be supported and developed and can reach the legislative goals.[113]

Regardless of the challenges, the biofuels industry is robust. Political support from farming states has generated a series of federal incentives including tax benefits and grant loan programs that have sustained the rapid growth of the industry. It has been estimated that federal incentives have expanded ethanol production from 175,000,000 gallons in 1980 to 6.8 billion gallons in 2007.[114] Further, the production of energy crops, rather than food crops, for ethanol production can be significant as approximately 400 million tons of these crops could be produced each year by 2030. Energy crops have a substantial advantage over food stocks. They can produce energy efficiently, require modest amounts of fertilizer and pesticide, and can be grown on less fertile soil. Additionally, energy crops can be integrated into agricultural systems, thus maximizing land use without distorting food markets.[115]

The operation of the RFS program has not been smooth. The current RFS2 program, for example, can be broken down into four categories: (1) total renewable fuels, (2) advance renewable fuels, (3) fuel-based diesel, and (4) cellulosic biofuels. The EPA sets the schedule for the amounts for each category that are to be produced to meet the mandate, and each fuel is required to meet a minimum lifecycle greenhouse gas threshold. The design of the program proved to be more challenging and complex than initially anticipated and reforms are necessary. Going forward, with financial supports, clear attainment standards, transparent administration, and R&D programs, a clean, nonfood biofuel industry has the potential to create jobs, positively contribute to the economy, and reduce carbon dioxide emissions thus serving as a clean power resource.[116]

Nuclear Power

Nuclear power is regularly cited as a necessary element of a clean and sustainable energy future[117] because nuclear power generation emits no carbon dioxide, yet the carbon footprint for the entire nuclear fuel cycle is not completely carbon neutral.[118] The environmental argument for nuclear power becomes more important as old nuclear plants are retired, because even if natural gas rather than coal is used to generate replacement electricity, more carbon dioxide emissions are generated from natural gas than throughout the nuclear power fuel cycle.[119] Further the case in favor of nuclear power is gaining public support[120] (certainly prior to the accident in Fukushima, Japan),[121] yet challenges remain and nuclear power is not included in this definition of clean power.

Today, we frequently hear that the United States is experiencing a "nuclear renaissance." Evidence of such a renaissance can be found in the fact that approximately 30 nuclear units are in some stage of planning and that the Nuclear Regulatory Commission has granted combined construction and operating license permits for two reactors in Georgia, two reactors in South Carolina, and one in Tennessee.[122]

Compared to the situation of nuclear power over the last 30 years, these new licenses indicate a significant change in the course of commercial nuclear power. Indeed, until recently, no new plants were built or ordered since 1978, and all plants that had been ordered since 1974 were canceled. Consequently, these new licenses evince a notable change in direction. It must be recognized, however, that this change has been facilitated by federal financial supports, including substantial multibillion dollar loan guarantees, authorized by EPAct 2005, which include nuclear R&D, funds for two demonstration projects, construction subsidies, operating subsidies, and the funds in the case of plant shutdowns.[123]

A strong argument can be made that nuclear power should not be considered as a clean power resource in our energy portfolio for two significant reasons. First, nuclear power cannot pass a market test. Two recent cases confirm this point. In Georgia, the Southern Co. is building a nuclear plant that is facing project delays as well as cost increases.[124] This plant and the Florida plant that were originally scheduled to produce power in 2016 and 2017 are now scheduled to operate in 2019 and 2020, respectively.[125] Then, Florida Power & Light Co. also announced that while it needs to add a new natural gas plant by 2019 to satisfy customer demand, it will delay nuclear expansion activities at its nuclear power plant near Miami due to the low-cost natural gas.[126] Second, and complementarily, we can achieve greater gains in energy efficiency and in reduced carbon emissions by investing in alternative and renewable resources.[127]

Even with new nuclear construction in Georgia and South Carolina, serious problems remain. In addition to high construction costs, the economic pressures on the nuclear power industry include sluggish electric demand, aging nuclear inventory, and lower natural gas prices as well as cost competition from renewable resources.[128] Indeed, the levelized cost of electricity (LCOE), that is, the total cost of construction and operation, is higher for nuclear power than it is for several resources including conventional coal, wind power, and natural gas.[129]

It should be noted, however, that LCOE estimates are difficult to make. Some levelized cost estimates of wind, for example, may not take into account subsidies or backup power needed when the wind does not blow, and therefore, wind may be more expensive than nuclear power. Similarly, the levelized cost estimates for nuclear power do not always include the subsidies that created the industry and continue to sustain it. Moreover, the estimates for nuclear power are often based on "advanced" designs that are not now in use and, therefore, do not provide reliable cost estimates. Consequently, LCOE estimates for nuclear power must be scrutinized carefully and are not always particularly favorable to that industry.

A major study of nuclear power by the Massachusetts Institute of Technology (MIT) indicated that the LCOE from nuclear power can become cost competitive only under very restrictive circumstances. According to the MIT study, nuclear power can compete with other generation sources if the country considers and adopts a standardized design, builds five prototype plants, imposes a carbon price, and addresses proliferation and nuclear waste issues.[130] Under those tight restrictions, nuclear generated electricity can become cost competitive. At this point, however, none of those circumstances have been obtained even though EPAct 2005 adopted many of the recommendations of the MIT report. Simply, not only is nuclear power not "too cheap to meter," as promised in the heydays of commercialization, but also nuclear power is too expensive to build and generate cost-competitive electricity.

Still, proponents argue that advanced nuclear reactor designs promise: (1) to be safer, (2) more efficient because they can use spent fuel, (3) more efficient to operate, (4) more environment-friendly because of zero carbon emissions, and (5) produce much less nuclear waste.[131] Supporters of advanced nuclear designs also argue that "fuel availability, waste disposal, and proliferation risk are not significant obstacles to nuclear deployment and lower costs."[132] At this point, though, the technologies are under development, yet are neither online nor projected to be so in the near to mid-terms. Further, advanced nuclear will be developed only with the support and funding from the US government.[133] To be clear, the clean power resources discussed in this book also receive government's support. The argument in favor of government support for them, though, is that traditional resources have received the lion's share of subsidies over time and that a transition to a clean future as outlined in this book can be made with temporary rather than long-term public funding.

Another dimension of the nuclear renaissance is the construction of small, modular nuclear units of less than 300 MW as defined by the DOE.[134] The attraction of smaller units is that they can be designed uniformly, are quicker and cheaper to build, and are more mobile, and licensing can be streamlined. Therefore, they can provide decentralized electricity generation. Proponents favor modular units because a uniform design makes construction less costly.[135] Proponents also argue that they are safer. Critics of modular design, however, disagree on both counts and questioned both the safety and the cost effectiveness of modular nuclear units.

There are two dimensions to the cost issue. First, this proposed next generation of nuclear power will require government financial support because the private sector will not sufficiently invest.[136] Currently, the DOE is supporting the development and deployment of small reactors through its Licensing Technical Support Program. This program has over $450 million available in matching grants to help subsidize the design and licensing of this technology.[137] Second, critics also argue that it is not necessarily true that modular units can be operated more cheaply than traditional larger units because traditional units have enjoyed economies of scale that will not be available to newly installed, smaller modular reactors because those units are untested and learning curve costs must be absorbed.[138] Again, advanced nuclear power is not market ready.

Additionally, critics continue to voice their concerns about safety. There is an inherent trade-off between safety and cost. In arguing for the safety of modular units, proponents miss a step in the logic process. Uniform reactor design will only be safer if the original design is safe to begin with, and as critics point out, such safety features are both unproven and constitute a trade-off with lower costs.[139]

Nuclear power proponents counter that safety standards are redundant and, therefore, costly, and that those costs must be reduced. It must be noted, however, that safety issues have become more significant after 9/11 when the Nuclear Regulatory Commission (NRC) required US reactors to be more secure against aircraft attacks. Additionally, Fukushima raised safety concerns that have been addressed by the NRC.[140] As part of the response to that disaster, an NRC task force made multiple recommendations to improve the safety of plants, given such unanticipated contingencies as those that occurred at Fukushima. Those recommendations address mitigation strategies, emergency preparedness, the regulatory framework, and flooding among others.[141] It must be noted that the NRC Fukushima review concentrated on safety and failed to look at broader issues of national energy policy. Instead, after the review, US nuclear power policy has been business as usual.[142]

Under the proposed CPP rule, nuclear power was included in Building Block 3 and could be considered in designing a state's best system of emissions reduction (BSER) because five new nuclear units were under construction. The proposed rule considered that some states could choose to extend the life of nuclear plants that could satisfy CPP targets. The nuclear power provisions were deleted in the final rule for several reasons. Some states worried that if nuclear was included, then their state goals might be more stringent than otherwise because some or all of the five plants under construction could be delayed. By simply delaying plant retirements, no additional contributions to emissions reductions were being made. Further, other comments indicated that nuclear plant retirements would not occur evenly across all states, and states with high rates of retirement would be disadvantaged. Ultimately, the final rule eliminated nuclear power from BSER considerations because of the high cost of nuclear investments and because renewable electricity was coming online at cheaper rates. In effect, the change from the proposed to the final rules simply means that states may not calculate nuclear power in their BSER; however, emissions reductions attributable to nuclear power can be used to calculate compliance.[143]

Given the choice between investing in nuclear power and cleaner energy options, the more effective and efficient solution would be to opt for renewable resources and energy efficiency. The issue becomes not so much the question of whether or not greenhouse gas emissions from nuclear power are negligible. Rather, the issue is whether or not investment in clean energy can be more effective in terms of both generating electricity and reducing emissions. One study, for example, concludes that "[f]or every dollar you spend on nuclear, you could have saved five or six times as much carbon with efficiency or wind farms."[144]

Today, the current fleet of nuclear units is cheaper to operate than many new renewable and efficiency technologies because those units have already recovered their construction costs through rates. There are, however, several significant open issues regarding new nuclear power and the cost of electricity that it will generate. The new plants in Georgia and South Carolina will not be online for at least half a decade or more. The United States is yet to solve the problem of long-term storage of nuclear waste. Similarly, the relicensing of older nuclear plants and the expansion of spent fuel pools have costs associated with them that are yet to be incorporated in the cost of electricity. And the cost to decommission a nuclear plant is about the same as constructing one. Simply, the nuclear fuel cycle has attendant costs that will have to be paid. Not only must we move away from fossil fuels but also we must acknowledge that our experiment with nuclear power has simply proven to be too costly to continue.

Shale Gas

Until recently, the US energy economy had a very specific trajectory. In 1970, domestic oil and gas production peaked, flattened, and then declined. Correspondingly, oil imports increased significantly over the period. In 2005, however, our energy picture began to change dramatically. Recall, the first prong in the nation's energy policy was energy independence from importing Middle East oil. With domestic production rising and imports declining, together with available oil resources from Canada, energy independence seemed closer to reality. Indeed, in 2012, Republican presidential candidate Mitt Romney ran on an energy platform stressing North American energy independence by 2020.[145] At the heart of the Romney plan was a reliance on the increased domestic oil and gas production that had already been occurring.[146]

Domestic oil and gas production has been on the rise.[147] The United States hit its peak oil production in 1970 at an average of 9.6 million barrels per day (mbd) falling to an annual average low of 5.0 mbd in 2008. Since then, domestic production has been rising to an average of 8.6 mbd 2014.[148] Similarly, natural gas production peaked in 1970 at 21.9 trillion cubic feet (tcf), falling to a low in 1985 of 17.7 tcf and projected to exceed 26.0 tcf for 2014.[149] Over the last decade, shale gas production has increased more than 10-fold and is expected to continue as production is expected to rise from 9.7 tcf in 2012 (40 percent of US dry gas production) to 19.8 tcf in 2040 (53 percent of US dry gas production.)[150] According to the EIA, shale gas contributes to our natural gas portfolio significantly with numerous benefits including: (1) generating 25 percent of US electricity, (2) providing heat to 56 million residences and businesses, (3) providing 35 percent of the energy and feedstocks needed by US industry, (4) employing over 600,000 jobs, and (5) generating over $250 billion in various revenues and taxes.[151]

Recently, the International Energy Agency (IEA) reported that new fossil fuel discoveries in the United States are having a profound impact on domestic and global energy policies and markets. According to the IEA, "[t]he global energy map is changing" and is being redrawn by the "resurgence of oil and gas production in the United States."[152] The IEA projects that by 2017 the United States will produce more oil than Saudi Arabia. In addition, the agency reports that the global energy map is changing as European countries retreat from nuclear power and replace it with rapidly growing wind and solar technologies. Other commentators, like Professor Richard Pierce, claim that shale gas addresses *all* of our major energy problems,[153] while still others treat this natural gas resource as a bridge fuel to the future.[154] In his 2012 State of the Union Address, President Obama cited experts who predicted that the natural gas industry will create 600,000 jobs by the end of the decade.[155] As remarkable as these claims are and even with the brightest projections, the United States is not scheduled to be energy independent without a robust clean energy economy.[156] Nevertheless, shale gas development is a "game changer" for our domestic energy profile.[157]

These new finds of natural gas have much to recommend them. First, recent discoveries reveal abundant reserves, and following abundance, consumers are enjoying low natural gas prices.[158] Second, natural gas emits about half of the carbon dioxide released by coal during burning. It has been argued that by replacing coal with natural gas, we can reduce greenhouse gas emission by 45 percent with attendant improvements in health.[159] Third, as a result of lower prices and less drastic environmental effects, natural gas is displacing coal for electricity generation.[160] Fourth, the increase in domestic production adds jobs to the economy. Fifth, the United States is beginning to reduce imports and increase exports, thus reducing our trade deficit as the country grows more energy independent.[161] Not only are we less reliant on imports, natural gas can be adopted for use in the transportation sector, further reducing our reliance on oil.[162] Finally, the new discoveries have the effect of smoothing out the price volatility experienced by the natural gas sector for the last two decades.[163] Unfortunately, the government policies that drive a "natural gas transition" will not adequately address the need for carbon reduction.[164]

If we look more closely at shale gas production, particularly when we consider hydraulic fracturing, we find significant environmental costs associated with developing this domestic resource. From a broader perspective, the role of natural gas in a clean power future must be closely considered. Will we continue to favor domestic fossil fuel incumbents at the expense of new entrants in renewable resources and energy efficiency markets?[165] Although shale gas releases lower carbon emissions than coal, it is still a dirty resource, and even given its current abundance, it is underpriced because the cost of carbon is not included in the cost of a million cubic feet of natural gas. Shale gas, then, is simply an extension of our traditional hydrocarbon economy favored by government and large energy firms for over a century, and it has serious environmental consequences that exclude it from being part of a clean power solution.

The success of shale gas production is directly attributable to horizontal drilling and hydraulic fracturing, which is used in approximately two-thirds of the natural gas wells in the United States and up to 95 percent of all oil and gas wells currently being drilled.[166] Regardless of the several benefits listed earlier, natural gas, particularly through horizontal fracturing, poses significant environmental costs and risks that cannot be ignored and that militate against including natural gas in a clean power portfolio.[167] More specifically, environmental harms occur throughout the fuel cycle from exploration and production through transportation and burning.

1 Air Pollution

The general argument favoring natural gas (including shale gas) as a "bridge" fuel is that it releases roughly half as much carbon dioxide as coal and that its substitution for coal to generate electricity will contribute to environmental improvements. However, this is not necessarily a long-run proposition. Natural gas is still a fossil fuel and to the extent that it becomes a substitute to coal for electricity generation, over the not so long term, a greater use of natural gas "could contribute to that sector's overall increase in carbon dioxide emissions."[168]

Shale gas drilling operations can cause air pollution from a number of sources. Diesel engines, rigs, trucks, and other equipment used in the production process emit greenhouse gases. Additionally, gases are released from operating the wells especially through venting and flaring. The production process and the various activities associated with it combine to "release large amounts of methane, fine particulate matter and [volatile organic compounds] VOCs. VOCs are ground-level ozone precursors, and methane is a highly toxic gas."[169] Gas leakage, especially methane leakage, from all of these activities has the potential for significant environmental harm.[170] Methane, a component of natural gas, gives the greatest cause for concern. Although the amount of methane emissions is much lower than the emissions of carbon dioxide, methane is 72 times more potent at the time of release and is 25 times more potent than carbon dioxide over a 100-year period.[171] Consequently, as new oil and gas exploration and production expands, methane leakage can occur throughout the development of those resources.

While the EPA initially concluded that the net environmental impact of methane emissions is likely to be small,[172] other studies show that non-CO_2 emissions from shale gas can result in lifecycle emissions higher than those of coal and conclude that shale gas does "not discernibly reduce the trajectory of greenhouse gas emissions" due to methane seepage during fracturing and drilling[173] and that previous studies had underestimated the amount of methane emissions.[174] Further, EPA white papers indicate that methane seepage does occur in the use of compressors,[175] the operation of completed wells,[176] and leaks[177] among other sources of pollution.[178]

As part of its Climate Action Plan, the White House has issued a white paper warning of the dangers of methane leakage. The report notes that methane accounts for 9 percent of greenhouse gas emissions, and although they have decreased since 1990, methane emissions are expected to increase through 2030 if no additional ameliorative actions are taken. The report also states that methane can be captured and put to economically beneficial uses.[179] To that end, the EPA has been directed to issue methane rules with the goal of reducing emissions from oil and gas production by 45 percent by 2025 from 2012 levels.[180] The EPA is expected to issue final regulations by 2016. Upon the closing of the public comment period, the EPA estimated that its proposed methane standards could reduce leakage of up to 400,000 short tons of methane by 2025, which is the carbon equivalent of 1 billion gallons of gasoline or shutting down two coal-fired power plants. While these reductions are sizable and necessary, they are insufficient covering as they do only 4–5 percent of 2013 emissions from petroleum and natural gas systems.[181]

2 Water Pollution

Water is a significant input in the hydraulic fracturing process. Consequently, several water issues emerge. First, drilling requires large volumes of water to be withdrawn from both ground and surface waters ranging from 2 to 5 million gallons per well. Second, during drilling, various chemicals are mixed into the water and consequent surface spills can affect drinking water resources. Third, well injection also has an impact on drinking water resources. Fourth, wastewater must be transported and stored and spillage from either can also have negative health effects. And, finally, wastewater needs to be treated and disposed of and, therefore, can also impact drinking water resources.[182]

In 2010, the EPA was directed by Congress to study and review the effects of hydraulic fracturing on drinking water resources. In December 2012, the EPA issued a progress report on its study.[183] In late 2014, the EPA announced that it would release a draft report in March 2015 and a final report in 2016.[184] During the study process, the EPA collected a series of academic papers reviewing such things as water acquisition, chemical mixing, well construction, flow back water, and wastewater treatment and disposal.[185]

The potential for water pollution involved in the hydraulic fracturing process is significant. Water that is injected into a well will flow back. Anywhere from 10 percent to 50 percent of the injected water can be returned to the surface and that flow back water contains chemicals used during the fracturing operation.[186] Wastewater chemicals are often toxic including organic pollutants, heavy metals, and radioactive materials, some of which are naturally occurring.[187]

Thus, water use involves several environmental issues including the amount used in injection and the possible environmental and human health effects that can result from the effects of the use of chemicals in the process. Noted risks include the introduction of invasive species between water resources, increased surface water temperatures, increased pollutant concentrations, harmful water to plants and wildlife, and reduction in water quality for all users. These effects will vary depending upon levels of toxicity, how the chemicals are introduced into the environment, and the routes by which humans, wildlife, and plant life are exposed to them including chemical spills.[188]

In most shale regions, flow back and produced water can be disposed of by injection into deep geologic formations; however, most notably in the Marcellus Shale region, those formations are limited. In such regions, flow back must be treated, recycled, disposed of, or delivered to water treatment facilities.[189] Consequently, these chemically tainted waters must be managed and treated properly. One regulatory option is to require the disclosure of the exact composition of the chemical fluids used in the process. Many producers have self-reported and use the public website FracFocus to disclose volumes as well as the chemical makeup of the fluids. Overall, though, industry has been reluctant to fully disclose the chemical composition of wastewater, thus hiding risks to environmental health.[190]

Unfortunately, the EPA pursuant to the EPAct 2005 is prohibited from regulating hydraulic fracturing operations under the Safe Drinking Water Act.[191] This gaping loophole is known as the Halliburton exception named for the oil and gas industry firm that lobbied for it and patented hydraulic fracturing in the 1940s.[192] In 2015, the Republican Senate voted to maintain that exemption.[193] Even with this obstacle, the EPA has initiated a rulemaking to set water discharge standards for wastewater from shale gas production.[194] Additionally, industry environmental groups and state regulators have devised a program, under the acronym STRONGER, to develop "guidelines for better management and disposal of oil and gas wastes."[195]

3 Community Disruption

Shale gas development is occurring in regions, particularly in the eastern United States, that are unfamiliar with oil and gas exploration and production. Developing sites require the use of trucks and other heavy equipment as well as the possible construction of new roads, drill pads, and gathering lines. These activities affect the immediate area and affect air emissions, odors, noise, spill risk, changes in land use, the disruption of wildlife, and the general changes in the life in these communities. Additionally, drilling in populated areas brings with it health risks including cancer, asthma, headaches, nosebleeds, and other health problems.[196] Concern about such disruption has led citizens to attempt to ban fracking in their communities.[197] And, concern in New York about respiratory health, safe drinking water, soil contamination, and seismic activity as well as climate change has led that state to ban fracturing.[198] Such activity, unsurprisingly, has resulted in pushback legislation by the industry.[199]

The shale gas boom has seen a significant increase in drilling activity. More wells are being drilled and with that increase there is a greater need for more surface usage. Operators need more access roads, habitats are disturbed, transportation activity increases dramatically, soil erosion occurs, and storm water quality is adversely affected. In addition to growing conflicts between local, state, and federal authorities regarding the extent of hydraulic fracturing and its regulation, conflicts about the use of and disruption to public lands are also increasing.[200]

Given the reality that shale gas production will continue and given the potential environmental consequences of hydraulic fracturing, fracturing operations must be conducted with greater environmental sensitivity. Fortunately, there is no shortage of recommendations regarding this drilling process. At the federal level, the EPA continues its research into the consequences of hydraulic fracturing on drinking water. Additionally, the Bureau of Land Management has issued a final rule to regulate fracturing on public and Indian lands. In particular, the rule requires disclosure of chemicals used throughout the drilling process, attempts to improve the well-bore integrity, and addresses issues on flow back waters.[201] That rule is now subject to legal challenge.[202]

Federal regulators should also reconsider the Halliburton exemption mentioned earlier as well as the exemption of fracking under the Resource Conservation and Recovery Act. Further, Congress has had various bills introduced, known as the Fracturing Responsibility and Awareness of Chemicals Act that promotes public disclosure.[203] National regulations have the advantage of making fracking regulation even across state boundaries and that uniformity should benefit the industry from having to comply with multiple regulatory schemes.[204] Further, additional study of methane emissions is necessary to understand the full environmental impact from shale gas development.[205]

Professor Hannah Wiseman has written extensively on hydraulic fracturing and makes several recommendations for improving the process. Her recommendations range from conducting environmental studies and developing spillage and response plans to adopting protections for surface water withdrawals and storage to better siting of well pads and improvements in the drilling process.[206] Other scholars recommend more extensive use of liability mechanisms such as bond requirements and insurance to shift damages away from the public and impose the costs on the polluters,[207] and there is evidence that environmental enforcement does have positive consequences by reducing violations over time.[208]

Natural gas, particularly shale gas, should not be included in the definition of clean energy. For all its asserted environmental improvements and economic benefits, shale gas continues our traditional fossil fuel energy model and we cannot allow it to distract us from a more important and economically promising clean power future.[209]

MEASURING CLEAN POWER

Because the CPP merged energy and environmental regulations, there is no accepted or standard metric to be used to measure progress toward a clean power future because the energy future is configured radically differently from our energy past. More pointedly, because of climate change and the energy responses to it, we cannot solve energy problems with policies or strategies that are linear and short-term. Instead, the clean power future is multivariate, spans generations, is not contained within usually recognized jurisdictional boundaries, and contains a host of technical, economic, and political uncertainties. There are markers that can be used to help us identify the direction of progress. Some of those markers are better indicators of changes in the direction of energy policy while others are more explicitly concerned with environmental improvements. Clean power gains must be tracked and metrics must be established to understand the monetary and nonmonetary values of: (1) investments in clean energy, (2) reductions in greenhouse gases particularly carbon dioxide, and (3) environmental and health gains.

A clean power future is, in part, driven by concerns regarding climate change. One set of metrics is based on reduction of carbon dioxide in the atmosphere. If carbon reduction was the only element of a clean power future, then a cap on emissions would be sufficient to reach that end. However, even though scientists agree that setting carbon targets is a desirable metric, the difficulties regarding how and at what level those targets should be set and then allocated has been prevented because of political disagreements.[210] Adding to the complexity, a clean power future is more than simply carbon reduction; it involves new sources of energy production. Consequently, an emissions cap alone is insufficient to measure a successful clean power transition.[211] Therefore, in assessing the transition, both environmental and energy metrics should be considered.

Environmental Metrics

From an environmental perspective, setting climate targets has been one way to measure developments in climate change. Two metrics are commonly used – changes in temperature and changes in the concentration of carbon in the atmosphere. In its most recent report, the International Panel on Climate Change (IPCC) found that "[h]uman influence on the climate system is clear, and recent anthropogenic emissions of greenhouse gases are the highest in history. Recent climate changes have had widespread impacts on human and natural systems."[212] Another study reports that the world has not seen such concentrations in hundreds of thousands of years.[213]

The IPCC report also noted that the Earth's surface has been successively warmer for the last three decades, more so than any preceding decades since 1850.[214] The report recommends that a global warming target of no more a 2°C increase above preindustrial levels be reached by the end of the century.[215] It also notes that without additional mitigation efforts, global temperatures can be expected to increase from 3.7°C to 4.8°C above pre-industrial levels by the year 2100.[216] The 2°C target is based upon a mid-nineteenth-century baseline and that since that time the Earth's temperature has increased about 1°C, thus not leaving much room for improvement.[217] It is also important to recognize that a one-meter rise in sea level endangers several island nations, and in response, the Paris climate talks set a more ambitious goal of keeping temperature increases at 1.5°C.

In addition to measuring increases in global surface temperature, the environmental metric also assesses the concentration of atmospheric carbon dioxide. As of November 2015, the National Ocean and Atmospheric Agency measures CO_2 levels in the atmosphere in excess of 400 ppm. Once a baseline is established, goals must be set and policymakers often use a range of goals. In addition to the IPCC recommendation of maintaining carbon levels of 400 ppm, the most frequently used carbon targets are 350 ppm, 450 ppm, or 550 ppm. There are climate activists who argue strenuously for a 350 ppm target which means, of course, a significant reversing of carbon emissions.[218] Others tend to favor 450 ppm as a more realistic, as well as acceptable, climate target.[219]

Notice that we currently exceed the 350 ppm target and that the 2°C target is also unlikely to be maintained without further climate strategies. Most significantly, mitigation measures are necessary if either or both targets are to be achieved and the clean power regulations must be considered an important part of a carbon reduction strategy.[220]

Energy Metrics

The most important energy metric is the reduction of carbon emissions. Carbon reductions can occur through three general strategies – increased energy intensity, decreased carbonization, and increased use of energy efficiency and conservation. Signs are promising as the country continues to improve its energy intensity by spending less money for the energy it consumes and is projected to continue these improvements for the next 30 years,[221] and over the last 25 years, carbon intensity has been reducing at an average rate of about 1.8 percent per year. While the trend is moving in the right direction, it must be more aggressively pursued.[222]

Energy intensity and energy efficiency have been discussed previously. Decarbonization strategy is central to the success of the clean power regulations. One study argues that effective decarbonization would require a 4 percent reduction in carbon emissions per year and that, while achievable, such a level would require a "strong push from government and strong public support."[223] Other analyses demonstrate that decarbonization is "both technically feasible and economically affordable."[224] The findings in that analysis indicate that it is technically feasible to achieve 80 percent greenhouse gas reduction below 1990 levels by 2015. Importantly, adequate decarbonization can be made with only incremental costs to the energy system and without noticeable changes in lifestyle.[225] The following chapters of this book present a series of policies that can be adopted by government and the private sector to help achieve greater decarbonization.

Consequently, the way that the cost issue is framed has a dramatic impact on analysis. If, for example, the clean power regulations measured against the cost of electricity with and without the plan, then it may very well, but not necessarily, be the case that electricity will cost more with the clean power regulations than without it, at least in the short term. Assume for the moment that this is true.[226] There is a strong, and necessary, argument that electricity costs with and without the clean power regulations is the wrong way to frame the issue of the importance of decarbonization. Indeed, the EPA's cost-benefit analysis weighed the health and environmental benefits over the long term. Therefore, the better framing of the issue is one that merges energy and environmental concerns such that not only will short-term electricity costs be assessed but also will long-term health and environmental benefits.

CONCLUSION

A clean power future requires a specification of the resources that will lead to a decarbonized economy. To have a solid and vibrant clean power politics, it is necessary to be precise about what constitutes a qualifying resource. For the reasons discussed in the chapter, renewable resources such as solar wind and geothermal as well as energy efficiency are clean power resources. Other resources, clean coal, shale gas, nuclear power, and biofuels have been treated as clean energy resources by different groups for different purposes. However, each of those resources suffers from one or more defects. In the case of food-based biofuels and natural gas, their carbon intensity disqualifies them from being treated as a clean energy resource. Nuclear power and clean coal, even if they can result in a substantial reduction of greenhouse gas emissions, both fail a market test and both continue the traditional hard path energy paradigm that must be abandoned in favor of more decentralized energy reduction and distribution. The proper definition and framing of the clean power regulations directly affect energy and the environment. More importantly, the clean power future is a matter of our broader political economy that is addressed in the next chapter.

3

The Political Economy of Clean Power

As politically desirable as a clean and environmentally friendly future may be, it is a future that is set in an economic context that cannot be ignored and that context is the central focus of this chapter. Throughout this book, data on the costs of energy, natural resources, and pollution as well as estimates of job increases or decreases, investment trends in clean energy, and the like are presented and point out the future direction of energy policy. Data trends in the United States, as well as in other developed nations, demonstrate the growing adoption of clean power policies and practices. These trends, in turn, shape an argument about our political economy that addresses the foundations of our economic life, how wealth is produced and distributed, how it is consumed, and how political decision-making power is allocated.[1] The political economy of clean power presented here is consistent with the data trends and embodies a set of normative and policy principles about the desirability of an energy transition to a clean future. That future must attend not only to the environment; it must also attend to the matter of economic growth.

BETTING ON A CLEAN POWER FUTURE

One way to consider a clean power future is as this generation's "wager": Will the political economy be better off investing now in a clean transition or should we continue a business-as-usual fossil fuel energy path? This clean energy wager reprises a bet made between neo-Malthusian Paul Ehrlich and his antagonist Julian Simon, which is recounted in Yale historian Paul Sabin's book, *The Bet*.[2] Paul Sabin uses Ehrlich and Simon as foils to explain today's dysfunctional politics surrounding energy and the environment. In 1980, Ehrlich and Simon bet each other on the price of five minerals (chromium, copper, nickel, tin, and tungsten). Ehrlich, the father of Zero Population

Growth, believed that thoughtless and unconstrained consumption of natural resources by an ever-expanding human population would literally doom the planet.[3] Ehrlich posited that by 1990, world population growth would exacerbate the scarcity of natural resources, and therefore, resource prices would rise and the economy would decline and suffer.

Simon, by contrast, asserted that population growth was an overall benefit to society and that "free market" innovation and pricing would cause resource prices to fall. Simon argued further that human creativity entailed in an increased population would spur economic growth and benefit human well-being through technological fixes. To Simon, a no-growth policy was unwise, was inefficient, and would itself doom the planet. As it turned out, ten years later, the prices of all of the named resources decreased and Ehrlich lost the bet. However, Simon's victory was more a matter of market timing rather than an inevitable confirmation of his pro-growth, free market ideology. As Professor Sabin points out, if different ten-year periods were used between 1900 and 2008, Ehrlich, not Simon, would have won the bet 63 percent of the time. So much for predicting an energy future.

Sabin, of course, uses "the bet" as a focal point for a larger story. Similarly, he uses Ehrlich and Simon as markers for a debate about energy development and environmental protection that has been ongoing for more than 40 years. The positions taken by pro-growth Simon and by environmentally conscious Ehrlich mirror the same disagreement between Yergin and Speth discussed in Chapter 1. Sabin's thesis is that not only has the debate continued; it has become shriller, more polarized, and more partisan as environmental concerns become an increasing part of the energy policy conversation.[4] Similarly, from Sabin's perspective, there is a widening rift between pro-environmentalists and pro-growth advocates as these opposing positions continue to harden. Such hardening, however, need not be the case. While each of the arguments by Simon, Yergin, Ehrlich, and Speth is more of a caricature than a full-blown policy prescription, elements from each can be forged into a clean power pathway. Quite simply, the divide between energy and the environment can be bridged by a transition to a clean power future.

Using Ehrlich as a marker, the liberal, environmental side of the debate tends to focus on resource conservation, environmental protection, species preservation, and, in some quarters, a slowdown in population. Critics of that position argue that environmental and ecological pessimism is unwarranted and point out that spaceship Earth has not yet imploded.[5] Critics also argue that the liberal environmental side is simply foolish to ignore economic growth and the lifestyle issues that are part and parcel of the American heritage. Critics further claim that the liberal call for widespread government regulation will kill jobs and ruin the economy. Those critics are, at best, slow to acknowledge climate change[6] and the reality of the costs of pollution when they are not denying those consequences altogether.

On the other side is Julian Simon's pro-growth, free market conservatism. Simon argues that an increased population will generate more innovation as long as markets are left alone unimpeded by pesky government regulations. The technological optimism of Simon's position is offered up as the antidote to environmental pessimism. Simon's critics, however, note that he ignored the market failure of negative externalities. Simon's argument mirrors the pro-market, anti-government ideology that has dominated discussion of the political economy for over 30 years and it contains a fatal category mistake. Markets do not exist without legal structures in place to allow them to operate and to fix them when they are broken. Government and markets exist in a dynamic, not static, relationship. The issue is never about a choice between government *or* markets; it is, rather, always a choice about how much of each can be used to improve society.[7]

The interrelationship between government and markets is never more obvious than in the case of energy. Energy is, and has been, heavily regulated for over a century. As a result of subsidies, financial supports, and market protections such as natural monopoly regulations and tax expenditures, there are no truly competitive energy markets, only those that are more or less regulated than others. Moreover, domestically as well as globally,[8] subsidies have heavily favored traditional fossil fuel resources over clean resources. While clean power resources receive government aid, they are not overly subsidized.[9] In short, government financial support and regulation of energy resources and industries have resulted in a dirty, fossil fuel economy from which we are now trying to extricate ourselves.[10]

At their extremes, both Ehrlich's and Simon's positions tend to stagnate. Ehrlich wants world population growth and resource consumption to stop so that we can catch up with nature. However, he ignores the fact that world population is growing, that countries are developing economically, and that the quality of life for billions of people is improving. Simon wants government to stop fussing with markets so that innovation can conquer whatever ills infect the planet. However, he ignores the reality that today tourists can see the Grand Canyon more clearly than they could 40 years ago; that Clevelanders do not have to read by the glow of a burning Cuyahoga River; and, that some species are preserved rather than thoughtlessly and automatically made extinct by human activity. All of these benefits have occurred because of government regulation, not because government has stopped intervening in markets. Simon is also mistaken about the relationship between private enterprise and innovation as conservatives and liberals concur that technological innovations in the energy sector require financial commitment by government.[11] This point will be discussed more thoroughly in the next chapter.

Simon's penchant for technological innovation is a worthy one that Ehrlich's followers tend to downplay. Ehrlich's penchant for environmental sensitivity is also a worthy one that Simon's adherents, in turn, denigrate. Both positions in their sound-bite, simplified versions are, of course, wrong.

Regulation does get things wrong. Regulation can be costly. And, regulation can protect incumbents at the expense of new entrants and competition. Think, for example, about farm subsidies for agribusiness, oil and gas subsidies, and traditionally structured electric utilities. And yet regulation has made the air and water cleaner, has stimulated markets, and has protected consumers from adulterated drugs and foodstuffs.[12] Similarly, even though markets can get things wrong, they can also get things right as easily demonstrated by the proliferation benefits of those technologies that we rely upon in our daily lives.

So we must sift the wheat from the chaff. Ehrlich is right to worry about the thoughtless use of our natural resources, the consequences of which may impair the health of our children, shorten our lives, and degrade the natural environment around us. Simon is right to extol human creativity and the economic value of innovation and competitive markets. However, neither markets nor human creativity are the exclusive province of the private sector.

Neither technological innovation nor market competition occurs in a vacuum. Private sector technological innovation is an essential part of a vibrant economy and of economic growth. Yet, there are sectors of the economy that cannot be supported by private investment alone. Public goods such as a clean environment, clean power, the energy infrastructure, and basic science, as well as complex and long-term technological demonstrations, are historically underfunded by the private sector. These public goods are also historically supported by government investment and other financial incentives and supports.

It would be a very good wager to make that the world will transition to a clean power future. A smarter grid, increased energy efficiencies, expanded use of renewable resources, greater consumer choice, and a broader array of clean technologies and markets will emerge. Importantly, a cleaner energy future will occur sooner and more effectively through thoughtful government regulation and leadership, especially for technological innovation.[13] The nation's traditional fossil fuel energy economy did not come about on its own; it developed with the helping hand of government, the same helping hand that is shaping the clean future.

The environmental or clean power skeptic may argue that government should not participate in shaping a clean future and point to the technological and information revolution that has transformed our use of computers as well as transformed the way we communicate and receive news, information, and entertainment. To the skeptic, the dot.com craze was the result of private innovation by guys named Jobs, Wozniak, Gates, and Allen just as people like Cuban, Bezos, and Musk transformed the delivery of retail products and services and people like Zuckerberg have created social networks. Private entrepreneurship has indeed been responsible for the remarkable expansion of those technologies and methods. But, the dot.com era did not emerge full-blown out of the heads of the private sector. Instead, that sector built upon prior government innovations and developments.[14]

Energy is different from the information sector and requires more, not less, government input. You cannot build a next-generation small nuclear plant at your computer desk as easily as you might develop a software app. Nor will large-scale clean power technologies become a reality without large-scale, government-supported demonstration projects. Utility-scale solar and wind arrays must connect to the electric grid, and universal energy service at reasonable and fair prices cannot occur by waving a free market wand. All of these achievements will be the result of government intervention.

Clean power addresses the negative externalities identified by the liberal, environmental side of the conversation. So too does clean power serve as a strong response to the dynamic, technological innovation model of economic growth through competitive markets.[15] A clean power wager is one that both Ehrlich and Simon could embrace; it is also one that we must embrace for a healthier environment, a strong economy, and an improved way of living.

At bottom, the Simon–Ehrlich bet is about what the future holds for the political economy generally and for economic growth more particularly. There are three economic growth scenarios that can be used to describe the energy future: (1) an economic growth path that relies on business as usual and is heavily dependent on traditional energy resources; (2) a path that adopts the precautionary principle as its central motif and can be considered a slow or no-growth scenario; and (3) an approach to economic growth centered on a clean power transition that embraces an aggressive adoption of renewable resources and energy efficiency as well as the creation and sustenance of new and more competitive energy markets through technological innovations and smart government regulation.

GROWTH I: THE TRADITIONAL PATH OR BUSINESS AS USUAL

Growth I, or the business as usual path (BAU), is clearly exemplified in the energy position papers from the US Chamber of Commerce entitled *Energy Works for US: Solutions for America's Energy Future*[16] and from the Business Roundtable entitled *Taking Action on Energy*.[17] The data and references in the reports are largely accurate, as far as they go, and the reports promote energy efficiency and renewable resources, which are welcome steps. Ultimately, though, the reports are unreliable because both envision the future too narrowly and are the result of incumbent industry capture. In particular, they inaccurately characterize government regulation and neglect the environmental consequences surrounding the production, use, consumption, and disposal of our energy resources.

The BAU frame balances the cost of energy with and without government regulation whereas the proper clean power frame balances energy costs against health and environmental benefits. *Energy Works* reads more like a political polemic rather than a reliable white paper and *Taking Action* describes the benefits of continuing our traditional energy path without acknowledging the costs of BAU. Basically, these reports fail to recognize the complexities and challenges necessary to fashion an energy future in light of climate challenges and in light of the promise of a more competitive and cleaner energy economy. Instead, the reports fall back on yesterday's energy strategies to the benefit of incumbent firms and to the detriment of new entrants.

Energy issues are more in the news today than they have been since the crises of the mid-1970s. In the 1970s, the cause for concern was the ability of Middle East oil producers to wreak havoc on our general economy by controlling the flow of oil, which had the consequence of increasing oil prices and contributing to double-digit inflation. Independence from foreign oil then became the major concern about our national economy, our energy security, and our future economic growth.

Today, concerns about Middle East oil are less severe than they were then. Global oil markets have been relatively stable, OPEC has lost its market share and influence,[18] and while the reports acknowledge our historic desire for energy independence, they do so as a way to encourage and promote the further development of domestic fossil fuels rather than more fully explore a clean power strategy. Both reports further assert that the more domestic energy we produce and consume, the healthier and more vibrant our economy will be. Indeed, echoing a theme of Mitt Romney's presidential campaign,[19] according to the Business Roundtable, North America can become energy self-sufficient "in coming decades."[20] This position is a narrow and inaccurate view of national energy policy and, ultimately, a poor plan for national economic growth for several reasons, not the least of which is that the reports ignore the country's increasing energy intensity.

Energy Works begins with the premise that optimism about domestic energy production must be tempered "by the realization that it has come about largely in spite of national policy rather than because of it."[21] This statement is false. The Chamber report attributes this optimism to technological advancements "most notably ... hydraulic fracturing, horizontal drilling, and precise multidimensional geologic imaging."[22] These technologies have advanced domestic oil and gas production; they have done nothing to broaden the energy portfolio with clean resources. What is wrong with the Chamber's antigovernment criticism is that it fails to recognize that US energy policy has greatly favored fossil fuels for over a century and continues to do so today. *Taking Action* takes a similar tack warning about a national energy policy that "has evolved through decades of ad hoc measures, resulting in an incoherent patchwork of subsidies, mandates and regulations" one consequence of which is that this "policy labyrinth ... is more likely to inhibit than to unleash the private-sector investment needed to transform the energy sector."[23] The concern about excessive and complex regulations must be taken seriously; however, both reports use their criticism of government to favor fossil fuels and disfavor clean power, thus preferring more limited, rather than more competitive, energy markets.

The Chamber criticizes federal energy policy as limiting access to resources and "regulatory overreach." According to the Chamber, these positions have created uncertainties that threaten to hold back "US energy production and investment and jobs to go with it."[24] According to the Roundtable, excessive government regulation will drive energy manufacturing overseas.[25] This parade of horribles is, quite frankly, nonsense. The federal government has not thrown up "roadblocks to domestic energy development";[26] rather, federal energy regulation has promoted domestic fossil fuel producers throughout the twentieth century. While it is fair to discuss whether more public lands should be available for energy production, it is disingenuous to suggest that government hinders that development altogether as both reports assert. Nor, as *Energy Works* states, has government "forced existing sources to prematurely exit the system."[27] If the reference is to coal-fired electricity, then look to low natural gas prices as the culprit; not "Obama's war on coal" as the fossil industry and its political supporters falsely claim. If the reference is to nuclear power plants, then look to plants that have reached the end of their useful lives as one cause; look to cheap natural gas and wind power as another; and look to multibillion-dollar construction costs as a third reason that the nuclear future is waning.[28]

Often, what the Chamber and the Roundtable do not say is as revealing, if not more so, as what they do say. Many of the issues about which the reports are silent are resounding. The most notable omissions are the phrases "climate change," "global warming," "carbon emissions," "carbon price," and "greenhouse gases." Today, no responsible conversation about our energy future can ignore the direct connections between energy and the environment. Richard Muller, a physicist from Cal Berkeley whose work was funded in part by the Koch Brothers, concludes his research with the observation that "[a]n excessive use of energy may be leading us into the greatest catastrophe in human history."[29] Yale economist William Nordhaus echoes that sentiment and concludes his recent book by saying that "global warming is a major threat to humans and the natural world."[30] And, British politician and economist Nicholas Stern assesses global warming as the largest market failure in history.[31] The BAU position is designed to serve incumbent businesses, but any thoughtful discussion of a future energy policy that ignores global warming or climate change is, at best, negligent.

The BAU strategy also extols the use of our most abundant resource, coal. It neglects to point out that it is also our dirtiest resource and that "clean coal" strategies are far from cost competitive.[32] The Chamber and the Roundtable bemoan the future of coal because of clean air regulations and low natural gas prices. There are two fallacies with their position. First, while it is true that new air regulations are coming online, coal's current decline as a fuel of choice for electricity generation began with the low price of natural gas before many regulations were enacted before the Clean Power Plan (CPP) was even proposed. Second, the real problem with coal is not too much regulation; it is too little. The Upper Big Branch mining disaster,[33] the recent release of chemicals into the Ohio River,[34] and inadequate health protections for miners[35] have occurred precisely because of lax oversight and underregulation, not because of overly intrusive government agents. The BAU approach does not adequately address these realities, let alone address the economic costs to remedy them.

Similarly, the reports are proud to champion the virtues of increased oil and gas production from hydraulic fracturing yet remain silent about the water resources used in the drilling process and the threats to groundwater and aquifers that hydraulic fracturing may present.[36] In the same vein, the reports are silent about current concerns about hydraulic fracturing and earthquakes.[37] Even accepting a BAU strategy, these reports provide incomplete analyses of the costs involved with pursuing it.

Another example of misinformation concerns nuclear power. The Chamber and the Roundtable promote nuclear power, as do some clean energy advocates,[38] but completely fail to mention the hard fact that without regulation, there would be no commercial nuclear power industry at all. Historically, industry executives were quite forthcoming in acknowledging that without the liability limitations of the Price-Anderson Act, they would not invest one penny in nuclear power. Those liability limitations continue. In addition, as noted in Chapter 2, under the Energy Policy Act of 2005,[39] nuclear power received a range of subsidies including production tax credits, regulatory lag insurance, loan guarantees, and direct payments for research and development. Without such supports, the current plants under construction would not have gotten off their engineers' drawing boards.[40] Further, any responsible discussion of nuclear power must address the overall costs of nuclear electricity including construction and operation costs as well as subsidies, not to mention waste disposal and decommissioning costs.[41]

In an aligned argument, *Energy Works* criticizes the use of renewable portfolio standards as well as wind and solar subsidies because of their negative effects on nuclear power. The report states that these efforts "have distorted wholesale power markets;" make it "difficult for existing nuclear power plants to operate, [and] discourage[s] new plant construction"; and threaten to "force out nuclear power."[42] This criticism of subsidies and incentives to renewable resources simply runs counter to the fact already noted that the commercial nuclear power industry would not exist but for a government support structure. To its credit, the Roundtable report is more favorable to renewable resources and advocates greater government funding for innovation in this sector while protecting traditionally structured utilities.[43]

Energy Works and *Taking Action* can be welcomed for their overviews of both fossil fuels and alternative resources including efficiency. Additionally, the reports, particularly *Taking Action*, state the need for smart regulation and the need for government support for energy innovations that can be brought to commercial scale. Nevertheless, *Taking Action*, as well as *Energy Works*, focuses on reducing environmental regulations in favor of fossil fuel production. Consequently, the reports can be faulted for their partial and, at times, misleading analysis of the energy future. The promotion of a fossil fuel economy takes pride of place in both reports.[44] As a consequence, they neglect the most serious environmental challenges to a vibrant clean future, along with attendant costs. These reports and the BAU approach are not reliable and do not provide the path to our energy/environment future, even from a solely economic perspective.

GROWTH II: A PRECAUTIONARY TALE

The news from the climate front is not good. In spring 2014, the United Nations' Intergovernmental Panel on Climate Change issued its Fifth Assessment Report entitled *Climate Change 2014: Impacts, Adaptation and Vulnerability* (AR5).[45] As the subtitle indicates, the report is concerned about the human, environmental, and economic consequences of continued carbon emissions and attendant global warming. Also in spring 2014, the White House released the third *National Climate Assessment* that reiterates the claims and warnings of AR5.[46] And, in a resounding encyclical, Pope Francis argues forcefully that climate is a common good, that the earth is subject to human degradation, and that ignoring environmental damage will not only affect the natural environment but have devastating effects on humanity, especially on the poor.[47] Then, in December 2015 the Paris Climate Agreement was signed expressly acknowledging that "climate change is a common concern of humankind" and that addressing climate change is part of every nation's obligations to respect human rights.[48]

We all are familiar with stories in the popular press, and even from common observation, that weather patterns and the natural environment are changing.[49] Melting ice caps, more frequent and intense storms,[50] flooding, drought, colder winters, hotter summers, and species migration are stories that are routinely reported. While scientists are careful to distinguish weather from climate, the UN and White House reports make clear that the anthropogenic contribution to global warming is a reality and that the environmental consequences are indeed dire.

AR5 confirms many of these observations with a high degree of confidence. The UN panel finds that glaciers continue to shrink, thus raising sea levels, and that permafrost continues to warm, thus releasing more methane. Many species have not only migrated but they have changed their seasonal activities. Also, species extinction has increased. Further, climate change has had a more negative than positive impact on crop yields and climate-related extremes such as heat waves, droughts, floods, cyclones, and wildfires expose the human and natural environments to significant hazards. Additionally, such climate-related hazards exacerbate other stresses including economic inequality that worsens the pollution that surrounds persons living at the poverty level.[51] Wood-burning by those living in poverty, as an example, impairs their life expectancy and the quality of their lives.

The consequences of all of these changes are severe. AR5 identifies with high confidence increased risk of illnesses and fatalities; severe disruption of livelihoods; systemic risks to infrastructure networks as a result of extreme weather events; food insecurity; disruption of rural livelihoods; population migrations; the loss of marine and coastal ecosystems; and, the risk of loss of terrestrial and inland water systems and biodiversity.[52] Costs are naturally associated with risks and the report estimates that the current cost of adaptation for developing countries to reduce or eliminate these risks runs in the neighborhood of $70–$100 billion per year.[53]

Given the reality of observable changes in weather, and most likely in climate, together with increased risks and costs to the environmental and human health, precaution is a reasonable response. The precautionary principle, popularized by the 1992 Earth Summit in Rio de Janeiro, has been discussed by environmentalists for over two decades. As stated in the Rio Declaration, the precautionary principle can be described as:

> In order to protect the environment, the precautionary approach shall be widely applied by States according to their capabilities. Where there are threats of serious or irreversible damage, lack of full scientific certainty shall not be used as a reason for postponing cost-effective measures to prevent environmental degradation.[54]

The sensible idea, of course, is that it is better to be safe than sorry. Unfortunately, simple principles and simple slogans are often difficult to put into practice. The core idea is that environmental and energy policies should be adopted that are calculated to avoid harmful outcomes. Similarly, it is a core concept of regulation that *ex ante* principles should be adopted to avoid harm rather than rely on *ex post* liability rules for compensation to be levied after harm has been suffered.

Clearly, the precautionary principle has its roots on the environmental side of climate change rather than on the energy side. However, given the natural physical connection between energy and the environment, the principle can provide guidance despite the multiplicity of criticisms that it has engendered. Criticisms of the precautionary principle run from arguing that the principle is too radical to the claim that it is too empty.[55] Nevertheless, the precautionary principle can guide us regarding the availability and use of evidence, decision making during uncertainty, and a commitment to prevention and mitigation rather than relying on adaptation alone in the face of grievous environmental harm as a result of climate change.

More specifically, the principle is triggered when there is a threat of serious or irreversible harm. The principle also acknowledges that given the configuration of climate change, there will be a lack of full scientific certainty about future harms. Nevertheless, the need for caution and prevention should override the tendency to wait until scientific data are complete.[56] Completion will never occur particularly within a dynamic system such as climate.

It should be clear, certainly from the AR5, that the threshold of irreversibility is upon us.[57] Indeed, as Professor John Applegate has noted "The objective of the Precautionary Principle being to prevent harm by taking early protective action, the short-term irreversibility of global warming makes a particularly strong case for taking strong emissions control and mitigation measures."[58]

The precautionary principle can serve precisely the function of pointing the direction of decision making while not necessarily determining substantive policies or positions. Still, what Cass Sunstein calls the "hard precautionary principle"[59] can have slowdown effects on economic growth. The question then becomes: Can an energy policy make a commitment to precaution while not necessarily disregarding economic growth? This section examines the precautionary principle in the form that accepts slow or no economic growth. The next section on the clean power approach argues that an energy transition need not inhibit economic growth.

The strong environmentalist position is that continued consumption of resources without more attention to the environment will continue to generate negative externalities to the long-term detriment of the human and natural environments. The antidote to continued environmental degradation is a reduction in the production and consumption of those goods that contribute to environmental damage and human injury.

There are two versions of the strong environmentalist position. The first, and the more extreme one, is that a materialist society is inevitably destroying itself. A misreading of E.F. Schumacher's *Small Is Beautiful*,[60] as well as a misreading of The Club of Rome's *Limits to Growth*,[61] brought critics exactly to that anti-materialist position. And yet, the core idea that continued, unrestrained consumption inevitably leads to unsustainable environmental degradation is not without its supporters. There are environmental limits to economic growth. Precautionists argue that environmental limits must be countered by an economic calculus that values restraint in consumption over continued economic expansion.[62]

Another version of the precautionary approach is that a slow or smart growth economy is one that reconceives the economic universe.[63] In part, this approach is sustained by two core ideas. First, the standard economic measure of gross domestic product (GDP) must be reevaluated and redefined. From this perspective, calculations of economic productivity do not properly account for all values in society. Consequently, GDP must be replaced by another measure such as capabilities, and human development. Efforts by scholars such as Amartya Sen[64] and Martha Nussbaum[65] examine and define human capabilities to build both an economic and a political case for redefining a country's wealth. The second idea is based on research about human happiness, which indicates that human happiness or individual well-being reaches a limit once basic economic needs are satisfied. After that point, happiness does not increase.

Economist Diane Coyle challenges critics of economic growth in a particularly useful way. She asserts that economic growth increases well-being and happiness. "I argue that economic growth does increase happiness and also contributes to other important aspects of welfare, especially freedom."[66] She does, however, challenge the ways in which we measure both well-being and happiness. Particularly, she argues that GDP must be supplemented by a wider array of statistics that measure social and economic progress. New measures should include activities outside the market economy such as caring within the household and valuing our time other than only our working hours. In part, the urgency with which Coyle writes about reassessing GDP is linked to the challenges presented by climate change. However, she recognizes other forces are at work to redefine GDP including rising national debt levels, a global financial crisis, and political institutions that go wanting.

Coyle states that GDP had its most significant usefulness to assess economic progress after the Great Depression and World War II and it should not be ignored altogether. Instead, it must be supplemented. GDP tells us about certain forms of economic productivity even if it does not reveal much about social welfare. Most importantly, economic productivity and social welfare are distinct measures and should not be equated. Instead, new measurements are needed to account for the complexity of the economy including assessing and valuing: (1) innovation and globalization, (2) the increasing share of services and intangibles such as information technology that advanced economies depend upon, and (3) issues of sustainability including the depletion of resources.[67] Coyle particularly argues that "governments have nothing to tell them whether the growth their policies are delivering is coming at the expense of growth and living standards in the future."[68] She further asserts that while GDP provides useful information about market production, it does not provide a useful picture of the economy as a whole that includes the environment and other human activities.[69]

For Coyle, economic productivity and human well-being are distinct measurements. An effort to capture well-being more broadly than GDP was undertaken in 2008 when Nicholas Sarkozy, then president of France, commissioned three economists to examine the limits of GDP as an indicator of economic performance and social progress. The commission, headed by Joseph Stiglitz and assisted by Amartya Sen and John-Paul Fitoussi, issued its report in 2009 and concluded, like Coyle, that GDP, as a measure of production, has its limits. Their report asserts that material well-being rather than economic production should be seriously considered and measured by governments as they develop social policies. As a measurement of well-being, the distribution of income and nonmarket activities must be considered as well as economic productivity. The report notes that well-being is multi-dimensional and should include such things as material living standards, health, education, political voice and governance, social connections, and the future environment and security.[70] A clean power economy fits comfortably within Coyle's and Sen's economic analyses. The clean economy must be measured by the market and the nonmarket costs of energy as well as the market and nonmarket benefits to the environment.

The aligned argument is that human happiness is not directly correlated with wealth. In other words, individual happiness is achieved by a certain level of economic comfort.[71] Above that level, the correlation between wealth and happiness breaks down. Think, for example, of how many consumer electronics we each have. How many computers or other electronic communications devices do we each own? How many televisions do we have in our homes? It is indeed quite easy to extend these questions through a long series of personal and consumer goods that many of us possess. The more direct point is that after a certain point human comfort and happiness are not increased by more material wealth.

The United Nations, for example, has developed a Human Development Index for a variety of goods. One index shows that after 4,000 kWh per year of electricity consumption, the quality of life flattens and stabilizes. Developing countries such as Ethiopia, India, and Indonesia show a sharp increase in human development below the 4,000 kWh range while countries such as Germany, Japan, the United States, Sweden, and Canada level off substantially even though their consumption ranges from 4,000 to 18,000 kWh per annum.[72] In other words, we can enjoy a clean power economy without threatening current lifestyles.[73]

We can call this alternative growth model either slow-growth or no-growth economics or sustainability. At its core, the idea that economic growth can continue unhindered is a fundamental tenet of "free market" economics. Any criticism of unlimited growth is often derided, yet basic economics tells us that economic growth often entails externalities that must be kept in check. As Columbia economist Jeffrey Sachs writes, while the relationship between long-term economic growth and environmental health has been debated "one thing is certain: *the current trajectory of human activity is not sustainable*."[74] The debate is not about whether limits exist or not; rather, the debate is about what those limits are and how economic growth and environmental protection can coexist. Today, the new economics movement is challenging this fundamental assumption that economic growth can continue without end.[75] We must accept the separation between economic growth and energy as, in Gus Speth's words: "The planet cannot sustain capitalism as we know it."[76]

Another way of putting the matter is to distinguish between "desirable" and "undesirable" economic growth. For students of ecological economics, growth that expands GDP but does so at the cost of impairing natural ecosystems is not a desirable form of economic growth. Instead, desirable growth is that which preserves natural ecosystems. Advocates of slow growth, then, take the position that "[p]lenty of evidence suggests that the global economy is now so large that it is undermining the natural systems on which it depends."[77] These advocates point to climate change, biodiversity losses, ozone depletion, deforestation, soil degradation, and other environmental and ecological harms. One consequence of such a precautionary approach will be a redistribution of wealth away from fossil fuel firms to energy providers who excel at renewable resources, energy efficiency, and energy storage, all of which directly reduce carbon emissions.[78] Opposition to this redistribution is one factor that underlies the Chamber and Roundtable reports, not sound economic analysis for energy future.

Slow growth advocates argue that the investments needed will be costly and to reduce threats to the environment will not keep pace with GDP even at 3 percent per year. They posit that significant investments in rapid technological developments to promote a clean environment are necessary and that "[a] major way to reduce pollution and consumption of natural resources while experiencing economic growth is to bring about a wholesale transformation in the technologies that today dominate manufacturing, energy, instruction, transportation, and agriculture."[79] Technological investments at such a scale will clearly be expensive; maybe too expensive to make without curtailing economic growth, at least from a short-term perspective.

Slow growth advocates have a larger target than the energy sector of our economy. The new economists challenge the central premise that GDP is the true measure of welfare and instead argue that a singular concentration on economic growth not only harms the natural environment but also decreases human welfare.[80] The new economists argue for changes in the basic structure of work including a shorter work week, longer vacations, greater job protection benefits, and such. In addition to technological improvements leading to clean power and a cleaner environment, investments in education and health are also promoted. "In the end, what has to be modified is the open-ended commitment to aggregate economic growth – growth that is consuming environmental and social capital, both now in short supply." As for social capital, investment is called for in "growth and good jobs and in the incomes of the poor; growth and availability and efficiency of health services; growth and education and training" among other social or public goods.[81] On the environmental front, investment is needed in a range of activities including public infrastructure and green technologies and to replace "America's obsolete energy system."[82]

The slow or no-growth movement has been part of the environmental discussion since the early years of environmental laws and regulations. The discipline of ecological economics, the concept of small is beautiful, and now emphasis on a steady-state economy, all challenge what some consider an obsession with economic growth. To be sure, we can accept the idea that economic growth cannot continue unabated without accounting for its harmful consequences. We can also accept the idea that BAU is counterproductive. We can also imagine a clean power economy that attempts to mediate the desire for continued economic growth with the desire for a healthier environment and healthier lives.

GROWTH III: THE CLEAN POWER ECONOMY

Growth I must be faulted for its failure to acknowledge the environmental costs attendant with unreflective economic growth. Growth II must be faulted for its failure to acknowledge the role of economic growth in our energy future. Fortunately, a clean power economy mediates the need for economic growth with the need for environmental protection and, therefore, draws on both scenarios for its guiding principles.

The model for a clean power economy is distinguishable from the traditional fossil fuel energy paradigm in several respects. The clean power economy acknowledges the natural physical connection between resource extraction and energy production. It also recognizes the connection between energy consumption and the production of harmful wastes. Additionally, the clean power economy recognizes that natural resources used for the production of energy are a primary input into the economy and that economic welfare is a value that is widely shared and is a core principle of a country committed to both democracy and capitalism.[83] A clean power economy, however, does contest traditional energy policy that has generated a century-old fossil fuel energy policy of ignoring costly externalities.

We can generate energy, enjoy economic growth, and reduce environmental harms. By way of example, the Regional Greenhouse Gas Initiative, which places a cap on carbon trading for nine Eastern states, has also shown that the states can cut their emissions more than the rest of the country and, simultaneously, can see their economies also grow more than the rest of the country.[84] Most simply, our current economic trajectory based on the traditional energy policy is unlikely to result in a sustainable economy.[85]

There is a serious political hitch in the transition to a clean power economy. Since 2005, our domestic energy profile has reverted to a greater production of fossil fuels, thus giving those who favor BAU a false sense of energy and economic security. The energy policies of President Obama's 2014 State of the Union address, for example, are consistent with the BAU approach described earlier. In that address, the president points to the domestic increase in oil and natural gas and sees natural gas as a "bridge fuel" to the future.[86] The administration also continues to subsidize nuclear power and invest in clean coal technologies.[87] The old paradigm continues to influence policy although that situation is changing with the clean power regulations. This section will outline the several reasons supporting a clean transition.

Although the 2014 State of the Union address reflects a BAU approach, there have been changes promoting clean and sustainable energy throughout the Obama administration. The administration's FY 2015 budget, for example, increases the Department of Energy (DOE) budget while holding other expenditures essentially flat. Within that budget, both the Office of Energy Efficiency and Renewable Energy and the Office of Electricity Delivery and Energy Reliability would receive 22 percent increases. In addition, the proposed budget for energy infrastructure resiliency will nearly double and smart grid R&D would receive a two-thirds increase. At the same time, the budget proposed to reduce funding for the Office of Fossil Energy as well as the Office of Nuclear Energy.[88] DOE funding over the years of the Obama administration has shifted from fossil fuels to clean energy. Notably, Obama administration's Climate Action Plan (CAP)[89] and the Third National Climate Assessment are expressly directed to climate change and those efforts are complemented by the clean power regulations and a moratorium on coal leases on federal lands.[90]

The CAP begins: "[W]e have a moral obligation to future generations to leave them a planet that is not polluted and damaged." This is the language of sustainability and President Obama weaves it into both his climate change and his clean power initiatives. The first item discussed in the CAP is to cut carbon pollution by monitoring power plants more closely, promoting renewable energy more aggressively, accelerating clean energy permitting; and modernizing the grid. As an adjunct to those initiatives, the CAP supports clean energy innovation investments including advance fossil fuel projects such as sequestration, undertaking a DOE Quadrennial Energy Review to assess effectiveness of innovation investments, continuing to increase fuel economy standards while promoting advanced transportation technologies, and engaging in energy efficiency activities across the board.[91]

Similarly, the National Climate Assessment describes both the threats and challenges of climate change and provides a broad set of policies. On the energy front, the assessment recognizes the need for investments in new technologies and it recognizes the fact that future energy systems will differ from those in place today. The future energy mix will change and that change will be driven by climate challenges, which, in turn, will present new opportunities even as we must confront new risks.[92] Economically and politically, it is better to be ahead of the curve than forced to respond to crises, and the administration's clean power and climate initiatives are supported with several political, policy, and economic arguments.

Policy Support. In *Ending Dirty Energy Policy*, I demonstrated that a new energy policy has been developing for over four decades.[93] In light of the energy crises of the 1970s, policy analysts focused on the increasing need for energy independence and security. In addition to national security, policy analysts recognized that the traditional energy model may have reached a technological plateau such that economies of scale may well have been reached if not exhausted. Also at the time of the energy crises, the country became more aware of the human and ecological environments. A rash of legislation from the National Environmental Policy Act to legislation to protect water, air, land, and species exemplified the new environmental sensitivity. It was only a matter of time before the connection was made between energy production, transmission, distribution, and consumption and the environmental consequences of all those activities as a natural consequence of the fuel cycle. There is no shortage of support for a clean energy economy in the policy literature, and government programming is beginning to implement those policies.

Energy Sustainability. Sustainability, like the precautionary principle, had its genesis with United Nations. In particular, the idea of sustainability was first developed by the Brundtland Commission, which defined "sustainable development" as: "to ensure that [current development] meets the needs of the present without compromising the ability of future generations to meet their own needs."[94] Like the precautionary principle, the concept of sustainability is grounded in a core idea – economic development should not ruin the planet; rather it must protect future generations.

The concept of sustainable development has also been adopted by economists more generally to include economic growth and it has been adopted by energy advocates seeking the transition to a cleaner energy future. To date, energy sustainability has not been an element of national energy policy.

President Clinton established a President's Council on Sustainable Development in 1993, which lasted until 1999 and issued a series of reports but no corresponding legislation.[95] Similarly, President Bush's *National Energy Plan*[96] uses the word "sustainability," but again, no sustainability legislation resulted from that plan.

During the Obama administration, the DOE has developed a sustainability plan for its internal use and has appointed a deputy secretary as a senior sustainability officer whose job it is to oversee department efforts including achieving greenhouse gas reductions, sustainable buildings, fleet management, smarter water use, efficiency, pollution prevention, the use of renewable resources, and climate change sensitivity among other initiatives. The central idea behind the plan is that DOE operations and activities will be undertaken with sustainability in mind and that the DOE, in turn, can serve as a leader for the federal government to integrate sustainability into all of its operations.[97] Energy sustainability means that energy systems should be "cleaner, more reliable, and affordable for all"[98] without undermining economic growth.

The United Nations has also embraced the concept of sustainable energy as part of its Millennium Development Goals[99] and sustainability is central to the Paris Climate Agreement.[100] To the extent that sustainability primarily focuses on the human and natural environments, sustainable energy is clearly perceived by the United Nations as "not just a moral imperative but a unique business opportunity – a huge market in itself and one that will create new levels of prosperity and demand for goods and services of all kinds."[101] For the United Nations, sustainable energy entails three objectives: (1) universal access to modern energy, (2) doubling the rate of global improvement in energy efficiency, and (3) doubling the share of renewable energy and the global energy mix all to be achieved by 2030.[102] The United Nations also perceives that these goals are both achievable and consonant with limiting the increase of the global temperature to 2°C in the longer run.

The private sector has been engaging in any number of initiatives to promote sustainability. Chief sustainability officers, sustainability investments, and corporate environmental and efficiency checklists are gaining traction among corporations. Notably, companies such as Google, Apple, Walmart, Microsoft, Unilever, and Kohl's have agreed to seek 100 percent use of renewables in their operations.[103] Still, more action can be taken by corporate boards, shareholders, and management to monitor an account for sustainability gains through governance, disclosure, and performance all along corporate supply chains.[104] The driving force behind the corporate move toward sustainability is not only the identification of environmental risks and possible liabilities from corporate waste but also protection against natural disasters.[105] They are also being driven by clean business opportunities.

Public Good. The dominant model of US energy policy has not only treated energy as a necessary input into the economy; it has also treated it as a public good. Most simply, a national energy policy evolved such that adequate supplies of affordable energy would be made universally available. Natural gas and electric utilities are primary examples.

Early in the regulation of natural gas and electric utilities, a policy was adopted that these utilities, in whole or in part, had characteristics of natural monopolies because private markets would not efficiently or adequately provide service to all customers. In part, the concern was that these industries could exercise market power that enabled them to reduce the amount of electricity to be put on the market while simultaneously raising prices above competitive levels if left unregulated. As a result, consumer choices would be constrained.[106] The regulation of these utilities was in part an economic argument. Economic waste could be reduced and service could be made more widely and more affordably available through regulation. This regulation also had a political or policy dimension. Electricity together with universal service was seen as a desirable public good that could be delivered reliably and cheaply through regulation rather than through private markets.

Similarly, fossil fuel subsidies such as favorable tax treatment, forgiveness of royalties, and resource depletion allowance as examples were intended to encourage (as well as reward) the development of those natural resources. The result of a widespread series of favorable government regulations and supports was to make fossil fuel energy cheaply available. Therefore, cheap, dirty energy has been treated as a public good and its environmental and health costs were not taken into account.

We can take the same analysis of public goods and apply it to clean power resources. A public good has at least two characteristics. First, government supports are used to provide a good that is deemed to be in the public interest because it is unlikely that private markets will provide that good in adequate amounts. It is true that clean power markets are developing and that clean energy investments are significant. It is also true that government supports exist to stimulate those markets, to invest in innovative energy technologies, and to restructure an energy portfolio.

The second attribute of public goods is non-excludability. Once the public good is provided, people cannot be prevented from benefiting from it. In the case of clean power, the fact that a clean economy reduces greenhouse gas emissions is a benefit to all persons regardless of whether they are consumers of particular energy resources. The fact that the United States treats fossil fuel energy as a public good has had the perverse economic consequence of generating more negative externalities in the form of pollution than private markets would have done on their own accord if energy products were properly and accurately priced to include those externalities.

Investment and Economic Value. Energy policy is changing because the economic value proposition behind it is changing. A century ago, energy policy was driven by economic growth without examining environmental injuries. Today, energy policy is still a factor in economic growth but that policy must also attend to the human and natural environments as well as to national and world security. A clean power economy acknowledges those parameters and understands the necessity for economic productivity. Aligned with a continued emphasis on economic growth is the idea that energy transitions have always been accompanied by technological changes as well as by needs for new energy sources. Those changes will be the intended consequence of public and private investments in clean power technologies that will facilitate the transition. Public–private partnerships are particularly suitable vehicles as public investments open new private markets, bring energy technologies to scale, and make them affordable as well as reliable.[107]

Clean power investments are making an impact and will be discussed in the next chapter. Notably, those investments are paying dividends. Globally, renewable resources contributed more than half of the net total additions in electric generating capacity, and, by the end of 2012, renewables comprised more than 26 percent of global generating capacity and supplied nearly 22 percent of global electricity.[108] Further, in 2013, solar photo voltaic capacity increased by 41 percent over 2012 and nearly ten times the capacity added in 2009. During the same time, wind capacity increased by 74 percent.

Domestically, under the American Recovery and Reinvestment Act,[109] the Obama administration dedicated over $80 billion for energy investments, most of which were in the clean power space. Clean energy investments hold the promise of developing clean energy manufacturing capacity, spurring job creation, and building a more sustainable economy particularly in light of threats of climate change.[110] In 2014, we find that wind and solar power contribution to the energy portfolio has more than doubled and constitutes 4.4 percent of US electricity capacity up from 1.9 percent in 2009.[111]

In addition to investment in renewables, energy efficiency investments[112] have yielded positive gains and investments in energy storage are increasing significantly such as Tesla's announcement that it plans to invest $2 billion in a large-scale battery factory by 2017[113] and its introduction of the Tesla Powerwall, a solar energy storage technology,[114] as well as Daimler's entry into the home energy storage market.[115] Overall, and despite declining fossil fuel prices, clean energy investments for 2015 reached over $328 billion worldwide, which is a 4 percent rise above 2014 investments and a sixfold rise for clean energy investments made in 2004.[116]

A recent study backed by 190 private investor groups describes a financial model that reduces emissions while generating positive investment returns averaging 33 percent.[117] Therefore, the future for clean power continues to look promising because of several factors: (1) wind and solar technology prices continue to decline, (2) clean energy manufacturers are operating profitably, (3) energy efficiency investments are increasing, and (4) markets in fast growing and developing economies are robust.[118] A clean power transition will increase and diversify investments in the energy sector as well as provide stable prices and markets.[119]

Lifestyle and Quality of Life. On February 2, 1977, President Jimmy Carter addressed the nation in a fireside chat. He sat before an open fire in the White House and, wrapped in a cardigan sweater, told the nation that we must all conserve energy. Later, on April 18, 1977, he delivered another speech in which he said that energy independence was the "moral equivalent of war."[120] That image of the president before the hearth may well have doomed his reelection. Consumers were already aggravated about having to wait in gas lines on alternate days to refuel their cars. The idea that energy security came at the price of the quality of life and existing lifestyles was too much for citizens and voters. While a clean power transition has much promise, clean initiatives must not threaten the quality of life or our existing lifestyles. Otherwise, there will be more political pushback than the existing partisan opposition to environmental protection.

Changes in consumption patterns must be gradual and they must not threaten energy budgets. Over the last few decades, the good news is that energy has been consuming a smaller portion of our household budgets. Still, when gasoline hits $4 per gallon, consumers react. Public opinion surveys show the public is favorably disposed to reducing greenhouse gas emissions, developing new energy technologies, and adopting energy efficiency as examples.[121] Cost, and therefore quality of life, is an important variable and consumers will support clean power initiatives, yet that support is price-sensitive.[122] On the positive side, survey data reveal that although consumers will put an upper limit on the price they will pay for an energy transition, that upper limit may, in fact, be sufficient to fund emissions reductions efforts.[123]

Over the last decades, consumers have adopted clean power habits such as recycling, purchasing energy-efficient household appliances, and monitoring energy consumption. These behavioral changes have occurred due to a variety of forces including discussion of the national need for energy independence, cost savings, and a cleaner environment. Incremental changes that improve efficiency and reduce emissions are simply easier to make than dramatic ones. Carpooling, for example, may be greatly efficient; however, it has not been widely adopted. On the other hand, weatherization and smart thermostats are easy fixes to make[124] as the advocates of "nudge" regulations would have it.[125] While consumers are sensitive to prices, often it is difficult to assess return on their investment. Thus clean energy investments may lag behind optimal efficiency without better public education[126] and the clean power transition can be facilitated by greater consumer information and awareness.

Social Cost of Carbon. Often, the elephant in the room in energy policy discussions, particularly discussions that support a BAU approach, is the absence of any consideration of the cost of greenhouse gas emissions. Policy discussions, for example, will readily compare current energy prices and point out that electricity produced from wind and solar installations is more expensive than coal-fired electricity even though the costs for those renewable resources are declining. This is not an apples-to-apples comparison because it ignores the health and environmental costs of emissions.

It makes great sense that future energy policies consider the interaction between energy and climate policies. "Poor policy integration can undermine energy policy objectives such as energy security and affordability, as well as making climate objectives more difficult to meet. Conversely, a well-integrated policy package can reduce the trade-offs and advance the synergies between energy and climate objectives."[127] Further, a "carbon price is generally considered necessary for enabling least-cost emissions reductions and should be a cornerstone element of a climate-energy policy package."[128]

When emissions costs are considered, they are generally discussed under different rubrics. A carbon allowance, for example, is a certificate that allows the holder the right to admit a certain amount of a particular pollutant. A carbon tax operates like any other tax and sets a rate that is theoretically equivalent to the damages caused. And, the social cost of carbon (SCC) refers to the social cost of current and future damages related to climate change. In effect, though, each configuration can be considered a form of a carbon price.[129]

Clean energy analysts agree that a true comparison among energy resources must account for the SCC in order to accurately assess the economics of energy.[130] They do disagree, however, on exactly what that price ought to be. The two major carbon pricing schemes are the imposition of a carbon tax or a cap and trade policy. In either case, a SCC will be reached either by setting the tax price or by arriving at a price through carbon trading markets, thus signaling to producers that they should move to cleaner energy alternatives.

Unsurprisingly, there are advantages and disadvantages to each pricing scheme. In brief, a tax is easier to administer, yet it must be assessed and adjusted over time to make sure that either climate change or clean power goals are being met. The chief problem with an energy tax is that the economic value of the damages to be attributed to carbon emissions is uncertain. Consequently, the difficulty in setting such a tax reflects that uncertainty.[131]

A cap-and-trade system opens up carbon markets and, in fact, may provide better price signals to producers and consumers than a tax. Ideally, a cap-and-trade system would "achieve emissions reductions at lower cost than is possible under direct regulations such as mandated technologies or performance standards."[132] However, setting emissions limits, providing offsets (i.e., exemptions), and creating the markets themselves can be complicated and can undermine policy goals. Economists have argued that both systems can achieve the same results; however, they recognize that poor design choices can reduce their effectiveness.[133] More notably, the design of any policy will be done as a result of a political process that favors some interests over others and is more likely to favor industry over consumers and, therefore, more likely to perform suboptimally from an environmental perspective.[134] Political reality also means that a talk of any tax, including a carbon tax, is verboten.

At present, the SCC is not accounted for in actual energy prices. However, both the public and private sectors attribute a carbon price, in effect a shadow price,[135] for planning purposes. On the public side, the Environmental Protection Agency (EPA) and other federal agencies attribute a sliding scale of costs (as well as different discount rates) to estimate the economic damages associated with increases of CO_2 in various rulemakings, thus resulting in a range of cost estimates for present value. In 2010, for example, the estimates for the year 2020 ranged from $7 to $86 per metric ton of CO_2 emissions reduction. And, with changes to the assessment model, in 2013, the 2020 figures ranged from $13 to $137.[136] The estimates include, but are not limited to, changes in agricultural productivity, human health, and property damage. The EPA recognizes that according to the Intergovernmental Panel on Climate Change, it is very likely that current SCC statistics underestimate the damages.[137] The EPA does not have to work from a clean slate. Ten states, representing 29 percent of the US economy, and two provinces, representing 32 percent of the Canadian economy, have been operating carbon markets.[138] These markets use different forms of cap-and-trade regimes and provide evidence and data for setting carbon prices.

On the private side, an independent consulting firm generates a series of carbon prices. Based upon the analysis of the current state of regulations as well as assumptions about the future, Synapse Energy Economics forecasts a carbon price beginning in 2020 at the low end at $10 per ton increasing to $40 per ton by 2040. Its mid-case forecasts $50 per ton in 2020 increasing to $60 per ton in 2040. And, its high case forecasts a carbon price of $25 per ton in 2020 increasing to approximately $90 per ton in 2040.[139] These estimates vary according to assumptions as well as according to the models used.[140] Regardless, the models consistently show that emissions reductions are not achievable in the absence of a governmental policy.[141]

Another private entity, CDP (formerly known as the Carbon Disclosure Project), administers a questionnaire to public companies on behalf of its signatories to disclose information about their carbon planning. Many major publicly traded companies have integrated an "internal carbon price" as an element in their ongoing business planning and strategies. Companies disclosing this information include consumer companies such as Walt Disney, energy companies such as Exxon, and utilities such as Duke Energy and Entergy among many others. The latest report from CDP reveals the prices range from $6 to $60 per ton.[142]

The SCC, as the key representative of the negative externalities generated by traditional energy policy, is one dimension, perhaps the most important one, that distinguishes the three scenarios just discussed. Under the institutionally conservative BAU scenario, externalities are, for the most part, ignored. The moral imperative of the precautionary approach emphasizes externalities as the most important variable to a healthy energy/environmental future. And, the more pragmatic clean power scenario attempts to properly price externalities so that energy markets can function while maintaining healthy and safe environmental standards.

A Clean Power Ethic. Another way of conceiving our energy/environmental system, in either Sarah Krakoff's analysis or in Pope Francis Encyclical,[143] is as a bounded system in which resources are limited and in which ill-considered human action can negatively affect well-being.[144] The idea that human activity generates negative externalities and affects limited natural resources may sound obvious but it has been controversial for decades. The strong critical reaction to the Club of Rome report *Limits to Growth*[145] in the 1970s decried any arguments suggesting limits to natural resources for fear of constraining continued economic expansion.[146] The idea of a bounded system comes into clearer view when we consider the antithesis of an unbounded planet in which all natural resource problems, including energy and the environment, are susceptible to technological solutions and that any argument about resource limits is an unacceptable argument against economic growth.

Krakoff's analysis provides an opportunity to present a frame of reference other than economic growth from energy production. The energy/environmental future has temporal and spatial dimensions that differ from past problems. Temporally, the environmental effects of carbon that was emitted a generation and more ago are just beginning to be registered. Consequently, the carbon that is released today will affect the environment beyond our lifetimes. Spatially, pollution released in Ohio is not contained within its borders; nor are the effects of pollution released in India, China, or the United States contained by the fiction of national borders. Energy production and its consequences span generations and extend beyond political boundaries such that waiting for climate harms to occur before addressing them will lead to economic harm.

For too long, energy and environmental policies have been based on an analytic method that narrowly hewed to a conception of an unbounded world. This analytic focused on short-term economic growth and a belief that such growth could continue indefinitely into the future. The analytic was further supported with a narrow cost-benefit calculus that generally overstated costs because they were more easily quantifiable and understated benefits because they were so difficult to monetize.[147] These analysts eschewed the bounded frame of reference, arguing that a growing economy would ultimately solve all problems created by negative externalities.

From such a positivist analytic, the bounded perspective leads to unacceptable conclusions. More specifically, in a bounded world, collective choice problems dictate that acting at either the local or the national level may be futile. Since no one state actor, let alone an individual, can have much influence on such large-scale environmental problems, according to such analyses, addressing them before harm is incurred is economically irrational. In other words, it is better to consume today rather than invest in tomorrow. It is precisely that sort of thinking that ignores the imperative for new frames of reference and new behaviors.

Our world and its environment are not unbounded. And, because the system is bounded, a belief in unfettered markets and perpetual economic growth as ends in themselves is an illusion that must be shed. Further, these analytic methods have limited value for addressing climate change precisely because they are focused on short-term gains and losses rather than more longer-lasting political responses to the complexities inherent in the clean power future. If we ignore long-term environmental harms and continue to burn fossil fuels, then incumbent energy firms will prosper and our grandchildren will suffer.

If, instead, we accept the bounded nature of our energy/environmental system, then a different range of regulatory solutions becomes available. Instead of market forces, government regulation is essential; instead of waiting for technical adaptations, mitigation measures will be necessary; and instead of allegiance to a constrained version of capitalism, we should have a more holistic view of democracy.

Put another way, if it is "rational" for actors to pursue cheap energy rather than reducing carbon emissions, then we are engaged in a true prisoner's dilemma.[148] Individual behavior may be self-maximizing; however, selfish self-maximization is detrimental to long-term collective welfare. Positive analytics, then, are limited in their approach to problems particularly of the sort presented by the energy/environmental complex. Instead, a broader array of social science analyses should be considered that concentrate on a new economics, new governance structures, and a broader array of political norms beyond immediate gain and the hope of indefinite economic expansion.[149]

Our clean power future requires a "new kind of moral calculus, premised on the idea that ecological interdependence is the condition of first importance in assessing human interaction with the natural world, and that it must imply a comprehensive reevaluation of economic life."[150] And, more significantly, new ideological commitments will lead to pragmatic applications that serve both energy and the environment.[151] The applications will be pragmatic as various actors in both the public and private sectors seek solutions that work rather than solutions that conform to an already received ideology. Further, a merger between energy and the environment can satisfy a progressive claim "that economic life should serve certain qualitative values … because those values are measures of a legitimate economic order."[152]

The list of arguments in favor of a clean power transition runs the gamut from policy and politics to economics and society. At the heart of the argument is the belief that transition is beneficial from multiple perspectives and that there is no reason to sacrifice comfort for conservation or to give up economic productivity in the face of an energy transition. The arguments, however, do have a significant and complementary consequence. The purpose of a transition is not only to move from fossil energy to clean energy, but also to engender a new way of doing energy business. An energy transition will embrace new business models described more fully in Chapter 5 and new regulatory structure more fully described in Chapter 6.

CONCLUSION

The dominant model of US energy policy has been in existence for over a century and it has had remarkable staying power.[153] The traditional model cannot last because it will be too costly. In order to reconfigure the US energy policy model, the new model must be set into the context of a new political economy. Regardless of the barriers that a clean power economy must confront, the new economy will have new, distinct, and desirable characteristics different from the traditional model. Most notably, a clean power economy will move away from fossil fuel resources, will be sensitive to harmful environmental externalities, and will depend upon a wider variety and diversity of resources, including energy efficiency, for a national energy portfolio. Diversity of resources will provide more options for consumers and will inject more competition into energy markets. A clean power transition, coupled with intelligent innovation policies and reliable regulations, will generate new technologies[154] and new markets with a proliferation of new market actors and firms.[155]

A clean power economy will be less capital-intensive and more decentralized than our traditional energy economies. The use of distributed energy resources or distributed power, as an example, will continue to expand as consumer choices increase. The advantages of decentralization include bringing energy closer to end users, thus reducing delivery costs; relieving stress and congestion on national energy infrastructures; scaling energy production more closely to the tasks needed by end users; and, reducing cyber security vulnerabilities through decentralized power production, transmission, and distribution.[156]

The governance structures in the clean power economy will likewise change. The federal government took the leading role in developing and supporting the traditional model. Large firms enjoyed economies of scale, constructed a national infrastructure, and regulation was therefore centered in federal and state capitals. The clean power economy will develop a different relationship with regulators. In addition to federal leadership via the clean power regulations, the new energy economy will be largely driven by market and local forces. Similarly, because a clean power economy will ultimately succeed when clean products reach commercial scale and are cost competitive with traditional fuels, they will need less regulatory support.[157] Moreover, to the extent that energy firms can wean themselves from public support systems, incumbency bias by regulators can be reduced.

The federal government has a necessary role to play in fostering the clean power economy. Most notably, in addition to clean power regulations, federal financial supports, including subsidies, tax breaks, and R&D funding, are necessary to bring these new energy sources to market scale. Most importantly, the transition will greatly benefit from the design of an intelligent innovation policy[158] discussed in the next chapter.

PART II

THE NECESSITY OF INNOVATION

4

Innovation Policy and Institutions

The second part of this book addresses the necessity of innovation in technologies, businesses, and regulations. Technological innovation is an important input to a healthy and vibrant economy. Some argue that it is the most important input.[1] Regardless, it is not the only input; a sound rule of law, robust infrastructure, educated workforce, and healthy citizenry, among other inputs, are equally valuable. Technological innovation, though, is an engine that can drive the economy further and faster than it would ordinarily travel; it can also hasten and advance the clean power transition.[2]

The American economy has flourished as both the public and private sectors have contributed to making innovation a strong part of the economy. Historically, the United States has "generally demonstrated an almost ruthless pragmatism in implementing the core principles of free markets and strong property rights, overlaid with decisive government investments in infrastructure, human capital, and new technologies."[3] Government action works in collaboration with market forces and serves as stimulant to create and sustain markets. Government also serves as a monitor to enforce market rules and fix broken markets.

Such positive roles for government are hardly novel. At the founding of the United States, the debate between the Hamiltonians and Jeffersonians over the role of government was not about whether government should be involved with stimulating markets or its regulation; rather the debate was about the locus and types of that involvement. The Hamiltonians preferred a strong central government so that the United States could become an actor on the world economic stage. The Jeffersonians preferred local government to a central one, believing that democracy works best at a smaller scale. Both factions, however, perceived government participation as necessary for a strong economic state. This public–private partnership was dubbed the American System by Henry Clay and it continues to operate.[4]

Through mercantilist practices, government facilitated the construction of roads, bridges, and canals in the yearly years of the Republic. The government was also actively involved in trade, customs, monetary, and other regulations on the way to creating a strong national economy. The development of infrastructure, as well as the development and provision of other public goods such as health, education, and war mobilization, became the rationale for innovation investments throughout the country's history. In the race for space, the private sector decidedly took a backseat to a pro-active government. Technological advances in the twentieth century from nuclear power to nanotechnology, to the Internet, and to the algorithm that sustains today's search engines, all began with government initiatives.[5]

This chapter begins by explaining the economics of innovation and describing the innovation system as a whole. The chapter then explains the key innovation actors and the roles that they play in moving to a clean power economy. Finally, the chapter concludes with an explanation of technological assessment as a way to measure whether or not innovation policy and the system it has created have succeeded in reaching their goals.

ENERGY INNOVATION AND GOVERNMENT

The demands of energy and the environment provide significant reasons for continued public support for technological innovation.[6] The United States needs to revive its mercantilist spirit and increase its innovation investments across the board from scientific and technological discoveries to infrastructure and manufacturing, and from education about energy choices to small business development. Such funding can occur through a range of strategies and organizations that are described next.[7]

Until recently, the United States had reduced its investments in energy innovation.[8] This recent return to energy innovation investment is consistent with the country's rich history of technological transformation through government support.[9] Over the last century, the country has "built large, stable innovation systems that drove extraordinary technological transformations in comparably vast regions of the economy, including agriculture, defense, health, and telecommunications." Given this time in our history, it stands to reason that "energy must now join this list."[10]

Energy technologies have characteristics that differ from classic R&D efforts such as the Manhattan Project and the Apollo Space Program. Energy technologies also have characteristics different from many telecommunications and information technology innovations that have disrupted and transformed those sectors. Accordingly, these different characteristics require an innovation policy that is more closely aligned with an energy transformation.

The core idea is that energy innovation will not take place on its own, which is to say that the private sector will not adequately fund clean power development. The private sector has said as much by calling for increased government funding for clean power research, development, and demonstration.[11] The announcement at the Paris climate talks by a group of CEOs, such as Bill Gates, George Soros, Jeff Bezos, and Richard Branson among other billionaires, about the formation of the Breakthrough Energy Coalition is a case in point. The Breakthrough Coalition's founding principle is that "technology will help solve our energy issues" and will do so with direct attention to climate change. More specifically, the Breakthrough Coalition will pursue an aggressive program of developing zero-emission energy technologies through public–private partnerships and government support.[12]

A successful clean power transition must be "underpinned and supported by a dense network of federal R&D programs and institutions."[13] Energy innovation policy will focus on marketability and will generate new technologies and markets.[14] Further, a full-fledged innovation policy is not just one thing; there is no single path to success. Instead, it requires a systemic approach that incorporates a variety of institutions, networks, and feedback and learning processes as well as new actors and organizations that reject business as usual.[15]

According to the usual textbook analysis of innovation processes, there is a continuum in which, at the front end, the public sector is almost exclusively involved in funding fundamental scientific and technological discoveries and inventions. Then toward the back end of the continuum, the private sector is almost exclusively involved in scaling up technologies and bringing them to market. The reality, however, is slightly different. Government involvement does not end at the initial R&D phase; instead, it has played a large role in moving beyond initial research as well as beyond demonstration projects to assisting private capital in traversing the valleys of death on the way to technological commercialization.[16] In fact, the central focus of government-sponsored energy R&D is commercialization, not research and discovery for their intrinsic values.

A full complement of regulatory instruments is necessary to effectively create and successfully implement an innovation system that is directed at accomplishing an energy transformation. In addition to R&D, intellectual property protection, training and education, public–private sector collaborations, and trade and competition policies, as well as financial incentives such as tax credits for production and investment, can be used to stimulate innovation and *push* new technologies into the market.[17] Further, energy efficiency standards, clean energy standards, and energy portfolio standards can all be used to *pull* innovations into the marketplace. This dual push–pull approach is a necessary component of an effective energy innovation system.

Technological energy innovations should stimulate economic growth, promote jobs, and increase competition by bringing more products to the market, thus expanding consumer choice.[18] Additionally, energy innovations should stimulate firms to adopt new business models, which, in turn, should increase efficiencies. Importantly, to the extent that the energy economy is changing in these directions, the sooner the change is fully engaged, the less costly it will be. As the White House recognized, the costs of waiting to address climate change will only increase.[19]

While clean energy initiatives and innovations are consistent with efforts to address climate change, the two are not mutually inclusive and it is useful to distinguish between them along three dimensions – the temporal, the political, and the financial. Temporally, clean power initiatives are more short- and mid-term strategies because the demand for energy is constant. Climate change innovation does not fit as comfortably with short- and mid-term economic strategies because addressing it is a long-term proposition. Indeed, critics of the Clean Power Plan (CPP) emphasize the drag on economic growth caused in the short term by those environmental regulations.[20] In the long term, however, if we do not address climate change, economic growth may be imperiled.

Politically, the goal of climate change innovation of reducing greenhouse gas emissions is contested along partisan lines. While the need for reliable and affordable energy is widely embraced, the need to address climate change is not. Consequently, innovation for the purpose of addressing climate change is treated differently than energy innovation. Climate change innovation is driven by the desire to promote the public good of a healthier environment, which, however desirable, is less visible to the ordinary consumer than greater energy efficiencies, cleaner energy, and reduced energy expenditures.[21] The point is a simple one. Clean power innovation is consistent with climate change innovation while climate change innovation is not necessarily consistent with the development of clean power technologies. While the policies are complementary, clean power is more visible than a clean environment and, therefore, more likely to be perceived positively by the public. Thus, we can and should distinguish between the politics of clean power and the politics of climate change.

Financially, public and private investments in clean power have been increasing. Clean power investments are discussed later in this chapter.

Climate change investments, however, have not become part of many financial portfolios. Although climate change is receiving more attention, particularly at the Paris climate talks, it is generally perceived as too long-term to attract significant investment dollars.[22]

Clean power innovations can be distinguished from other forms of technological innovations as well. We all marvel at the rapidity of technological change in the information and telecommunications (IT) sectors. It was not that long ago when people used landlines and had never heard of an iPad or an Apple Watch. Today, cellphones and iPads are ubiquitous. As consumers, we can barely anticipate the next consumer products on the horizon. Clean power innovations do not share the same characteristics as those in the consumer electronics arena. The economic benefits of clean power are simply less visible.[23]

Clean energy innovation is longer-term than IT innovation. And, longer-term change strategies are not quickly embraced by incumbent energy firms that prefer to focus on short-term shareholder value, and that short-term focus is a roadblock to change. Although, clean power innovations may be as simple as the design of a new thermostat, for significant change to take hold, large-scale and systematic changes are necessary. Those innovations are slowly embraced, if at all, by incumbent energy firms that are set in their ways because of the sunk costs of past investments and because such firms are comfortable with and dependent upon past ways of doing business.

By way of example, the most significant change in the energy sector will be to breach the divide between our two major energy systems – transportation and electricity – through electric vehicles and alternative fuels. Such a change will necessitate disruptive technologies, and those technologies will be large and complex and will invite a wide variety of associated and complementary applications and other technologies to the sector. While the promise of a disruptive technology is attractive to some—consider Tesla for a moment—it is a threat to other energy firms such as major oil companies, car manufacturers, and traditionally structured electric utilities, although even these industries are changing – slowly.

There is also a degree of consumer buy-in that distinguishes energy from IT. Consumers have been quick to understand that they can exercise choice in buying cellphones, computers, electronic games, and other consumer products. Consumers have not been quick to understand the energy choices available to them and have not been quick to understand the value of clean power and then demand it.

As a consequence of an underdeveloped market for clean power, there is a necessary role for government. Free market advocates argue that if a clean transition is to take place, then it should take place from out of the guise of government and it should take place in the hands of the private sector. The argument that the market can, and will, effectuate an energy transition is too simplistic.[24] First, the energy sector has enjoyed the involvement and support of government for all of its modern life much to the benefit of fossil fuel firms. Second, as it has developed, the energy sector has generated negative externalities, the costs of which have generally been ignored and now appear to be becoming prohibitive. Government has subsidized dirty energy resources for over a century and to now argue that government hands should be taken off the clean power sector is, at best, unwise. At worst, it is hypocritical and only exacerbates a growing environmental problem. Third, government support for clean power simply perpetuates an already unlevel playing field and contributes to the further increase of the social costs of fossil fuels. If left to private markets and firms alone, then the pace of energy innovation would be too slow to address the multiple needs of energy, the economy, and the environment.[25] Further, the argument in favor of government support for clean power innovation is amply buttressed by basic economics.

THE ECONOMICS OF INNOVATION

Standard economics tells us that the private sector will underinvest in innovation funding for four reasons. First, because inventors may not always be able to capture all of the gains to be made from their inventions, they have a disincentive to invest. The economic idea is that because at least some of the "positive externalities" of an innovation can be taken and exploited by others once the idea is out in the world, the disincentive exists. The second, and complementary, reason is that a firm is unlikely to invest too much money in innovation or R&D if that investment is likely to put it at a competitive disadvantage and at the risk of losing market share.[26]

There is a third financial reason that private firms promote government-sponsored R&D. Private firms prefer to free ride as government investment reduces their cost of doing business by reducing the risk of new ventures while not increasing the risk of losing competitive advantages. Private sector organizations such as the American Energy Innovation Council, a trade association comprising venture capitalists and chief executives from Lockheed Martin, General Electric, and Xerox, as well as former executives such as Bill Gates, enthusiastically endorse increased R&D spending in the energy sector.[27]

A fourth reason for government support is related more closely to energy innovation. Energy technologies have specific characteristics that weigh against a firm making significant innovation investments. Major technological changes in the energy sector require long lead times from initial concept to commercialization because the process "entails institutional changes, new business models, and evolution of social norms."[28] Additionally, energy system innovation entails innovations in science, technology, business, and education.[29] Unsurprisingly, because of the complexities (and costs) of energy innovation and because of the trillions of dollars of already sunk costs, incumbent industries and incumbent regulators tend to resist change because of path dependency in old ways of doing business and in regulating those businesses.[30] Thus, "[l]arge incumbent energy firms have little incentive to create new options, especially in the absence of any signal from the government that climate change or other energy policy goals will be taken seriously."[31]

Public funding is needed to overcome these barriers.[32] Other more policy-oriented arguments for government involvement in energy innovation are that public monies can, and do, leverage private sector investments and that energy, especially clean energy, as an important public good that deserves government support.

We can conceive of energy as both a private and a public good. Energy is largely supplied by the private sector; however, the entire energy sector has been subject to government regulation for over a century. Energy can be considered a public good in two senses. First, US policy has made it a priority that energy be widely, reliably, and cheaply available. Second, the public good nature of clean power entails the added benefits of environmental protection, domestic security, and the opening of new markets. Consequently, regardless of whether we treat energy as a private or a public good, government support systems are necessary.[33]

In the case of energy technologies, economic theory and practice coalesce. The energy industry has notoriously underinvested in research and development.[34] It has been estimated that all industries in the United States invest 3.1 percent of their domestic sales into R&D. Estimates also reveal that communications investments exceed 25 percent and pharmaceutical investments nearly 12 percent as compared with energy investments of 0.3 percent.[35] Additionally, the United States spends approximately 0.03 percent of its GDP for energy R&D as compared with other countries such as China at 0.11 percent and Canada and Japan at 0.09 percent.[36] It has also been reported that private electric utilities, on average, spend less than 0.2 percent of their revenues on R&D, which is significantly below the average R&D investment by high technology firms.[37]

Reduced funding from the private sector unfortunately comes at a time when public investments have also been reduced. Another study reports that

US companies spend less than 0.5 percent of their sales on new R&D and US government commitments to clean power are at about the same level. These spending levels contrast with information technology in which US R&D is 20 times that figure and pharmaceutical investments are 40 times that figure.[38] In the United States, after the 1970s oil crises, energy R&D investments collapsed with only gradual recovery after 2000 with a notable capital infusion as a result of the American Recovery and Reinvestment Act (ARRA).[39] Even with that infusion, additional financial support is warranted. Simply, the case for public investment in clean power innovation is substantial.

A GENERAL MODEL FOR CLEAN POWER POLICY

A policy model for clean power in general and energy innovation policy in particular must be driven by specific policy principles and goals,[40] principally aligning economic growth with environmental protection.[41] In response, energy innovation policy should focus on building infrastructure; developing new and visionary technologies; and, investing in human capital[42] as well as facilitating the development and diffusion of a panoply of new and existing clean power technologies.

We can identify a set of principles for the development of energy technology innovations. First, we should develop a clearly articulated clean power policy at the federal level. Second, a core principle of that policy must be that all energy actors must play on a level field. This issue is complicated by the fact that the country's energy history is one of uneven subsidies between fossil fuels and other energy producers. Third, the goals of the innovation policy must be scalability and commercialization. Energy innovation, even by the public sector, must be driven not by research for the sake of research, but with an eye toward marketability. Fourth, the energy innovation system must set clear goals and benchmarks, and must use assessment tools to measure progress and success. The simple point is that if innovation investments are not meeting goals, then they must be discontinued. Fifth, it will be a goal of innovation policy that resources are shifted from public to private sectors along the innovation continuum as new technologies reach commercial markets. Finally, feedback loops must be built into the energy innovation system so that continuous learning becomes a part of it. These principles are developed through the following discussion of the general model of clean power innovation. With these principles, innovation policy can serve several economic and social ends.[43]

There are several models of energy information systems in the literature and they are largely consistent.[44] The fundamental idea is to create an environment where inventions can occur and then move those inventions into the commercial marketplace. The focus on commercialization distinguishes the energy innovation model from other R&D projects such as the space race in two significant ways. First, the space race did not focus on commercialization; rather its goal was overtly political; the United States had to beat the Soviet Union to the moon. Second, the focus on winning the space race was a singular technological objective whereas energy innovation does not have such a singular focus; instead, the target is to generate a wide range of low- or no-carbon technologies. Also, along the innovation continuum, different public and private actors have distinct roles to play and the dynamic interaction between government and private firms is not only central to the full development of useful energy technologies, it is also essential. Figure 4.1 demonstrates two ideas. First, it represents the four stages of the innovation process. Second, it represents the relationship between government and private investments in energy innovation.

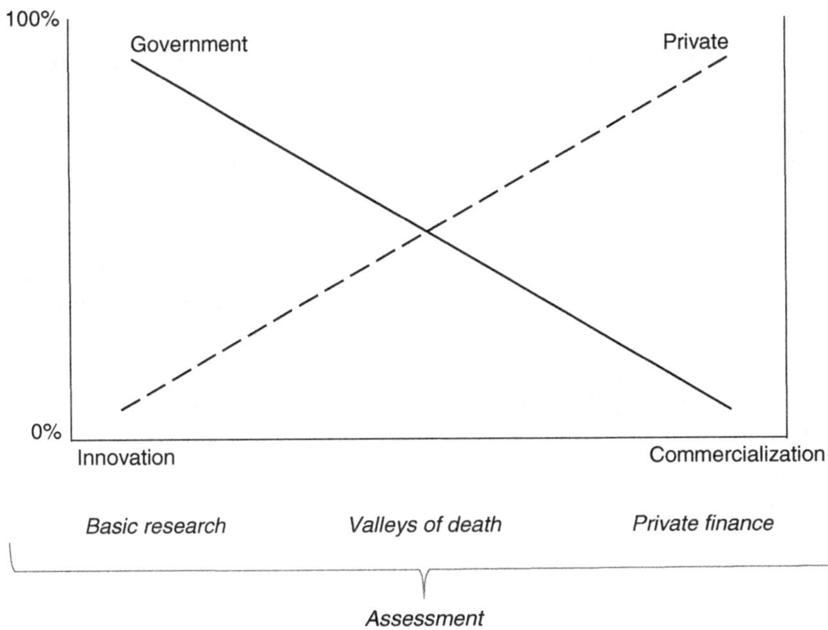

FIGURE 4.1 Government and Private Investment in the Energy Technology Innovation System

At the extreme left hand edge of Figure 4.1, one can envision a point at which the government is the only actor/investor in an innovation system. Here nuclear fission is a prime example. Similarly, at the other extreme on the right hand edge of the figure, one can envision a point at which the private sector actor/investor operates without government involvement. Edison's electric light bulb is as good an example as any. In a general scheme of innovation, both of those extreme positions are theoretically possible and even sound. Government researchers, for example, may be the only ones looking at a particular vaccine or military application. At the other end, private actors can dominate a particular market such as the manufacture and sale of cell-phones. In the energy sector, such extremes are rare; instead, public–private partnership is the norm. Nevertheless, along this continuum, there will be points at which one sector is dominant over the other.

At the beginning of the innovation cycle, it may be necessary for government to invest in fundamental science and technological research largely, for reasons stated before, because the private sector is reluctant to invest. In the initial stages of the innovation system, government bears more risk than private actors and reaps little to no reward for those risks.[45] At the other extreme, after the system has run its course, as specific technologies reach market, private actors control the commercialization of the new technologies. In short, "[a]s an innovation approaches deployment and investment prospects begin to rise, it is typical for private sector involvement to increase and public sector involvement to decrease."[46]

At the commercialization stage, government may no longer be involved and the gains to be made from market trades go to private actors. There is no ineluctable reason that those gains from trade cannot be shared between the public and private sectors. There is, though, a general reluctance to have government ownership of energy technologies. Instead of sharing gains, private actors are rewarded for their ability to bring products to market. Regardless to which sector the gains from trade do go, the energy innovation model runs through identifiable stages and at each stage there will be a different mix and different levels of public and private participation.

The first stage addresses *basic research*. Initial research involves scientific investigation as well as the initial application of a scientific discovery through the development of a new technology. The second stage addresses two *valleys of death* that must be traversed as a new technology moves from idea to market – the technological valley of death (i.e., moving from idea to demonstration) and the commercial valley of death (i.e., moving from demonstration commercialization). Both valleys involve financial risks that many entrepreneurs are unwilling to bear.

The third stage is referred to as either deployment or full commercialization at which time government involvement recedes and private involvement expands. At this point, *private finance* replaces government funding. Finally, if the innovation process and the innovation system are to work properly, then they must internalize the lessons they have learned through *assessment*. Each of these stages will be addressed next.

Basic Research

The idea that government fully funds basic science and technology is something of a caricature. In a certain sense, it is often the case with many energy technology projects that the government plays a significant and often dominant role. However, government most often fund private sector actors such as universities that make their own financial contributions to innovation projects to facilitate research as shown in the country's national laboratories and in other Department of Energy (DOE) activities.

National Laboratories. The DOE runs 17 national laboratories that are dispersed throughout the United States and they take on a variety of configurations and have an annual budget of $14 billion. Historically, most of the research conducted by these laboratories was for defense purposes. Today, defense is still the primary focus for many of these labs; however, energy innovation is gaining increased interest, as well as increased government funding. Additionally, while clean energy R&D conducted by national laboratories is gaining in importance, recent studies indicate that improvements can be made to accelerate that work.[47]

The Argonne National Laboratory outside of Chicago, Illinois, may be the quintessential example of a US investment in basic science and technology. The lab began life as an essential part of the Manhattan Project. On December 2, 1942, under the University of Chicago's Amos Alonzo Stagg football stadium, the scientists of Argonne Lab created the world's first nuclear reaction, which, in turn, led to the successful construction of the atomic bomb. After the war, at the direction of the Atomic Energy Commission, Argonne National Laboratory began developing reactors for the generation of commercial nuclear power. In addition to its work in nuclear and particle physics, Argonne conducts research in advanced computers, applied mathematics, and material sciences and engineering among other projects. Today, with a budget of $722 million and 3,350 employees, Argonne is a multidisciplinary science and engineering research center, which addresses matters of clean power and the environment as well as national security.

Similarly, Ames Lab, in Ames, Iowa, began in the 1940s as a government facility dedicated to producing high-quality uranium for atomic fission. From that initial project, Ames Lab has expanded its research into the areas of material sciences and engineering, chemical, and biological sciences, as well as applied mathematics and occupational sciences. Additionally, Ames Lab engages in technological research to address environmental challenges.

National labs conduct high-level scientific research such as that done by the Princeton Plasma Physics Laboratory (PPPL) in Princeton, New Jersey. PPPL is a collaborative national research center concentrating on fusion energy and plasma physics. Plasma physics has applications for use in particle accelerators, propulsion, and the synthesis of nanomaterials, and for medical diagnostic testing. Fusion has been a long-time dream of physicists who foresee it as a safe, economically efficient, and environmentally sensitive source of energy. Through the creation of a fusion facility, or tokamak, the fundamental idea is to literally smash atoms together to generate heat that can be used in the production of energy. Currently, PPPL together with representatives from the European Union, China, India, Japan, Korea, and Russia is building a demonstration fusion reactor in France that will be designed to produce 500 million watts of fusion power for at least 400 seconds by the late 2020s. Clearly, fusion is a long-term investment in a new energy source and that research is government funded.

Ames and Argonne are two examples of defense laboratories expanding their research missions. The Lawrence Berkeley National Laboratory is an example of joint government–university partnership. The Berkeley Lab began its research in particle physics, which resulted in the construction of a particle accelerator before World War II. During the war, the scientists associated with the lab, notably Ernest Lawrence and J Robert Oppenheimer, made significant contributions to the Manhattan Project. With a budget exceeding $800 million with over 4,200 employees, it has been estimated that its research contributes nearly $700 million annually to the San Francisco Bay area and is responsible for creating over 12,000 jobs nationally.

Brookhaven National Laboratory on Long Island was established right after World War II specifically to examine the peaceful applications of atomic energy. Now, the lab engages in basic and applied research in nuclear high-energy physics, nanoscience, national security, and nonproliferation, as well as energy and environmental research.

The National Renewable Energy Laboratory (NREL) is DOE's primary research facility for renewable energy and energy efficiency. NREL focuses on the production of fuels, transportation, and electricity generation and its delivery. NREL is committed to sustainability and partners not only with the

DOE but also with the Department of Defense, private industry, and various academic institutions. NREL research involves bioenergy, buildings, and hydrogen fuel cells, together with geothermal, solar, and wind energy among other projects.

NREL began as a dedicated energy research laboratory in 1977 under the name of the Solar Energy Research Institute created in response to the 1973 oil embargo. Since then, NREL's focus has shifted to broader areas than just solar power as its work on renewable resources has contributed to the cost decline in both solar energy and wind power. Similarly, the lab has contributed to the declining costs involved with converting biomass into cellulosic ethanol as a result of its work on enzymes. NREL partners with utilities, other industry actors, and other governments in exploring clean power.

NREL claims a significant number of successes including approximately 300 patents issued by the United States and foreign countries with almost 300 patent applications pending. NREL boasts over 650 partnership agreements and with those public and private partners has noted successes in solar technology, lowering the cost of plug-in electric vehicle batteries, energy audit tools, and pioneering work in wind energy. Its research mission has also generated a number of significant studies including its Renewable Energy Future[48] report, which concluded that by 2050, renewables, together with an improved electric delivery system, can supply 80 percent of US electric generation with commercially available technologies. Additionally, NREL has constructed a state-of-the-art "Laboratory of the Future," which is a model for sustainable building design intended to concentrate on energy technology innovations.

The national labs were predominantly created to deal with the scientific and technical challenges surrounding national security and atomic energy. The labs also focused on weapons development. And, with the exception of NREL, none of the labs are exclusively dedicated to energy research although many of them are conducting research that will impact the energy sector as their research activities become more cross-cutting. Another distinguishing factor about the national labs is that generally they are not dedicated to the commercialization of the energy innovations. This lack of a commercial focus has been a source of criticism as well as a challenge to a more robust energy transition.[49]

In response to that criticism, it has been recommended that the national labs give greater attention to commercialization and that they do so through greater cooperation with other innovation systems operating in the country. The recommendation is for national labs to form regional innovation clusters with a decided mission toward economic growth.[50] One way to facilitate economic growth is to increase technology transfer through licensing agreements, patents, and revenue agreements. In this way, economic growth can be part of the national labs' missions. Even though the national labs can be criticized for their lack of a commercial focus, the next federal research activity is decidedly so focused.

Department of Energy. In 1958, as a response to Russia's *Sputnik* launch, the Department of Defense created the Defense Advanced Research Projects Agency (DARPA) intentionally for defense purposes. DARPA has made major contributions in precision guidance, unmanned aerial vehicles, and communications technologies that have directly altered the face of war and daily life. In addition to military applications, DARPA's work, particularly in cybersecurity and communications, has advanced the state of information technology significantly. Most notably, the agency played a major role in the development of ARPANET, which played a major role in the development of the Internet. More recently, DARPA's early work in global positioning and artificial intelligence is manifest today on our iPhones through Google maps and by Apple's SIRI as examples.[51]

DARPA's success has been attributed to certain key institutional characteristics. The agency relies on relatively small offices in which scientists and engineers are given budget autonomy and encouraged to be proactive. "The goal is to create a scientific community with a presence in universities, public sector and corporations that focuses on specific technological challenges that have to be overcome."[52] Additionally, funding is not directed to single actors; instead funding is distributed to various universities and private firms as well as industry consortia. Importantly, DARPA managers are encouraged to terminate funding for groups not meeting their benchmarks.[53] Because the mission is technological improvement for pragmatic purposes, work is targeted for commercialization rather than scientific progress for science's sake. Finally, the agency sees its role as facilitative by connecting resources and actors across different research and development projects and facilities.[54]

As a result of the successful contributions to science and technology developed by DARPA, Congress asked the National Academies of Sciences, Engineering, and Medicine together with the National Research Council to undertake a study addressing the country's most urgent challenges in maintaining leadership areas of science and technology. Congress also asked the National Academies to recommend specific policies to be considered by Congress. In response, the National Academies published an influential report entitled *Rising Above the Gathering Storm.*[55]

Among its many recommendations the report urged Congress to establish the Advanced Research Projects Agency – Energy (ARPA-E) specifically modeled after DARPA. The agency was created by the America Competes Act in 2007[56] and housed in the DOE. ARPA-E was first funded in 2009 by the ARRA with an initial allocation of $400 million.[57] Since its inception, ARPA-E has funded over 400 potentially transformative energy technology projects.

The agency's mission is to "enhance the economic and energy security of the United States through the development of energy technologies that result in reductions of imports of energy from foreign sources; reductions of energy-related emissions, including greenhouse gases; and improvement in the energy efficiency of all economic sectors; and to ensure that the United States maintains a technological lead in developing and deploying advanced energy technologies."[58] The goals of ARPA-E projects are consistent with the consensus clean power policy to advance national security, economic prosperity, and environmental sensitivity.

ARPA-E funds early-stage energy technologies that are projected to have a high impact and can reach commercial scale. The agency has funded projects by small businesses, universities, large businesses, and federal research and development centers as well as nonprofit organizations with an eye on energy markets. Awardees are required to provide a market plan, and while working with ARPA's market advisors, the awardees develop strategies including training and business practices intended to provide a clear understanding of market needs as projects advance. The agency is aware of the increase in the domestic production of natural gas and it has developed a program to use methane as a vehicle fuel. Similarly, the agency has been actively involved in developing fuel-cell technology to expand the use of distributed generation and it has developed programs for grid modernization in coordination with industry actors.

Fiscal year 2013 and 2014 programs have been directed to such projects as next-generation storage systems to improve driving range and reliability through EV battery improvements. ARPA-E also funds biological technologies for the purpose of converting gases to liquids for transportation. ARPA-E is also involved in recycling by developing innovative technologies to recycle such metals as aluminum, magnesium, and titanium. Grid improvements, including green electricity integration into the network, are funded through projects that improve electric switching to enhance temperature control, reduce power losses, and otherwise improve grid performance. ARPA-E continues its investments in solar power programs to continue to deliver cost-effective solar energy when the sun is not shining and to develop advances to current photovoltaic and concentrated solar power systems.[59]

Like DARPA, ARPA-E employs a series of strategies intended to generate new ideas and new technologies rather than fall victim to path dependencies.

Both agencies will terminate projects that are not working. Both agencies give project managers significant degrees of discretion rather than setting top-down agendas. Additionally, both agencies routinely change project managers to avoid staleness and silo thinking. While government funding plays the predominant role, private sector capital is also leveraged for specific projects. To the extent that these strategies work together, it is to form communities of scientists, engineers, and technicians that generate ideas as well as design solutions to energy problems.[60]

ARPA-E is engaged in creating transformative energy technologies and measures the success of its investments by their market impacts by using various metrics including project milestones during the development phases, patents, and publications, and the formation of new companies as well as the creation of public and private partnerships designed to move projects to market. In its FY 2015 budget, ARPA-E reports that project teams have formed at least two dozen new companies, sixteen partnerships with other agencies for further project development, and at least four technologies have reached commercial sales.[61]

One of the requirements of the initial grant of authority to ARPA-E was the obligation to issue periodic reports to Congress on the strategic vision of the agency. The vision statement describes a three-year funding cycle. In its latest report, the agency reiterated its commitment to innovative technologies designed to reach market. It also reaffirmed its commitment to hands-on engagement with awardees to provide them with funds and technical assistance so their projects move from early-stage development to commercialization. ARPA-E envisions that future projects will concentrate on the development of new transportation fuels including those from renewable resources; the development of new materials to improve energy conversion processes through real-world applications such as motors, HVAC, solar cells, and wind turbines; energy storage that not only will provide lighter and more longer life batteries but also can address intermittency problems with renewable resources; and, the development of information technologies that can collect, analyze, standardize, and protect energy information to create smarter and more resilient energy systems.[62]

Hubs and Frontiers. In 2010, the DOE established a series of Energy Innovation Hubs. Currently, there are four hubs in operation. The hubs constitute a new configuration for technological innovation research. The idea behind the hubs is to bring together top scientists and engineers from the academy, industry, and government. Their charge is to collaborate for the purpose of overcoming known barriers to technological innovation in the energy sector and to reduce the time from technical laboratory innovation and technological development to commercialization for the purposes of energy security and economic growth.

The Joint Center for Artificial Photosynthesis (JCAP), for example, is conducting research on finding a cost-effective way to produce fuels using only sunlight, water, and carbon dioxide as inputs. JCAP is led by a team of scientists and engineers from the California Institute of Technology in partnership with the Lawrence Berkeley National Lab. Other key partners include Stanford University, the Stanford Linear Accelerator, and other campuses from the University of California. The project has a five-year budget of $122 million and its mission is to develop a renewable fuel source while reducing carbon dioxide emissions. JCAP's principal project is to develop a solar-fueled generator that can be manufactured and distributed.

Another DOE hub, the Consortium for Advanced Simulation of Light Water Reactors (CASL), is creating a virtual environment to study nuclear reactors. The purpose of virtual reactor monitoring is to see how the industry can achieve greater outputs of power, longer reactor lifetimes, and improved energy efficiencies through fuel performance while maintaining the highest safety standards. CASL is operated under the auspices of the Oak Ridge National Laboratory with oversight by an independent and external board of directors. The hub has also entered into partnerships with other national labs such as Los Alamos, with universities such as MIT, the University of Michigan, and North Carolina State University, and with private partners such as Westinghouse. CASL outreach includes the publication of journals and conference papers, technical reports, and invited presentations.

As its name indicates, the Joint Center for Energy Storage Research (JCESR) is dedicated to conducting research in improved energy storage with the goal of having 25 percent of all electricity consumed in the United States generated by solar and wind by 2025 and having 1 million all-electric or plug-in hybrid vehicles on the road by 2015. In order to accomplish both of those challenges, more efficient and reliable energy storage systems are necessary. JCESR, in conjunction with the wide variety of large and small companies, universities and colleges, and other state and federal actors, seeks to advance energy storage so that batteries operate more efficiently, for longer periods of time, at lower costs, and at a wider range of temperatures.

Finally, the Critical Materials Institute (CMI) is also a consortium of laboratories, universities, and private industry actors that focuses on technologies that make better use of domestically produced materials for use in wind turbines, solar panels, electric vehicles, and energy-efficient lighting. The DOE has been concerned about the availability of rare earth metals, and to this end, the CMI looks to diversify supplies, develop substitute materials, and use available materials more efficiently with reduced waste. The main focus of CMI, then, is to secure supply chains of materials necessary for a clean energy transition as well as for energy security.

Energy Frontier Research Centers (EFRCs) are another configuration of energy research projects conducted by the DOE. Housed in the DOE's Office of Basic Energy Sciences, the EFRCs were created to accelerate transformative discoveries in energy science and technologies by recruiting a national scientific workforce that examines a new generation of tools that operate at the atomic and molecular levels. The work of the centers is dedicated to basic research needs as identified by the scientific community at large. The grand hope is that the EFRCs can contribute to a concerted effort to establish a sound scientific foundation for a transformed domestic energy economy that will not only enhance energy security but will protect the global environment.

At present, 32 EFRCs are operating in 32 states and they are conducting basic research along a number of fronts. The goal of the centers is to perform research that can contribute to development of disruptive technologies on the frontiers of science. The centers, similar to the hubs, constitute partnerships among universities, national laboratories, nonprofit organizations, and for-profit firms. To these ends, the centers have multiple investigators and operate on an integrated mission. Fundamental research is being conducted on a wide range of energy initiatives including biomass conversions, biofuels, nanotechnologies, energy storage, superconductors, and light materials.[63] Thus, the DOE has a robust program of innovation and is establishing a solid set of innovation institutions and policies.[64]

The Two Valleys of Death

In the initial phases of the innovation cycle, government involvement is at its height. Most often in the early stages, the private contributions are often significantly less than those of government. Private actors have little "skin in the game." In terms of risk and reward, government is less risk-averse than private actors who have financial obligations to their institutions, their funders, and their shareholders. Often, energy innovation presents financial risks that cannot be surmounted by many private investors; government investment is needed to induce private firms to engage in innovation.[65] Still, in order to bring energy innovations to market, the innovation cycle must run its course. After initial successes in science and technology, energy innovations must demonstrate their potential commercial viability.

The next stage in the innovation cycle involves development and demonstration, which is still in the early stages of the energy innovation cycle and presents a challenge that is sometimes referred to as the "technological valley of death." Once a particular energy innovation has achieved proof of concept, further capital is needed for the purpose of undertaking a "process of developing, testing, and refining ... technologies in order to prove to private funders that the technologies will be viable in markets rather than just successes in the laboratory."[66]

As a general matter, the technological valley of death refers to innovations that look good in the lab, yet presents unacceptable financial risks to private investors. In the energy sector, however, those risks are increased. Think, for a moment, about an information technology innovation. More specifically consider a software application. Initial investments for software apps are not particularly large. More significantly, the time horizon between the idea for the app and its execution can be relatively short. Or consider the pharmaceutical industry. While the initial investments are high and time horizons are often longer than those in information technology, the pharmaceutical industry has demonstrated a high tolerance for risk largely because potential rewards are significant and revenue is reliable. Once a pharmaceutical has proven to be marketable and has received the approval of the Food and Drug Administration, that drug is protected by an intellectual property regime and profits are directed to rights holders.

The energy sector can be differentiated both from information technology and from the pharmaceutical industry. Where information technologies often involve low-capital investments within short time horizons, energy technologies instead require significant investments and the time horizons from proof of concept to market are considerably longer and, sometimes, are simply unknown.[67] A successful energy innovation, for example, often requires major capital investments in infrastructure, new plants, and new storage.[68]

While the pharmaceutical industry requires large capital investment and longer time horizons, pharmaceutical firms are significantly less risk-averse than traditional energy firms that face greater competition and that may not be able to protect their innovations through an intellectual property regime to the same extent as pharmaceutical firms. Further, some energy firms, most notably investor-owned utilities, must answer to regulators in order to earn returns on their investments, and regulators are often reluctant to include the high innovation investments in rates if it means higher cost to consumers. Consequently, energy innovation is perceived as having greater risks and smaller profit margins than other industries.[69] Thus, at the development and demonstration stage, an infusion of private capital from either commercial banks or venture capital (VC) and private equity (PE) firms as well as from risk-averse traditional energy firms often goes wanting.

Government investment in demonstration projects is made for the same reason that private actors do not commit significant amounts of capital in the early stages of innovation. Currently, demonstration projects are under way on a variety of activities including the smart grid and offshore wind power, and to some extent to carbon capture and sequestration and advanced nuclear power, both of which have proven to be expensive and a long way from marketability, given their high costs and canceled or inactive projects.[70]

Wind and solar demonstration projects have met with more success than clean coal and nuclear power. The DOE has selected seven offshore wind demonstration projects with each to receive $4 million for the first phases of those initiatives.[71] These grants will help fund engineering, site evaluation, and planning. Of those seven projects, in May 2014, the DOE selected three projects to advance to the second stage of demonstration. During that stage, each project is eligible for $46.7 million to engage in follow-up design, fabrication, and deployment. As part of the DOE's wind strategies, the department works with both government agencies and private actors to address the technical and market challenges to the installation and operation of wind power and its connection to the grid. Similarly, DOE and state government agencies have been actively involved in solar demonstrations at a variety of scales ranging from utility-type solar demonstrations to solar power for buildings.[72] Clearly, the way to traverse the technological valley of death is through an infusion of government funding combined with private financing even if at a lower scale.

The second financial challenge is known as the commercialization valley of death. Even though an idea in the lab may have proven itself in government-sponsored demonstration projects, it remains to be seen whether the innovation is marketable and, therefore, profitable. It is this stage in the innovation cycle that begins to attract more substantial private funding because of its profit potential. At this stage in the process, VC and PE are seen as the vehicles to bridge projects to bring them to the point of commercial investment. The challenge is to accumulate "enough capital for the commercialization, production, and manufacturing processes associated with demonstration and market launch."[73] Commercialization efforts for energy technologies are costly, easily running to hundreds of millions of dollars. Too often, these financial requirements are perceived as too risky for most VC/PE firms. Consequently, it is often necessary for government regulations to establish incentives to make commercialization more likely. Government incentives, such as subsidies and tax breaks, that reduce the cost of doing business can push technologies into the market.[74] Innovation policy can also stimulate market activity through standard-setting or technology requirements, which have the effect of pulling those technologies into the market. In the clean energy sector, innovation policy employs both devices. R&D funding, for example, can help push new technologies such as smart meters into the market while pollution control requirements will have the effect of pulling technologies into the market.

While VC/PE firms do get involved in energy innovation, they tend to become involved after the technology has been fully proven and marketability is on the near horizon. VC/PE funding tends toward investments in safer technologies rather than more scientifically and technologically risky innovations.[75] It is more likely, for example, to see VC investments made in wind and solar components of proven technologies, building materials, and energy efficiency services rather than more unproven energy innovations such as advanced biofuels or carbon capture and sequestration.[76] In the past, such investments often have proven to be too risky for most VC/PE money. "[R]eliance on capital markets means that private financing is impatient and venture capital and private equity provide minimal support, at best, for long-term, science-based, technological innovations in the absence of perceptible market signals."[77] In 2013, for example, VC/PE firms that invested in energy technologies invested over two-thirds of their capital in wind and solar projects, which are both proven technologies[78] with some signs of expanding those investments to other clean power technologies.[79]

Barriers remain for clean power investments. Clean power projects, for example, can run from $100 million to $500 million with long project time frames. VC/PE firms prefer a three- to five-year time frame with proven technologies at substantially lower investment levels and at substantial returns.[80] Thus, VC/PE funds "tend to be concentrated in areas of high potential growth, low technological complexity and low capital intensity."[81] Clear examples of such lower-risk investment would include VC/PE investments in Tesla Motors and in SolarCity. Both of these ventures are headed by Elon Musk, which has developed a reputation for bringing projects to scale.

We have moved along the innovation continuum from idea to proof of concept, to development and demonstration, and we are now poised for marketability and commercialization. This last stage, sometimes referred to as diffusion or deployment, can only successfully occur with large-scale private sector involvement as the process moves toward the right margin of Figure 4.1. The goal of energy innovation is commercialization, and commercialization means private sector involvement and ownership even though government involvement occurs from R&D through demonstrations and deployment right through to commercialization.

Private Finance

Given large capital needs, long time-horizons, competition from incumbents, and regulatory uncertainties, among other risks, private financing of clean power projects remains risky. Yet, commercialization is the end goal of the innovation process and private finances are necessary. While VC/PE firms will fund energy innovations to some degree, at the back end of the innovation continuum, commercial finance is mandatory.

Private sector involvement must take over once an innovation is ready for commercialization. The private sector's profit motive, managerial experience, and investment acumen are necessary for the diffusion and deployment of clean energy technologies. Even at this late stage, there are steps that government can take to increase the comfort level of private investment. Consistent regulations, more stable intellectual property regimes, joint public–private projects, and clear price signals are steps that government can take to help stabilize the investment environment and, therefore, reduce financial risk.[82]

The market for private clean energy investments is promising, robust, and affordable. It has recently been estimated, for example, that in order to fully combat climate change and reduce greenhouse gas emissions by 40 percent from 2005 levels by 2035, a $200 billion annual investment of both public and private resources will be needed. While significant, $200 billion is equal to about 1.2 percent of GDP and about 6.5 percent of total US investment for 2012.[83] A report by the Center for American Progress supporting that estimate argues that such funding can both stabilize the climate and improve the domestic economy. The report goes on to recommend that public expenditures, at all levels of government, would amount to roughly 25 percent of the recommended funding with the private sector contributing the remainder, thus revealing profit opportunities.

The report breaks down those investments into $90 billion per year for raising efficiency standards and the remaining $110 billion invested in renewable energy resources that generate low to zero emissions such as solar, wind, and geothermal. Those investments are manageable, and adopting an assumption by the Energy Information Administration, the report states that most clean renewable resources will be at cost parity by 2017. These figures provide useful benchmarks.[84]

There are positive signs for a growing interest in clean power investments. Energy investments in the United States and globally have been on the rise in absolute terms, and they have outpaced other types of investments in relative terms even during the economic downturn.[85] Clean power investments, however, have rebounded from the recession and are projected to continue to do so.[86] The first quarter 2014, for example, shows nearly a 10 percent uptick in global clean power investments from the same period in 2013.[87] More impressively, in the third quarter 2015, US clean energy investments were up by 25 percent for a total quarterly investment of $13.4 billion, second only to China's investment of $26.7 billion.[88]

Global investments in renewable energy have had a significant impact particularly relative to investments in fossil fuels. In 2013, for example, investments in new renewable generation capacity amounted to $192 billion, while net investment in new fossil fuel capacity was $102 billion.[89] REN21 similarly reports that global net additions to electric-generation capacity from renewable energy have exceeded those of fossil fuels since 2009.[90]

Globally, renewable resources contributed more than half of the net total additions in electric-generating capacity. By the end of 2012, renewables comprise more than 26 percent of global generating capacity and supplied nearly 22 percent of global electricity.[91] Further, in 2013, solar photovoltaic capacity increased by 41 percent over 2012 and nearly ten times the capacity added in 2009. During the same time, wind capacity increased by 74 percent. The investment climate for clean power is clearly healthy.

As the economy improved in 2014, so did investments in clean energy. Bloomberg reports that global investments in renewable energy projects reached $175 million for the first three quarters, which constitutes a 16 percent increase from the same period.[92] Globally, in 2015, clean power investments reached historic highs and were also predicted to increase.[93] Domestically, there has been a similar increase in clean energy investments. In the first two quarters of 2014, the United States invested $18.5 billion in this space, which is an increase of $4 billion over the first two quarters of 2013.[94] It should be noted that these figures exclude new hydroelectricity projects, which would reflect another $35 billion of investments for a rough total of $227 billion. With the publication of the final CPP rules, the investment climate was more reliable and investment in the clean power sector should experience a notable increase.

Given a positive investment climate, it is of central importance for the successful adoption of energy innovation technologies that commercial financing is available. Commercial banks such as Citigroup or Deutsche Bank have been actively involved in developing their green investment portfolios. Deutsche Bank offers an array of banking services to support an energy transition. It has reported that as a financial intermediary it has been involved in $1.23 billion of large-scale renewable energy projects in 2013 and that it manages assets that are sensitive to environmental goals of approximately

$7 billion. The bank has adopted an energy and climate strategy that includes the development of sustainable products, carbon neutrality, and green building investments as well as clean energy technology innovations.[95]

In 2009, Citi Group created its Citi Climate Change Universe to assess how to satisfy global energy needs. Citi estimated that global GDP was expected to quadruple over the next 50 years and to do so would require a $37 trillion investment in energy needs. Of that $37 trillion, $24 trillion is forecast to be satisfied by clean energy sector including natural gas. Citi also estimated that $6 trillion will be required renewable power generation alone.[96] This long-term trend analysis is intended to identify equity investments at acceptable risk levels. Citi then identified 175 stocks that are participating in the energy transformation. In the electricity sector, solar and wind investments, as well as natural gas investments, are one area of investment. In the transportation sector, fuel efficiency was another investment area together with resource efficiency.

Citi's analysis is consistent with the main theme of this book that a clean power transition is occurring and will only expand in the future. By way of example, Citi projects that of the $9.7 trillion in global investment needed in power generation, only 29 percent of that investment will be in conventional generation technologies of coal, gas, oil, and nuclear power. The remainder of the investment will be in renewable technologies.[97]

As a final example of commercial and investment banking activity, in April 2014, J.P. Morgan Chase & Co. published its *Environmental and Social Policy Framework* (E&S). The E&S policy examines environmental and human rights issues for the express purpose of identifying risks to investments as well as exhibiting corporate responsibility. Morgan has adopted a series of best practices that are used to measure a transaction against its E&S policy.

For example, hydraulic fracturing, oil sands development, and exploration in the Arctic, all require enhanced risk review by the bank. In the electric sector, coal-fired power generation must be measured against greenhouse gas impacts and other pollution controls before a recommendation for investment will be made. Note that Morgan is, and has been, heavily involved in the fossil fuel sector. According to its E&S policy, however, it takes the International Panel on Climate Change's assessment of the impact of carbon dioxide on climate change seriously and incorporates it into its portfolio review process.[98]

Claims of corporate responsibility, such as those made by commercial and investment banks, are not new. To be sure, most commercial and investment banks are heavily involved in the fossil fuel sector. However, these brief examples reveal two important things about a clean energy transition. First, commercial finance is taking into account environmental protection, sustainability, and climate change as part of its risk assessments. Second, and more important for those institutions, there are profitable investments to be made as well as risks to be managed. Relative to energy innovation technologies, the fact that these private institutions have an eye on a clean energy transition will benefit emerging clean energy technologies.

Assessment

Assessment is an integral and necessary part of the innovation system and must occur throughout each stage of the process. An effective innovation system must employ methods to determine successes and failures as well as measure whether or not particular investments are moving in the right direction. Assessment accomplishes this through performance standards, benchmarks, and metrics that fund a range of technologies.[99]

Earlier, the argument that "government should not pick winners and losers" was noted.[100] In support of that critique, particularly during the 2012 elections, reference was regularly made to the example of Solyndra, a company that was developing photovoltaic panels. Solyndra received a $535 million loan guarantee by the government and went bankrupt. No doubt the government made a bad bet on Solyndra, which had borrowed $528 million of the amount allotted to it. However, extending this bad example to argue that no government investment in technology should be made is both illogical and inconsistent with the facts. The argument against Solyndra is wrong on two counts. Although that firm failed, the innovation program under which it was funded has not as government regularly assesses the progress of the innovation program.

Solyndra failed for several reasons but it does not stand for the proposition that government should not fund innovation. First, Solyndra was one of 24 firms that received loan guarantees under the same program, and 22 of them, as of mid-2014, were still in operation.[101] Second, the early exit of VC investment in solar contributed to Solyndra's demise. Third, changes in global solar markets also prevented Solyndra from capitalizing on its investments as the cost of raw silicon, the major input into its solar panels, collapsed. Fourth, a contributing factor to collapsing prices was the Chinese government's investment in photovoltaic technology, thus putting Solyndra at a competitive disadvantage.[102]

One measure of assessment is whether the government investment actually pays off. Here again, the Solyndra example is instructive. The other firm that defaulted under the same loan guarantee program was Abound Solar. Abound was eligible for $400 million in loan guarantees but had only borrowed

$68 million. Under the ARRA, approximately $14 billion of loan guarantees were allocated and the two defaults amounted to 4.3 percent of that amount. Note also that clean energy investments are not made solely by government; instead, the government also leverages private funds. Relative to the loan guarantee program under discussion, "[t]he leverage rate ... amounts to nearly $50 of private clean energy investments for every one dollar federal government spending."[103]

The DOE also funded several successful projects including the world's largest wind farms, two all-electric vehicle manufacturing facilities in the United States operated by Ford and Nissan, a commercial-scale cellulosic ethanol plant, utility-scale photovoltaic plants, and the world's largest concentrated solar plant. Simply, popular press accounts and critics of Solyndra offer a misleading and incomplete picture of the larger, successful role government plays in developing new energy technologies.

This brief discussion of Solyndra is offered here to refute the argument that government should not pick winners and losers. Government has not placed all of its money on one clean power bet. Instead, government investment in clean technologies is done through an array of agencies and in a variety of configurations, and directed at a broad spectrum of technologies.[104] There are multiple reasons for a broad range of investments. Most obviously, uncertainty about the future prevents any sure bets. Next, given the scope, as well as the scale of the energy sector, there will be no single disruptive technology. Instead, a range of technologies is necessary for a successful energy transition and that range of technologies is most likely to come about through technology clusters that create significant positive externalities, generate network effects, and avoid technological lock-in.[105]

Assessment can take many forms but it is integral to a robust innovation system because it provides feedback loops for improving investments, learning about innovation systems and processes, and measuring successes and failures.[106] The success or failure of projects can be measured through the amount of leveraged funds and the number of patents, public–private partnerships, commercial ventures, start-ups, initial public offerings, or demonstration projects. Success or failure can also be measured by the number of technological breakthroughs and the amount of new knowledge about innovation and innovation processes.

The DOE uses a variety of assessment tools. Cheryl Martin, the director for ARPA-E, has said that her agency uses both performance metrics and cost metrics to assess the investments. Once funds are allocated, the agency sets milestones every quarter over the three-year funding period and the agency meets with the recipients quarterly as assessment is an "ongoing process rather than a discrete event."[107] Also, projects that do not meet milestones are terminated.[108] Additionally, many of the recipients have corporate partners and/or partnerships with universities or other government agencies. As a result of those partnerships, Martin estimates that her agency has invested $95 million and has leveraged an additional $625 million of funding. Of the 22 projects that constitute that $95 million investment, four have attained preliminary commercial sales.

To the end of assessing the progress of the government's involvement with energy technology innovations, the DOE has embarked on two major assessments, the Quadrennial Technology Review (QTR) and the Quadrennial Energy Review (QER).

Quadrennial Technology Review. In 2010, the President's Council of Advisors on Science and Technology recommended that the DOE carry out a technology review every four years.[109] The first report was released in September 2011[110] and it established two basic themes. First, the report recognized the need to balance more "assured activities" against higher risk of more transformational work. Second, private sector involvement is directly relevant to assessing progress. The first report set six strategies to address the country's energy needs and challenges: (1) generate clean electricity, (2) modernize the grid, (3) increase building and industrial efficiencies, (4) develop alternative hydrocarbon fuels, (5) electrify the transportation sector, and (6) increase vehicle efficiency.

The report went on to note that the DOE had underinvested in the transportation infrastructure and that the electrification of transportation and greater fuel diversity were priorities.[111] Additionally, energy efficiency was seen as a high priority for future energy deployment. The report also noted that the DOE has underinvested in grid modernization as well as in building and industrial efficiencies. The QTR is intended as an assessment tool rather than as a tool used to set budgetary priorities although the information that it generates will inform the budget process. Further the QTR intended to focus on energy technologies rather than on national energy policies and priorities. National energy strategy is to be the focus of the QER discussed next. Finally, the QTR will establish the conceptual framework for energy technology programming as well as for establishing energy technology priorities.[112]

In an interim report to the DOE, the Transition Task Force recognized that government support is needed throughout the innovation chain from the creation of new ideas to development and demonstration and finally to deployment through financial assistance or regulatory mandates. The Task Force also offered four recommendations for improving the DOE technology innovation program, which the Task Force saw as consistent with the QTR. First, the United States should have a strong energy policy with the capability of undertaking systems analysis that includes economic analyses, policy studies, an understanding of market trends and prices, effects on economic performance and competitiveness, and a cost analysis for major projects. Second, a technology demonstration board should be established to manage and select demonstration projects. This board would then undertake rigorous evaluation of technical readiness and expected costs and outcomes for each project. Third, ARPA-E should remain focused on supporting potentially disruptive technologies. And, fourth, the report recommended that DOE laboratories should be strengthened in their efforts to commercialize energy innovations.[113]

Quadrennial Energy Review. The Obama administration has set out a Climate Action Plan as well as a Clean Power Plan. In an effort to coordinate environmental and energy policies, the president established the QER in January 2014 through a presidential memorandum that proposed to establish a comprehensive and integrated national energy strategy initially focusing on infrastructure for transportation, transmission, and delivery of energy. [114] The QER established a task force comprising a wide array of government agencies and departments ranging from the DOE and the Environmental Protection Agency to the Army Corps of Engineers and Homeland Security and from the National Science Foundation to the National Economic Council. The QER is issued by the White House and is intended to establish an integrated approach to US energy policy in the context of the nation's economic, environmental, security, and safety and health priorities in consultation with state and local governments as well as businesses, universities, and nongovernmental organizations.

The first report, published in April 2015, provided a multiyear road map and an agenda for R&D programs, funding, and financial incentives for energy transmission storage and distribution infrastructure.[115] The scope of the infrastructure review is extensive including the electric sector; traditional fossil fuels such as coal, oil, and natural gas; and alternative fuels including solar, wind, biofuels, and biomass.[116] The QER process starts with developing a baseline scenario and then establishing a reference case. Infrastructure needs will be tested against the reference case in order to develop policy alternatives. Once those alternatives are analyzed, the QER will make recommendations for legislative and executive action as well as recommendations for future research.[117]

The first QER addressed electricity and fossil fuel infrastructures as intended,[118] noting that the country's energy transmission, storage, and distribution systems are complex as well as interdependent. When a natural disaster, such as Superstorm Sandy, knocks out power lines, gas stations are affected because they lack the electricity to pump gasoline. The QER, then, identified current trends in the energy sector including increased domestic production of oil and natural gas; increases of electricity provided by variable sources such as solar and wind; the need to reduce greenhouse gas emissions including methane; and the failure of timely investment in upgrading and improving transportation systems. Each of these issues presents infrastructure challenges.

To meet those several challenges, the QER made a series of detailed findings and recommendations. Those recommendations include: (1) increasing the resilience, reliability, and safety and security of the infrastructure; (2) modernizing the electric grid; (3) improving energy security; (4) addressing environmental aspects of the Internet structure; (5) integrating North American energy markets; and (6) examining the siting and permitting of the transportation infrastructure among other issues. The report also noted that meeting those challenges would require federal investments of between $13 billion and $17 billion.

As part of outreach activities, the DOE requested the Institute of Electrical and Electronics Engineers (IEEE) to report on a range of priority issues such as the effects and use of intermittent resources on the electric grid, electric storage, new utility and business models, and distributed generation among other issues. The IEEE submitted a report that addressed each of these issues. The report recognized that renewable intermittency can be accommodated by the bulk power grid but present challenges to the distribution system. The report also noted that microgrids and other distributed resources must be perceived as integral parts of the electric grid and that value can be created both for providers and for consumers of distributed resources. Electric vehicles can be supported by the grid; however, the timing of additions and scope of penetration must be monitored. Finally, the age of the infrastructure must be adequately assessed and the education and training of a new energy workforce must be addressed.[119] The QTR and the QER, as well as internal DOE and ARPA-E operations, apply an assessment tool throughout their processes. The assessment, in turn, contributes to policy formation and to energy/environmental agenda-setting.

CONCLUSION

The innovation infrastructure in the United States has four notable characteristics. First, over the last few decades, government R&D has shifted funds from defense to energy and the environment in its national labs. Second, in recent years funding has also moved from defense energy to nondefense energy initiatives as best exemplified by NREL, the national lab that promotes renewable energy. Third, the energy innovation system is consciously designed to promote commercialization of a variety of technologies rather than solve perplexing scientific or technological problems for narrow applications. Fourth, the system is built with public–private cooperation and with the use of multiparty consortia. Fifth, and most significantly, history demonstrates that private markets respond well and adapt to regulatory initiatives. In other words, the clean power regulations are more likely than not to stimulate private sector investment to further its goals.[120]

Our energy innovation infrastructure is robust, although not without its challenges. Chief among the challenges is the need for greater coordination as well as increased public and private investment. Although much is happening in the private sector in terms of increasing clean energy investments, more needs to be done. Also, public investment must overcome the political reality of the energy transition that incumbent energy firms either are reluctant to change or simply oppose the clean power transition. Nevertheless, clean power proponents should find signs of hope in the shift that the federal government is taking toward clean energy as well as the investment interest demonstrated by the private sector.

Finally, energy innovation will not take place in government laboratories alone; it will occur with private sector managerial expertise and inventiveness. More significant, perhaps, is the fact that innovation initiatives directed toward commercialization will have repercussions for both industry actors and their regulators. Energy firms, most notably private utilities, must adopt innovative business practices in order to become an integral part of the clean power transition. So too must regulators support those practices and further the transition. Innovations in business and regulation are addressed in the next two chapters.

5

Clean Power Systems

To hear traditional investor-owned utilities (IOUs) tell the story, the end is nigh.[1] The IOUs' chief worry is symbolized by the simple rooftop solar panel. A homeowner's installation of rooftop solar, in and of itself, is little or no cause for concern. Even if it were a threat to IOUs, a property owner has every legal right to generate their own electricity.[2] Rooftop solar, however, is significant for what it represents more broadly – distributed generation and distributed energy resources.[3] IOUs are correct in recognizing that the electricity landscape is changing and that the status quo will not last and that they ought to embrace these inevitable changes rather than bemoan them.

Distributed generation (DG) means that a generator is located close to the consumer such as rooftop solar or a heat pump. Similarly, distributed energy resources (DER) have been defined as "demand- and supply-side resources that can be deployed throughout the electric distribution system to meet the energy and reliability needs of customers served by that system."[4] DER operates on both sides of the electric meter[5] and encompasses a variety of applications. On the demand side, for example, LED lighting and smart appliances reduce demand. And, on the supply side, customers can also generate their own power through solar photovoltaic and combined heat and power. Additionally, storage options are available such as electric vehicles and improved batteries that can store cheap electricity and sell it back to the grid when prices rise. And, smart and distributed intelligence applications such as home area networks and microgrids can both achieve efficiencies and improve reliability.[6]

From an IOU's point of view, DG and DER mean that it can lose sales, and therefore, lose revenue.[7] Fortunately for IOUs, at this point, distributed solar electricity constitutes a very small percentage of the total electricity load and is not an immediately significant contributor to load loss.[8] However, the signs on the horizon are not necessarily rosy for IOUs that have dominated the power market for over a century.[9]

The electricity market is changing[10] even to the point at which a utility expert can declare that "[t]he age of the 'natural monopoly' is over."[11] The market is more competitive today than it has been historically, and consequently, traditionally structured IOUs face real financial challenges as new technologies with decreasing costs "directly threaten the centralized utility model."[12] Although the electric industry has faced challenges in the past, the twenty-first-century challenge is different in kind from previous ones. Historically, federal and state regulators served incumbent IOUs by protecting their revenue streams. That response is inadequate to meet the convergence of demands posed on IOUs by new technologies, new markets, and new regulations. The twenty-first-century challenge of a clean power transition requires a dramatic response as traditional electric utilities face a new economic order even as they seek assurances of financial stability from their regulators for satisfying their service obligation to their customers. Now, what should an IOU do? Two responses are readily available. IOUs can either fight or switch.[13] The first response is the one given by incumbents: stay the course, tweak the regulatory system, and continue doing business as usual (BAU). The BAU strategy relies on maintaining a rate-making formula favorable to IOUs. The second, and better strategy, is that IOUs must change their business models in significant ways.[14]

Traditional IOUs served the country well for most of the twentieth century as demand continued to grow. Now with flattening demand, together with the need for investments in grid improvement, smart grid technologies, access to the grid by variable resources, reliability, cybersecurity, and pushes for greater use of renewable resources and energy efficiency, the utility of the future must acknowledge that the IOU model will not function as effectively in a transforming world as it had.[15] As former Federal Energy Regulatory Commission (FERC) chair Jon Wellinghoff has stated, "utilities are going to have the ability to morph into those roles of entrepreneurs and marketers and deliverers of these energy services to be able to effectively compete with all the other people in the space."[16]

The country is making a "revolutionary" transition to a clean energy economy[17] and there are several drivers to that transition including: (1) a developing policy consensus,[18] (2) positive economic indicators,[19] (3) the need to diversify fuel resources, (4) new financing techniques, (5) clean power regulatory proposals at the state and federal levels, and (6) technological innovations.[20] Indeed, "[t]echnological innovation is for the first time in history making it possible to realize cost-effective, reliable, *and* clean power systems."[21] Existing electric utilities must be able to take advantage of innovations that provide electricity and other electric or energy services;[22] or, competing power and service providers will enter the market, thus increasing competition and reducing the market share of incumbent utilities.

The electric industry is in a state of transition that will require utilities to seriously consider and adopt new business models and practices. This chapter will first explore the traditional industry characteristics and then discuss the past challenges faced by IOUs. While for over one hundred years the industry has been resilient regarding those challenges, climate change and clean power regulations are a challenge of a new order and magnitude. The chapter closes with a discussion of the contours of that transition and presents examples of the business models that can both weather the transition and promote a clean future.

THE TRADITIONAL ELECTRICITY INDUSTRY

Historically, the electric industry has been dominated by vertically integrated, investor-owned electric utilities because IOUs were able to capture economies of scale and scope and reliably deliver affordable electricity. For more than three decades, that model has been questioned as the cost of IOU electricity has increased, as demand has decreased, and as competition has expanded.[23] The IOU electric system of the past must necessarily transition to a more diverse and competitive clean power system of the future.

The electric industry operates just as it did on September 4, 1882, when Thomas Edison flipped a switch at his Pearl Street generating station in lower Manhattan and lit 400 incandescent light bulbs. With that flip, the electric industry was born and it existed for one purpose – to sell electricity. Electric utilities today mostly behave in the same way and for the same purpose; however, that situation must change even though electricity has property characteristics that make it unique. We expect electricity to be always available. Electricity is not easily and readily stored, as we know from charging our cellphones. Also, electricity is completely fungible, which is to say that electricity from solar power functions exactly like electricity from a nuclear power plant. Further, because electricity travels virtually at the speed of light, it does not follow a defined path, which is to say that we cannot exactly identify the source of the electricity that we use. Most importantly, the electric system must stay in balance or it will crash. Because of these property characteristics and because of our reliance on electricity, a reliable utility business and its proper regulation are essential.

Throughout the twentieth century, the industry was regulated with the intent to capture its benefits; as a consequence, the industry enjoyed specific protections. At the end of the nineteenth century, an agreement, known as the regulatory compact, was made between utilities and local and state regulators.[24] Electric utilities agreed to have their prices regulated by government and they took on an obligation to provide electricity to all customers within a specified service territory. Another way to regard the relationship between utilities and regulators is to say that electric utilities traded the power to set their rates in exchange for a virtually guaranteed monopoly within a geographic area.

Under this arrangement, regulation protected IOUs from competition. During its formative years, the electric industry enjoyed increasing demand and improved economies of scale as a result of technological innovations, both of which contributed to lower costs of production. Those lower costs, in turn, generated increased demand and increased profits. In order to optimize those economies and returns, industry actors developed a particular corporate structure. More specifically, private IOUs were vertically integrated. Electric utilities owned and operated generation, high-voltage transmission, and lower voltage local distribution.

Vertical integration and the regulatory compact served the electric industry quite well for most of the twentieth century. Particularly after World War II, as home construction expanded and as electricity demand increased, customers enjoyed relatively low and stable prices; utilities enjoyed regular, predictable returns and reaped their rewards; and regulators were fairly complacent. However, starting in the mid-1960s electric utilities began to encounter a series of challenges.[25] IOUs successfully responded to those challenges and the industry remained healthy. We will see, however, that the issue now confronting the electric industry is how to transform the latest and more complicated climate challenge into opportunities in a changing energy environment.

CHALLENGING THE ELECTRIC INDUSTRY

The electricity industry has been roiling for decades.[26] For the first two-thirds of the twentieth century, the industry continued to realize growth and, with it, increasing sales and profits. By the mid- to late 1960s, however, things began to change: a national electricity infrastructure was completed, electric generation plants reached a technological plateau, and the cost of electricity from traditionally structured electric utilities began to rise. These events, among others, shook the industry from its complacency and presented three significant challenges both to industry actors and to their regulators. During that period, the industry had to wrestle with increased prices, the collapse of the nuclear power industry, and regulatory attempts to first deregulate and then to restructure the industry in order to make cheaper electricity more readily available to consumers. Each of these challenges is briefly described next.

Increased Prices. The first challenge began as electricity prices rose. Price increases were inevitable and were the direct result of how the regulatory compact was applied.[27] The most attractive aspect of the regulatory compact was that utilities could earn a rate of return on their investments that was comparable to the rates of return earned by other private firms with similar risk profiles. Competitive returns were necessary for IOUs to attract investors. Rates were set according to a standard price-setting formula, known as cost-of-service (COS) ratemaking that reimbursed IOUs for their costs and allowed them to earn a return on invested capital. As a result, this pricing method encouraged utilities to continue to invest in and build more plants. The problem with increased construction was that once demand flattened, utilities had increased costs because of excess generating capacity and the cost of electricity began to rise.[28]

The price rise from IOUs suggested a profound change in the industry. More specifically, it indicated that electricity from IOUs might be overpriced and that other electricity providers might be able to produce electricity more cheaply. Less expensive electricity was available because of an increase in the number of nonutility power producers. However, the then existing structure of the electric industry imposed two significant hurdles to increasing competition by nonutility electricity providers. First, IOUs, as encouraged by the regulatory compact, had sunk trillions of dollars into plant and equipment and were locked into those investments. Second, those same firms owned the transmission and distribution networks necessary to transport electricity from providers to end users and they were not willing to share those assets.

The solution to the problem of making cheaper electricity available to consumers is conceptually simple – provide open access to the grid at reasonable rates for all electricity providers. The reality, however, is not so simple; because IOUs owned transmission and distribution, they opposed competition from new entrants. In an attempt to promote cheaper electricity, Congress passed legislation that encouraged non-IOU electric generation. And, in an attempt to open access, the FERC engaged in a series of regulations that has restructured much of the electric industry.[29] Together these statutory and regulatory changes have made the industry more complex on the road to greater competition that IOUs must now navigate.

Nuclear Failure. The second challenge came from the failed nuclear experiment. Nuclear power was never "too cheap to meter"; instead, it was too expensive to produce. From the mid-1970s into the 1980s, the expansion of the nuclear industry collapsed with significant repercussions for both shareholders and ratepayers. Utilities that had invested in nuclear power found themselves with excess capacity, canceled plants, or the conversion of nuclear plants to coal-fired plants – all at great expense. These nuclear investments ran into the billions of dollars and federal and state regulators had to apportion those costs between ratepayers and shareholders.

The question "Who pays?" was a real one for utilities, for regulators, and for consumers. The response to the question was generally some form of cost allocation between ratepayers and shareholders.[30] In some instances, regulators simply amortized the investment and allowed the utilities to recover their principal but did not allow them to earn a return on their investment or to recover their full costs of capital.[31] Amortization was simply a way to share the pain between ratepayers and shareholders. In brief, the regulatory response to the nuclear crisis was to protect some of a utility's investment and to maintain its financial stability while not overburdening consumers.

Industry Deregulation. The third challenge came with another financial shock wave in the 1990s with efforts to deregulate the electric industry and, when that failed, to restructure it. During the 1980s through the 1990s, following the general deregulatory mood in this country, regulators attempted to deregulate wholesale and retail electricity markets. Those deregulatory efforts were only partially successful for wholesale sales and much less so for retail sales.

As a primary input into the economy and as a service relied upon by everyone, reliable and affordable electricity was a necessity and complete deregulation threatened that reliability and affordability. At the wholesale level, deregulation looked promising and has occurred to a significant degree through market-based rates managed by FERC. At the retail level, the continued natural monopoly characteristics of the distribution and transmission segments prevented full deregulation from occurring.[32] Many states did attempt retail deregulation but California's notable failure threw two major utilities into insolvency, with Pacific Gas & Electric declaring bankruptcy.[33] With that failed experiment, restructuring effectively ended,[34] yet not without threatening the financial integrity of IOUs.

It must be noted that industry restructuring continued and significantly altered electricity markets. Through a series of FERC regulations, regional electricity markets developed and were managed by nonprofit system operators known as regional transmission organizations (RTOs) and independent system operators (ISOs). These regional organizations, together with regulations that began to open access for other electricity providers, have transformed the electric industry but IOUs have remained central actors in that system.[35]

Each of these three challenges can be considered one-off events. In other words, once the financially threatening event ended, the financial consequences needed to be addressed and regulators and industry did so. In each of these instances – higher electricity prices, the nuclear collapse, and failed deregulation – IOUs and regulators were able to respond to those challenges through various adaptations of traditional COS ratemaking.[36] Even though COS ratemaking was the contributing factor to excess capacity, higher priced electricity, and nuclear construction, there was enough flexibility in the formula to address those financial challenges.

Because utilities recouped expenses and could earn a return on investment, federal and state regulators could adjust the COS formula by deciding whether to treat a cost as an expense or place it in the rate base so that it could earn a return. Further, regulators could move the rate of return either up or down as long as it was "reasonable" and not confiscatory. As noted, in the case of nuclear power, regulators routinely applied various amortization schemes within the COS formula that effectively split the cost of investments between shareholders and ratepayers even though those investments resulted in generating no nuclear electricity.[37] Similarly, regulators would protect a utility's "stranded costs" so that prudently incurred investments in assets that were no longer useful or needed would result in some compensation to the utility.[38] In the name of the regulatory compact, regulators generally allowed 100 percent recovery on those "prudent" investments.[39]

The challenges facing the industry today are distinguishable and, more importantly, unprecedented,[40] thus raising questions about cost recovery and the wisdom of continuing reliance on the COS model. Instead, in the face of challenges that come with the clean power transition, IOUs should be encouraged to reconfigure their business operations, as discussed next.

A CHANGING INDUSTRY

Those previous challenges affected both the industrial structure of the electricity sector and its regulation. Prior to 1978, IOUs generated about 70 percent of US electricity.[41] Today, IOUs continue to generate 42 percent of the country's electricity with another 42 percent generated by private non-IOU firms. The remainder is provided by various local and federal power sources.[42]

A drop from 70 percent of IOU market share to 42 percent is less dramatic than it may appear because private electricity firms continue to dominate the sector.

In response to changing regulations, an increasing number of various non-IOU electricity actors entered the electricity market under several names including independent power producers, merchant generators, qualifying facilities, and exempt wholesale generators among others. The key characteristic of these new actors (and many restructured IOUs) is the separation of generation and transmission either through a functional unbundling or actual corporate divestiture of those business units. The single driving force behind the separation of generation and transmission was the desire by regulators and policymakers to open the market to cheaper electricity and to increase competition by opening access to the transmission system of which 66 percent is owned by private IOUs, thus making electricity restructuring as difficult as it has been.[43]

Although regulators are responding to industry changes, that response is far from uniform. At the federal level, FERC continues to regulate wholesale interstate electricity sales and does so by regulating individual utilities and by regulating regional transmission organizations, which are tasked with the responsibility of maintaining a reliable and balanced power supply and creating competitively priced transmission and capacity markets. At the state level, some states continue to regulate IOUs as they traditionally have (these are known as "regulated states") while other states have encouraged the separation of generation and transmission (these states are known as "deregulated states").

In the new electricity world, traditional utilities must attend to climate change, greenhouse gas emissions, and clean energy policies. They must also satisfy renewable resources and energy efficiency goals.[44] Additionally as new generation and transmission technologies take hold, the role of central power diminishes. Looking down the road, the expansion of electric vehicles and electricity storage will disrupt the old system[45] even to the point at which customers live completely off of the grid.[46] To better understand the direction of that transformation, it is necessary first to understand key drivers that necessitate these changes.

Increased Competition. IOUs find themselves in a double bind regarding increased competition. Over the last three or more decades, IOUs have witnessed the proliferation of nonutility electricity providers. In large part, increased competition has been the result of high priced traditional IOU electricity and the availability of a less expensive resource. In another part, increased competition has been the result of regulations that have attempted to open the market to not only nonutility electricity but also efficiency and conservation. Consequently, incumbent IOUs must engage new competition particularly from nonutility generation and from distributed energy services.[47]

Regulations promoting renewable resources and energy efficiency further complicate the plight of IOUs. To the extent that greenhouse gas emission reduction is a regulatory goal, as it is with the Clean Power Plan (CPP), IOUs are faced with abandoning cheap coal for higher cost renewables or nuclear power. Currently, IOUs are switching from coal to natural gas to generate electricity because of low natural gas prices. However, as discussed earlier, natural gas presents its own emission problems. And, to the extent that regulation seeks to promote efficiency through such devices as net metering, demand response, and other efficiency and conservation measures, IOU electricity sales will decline. Consequently, IOUs face competition from third-party electricity providers, from firms that sell efficiency products, and from regulations intended to reduce demand. All of these forces mean that IOUs must cope with a radically changing energy sector. More particularly, IOUs must invest either in new forms of generation and energy efficiency or in energy innovations or in new business models. IOUs must consider all of these options while facing their service obligations for reliable and affordable energy.

Aging Grid. Significant investment is needed in the electricity infrastructure to upgrade the current grid and to promote interconnections with renewable resources as well as make the grid safer, smarter, and more resilient.[48] Even though the electric grid is in dire need of upgrades and improvements, IOUs have been reluctant to invest in their own transmission systems for two reasons – lack of clear governance authority over transmission and uncertain cost recovery. Regulatory authority over transmission is awkwardly split between federal and state regulators and the extent of federal regulation is open to question, thus contributing to a lack of governance clarity.[49] And, while the federal government has promulgated rules for cost recovery for transmission investments,[50] those rules have not satisfied judicial review and are being reconsidered by FERC.[51] Consequently, with uncertainty over governance and financial returns, IOU investment lags and will continue to do so until federal and state regulatory authorities are able to assure IOUs that their investments in grid and innovation can be recovered.[52]

Declining Demand. Demand for electricity has flattened.[53] For most of last century, electric utilities enjoyed a growing market and, therefore, regularly enjoyed increased sales. Today, demand for electricity has slowed each decade from the post–World War II "golden age" until now.[54] In the decade of 1949–1959, electric utilities enjoyed an annual growth of 9.8 percent. That growth has declined to an annual rate of 0.7 percent in the first decade of the twenty-first century. In fact, electricity demand has declined every year except two since 1996.[55] Further, for the last two years demand has fallen, and in 2012, demand was down by 1.7 percent compared with 2011.[56]

According to recent Energy Information Administration estimates, demand is scheduled to decline for the third year in a row and it is at the lowest level since 2001.[57] Nevertheless, the Department of Energy projects that for the next three decades, from 2011 to 2040, overall demand will increase by 28 percent.[58] Even with such modest growth in overall demand, individual consumers are, in fact, consuming less electricity.[59] More problematic for traditional IOUs is that projected demand for central power station electricity is predicted to fall dramatically "due to a combination of energy efficiency and competition from new technologies, which collectively could impact their addressable markets by 50% over the next two decades."[60]

Why has the demand for electricity changed so noticeably?

According to FERC, electricity demand declined due to reduced retail sales and a lack of demand growth in the commercial and industrial sectors as a result of a soft economy.[61] A slow economy due to the Great Recession, though, is only one reason among many. Other reasons include increased energy intensity, the transition from a manufacturing and heavy industry economy to an information economy, and growing consumer awareness of electricity prices. Consumers, for example, are aware of increased energy efficiency in appliances[62] and buildings, smarter meters and temperature controls, more choices about using cheaper off-peak energy, and the growth of DG/DER so that consumers can obtain power on-site.[63] These technological and market changes, however, did not come about on their own. They were aided by state and federal regulations that were intentionally designed to increase competition and change the fuel mix in the electricity sector largely because cleaner, cheaper power was available than that generated by IOUs. Further, these regulatory demands clearly point to a clean energy future rather than to a continued expansion of coal-fired, or even natural gas–generated or nuclear-generated electricity.

Clean Power Plan. Finally, the CPP put pressure on utilities to change their generation mix and reconfigure their business models in the face of increased competition and reduced market share as discussed in Chapter 1. Unsurprisingly, IOUs are not embracing the CPP.[64] The most crucial issue for utilities, then, is to design a new business model that will allow them to function in this new environment.

The electricity market is changing.[65] It is more competitive today than it has been historically, and consequently, traditionally structured IOUs face financial challenges as new technologies with decreasing costs affect settled ways of doing business.[66] The century-old electricity industry is now confronting new technologies, new markets, and new regulations[67] as the country makes a "revolutionary" transition to a clean energy economy[68] and IOUs must respond.[69] They can insist on BAU and on maintaining COS ratemaking as central to the regulatory compact; or, they can change.[70] In either case, the successful IOU, the utility of the future, will be measured against a business model that is organized in such a way as to create, deliver, and capture value to the benefit of producers as well as of consumers.[71]

THE UTILITY OF THE FUTURE

A significant literature regarding the future of the electric utility is emerging. The Massachusetts Institute of Technology (MIT), as part of its multidisciplinary Energy Initiative that has published studies on the future of nuclear power, the electric grid, and coal, is now engaged in an international, comprehensive, and multiyear *Utility of the Future Study*.[72] The MIT study will "address the technology, policy, and business models shaping the evolution of the delivery of electric services."[73] While it is clear that IOUs will no longer dominate the electric sector, most observers take the position that they will continue to be central actors and that their ability to adapt to the new environment will be central to the success of the clean energy transition.

This section will concentrate on three likely business models that IOUs may likely adopt and that will be designed to create producer and consumer value.[74] Preliminarily, however, three observations must be made. First, not only must IOUs invest in technological innovation, they must also invest in business innovation. Second, and complementarily, because IOUs will continue to be regulated for the foreseeable future, the transition will not occur without associated regulations to support it.[75] There are two reasons for regulatory support. In the first instance, regulations are necessary to protect past utility investments as a matter of the regulatory compact. Additionally, regulations can help stimulate the transition through financial incentives and other legal supports. Finally, there will be no utility of the future if by "utility" we continue to refer to traditional IOUs. Instead, the electricity future will have a wider range of providers and consumers will have more purchase options than they have had in the past. The future of the electric industry is not necessarily the *utility* of the future; instead it is a future clean power system.

With industry restructuring over the last decades, utility executives acknowledge that the expansion of vertically integrated IOUs is unlikely.[76]

Nevertheless, even though IOUs will no longer dominate, a fully competitive electric industry at the wholesale and retail levels will not develop in the near-term if for no other reason than the fact that the grid is a necessary component to an electricity future, and that grid, for the most part, was constructed by and is owned by incumbent IOUs. Consequently, as the three models discussed next indicate, although the future will be a mixed future of regulation and more competition, forward-thinking IOUs should be able to compete in these new and emerging markets.

The utility of the future must conform its business practices to three current and expanding trends. First, on the supply side, the cost of producing energy from renewable resources, most particularly wind and solar, continues to decline as cost parity is in sight. Another supply-side feature is that the scale of electric power production is shrinking as DG and DER technologies proliferate.[77] These distributed systems pose a direct threat to traditionally structured IOUs. Second, on the demand side, while projected future demands are relatively flat, consumers are using electricity in different ways including charging vehicles, increasing storage, self-generation, and responding to demand response regulations. The third trend involves information and communication technologies (ICT) that radically reconfigure the traditional delivery of electricity.[78] ICT systems of the future will have two-way information flows, which, in turn, improve price signals in real time and can improve grid security and reliability.[79] Each of these trends is transformative for traditional IOUs and each of these trends has the potential for improving customer control as well as increasing industry competition.

One way of conceptualizing the new utility model is that a utility's primary business will be to focus on distribution and customer service rather than maintain a singular focus on generation and the electricity sales. The new utility's primary business will be to serve as a grid operator in an environment of increased wholesale and retail competition.[80] Innovative utilities will become more sensitive to customer needs and will be rewarded for it.[81] Demand studies show, for example, that consumers are responding to price information and that they are reducing consumption at peak times. In addition, behind-the-meter technologies such as home displays, programmable thermostats, and other appliances together with social networking create a new environment as more information about energy use and price is available for providers and consumers. Providers can use that information to develop better business plans and consumers can use that information to better understand how to use energy more efficiently.[82]

What should be most clear from this brief description of industry trends is that the utility of the future will not involve unilateral transactions in which electricity providers exist only to sell electricity to consumers who, in turn, pay for that electricity. Rather, the future industry will involve a variety of two-way transactions in which traditional providers will also purchase energy services from traditional consumers. Customers will pay for the electricity that they consume and they will also sell energy and services, such as storage, to those same providers. Thus, "the challenge for incumbent utilities is to find innovative ways to retain the value proposition of their assets while capturing the opportunities presented by [distributed energy systems] and their component technologies."[83]

Another way to frame the issue regarding the utility of the future is to acknowledge that IOUs cannot depend upon regulators to satisfy all of their revenue requirements. Instead, the utility of the future is better understood as an electricity system comprising multiple actors within multiple regulated and nonregulated markets. Tomorrow's electric industry will comprise a wider variety of providers at different scales, generating electricity from different resources and in more competitive environments. Moreover, this new array of providers, by competitive necessity and with a desire for market share, will be more responsive to consumer interests in energy services as well as their demand for power. Additionally, the system of the future is, and will continue to be, driven by technological changes, business value opportunities, and, most importantly, supporting regulatory initiatives as explained in more depth in the next chapter.

PLANNING FOR THE FUTURE

IOUs do, indeed, face unseen challenges that must be met if they are to stay viable and be active participants in the clean power transition, and there are steps that they can take to meet those challenges. First, they must accept certain planning assumptions both about the future of the industry and about a firm's ability to participate in that future, which will lead to the adoption of appropriate business models.

Firms in the electric industry, indeed firms in most industries, are driven by a combination of factors including: technology, the economic environment (particularly the degree of competition), and the applicable regulatory scheme as well as their existing business practices.[84] These drivers must be taken into account as a firm plans for the future. For IOUs, planning entails a range of assumptions about rate structures, investment opportunities, environmental and efficiency goals, and consumer needs.[85] Most importantly, an IOU must deeply consider what its core business actually is. Simply, an IOU's future business will differ markedly from the business it has engaged in the past.

The utility of the future will not depend upon continuous large-scale generation investments and volumetric sales to provide its revenue stream.[86] Instead, diverse energy resources, energy efficiency, demand response, DG/DER, environmental sensitivity, and new rate schemes will be necessary components for the future utility.

The first driver of the future utility involves the technological innovations that are available and that must be managed.[87] Technologies such as the smart grid, microgrids, smart meters and two-way information energy flows, third-party and nonutility energy providers, improved storage, and electric vehicles are currently available as new and emerging technologies continue to develop. Notice, most importantly, that some of these technologies, most notably third-party and nonutility energy providers, pose a clear threat to the market share currently enjoyed by many IOUs. To the extent that customers can purchase nonutility power, the IOUs will lose sales. The existence of such alternative providers directly implicates the second driver – competition.

Greater competition in the electric industry is as much a consequence of changing regulatory requirements and ideas as it is about the development of new technologies. Regulation helped stimulate technological change as well as change in the competitive landscape. New technologies together with a climate of competition and associated regulations now drive IOUs to reconsider how they do business in a way that is responsive to all of those drivers.

The IOU, as a publicly regulated entity, serves two masters. As a privately owned entity, it is obligated to provide value to its shareholders. As a regulated entity, however, it is also obligated to serve the public in various ways. Historically, the sole role of the IOU was to provide reliable and affordable electricity to its consumers.[88] Today, however, the public service obligations have expanded. In addition to reliable and affordable electricity, IOUs must satisfy environmental requirements as well as anticipate future needs and new technologies to satisfy those obligations.[89]

Electric utilities must satisfy both public and private obligations, and in this new economic environment, a firm must consider not only increasing profits but also increasing consumer, as well as investor, value. An IOU's shareholder value will increase only to the extent that a utility's business model can satisfy the private and public obligations imposed upon it. Such a model will be one that "aligns utilities' financial interests in such a way that they can promote increased use of more socially desirable energy resources."[90]

The utility of the future, for example, must consider competing pathways through either greater consolidation or greater diversification.[91] On the one hand, utilities can continue to divest generation or transmission or distribution or they can create independent business entities for each of those functions.

On the other hand, a utility of the future can consider diversification. Part of its business will continue to be to provide regulated electricity services while another part of its business will provide unregulated energy services including behind-the-meter technologies that expand consumer control over usage and demand. Pursuant to this path, a utility of the future will expand its business enterprises, acquire competitors such as solar providers, use their special expertise in managing the electric system, and engage in constructing and managing large-scale and complex energy projects such as utilities-scale solar and wind and microgrids.[92] An IOU, for example, may consider providing electricity and other energy services to large residential developments, military bases, gated communities, or other discrete and segmented consumer groups. In this way, a utility stays in the electricity business and diversifies into energy services more generally.[93]

Regardless of either path, a utility must focus on system optimization in which the provision of electricity and other energy services corresponds to the more particular needs of various customer groups with the goal of maximizing efficiency and managing supply and demand.[94] Central to satisfying both supply and demand is adopting ICT capabilities that can gather information about customer usage in real time and better understand and manage the availability of power and efficiency mechanisms from diverse providers for the purpose of managing and balancing load. Additionally, data analytics can be used to provide information about investments in existing plants and technologies, about new business opportunities, and about ways to provide cybersecurity and privacy protections.[95]

Utilities must also be involved in customer engagement in new information-sensitive ways. In the past, demand was the only data point utilities needed. Today, utilities must understand customers' desires for savings, increased use of smarter appliances and other technologies, expansion of self-generation, and, not least, the growing market for electric vehicles.[96] Through all of these applications, customers ask more from utilities than only buying electricity.[97]

Greater consumer awareness directly implicates the role that energy efficiency will play in the future. Energy efficiency also has the benefit of being more sensitive to environmental regulations. "Utilities can help their customers use energy more efficiently as a way to moderate utility risks and customer bills while also providing valued customer services and protecting the environment."[98] The hard reality for IOUs is the acknowledgment that expanded generation and depending on revenue solely from volumetric sales cannot continue. Instead, utilities must incorporate efficiency as part of the energy services that they offer to consumers, perhaps even to the point of creating, as has Vermont, an entity that sells energy efficiency.[99]

Energy efficiency is not costless even though it is cheaper than buying electricity. Energy-saving devices and appliances must be purchased. In some instances, utilities can be involved in financing those purchases and recover those investments through rates that are below the marginal cost of electricity. In turn, those savings can enable a utility to invest in its core businesses without imposing rate shock on consumers.[100] Utilities can continue to invest capital as they historically have in generation and transmission as needed and they can begin to invest in consumer facilities and services.[101]

Utilities are confronting an economic future that represents multiple options as well as challenges. It becomes necessary, therefore, for a utility to engage in long-term planning as an essential element of its business. In some instances, the need for planning comes as a part of the regulatory requirement for integrated resource planning. In other instances, planning is a necessary component to participate in regional transmission initiatives. Such planning will involve preservation or extension of core capabilities, identification of new business opportunities, and the exploration of various partnerships, joint ventures, and acquisitions.[102]

THREE BUSINESS MODELS

IOUs enter this new environment with substantial assets including managerial expertise and experience. Since the beginning, IOUs have been the premier builders and operators of the entire electric system. Through various regulatory environments, they have adapted their services and their ability to balance load and deliver reliable and affordable electricity. In that process, they have developed a reputation for trusted reliability, solid financial reputations with which to attract capital, and they have been able to communicate with millions of consumers. In short, as reported by the MIT Utility of the Future project, a viable power system must provide primary services defined as energy, operating reserves, black-start capability, and firm capacity together with network connections, voltage controls, and other minimum requirements to manage the growing multiplicity of the increasing diversity of energy sources including distributed resources and demand response.[103]

Today, though, utilities of the future must pay increasing attention to (1) the services they provide, (2) their customer targets, and (3) their revenue streams particularly from distributed energy resources as well as providing firm capacity, operating reserves, and energy.[104] Additionally, although their ICT systems have traditionally been limited to billing, those communication systems are changing. IOUs can accumulate information on demand and customer usage as they reconfigure their business operations.[105] In other words, the clever IOU will learn how to manage big data to increase value for their shareholder as well as increase consumer value. With these assumptions and opportunities in mind, the utility of the future must make a decision about its optimal business model. Although there is no single conception, there are three prevalent models for the utility of the future – a wires-only system operator, a smart integrator, or an energy services operator.

Wires Only. The traditional IOU developed expertise building generation plants as well as transmission and distribution systems. The traditional IOU also developed expertise in managing that system and maintaining grid reliability either on its own or through cooperative ventures such as voluntary power pools. It is an easy move for an IOU, particularly in deregulated jurisdictions, to separate generation from either transmission or distribution and then run the transportation segments. To the extent that the traditional IOU divests generation assets, its ability to manage transmission and/or distribution makes it a "wires-only" company.

A utility of the future can consider building and improving transmission as a profit center. The smart grid will incorporate new two-way information technologies that will require greater expertise to operate. Further, as variable resources play a larger role in power generation, new transmission lines will be needed to connect wind and solar installations to the existing grid. Additionally, a wires-only utility will serve a backup role for a variety of distributed energy resources.[106]

There can be two types of wires-only companies – a high-voltage transmission system operator (TSO) and a lower-voltage distribution company or distribution system operator (DSO). Today, over half of the country's electric consumers are served by regional organizations. RTO/ISOs manage capacity markets to ensure that enough electricity is available to serve demand. RTO/ISOs own no assets. Transmission lines continue to be owned by private utilities that agree to the terms for RTO/ISO participation as established by each regional organization together with FERC. RTO/ISOs conduct auctions for the purchase of energy capacity that is then placed on the grid and managed by that entity. Within this system, the TSO can be an active participant and can continue to provide transmission lines and services as well as be responsible for load-balancing, frequency modulation, dispatch, and reliability.

To keep the system in balance and operating reliably, there must be a clean interface between the TSO and the DSO. The TSO will remain largely responsible for aggregating enough electric capacity to be sold to all customers and must maintain the high-voltage portion of the grid. The DSO will obtain power from the regional TSO, as well as other power providers, and will be responsible for satisfying customer demand and maintaining the reliability of the local grid.[107] Long-term planning between these entities is crucial for the purpose of maintaining supplies, grid reliability, and security, and, increasingly, meeting environmental obligations.[108] The DSO, in contrast with the TSO, directly connects to end users. The main task of the DSO is to "ensure that the distribution system can securely, efficiently, and economically distribute electricity to end-users."[109] The DSO is responsible for network infrastructure and will recoup its investments through sales of electricity and other services. Additionally, and more significantly, the DSO enters into contracts with power providers to sell their electricity. Given the growing array and variety of providers, a DSO can be the linchpin for gathering a growing portfolio of distributed and renewable energy and for coordinating electricity sales through TSOs. Under this model, the DSO becomes the retail-level market operator using dynamic pricing signals to serve customers as well as invite marketers and other providers to participate at that level. The DSO, because of its necessary connection with the TSO, will also use more sophisticated ICT to understand real-time pricing and customer usage, keeping an eye on innovations that can improve the system for greater efficiency and reliability.[110] The DSO, then, serves as a grid-connected firm that responds to the demand for electricity and provides energy storage and generation through the use of advanced metering controls and information technologies at the local level.[111]

The DSO market becomes a decentralized electricity ecosystem that is more consumer responsive, is more open to innovation, and provides opportunities for a greater variety of actors than traditional IOUs. The DSO can also serve as an aggregator for DER, thus increasing system efficiencies.[112] The DSO can also act as an integrator of distributed energy resources including storage and connection to electric vehicles. To the extent that the DSO directly connects distributed resources, it becomes a node for the purchase and sale of electricity and its storage. Customer-owned power such as solar photovoltaic can result in sales to the DSO through either net metering or feed-in tariff rules. Similarly, electric vehicles or other storage systems can contribute to grid stability and, therefore, provide value to the DSO as well as to system users more generally.[113] Because the DSO is closer to customers, it can use its ICT architecture to measure and verify transactions so that they correspond as closely as possible to actual services delivered. This market data, in turn, can be used to inform investors about value propositions in this sector.

The DSO can take on different corporate forms. It could work as an independent nonprofit entity that operates and manages the distribution portion of the grid. Or, a DSO can be a legacy utility that simply adopts a different structure to serve the retail market only. The DSO can also be the default electricity provider to those customers who will become significant self-generators. Or, the DSO can take on a for-profit configuration that offers a range of energy services and sales in competitive markets. The DSO, for example, can engage in home energy management services or even financing and installing distributed generation[114] and storage.[115] At the local level, it will remain "responsible for efficient construction, operation, and maintenance of the safe, reliable, and affordable electric distribution network within their service territory."[116] The DSO, then, can be a hybrid organization in which portions of its business are regulated while others are competitive. Given this wide range of responsibilities, the DSO must remain flexible and open to new energy sources and services in fulfillment of its obligation to provide reliable and affordable electricity.

Smart Integrator. The wires-only TSO or DSO closely represents one segment of the traditional electric utility – transportation. This new energy actor draws on its experience managing complex systems and operating in a regulatory environment. The wires-only company differs from an IOU in that it is neither vertically nor fully integrated, must draw on a variety of electricity providers, will offer a wider variety of services, and must manage the integration of variable and efficiency resources. Moving away from the TSO or DSO, another model of the utility of the future will be more diverse in its products and services while also operating in regulated as well as more competitive marketplaces.

One such new actor is known as a "smart integrator." The hallmarks of such a firm are that its revenue will be decoupled from electricity sales and it will be expected to fulfill energy efficiency and other environmental mandates.[117] This firm will operate the local power grid through its mastery of ICT systems necessary to deliver electricity although the integrator will not generate its own power for sale. Instead, the smart integrator will own and maintain the assets necessary for transmission and distribution, improving those services as it collects information about consumer demand and other needs.[118] The primary business rationale for the smart integrator is to bring innovative technologies to the energy system in order to satisfy the multiple goals involved with a clean power future. Its core competency will be its effective use of ICT specifically designed for two-way communications. In this regard, it must operate an open architecture that is available to a variety of providers and consumers alike in order to optimize the availability of information to enrich consumer and producer choice.

The smart integrator has also been described as a firm that creates partnerships between utilities and innovative energy firms for the purpose of bringing new technologies and services online through new business practices and processes. While traditional utilities would continue to either generate or transport electricity or both, the smart integrator will facilitate those transactions. As regulators adopt interoperability standards among providers and transportation system operators, the smart integrator can facilitate the adoption of the new regulatory regime and can rationalize interconnections between new technologies and the existing grid as well as integrate new generation into the system.[119] The smart integrator can also take on the role of backup power provider or provider of last resort by contracting with producers. Consumers will look to the smart integrator not only for new forms of energy and services but also for the reliability and security of electric service itself. Concomitantly, the smart integrator will be the go-to source of power in case of emergencies.[120]

The key attribute of the smart integrator is their knowledge of and ability to adopt new and innovative energy technologies for developing markets. The integrator can do so by running pilot demonstration projects specifically for the purpose of traversing the innovation "valleys of death" as discussed in the previous chapter. Also as noted, innovations by private entrepreneurs are often stymied by an inability to move from proof of concept to the marketplace. To successfully navigate that valley, private initiatives often require government support. Smart integrators can serve as project managers for demonstration projects and can receive the necessary public support through the rate-making process. To the extent that such pilot projects are successful, financial risk is reduced for the firms involved and consumers should benefit from advances made in the energy sector.[121]

Under the model of the smart integrator, the focus on innovation translates into an increase of consumer choice. Utility customers will then have a vendor for rooftop solar, energy saving and efficient appliances, financing, energy audits, and net-zero energy homes among other products and services. The smart integrator can also operate microgrids and serve more localized communities.[122] In these ways, the smart integrator provides electricity to satisfy the demands of customers as it customizes access to energy based on consumers' various needs.[123]

The integrator's mastery of ICT can be used to send accurate price signals directly to consumers' programmable thermostats, central air-conditioners, electric vehicles, and other appliances in real time. Simultaneously, the smart integrator can help consumers plug in their cars and solar panels directly into the grid.[124]

The smart integrator is a gateway for energy access for providers as well as consumers. The smart integrator will monitor the needs for grid expansion and will play a role in community energy planning. In terms of grid expansion, the integrator plays a bottom-up role connecting providers and consumers to the grid as distinguished from the traditional top-down role played by IOUs that constructed, owned, and operated the grid.[125] The smart integrator will also manage the connection of variable resources to the grid. The smart integrator model works well with existing state plans, such as those in most of New England, that allow for retail choice by consumers.[126]

Further, because of the central role that ICT plays in the smart integrator framework, the integrator will have a vested interest in developing the smart grid to capture efficiencies made available through big data. The idea of customized energy choices for consumers and the collection of information necessary to accommodate a variety of power providers may appear daunting, but it is not dissimilar to the types of two-way information flows that consumers experience daily on the Internet. Accordingly, energy ICT systems must serve customers as if they were everyday commercial transactions[127] and they must be adapted by the firms that provide the content and services that consumers purchase. Such a reconfigured energy system that emphasizes a multiplicity of providers and greater consumer responsiveness should create new value propositions as "customers [play] a larger role in producing and managing their energy may also help to provide electricity services to the grid to enable better economic optimization of resource use across the entire system."[128]

Electric Services Operator. The electric services operator (ESO) most closely resembles the traditional IOU. The ESO will preserve and extend core capabilities of generating and delivering electricity, identify new technologies, and explore a variety of new business opportunities to succeed in the new market.[129] The ESO retains aspects of vertical integration and its business is to provide electricity within a large service territory. The principal responsibility of the ESO will be to provide low-cost, reliable energy services to its customers.[130] While the ESO may own generation and other assets, it will also be required to open access and purchase or transmit power from a variety of providers.[131]

The regulation and operation of an ESO will differ from that of the IOU. The ESO will offer new services and products that are properly priced and aligned with regulatory incentives, will incorporate DG and DER resources, and will invest in a wide variety of new technologies and business opportunities.[132] Some ESOs will maintain their vertically integrated role in the power system but regulation will shift from rewarding increased sales to rewarding increased performance. In this way, the ESO maintains its monopoly and will be motivated to incorporate new technologies, some of which reduce sales through efficiency gains.[133]

This model will be recognizable to state regulators and, therefore, should be attractive to them. Most particularly, regulators can continue to apply COS ratemaking for the regulated portions of the ESO's business. In other words, although the ESO "still has an incentive to build its rate base through new capital projects, the nature of investments [will shift] significantly from bulk power production and delivery to investments that promote smart and resilient grids, centralized management of DERs and price-responsive consumers."[134]

The ESO must also take on the responsibility for adopting new technologies, especially in information and communications, which are particularly important for the development of the smart grid. In this scenario, existing utilities "might be encouraged to expand their business scope and scale by buying up innovator firms, acquiring their competitors, and making the most out of their special competence in managing large-scale, complex engineering and construction projects."[135]

While the basic structure of the ESO will be familiar to traditional IOUs, they will adopt different roles and, depending upon the regulatory scheme, will serve different customer segments in different ways. The ESO, for example, can provide more localized[136] energy products and services such as serving college campuses, military bases, residential developments, and large commercial facilities that already have access to power.[137] The ESO would provide energy services together with backup power. The ESO will have a greater diversity of products and services that can be offered and sold on bundled or unbundled bases not unlike consumer arrangements for their cellphones and TV/Internet subscriptions.[138] The ESO, for example, could charge for the electricity consumed as well as impose a fixed charge for network usage and backup power. At the same time, the ESO will set a price for electricity purchases from customers while giving credit for the value added by customers for grid stability and other savings.[139]

The ESO will also have elements of the smart integrator insofar as it will be managing a more complex grid involving more actors. Consequently, it will be required to manage big data and engage in more sophisticated mid- and long-term planning. Further, the ESO will be tasked to meet other social policies including environmental and efficiency regulations that will reduce their sales revenues. Thus, an ESO and its regulators must develop a rate scheme that allows the new utility to move in both directions, that is sell electricity and "sell" efficiency and conservation.

The ESO concept "puts electric utilities into two diametrically opposed businesses, one selling their traditional product and one helping customers buy less of it. It combines the old product and service model with selling investments and services inside customer premises."[140] To do this successfully, the ESO must learn about the customer's side of the meter and should encounter increased competition along the way.[141] Consequently the ESO must meet new customer needs, understand real-time customer end-use data, work with customer-side energy storage and generation, and facilitate behind-the-meter appliances, applications, and controls.[142] Further, the ESO and its regulators must also develop policies for integrating into the ESO system other energy providers including energy provided by ESO customers and must adopt incentives and rewards for expanding the availability and capacity for energy storage.[143]

The key to the success of this model, as is true of the other models as well, is for utility managers to identify new profit centers. Clearly, electricity sales will continue to bring in revenue. Can the smart ESO, however, develop energy-efficient products that also earn returns?[144] The ESOs will sell electricity and they will also operate the smart distribution platform and will provide value-added services to consumers.[145] Additionally, ESOs will advance the use of DG/DER and expand the use of variable energy resources by building utility-scale solar and wind projects, owning their own distributed generation business units, and/or partnering with third-party vendors.[146] In short, an ESO will make money through cost-competitive tariffs, reliable grid services, and financially attractive pricing for energy, as well as for the provision of demand response and other services for customers.[147]

The ESO must be provided with incentives to innovate and diversify.[148] Another way to put the matter is that ESOs must be able to monetize their services and realize profits from them.[149] It seems likely that as competition increases, as innovative energy technologies gain markets, and as the utility of the future expands its capacity to manage more customer and market information, then, as has occurred in telecommunications, services and products can be priced and profits can be taken. These initiatives, as the next chapter discusses in more detail, will depend upon the regulatory regime that rewards the ESO, does not impose excessive costs on consumers, and avoids inequitable allocations of costs among customer classes, some of whom generate their own power while others do not.[150] The ESO will operate an energy "platform" best defined as a "system that supports value-based interactions among multiple parties and a set of rules – including protocols, rights, and pricing terms – that standardizes and facilitates transactions among multiple parties."[151] This platform can increase innovation and competition in the electric sector by reducing transaction costs, increasing transparency relative to pricing the value of services of various assets, and developing "integrated solutions" in this evolving sector.

CONCLUSION

What model is any particular IOU likely to adopt? Will it maintain its traditional IOU form or adopt any of the three models discussed earlier or some hybrid thereof? The most likely answer is all of the above. Different regions of the country have different energy needs. Each state has a different regulatory regime. And, each utility has specific core competencies, business acumen, and industry foresight, which indicates that a multiplicity of models is most likely. What can be said with certainty is that BAU across the industry is unlikely to be a sound strategy as new business practices are developing and will continue to do so.

One need only look at the technological advances in telephony and computers to realize that the world has changed in ways that will not return. Landlines and desktop computers have largely become relics of the past. Electricity providers are proliferating, energy-efficient appliances and buildings are reducing per capita energy costs, and competition and consumer options are increasing. IOUs, simply, are in a new market. Indeed, electric utilities can learn from the telecommunications playbook and invest in change rather than continue to resist it.[152] Utilities must offer a wider array of energy products and services, ranging from renewable energy and energy efficiency to performing energy audits for its customers and broadening the array of power providers.[153]

As examples, NRG Energy[154] and NextEra Energy[155] are developing utility-scale solar and other renewable projects; firms like Direct Energy[156] and Veridian[157] have partnered with Solar City to offer solar installations to their customers; and Duke Energy and PSE&G have been investing in residential solar, microgrids, and energy storage in smart grid technologies.[158] Similarly, rooftop solar offers a low-carbon alternative to baseload power, and it is being offered by such companies such as Solar City that finance, install, and maintain the systems at a lower cost to the owner than traditional utility service under long-term power purchase agreements.[159]

Opportunities abound for forward-thinking utilities such as San Diego Gas and Electric, which has proposed a strategy to: (1) generate and sell electricity to serve customers' real-time needs, (2) provide distribution services, and (3) help customers manage electricity use through programs that promote efficiency, smart appliances and meters, electric vehicle charging, and the like. Through this program, San Diego Gas and Electric can transform itself into becoming a successful ESO.

The utility of the future must start by recognizing that its primary business is not merely selling a commodity; it is providing and managing an infrastructure and providing other services. "The entrepreneurs who put that competitive solar power on your roof with no money down can provide a portfolio of other equally unregulated products, like efficiency, demand response, storage, and so on, that could ultimately add up to a virtual utility providing the same services that utilities now provide – quite possibly with lower-cost and greater reliability and resilience."[160]

Another, and similar, way of conceptualizing the utility of the future is to see it as a network entity that operates and maintains the grid, creates markets and manages transactions, and connects buyers and sellers within the network.[161] Of central importance to this new utility will be its ability to manage demand and incorporate DG/DER rather than continue to make capital investments as a primary business strategy.[162]

Such new business approaches are responsive to any number of issues. If large capital investments are too financially risky, then they can be scaled down. Investments in efficiency and in DER are less costly and less risky than building a new plant or making significant additions to transportation. Similarly, if the concern with upgrading and modernizing the grid is cybersecurity, then reducing the scale of generation and multiplying power sites rather than concentrating them will reduce those risks. Also, if natural disasters threaten the grid,[163] then, DER, microgrids,[164] and other small-scale options are valuable alternatives.

As new technologies and new strategies develop, the utility of the future must integrate them into its portfolio and into its pricing schemes. Strategic investments as well as strategic partnerships will be necessary components of a utility's new business model. Investments in distributed generation such as fuel cells[165] or rooftop solar, as examples, can in some instances produce greater efficiency and in both instances reduce carbon emissions. Companies such as Bloom Energy[166] and Fuel Cell Energy[167] are actively in the market of constructing fuel cells on-site as well as developing them for traditional IOUs and these are examples of partnership opportunities.[168]

The utility of the future will see itself not as a stand-alone actor in the market but as part of a network that provides a "platform for the economic and operational integration of distributed resources."[169] The new utility will use more transparent costs, develop new technical standards such as those needed for interconnection, and adopt new economic standards such as those used in making value determinations and pricing goods and services generally.[170] The new utility will be a value creator by serving as a distributed system operator,[171] an integrated resource planner,[172] an energy services provider, and an energy financier for consumer products.[173]

The new utility will proactively respond to a new business environment. Utilities, however, cannot and will not act on their own. They must be assisted by regulators who will adopt new rules for their relationship with utilities that they regulate. Those new rules will be sensitive to the market, sensitive to the demands of customers, and sensitive to the needs of utilities. The sensitivities are not only responsive to changing market conditions; they are also responsive to a fundamental change in energy and electricity policy. Traditional fossil fuel policy is no longer viable. The future demands a clean power economy and innovative IOUs can play a transformative role. The clean power future should encourage competition, consumer choice, and technological innovation as well as economic growth. Although the challenges are real, the direction of the future should be clear. Regulators and IOUs alike must play leadership roles in building out the clean power world.

6

Regulatory Innovation

In the last chapter, new business models for the utility of the future were discussed and none will be successful unless it is supported by a complementary and innovative regulatory regime. For virtually all of its history, the electric industry has been governed by a series of economic regulations, the chief purpose of which was to monitor the market power that could be exercised by utilities that exhibited natural monopoly characteristics. Today, as the industry becomes more competitive, the need for heavy-handed price controls lessens; however, it does not disappear entirely – rates must be set that balance the interests of producers and consumers in today's fluid energy environment.

Regulators have an array of tools that can be deployed to shape the new industry. In Chapter 5, cost-of-service (COS) regulation was shown to be flexible enough to help the industry weather a series of economic challenges. COS ratemaking may still be used in the future but on a more limited basis because it is unsuited for the developing electricity markets. COS ratemaking makes it difficult for investor-owned utilities (IOUs) to respond to distributed energy resources (DER); provides weak incentives for innovation, and provides regulatory risks to the extent that regulators either highly scrutinize or are unwilling to compensate IOUs for investments in capital expansion and innovation.[1] Consequently, COS will not be the only rate-making method employed. Instead, regulators will draw upon performance-based rates, decoupling, connection tariffs, surcharges, add-ons, various forms of marginal cost pricing, and other tools to maintain the availability, affordability, and reliability of electricity. The more precise issue is whether or not existing tools are adequate or whether regulators must more comprehensively redesign the scheme of electricity regulation that has existed for the last century.

The need for innovation affects regulators as much as it does utilities and will be required to address changes in the industry, develop energy plans, and incorporate economic and environmental goals for a viable clean power future. Instead of business as usual (BAU), public utility commissions (PUCs) must now engage in more extended planning and forward thinking. And, instead of BAU, utilities must now more proactively pursue new business designs by assisting PUCs as they develop their new regulatory regimes. This chapter will discuss the reasons and assumptions upon which traditional regulation was based. This chapter will argue that the changes now being experienced by the electric industry, most notably reduced demand, increased competition, and clean power requirements, disrupt the traditional model and require notably different regulatory approaches. We will see that the old regulatory system of adversarial rate cases is giving way to broader, more systemic regulatory frameworks that will contribute to industry restructuring and system redesign. As examples, the broad-based regulatory initiatives in Minnesota, Maryland, and New York will be emphasized.

THE "NEW NORMAL"

A constrained electricity market now represents the "new normal" for vertically integrated IOUs.[2] This "new normal" must be recognized as different in kind from previous economic challenges faced by the industry. Today's challenge, unlike the past challenges of increased prices, the collapse of nuclear power, and industry restructuring described in Chapter 5, is systemic, long term, and driven by multiple events. Consequently, two structural changes are necessary – the regulatory compact must be renegotiated and traditional COS ratemaking must be redesigned.[3] To better understand the new electricity market, it is necessary to examine the economic and policy assumptions behind the traditional regulatory model and then explain the economic and regulatory climate that has altered that market.

Traditional Economic Assumptions

In the early years of utility regulation, the relationship between utility and regulator was based upon what, in 1898, the infamous Samuel Insull proposed as a "grand bargain in which local electric companies would receive exclusive franchise service territories, '. . . coupled with the conditions of public control, requiring all charges for services fixed by public bodies to be based on cost plus a reasonable profit.' "[4] Nearly 100 years later, then judge Kenneth Starr defined that grand bargain as a "regulatory compact" that has prevailed since electricity regulation began.[5] The regulatory compact was indeed a grand bargain for the utility. As it turned out, the regulatory compact was also something of a bargain for consumers and for regulators.

Utilities greatly benefited from the regulatory compact because they were given an exclusive service territory. Utilities could block competition from other utilities because they were now operating under a government-protected monopoly. Utilities also benefited from a rate-making formula that operated like a cost-plus contract. Utilities would receive all of their reasonably incurred expenses on a dollar-for-dollar basis and they would be able to earn a reasonable rate of return on prudently invested capital. While it is inaccurate to say that utilities were "guaranteed" a profit, in effect though, as long as they operated prudently, profits were assured. Consumers also benefited to the extent that rates were set at more or less competitive levels rather than at monopoly levels. Consumers and regulators benefited because the industry was expanding and utilities were realizing economies of scale as rates stayed relatively flat and, in some instances, declined. In other words, rate hearings were largely noncontroversial affairs and the life of a regulator was fairly easy.[6]

The regulatory compact was implemented through the application of COS ratemaking that required regulators to balance the interests of the utility and its shareholders by providing a reasonable return on their investments against the interests of ratepayers in not being charged confiscatory, or discriminatory, rates. The balance was intended to satisfy the Fifth Amendment constitutional prohibition against takings of private property without just compensation. COS ratemaking works well in an expanding economy. As long as electric demand continues to grow and as long as utilities continue to make technological improvements and achieve scale economies, utilities can be rewarded for their prudent capital investments and customers do not suffer rate increases due to a "virtuous growth cycle in which increasing electricity consumption was viewed as synonymous with the public good."[7]

The danger in such a formula, however, should be apparent. As long as utilities receive a return on capital expenditures, they have an incentive to build. Again, during a period of economic expansion and growth in electricity demand, building is a necessary and economically valuable strategy. Today, discussion of the need for grid improvements and for the smart grid puts pressure on IOUs to make new capital additions at a time of declining sales growth and reduced creditworthiness.[8] If the economy slows or demand falls, then capital investments may not be economically valuable because the market is saturated and electricity sales flatten, which means that revenues decline for IOUs. Now, IOUs face just such a slow economy, weak demand, and nervous regulators.

Traditional Policy Assumptions

Energy policy generally, and electricity policy more specifically, was grounded in the central and important idea that the more energy that a country produces and consumes, the more vibrant its economy will be. Indeed, the twentieth century witnessed unprecedented economic growth for the United States as does any developing country with a robust energy infrastructure.

There are other policy ideas associated with the belief in the direct positive relationship between energy and the economy. First, it is more efficient to use cheaper inputs to produce a product such as electricity than more expensive ones. In this way, the electric industry has relied predominantly on cheap, but dirty, fossil fuels, particularly coal. Second, scale economies could be realized through larger plants and greater centralization; therefore, an IOU should make as many capital investments as possible – to a point. Parenthetically, this principle was exactly the reason that utilities invested in nuclear power – to realize scale economies. Unfortunately, that strategy proved to be quite costly. Third, as utilities moved from local to regional and, ultimately, to interstate transmission and distribution (T&D), regulation also moved from municipal to state and then to federal authorities. The development and the structure of the industry and its regulation moved in tandem as industry actors and regulators mimicked how each conducted its business, thus reinforcing the traditional energy paradigm.[9] In other words, regulators encouraged and supported IOU expansion into a national electricity infrastructure.

As a result of these assumptions, the industry and its regulation developed a pattern that exists today, and it is a pattern that has witnessed the investment of trillions of dollars over the century. Unfortunately, the traditionally structured industry and its regulation do not fit with the current economy nor are they aligned with contemporary energy policy assumptions.

We have significant reason to question the underlying assumption about the direct relationship between energy and the economy as our previous discussion of energy intensity demonstrates. Most particularly, even though electricity demand is projected to increase overall, albeit slowly, individual consumption is declining. The traditional belief in the direct linkage between energy and the economy is now experiencing a reversal. Individual consumers can continue to enjoy the lifestyles they have while consuming less electricity. Further, industrial and commercial, as well as residential, consumers are less dependent on the local IOU for their electricity because other electric providers are available.

Regulatory Changes

The regulatory landscape for the electricity industry and its markets has been undergoing dramatic change for over 40 years at both the federal and state levels. It is this regulatory twist that has given IOUs cause for concern and it is something that they must now confront.

As economic dislocations occurred in world energy markets and in the domestic economy in the 1970s, President Carter proposed, and Congress enacted, the National Energy Act[10] with the intent of stabilizing the domestic economy. One part of the National Energy Act was the Public Utility Regulatory Policy Act of 1978 (PURPA),[11] which was intended to encourage states to move away from rate designs that encouraged consumption and move toward marginal cost pricing because it would reduce demand, promote more accurate price signals, and achieve greater efficiencies. In addition, PURPA promoted independent power production, cogeneration, and small power generation. Known as "qualifying facilities" (QFs) under the act, these non-utility generators were able to produce electricity that was less expensive than electricity generated from traditional IOUs.[12] These QFs were more successful than policymakers imagined. Not only did QFs produce cheaper electricity, but also there were more non-IOU generating facilities than anticipated, and consequently, it was revealed that a significant amount of cheaper power was available for electric consumption.

QFs had a very attractive economic incentive to generate electricity up to the maximum amount allowed under law. Not only could QFs generate cheaper power for a customer's own use, but also any excess power could be sold back to the local utility at the utility's "full avoided costs."[13] The local utility had to allow grid access to QFs and it was obligated to purchase excess QF electricity at its marginal cost of electricity. The local utility had to pay the QF the cost that it would incur to generate one more kilowatt hour of electricity. In other words, the utility had to pay the QF not the prevailing market value, but the utility's own higher cost of producing electricity. PURPA discovered a new generation market and set the stage for competition in a formerly noncompetitive industry.

Traditionally regulated IOUs, following the traditional regulatory structure and rate formula, earned favorable, stable rates but had overbuilt. Excess capacity raised utilities' fixed costs, which had to be recovered from ratepayers. Consumers were not unaware of these market developments. They did not want to pay for higher cost electricity and sought lower-cost options. While the existence of lower-cost electricity did not surprise large customers, the market was surprised by how much new nonutility-generated electricity was available and how eager new generators were to enter the market. These new unregulated producers were willing to supply the market with electricity at prices lower than those charged by incumbent IOUs and they today provide over one-third of the country's electricity.[14]

PURPA opened electricity markets but other state and federal legislation entered that arena and further expanded competition. Under the Energy Policy Act of 1992, Congress created a category of "exempt wholesale generators." These entities generated electricity to be sold at wholesale and they were exempt from some of the regulatory provisions contained in the Public Utilities Holding Company Act of 1935, which was later repealed by the Energy Policy Act of 2005. That repeal was deemed to be a significant boost to independent power production because it opened the electricity market to a wider variety of business activities.[15] Then under the Energy Policy Act of 2005, Congress required electric utilities, under certain restrictions, to offer net metering services to electricity consumers, which means that consumers can generate their own electricity and either sell any excess generation to the local utility or receive a credit on their electricity bill.[16] To date, 43 states and the District of Columbia have adopted some form of net metering.[17] Additionally, for over three decades federal tax incentives in the form of production tax credits and investment tax credits, among others, have spurred production of electricity from renewable resources.[18] Finally, as federal and state regulators pursue methods of pollution control, the cost of fossil fuel power production increases.[19]

Federal regulation was a boon to independent power production. State regulation was more varied and in many instances went quite a bit further. Instead of focusing exclusively on production, state regulators started to focus on consumption and sought ways to reduce demand through such initiatives as demand-side management requirements; integrated resource planning requirements; and, energy efficiency standards. Each of these devices has the intent and effect of constraining demand and, therefore, reducing sales. Additionally, in an effort to stimulate nonfossil fuel generation, 38 states and the District of Columbia have adopted renewable portfolio standards that impose requirements on local utilities to sell electricity generated by renewable resources and these resources are produced by non-IOU electricity providers.[20]

States have also adopted regulations that encouraged nonutility generators to produce electricity from renewable resources. Feed-in tariffs, for example, are long-term contracts that utilities enter into with renewable resource providers, which enable providers to have an assured income stream enabling them to provide renewable energy to local utilities. Additionally, efficiency programs and zero net building standards are intended to reduce consumption by capturing energy efficiencies. States also have tax credits available that have made the installation of photovoltaic solar and other alternatives more affordable for more consumers.

Consequently, an array of federal and state legislation has had two dramatic consequences for the industry. First, competition in the electricity market has increased, and second, regulations have promoted renewable resources and energy efficiency that have reduced demand for IOU electricity. This new regulatory scheme has caused a reevaluation of regulation at both ends of the electric meter. At the generation end, the market is more competitive than once assumed.[21] At the consumption end, consumers want cheaper electricity and want more choices among providers including self-generation.

Since the late 1970s, regulators have been trying to restructure the electric industry with only partial success as several problems persist including: (1) getting cheaper electricity to consumers, (2) continuing to diversify generation sources, (3) dealing with intermittent sources such as wind and solar power, (4) redesigning electricity markets, (5) opening access to the grid, and (6) encouraging traditional IOUs to rethink their business models as discussed in the last chapter. IOU business innovation will only occur with complementary and supporting regulations.

The electricity market is indeed changing. As the Edison Electric Institute, the trade association for IOUs, puts the issue: "While every market-driven business is subject to competitive forces, public policy programs that provide for subsidized growth of competing technologies and/or participant economic incentives do not provide a level playing field upon which generators can compete fairly against new entrants."[22] It is important to distinguish between technologically driven changes that result in increased competition and competition that results from new regulatory requirements on incumbent utilities and on regulatory incentives that promote new entrants. It is equally, if not more, important to realize that the dividing line between markets and their regulation is fuzzy at best.[23]

The Edison Institute is partially correct to distinguish between market-driven technological change and public policies that promote competition. This distinction, though, fails to recognize that the electric industry has been a regulated industry and has enjoyed the fruits of that regulation for over a century. In other words, the divide between market changes and government regulation is not a particularly neat one. The fact that the electric industry has been the beneficiary of regulation and is now in a posture of contesting competition that has come about through regulation reveals that a solution or response to the industry's concerns involves political and policy as well as economic considerations including renegotiating the regulatory compact.

RENEGOTIATING THE REGULATORY COMPACT

The core of the traditional regulatory compact is that the government sets the utility's rates (and, consequently, its profits) in exchange for protecting the IOU's service territory. When the compact was made, the exclusive business of the IOU was to sell as much electricity as it could. Now that the electric market is changing in significant ways, a new regulatory compact is necessary.[24]

The new compact must be based on a set of assumptions. First, large-scale central power stations will continue to be important generators although on a diminishing scale. Second, an increasing number of non-IOU power providers will be part of a more competitive electricity market. Third, the T&D segments of the industry will continue to be regulated as long as they exhibit natural monopoly characteristics. Fourth, IOUs can no longer be devoted exclusively to electricity sales. Instead, IOUs must be seen as actors in a broader energy business that provides a wider array of energy services and products including renewable resources and energy efficiency. Finally, because IOUs will continue to be regulated, some form of regulatory compact will continue, yet it will be based upon a new set of regulatory principles including the following.[25]

Stranded Costs. Utilities should not be put in a position of incurring excess costs that, due to regulatory or policy changes, may become stranded and generate little or no electricity. Regulations that put an IOU in this position may well give rise to a regulatory takings claim. This principle of avoiding stranded costs is a two-edged sword. On the one hand, investors should not be deprived of a return on their investments due to regulatory or policy changes that they could not anticipate. Therefore, prudent investments that result in stranded costs should be afforded an opportunity to earn a return.[26] On the other hand, consumers should not pay for investments that yield either no electricity or expensive electricity. As discussed in Chapter 5, in the past, regulators provided relief to utilities from previous financial challenges. To the extent that IOUs invest in reliance on regulatory requirements and lose customers as a result, some protection must be provided.[27] Nevertheless, as contemporary energy policy changes, the problem of stranded costs should be anticipated and, if possible, avoided.[28]

The stranded cost problem in the context of a clean energy transition is distinct from the problem of nuclear power cancellations or from government ordered divestment under earlier regulatory restructuring efforts. In the nuclear power and divestment situations, stranded costs were more or less identifiable and they occurred at a very time-specific point. A clean energy transition is distinguishable in that it will not occur at a point in time but will occur over decades. This fact alone should allow utilities to plan for changes in the industry and changes in their own business models and investments. Next, as a utility's customer base declines, the downward spiral in lost sales will mean that there will be a smaller group of ratepayers to pick up increasing costs.[29] That scenario is not sustainable and regulators must be cognizant of these risks.

Although the law regarding regulatory or deregulatory takings remains opaque, the risks are real.[30] Investors will be reluctant to invest without reasonable assurances that a return on that investment will not be negated by prudence hearings, regulatory changes, or legislation that diminishes the value of their investments to the point at which their investment-backed expectations go uncompensated. Today such financial risk is reflected in the downward movement of credit ratings for the electric industry.[31] Thus, non-IOU generation, particularly coupled with an IOU's obligation to purchase excess generation, can pose a real risk to capital unless the utility recalibrates the way it does business and regulators rethink their rules.[32]

Legacy Financing. Regulators should avoid legacy financing. Traditionally structured utilities should not continue to be rewarded as they have been in the past if they take a BAU path. Any argument that utilities should continue to earn the same revenue because demand is down is not sound. Decreased demand alone is no cause for continuing to allow a regulated firm to earn a return on unproductive investments. The problem is complicated because the current challenge to IOUs is the consequence of both market and technological changes as well as regulatory requirements. No utility has any legal claim to continue to maintain its revenue requirement just because it loses sales.[33] The idea that the revenue requirement must be maintained as embedded in a COS mentality to cover a utility's costs regardless of the amount of service that it provides is no longer tenable.

COS ratemaking had its place but it should not be used to allow utilities to continue to build dirty coal-fired plants nor should it be used to reward utilities for embarking on financially risky nuclear projects precisely because "investment in conventional generation [is] hard to justify" in the new market.[34] Financial analyses indicate that solar-, wind-, and natural gas–generated electricity are showing increasingly positive cost signals, particularly against nuclear power. As a result, continued investments in coal and nuclear power will be viewed skeptically by the market while investments in new fuels and technologies are becoming increasingly attractive. Traditional investments must also be viewed skeptically by regulators. Instead of maintaining the status quo, regulators must manage the changing role of IOUs and encourage innovation in their business models.[35]

Equity. The new regulatory compact should encourage, rather than inhibit, competition and the development of innovative energy technologies including sales-reducing technologies such as DER.[36] Indeed, the alternative energy and energy efficiency markets are attracting significant investments and will only expand.[37]

DER is becoming an increasingly important actor in electricity markets and it has the potential for unfair cross-subsidization. With the expansion of distributed generation and energy-efficient improvements, some customers will be placed at a disadvantage because DER customers will be using less electricity, which puts pressure on utilities to raise rates to the customers that remain in that service territory. Regulators must be careful to ensure that non-DER customers do not pay more than their fair share of a utility's remaining fixed costs. To the extent that net metering rates generate an unfair cross-subsidization, they should be changed.[38] However, net metering benefits must also be accounted for in rates.[39] Further, regulators must be careful to avoid designing net metering rates that slow DER penetration or act as a drag on innovation and competition. The smart utility will become actively involved with DER as well as with the development of utility-scale solar wind and other renewable projects.[40]

Universal Service and Reliability. Regulators must be attentive to maintaining reliable universal electric service. The provision of universal and reliable service presents challenges all of its own. However, an increase in electricity providers does have the potential for bringing significant benefits to a utility's T&D segments. Reduced load should reduce congestion, should assist balancing, and, for a larger number of providers, should lower cybersecurity risks. Questioning reliability is an argument made against the Clean Power Plan and DER, and often, that argument should be recognized for what it is – a political argument in favor of the status quo, not necessarily a technical nor economic one as discussed in Chapter 1.[41]

Mitigation. Despite dire predictions of the death spiral, IOUs are well aware of changing electricity market conditions and a policy landscape shifting toward clean power. As a consequence, utilities cannot rely on past practices for future revenue. Instead, because IOUs are well aware of the political economy of a changing energy market, they cannot continue to do business as usual. To the extent that they can avoid incurring expenditures based upon past assumptions, they must do so in an effort to mitigate damages as is required by any contract.

During the period of electric industry restructuring, New Hampshire, for example, passed legislation intended to introduce competition into retail electric markets. As part of those efforts, the New Hampshire plan treated generation and retail marketing as functionally separate from T&D services, and the legislature expressed a preference for the divestiture of a utility's generation and transportation assets. Utilities operating under the previous statutory scheme were concerned about stranded assets. More specifically, regulators recognized the fact that if retail customers could purchase lower-priced electricity from sources other than the IOU, then a portion of the IOU's investments may not be recoverable.

The New Hampshire PUC recognized this possibility and made provisions that would allow a utility to recover its stranded costs if those costs were found to have resulted from a government regulation. The utility, though, would not be able to recover stranded costs if they were not prudently incurred. Concomitantly, the legislation required utilities to mitigate their stranded costs. New Hampshire took an aggressive approach regarding mitigation efforts that a utility should undertake. Those steps included, among other efforts, the sale of excess generating capacity and the renegotiation of service contracts.[42]

By adopting these principles, the regulatory compact will continue to balance utility/shareholder interests with customer/ratepayer interests by maintaining reasonable and fair rates from both perspectives. At the same time, the new regulatory compact will encourage utilities to adopt new business models, promote technological innovation and competition, expand market opportunities, and increase consumer choice. The regulatory compact, however, is not self-executing. Instead, PUCs must adopt a forward-looking approach to ratemaking.

REDESIGNING RATEMAKING

Like the regulatory compact, ratemaking is based upon a set of principles. The classic formulation of those principles was set out by James Bonbright in 1961 and they are still in use. Bonbright wrote that rates should be practical, simple, and understandable; maintain the viability of utilities through relatively stable and reliable revenue; maintain fair rates to consumers; fairly apportion costs among different classes of ratepayers; and, promote economic efficiency and reliability.[43] Bonbright further specified four functions for utility rates; rates should: (1) attract capital, (2) set reasonable energy prices, (3) promote efficiency, and (4) control demand through consumer rationing.[44] Each of those functions addresses the economic stability of IOUs.

At the time of the classic formulation, the electric industry was dominated by IOUs and was experiencing growth and realizing economies of scale. Today, neither of those conditions is operative – IOUs neither dominate nor continue to experience scale economies. Therefore, a new set of rate-making functions is necessary as IOUs must also respond to social goals such as carbon reduction.

Ratemaking is the mechanism that drives the regulatory compact. Even when the electric industry was challenged by nuclear and restructuring failures, regulators relied on cost-based ratemaking. Also, in times of financial stress, when utilities confronted volatile costs for fuel or wrestled with inflation, they sought refuge behind automatic fuel adjustment clauses that allowed rates to escalate in tandem with those rising costs.[45] Similarly, regulators have relied on the COS formula and, in some instances, have expanded its use through devices such as future test years,[46] multiyear rate structures,[47] and cost trackers. Each of these mechanisms is revenue-based; they are not performance-based.

As noted, cost-based rate-making functions well when the market is expanding and demand continues to grow. Once the market slows or stalls, cost-based ratemaking contributes to excess capacity, high prices, and other economic dislocations.[48] Further, "cost of service regulation can slow the pace of innovation and may offer little incentive for utilities to improve operational efficiency or service quality beyond the minimum levels set by regulators."[49]

Still, COS ratemaking has a strong hold on the regulatory structure. "The regulatory framework has been resilient in the face of the flux brought about by economic, technical, and financial shocks that often nullified one or more of the assumptions underlying the original framework, precisely because of the willingness to adopt incremental changes to the process."[50] Another way of analyzing the situation of "resilience" is to see the regulatory framework as resistant to change, not resilient. For the clean power transition to take hold, ratemaking must be redesigned and adapted to today's changing market conditions and policy preferences.

The most immediate problem is that COS ratemaking was dedicated to covering a utility's prudently incurred costs. Now the problem is that most of those investments are "more necessary than productive. But upward rate pressure plus stagnant or falling sales could shrink the domain of financial stability"[51] of an IOU. Traditionally structured electric utilities, as well as their regulators, must figure out how to earn money by selling less electricity while promoting other energy services and products. Most notably, increased use of DER challenges regulators to accommodate increased DER adoption through ratemaking while also encouraging IOUs to take advantage of opportunities to reduce network costs and improve service quality.[52]

There is no shortage of new rate designs[53] including (1) performance-based ratemaking,[54] (2) incentive rates,[55] (3) alternative regulation,[56] (4) market-based rates,[57] (5) decoupling,[58] (6) feed-in-tariffs,[59] and (7) results-based regulation as examples.[60] In choosing among new rate designs, regulators must "address the fact that in an efficient, modern utility, conventional revenue recovery may no longer keep pace with utility system costs, investment needs and the changing dynamics of customers which have a growing range of energy related choices ranging from DG to demand response."[61] Further, rates should be seen as a "means by which energy companies communicate their value proposition to their customers, and not merely the process by which they collect revenues."[62] While a wide variety of approaches can be adapted for a new electricity market, any rate design should be based upon a set of new functions.

Costs. While cost recovery will play a role in any new rate design,[63] a move away from using historically embedded costs, or even future tests' year costs, as the central element of a utility's revenue requirement must be adopted. A key move away from cost-based ratemaking is decoupling. At its simplest form, decoupling means that rates will not be based on the volume of electricity sales; instead, rates will be based on other indicators such as the number of customers served. There are a variety of decoupling mechanisms. "Some mechanisms use the revenue authorized in the utility's last general rate case; others adjust that for specific cost changes or according to a formula and still others calculate revenue on a per-customer account basis rather than as a single dollar amount."[64] A basic element of several decoupling schemes is that they allow for periodic rate adjustments to compensate for unanticipated cost increases.[65]

The tricky issue with decoupling is a utility's fixed costs. How should rates treat those capital investments? Variable costs, such as the amount of energy, are easily recouped through sales. Fixed costs, however, are more difficult to assess because capital investments are often expensive, are incurred over a period of years during which the number and identity of customers vary, and do not necessarily serve specific individuals for specific customer classes. Revenue-based rate structures must give way to a new and dynamic electricity market. New rate designs should treat variable costs variably and set fixed costs fairly and rationally so that stable rates and price signals are generated without diminishing customer incentives to invest in new technologies.[66]

Innovation and Transition. Rate designs can promote innovation and assist in the clean power transition by allowing utilities to recover investments in innovation, energy efficiency, or renewable resources. Smart grid investments and pilot project costs should be recouped, as examples. Similarly, investments in smart meters, energy savings appliances, energy audits, and the like should be encouraged and included in a utility's revenue requirement. Regulators, of course, will have a great degree of discretion. Some investments can be included in the rate base and can earn a return for shareholders. Other investments can be treated as costs and recouped dollar for dollar.

In the United Kingdom, for example, the utility regulator has adopted a RIIO rate design (revenue set to deliver strong incentives, innovation, and outputs). The intent is to have utilities focus on delivering long-term value to customers. Revenues will be set based upon a review of the utility's business plan including its planned operating expenses as well as an assessment of future capital investments. The rates are then set on a multiyear basis and are intended to provide an incentive for the utility to pursue efficiency improvements by allowing the utility to retain some of the cost savings.

Cost-sharing can incentivize utilities to earn savings that can then be shared with customers. Again, regulators will have discretion on the proportion of cost-sharing between the parties, but the idea is to create incentives for innovation and efficiency.[67]

> In the same way that revenue decoupling and shared savings policies together can provide strong incentives for utilities to invest in energy efficiency, a similar approach could strengthen incentives for utilities to invest in distributed generation, storage, microgrids, smart electric vehicle charging, smart inverters, or other distributed technologies to reduce operating costs and/or to defer or avoid the need for investments to expand capacity of distribution feeders or invested other electricity supply, transmission, or distribution assets.[68]

An effective rate design may require hybrid pricing models that apply to different investments, different expenses, or different customer classes. Electricity rates can be unbundled for different purposes such as for reliability, standby power, a certain level of service quality, and ancillary power services.[69] Smart rate designs "may ultimately create a nimble system that pays for required services, maximizes value, and allows for effective implementation."[70] The core idea behind moving away from COS to rate designs that are more sensitive to the market and to technological developments is to encourage competition and enable utilities to capitalize on new opportunities.[71]

Balance of Interests. Shareholders, naturally, will only invest if they earn a reasonable return on their investment. That return must be comparable with investments of similar risk. Still, shareholders do take on some investment risk and they should not be guaranteed a return at the expense of customers who may receive little or no benefit. The trick lies in clearly identifying the risks to shareholders as well as the costs and benefits to consumers. Rates should send clear price signals that account for both fixed and variable costs;[72] avoid cross-subsidization as much as possible;[73] and, represent the value of services provided to the customer by the utility.[74] "Building a shared understanding among stakeholders and regulators in the electricity sector about the full range of costs and benefits of distributed energy resources and the implications of net energy metering is an essential first step toward devising rates and incentives that will create the greatest benefit for all."[75]

Prudence and Need Reviews. Prudence reviews became a matter of concern to utilities with the collapse of nuclear power. The possibility of a prudence review constitutes a risk to investors; however, all risk cannot and should not be eliminated. The fact that a utility's capital investment will be reviewed for prudence should be considered simply a matter of bringing business discipline into the electricity market. A prudence review should work hand in hand with the obligation of a utility to mitigate the costs of unwise investments. In that regard, then, two reviews should be considered. In effect, such reviews will occur before rates go into effect and then again after they have operated for a period of time. The *ex ante* review will set forward-looking benchmarks in an attempt to achieve efficient network expenditures, particularly in an era of greater DER penetration. The second, *ex post*, review will be used to make revenue adjustments to accommodate the uncertainty involved with changing network use as well as because of forecast errors.[76]

First, an *ex ante* prudence review should occur at the time a utility wants to include specific investments in the rate base as part of a rate hearing or negotiated settlement. This first prudence review should occur before the investment is made rather than after the completion of a project when policy and economic circumstances may change. The problem with *ex post* reviews of investment decisions should be apparent. At Time One, for example, a utility assesses the need for a capital investment. Construction projects, particularly nuclear plants, take years and up to a decade or more to complete. Consequently, the decision to include that investment in the rate base will occur at a time when future market and financial conditions, as well as the need for energy, can change significantly. One way of mitigating the risk of a disallowance at Time Two, when the second prudence review takes place, is for regulators to aggressively assess the need for power before the investment is made.[77] Nevertheless, a review that assumes the prudence of an investment when made should not preclude a second *ex post* review to assure that the project was constructed as advertised.

Market Power. Finally, regulators will be called upon to exercise an additional review of rates to ensure that utilities are not unfairly exercising their market power. The emergence of more competition in the electric industry and the development of utility business models which encourage them to participate in those markets by, for example, selling energy services and products that are also being sold by third parties may present market power problems. As an incumbent, a utility will have a leg up with customers because of their business dealings with them. The more complicated problem is that because utilities will be receiving government-protected rates, they should not be able to favor the competitive arms of their businesses through those rates. Utilities should not be in a position to exercise market power on the competitive side of their businesses nor should they be able to engage in market manipulation[78] certainly of the sort experienced during the Enron scandal by manipulating the way that rates are constructed.[79]

Such review is a form of antitrust analysis. Regulators must carefully assess whether or not the incumbent utility has an unfair advantage due to its regulated status in certain competitive markets.[80] More particularly, third parties that sell energy products and services should be able to operate on a level playing field, and utilities should not be able to reduce their financial risk in those markets through rate protection. Therefore, regulators must examine rates to ensure that they do not facilitate the exercise of market power in those more competitive markets.

THREE MODELS OF THE UTILITY OF THE FUTURE

The electric grid is the single most important component of the electric system. Given the changes in the industry that we have discussed, including changes in business models of IOUs, the grid will necessarily be affected especially in its accommodation of a wider variety of energy resources.[81] While the grid will maintain its centrality in the electric system, the grid of the future will have to be more flexible, more resilient, and more secure while maintaining reliability. The grid of the future, also referred to as the integrated grid in a concept paper by the Electric Power Research Institute (EPRI),[82] must be capable of balancing and transporting a wider variety of power sources including central power, DER, energy storage, renewable resources, microgrids, and other new technologies that come online. As also noted by the

Department of Energy, the grid of the future will operate advanced information and communication technologies (ICT) for the purpose of managing a multiplicity of transactions among utilities, consumers, and third parties in regulated and unregulated markets.[83]

In addition to its concept paper, EPRI's future grid project includes two other phases: the institute will develop a framework for cost-benefit analysis of integrating DER into the grid[84] and then engage in a series of demonstrations and modeling programs to provide data needed for cost-effective system-wide implementation of integrated grid technologies. In combination, the three phases of the project will yield a guidebook of analytic tools and resources for evaluating various combinations of technologies and resources that will be part of the new grid and will enable IOUs and regulators to adopt complementary business models and practices.[85] The guidebook will describe technological approaches, provide tools needed to assess performance, and explain the relationship between DER owners and grid operators. It is intended that the project will generate the analytics necessary to assess the various values inherent in the smart grid including producer and consumer value and the value contributed to the grid by DER owners.[86]

California is pursuing energy policies consistent with EPRI's integrated grid project. Policymakers have recognized that the roles and functions of the grid have changed as a result of new customer expectations, environmental objectives, and the rapid advancement and deployment of new technologies including efficiency. They have concluded that a modernized grid is essential to achieve those policies as well as necessary for the transformation of the electric industry. California's approach links technological innovation, regulatory reform, and new business practices together in a strategy intended to bring the grid into the twenty-first century.[87] California has been in the forefront of the energy transition for over two decades and the lessons learned are valuable. Other states, such as Hawaii, Vermont, and Maine,[88] have also engaged in developing regulatory models that will transform the electric industry and energy policy more generally. Here we discuss three other system-wide approaches to redesigning electric markets within those states.

Minnesota e21

In February 2014, a group of energy consultants, academic institutions, and utilities convened what is known as the e21 Initiative for the explicit purpose of developing a "more consumer-centered and sustainable framework for utility regulation in Minnesota that better aligns how utilities earn revenue with public policy goals, new customer expectations, and the changing technology landscape."[89] Currently, electricity regulation in Minnesota is based upon the traditional model. The market is dominated by IOUs that operate in a regulated market under COS regulation. Consequently, utility revenue is earned through prudently incurred expenses with an opportunity to earn a reasonable rate of return sufficient enough to attract capital.[90] Minnesota utilities, then, are still driven by regulation to sell electricity and build more plants.

Because of changes in the industry, e21 recognized the need for a new regulatory framework. More particularly, declining sales, increasing investment and operational costs, the increased use of distributed generation and other alternatives, and environmental regulations, all contributed to the need to rethink the old model.[91] Minnesota already had on the books a set of regulatory tools to address the effects of those changes such as using future test years rather than historic test years, the ability to file for interim rates in the event of unforeseen costs, multiyear rate plans, automatic adjustment clauses and fuel trackers that allow utilities to recoup expenses above and beyond the filed base rate; the ability to recover construction work in progress in the rate base, and revenue decoupling. Even with this array, these tools appeared insufficient to the task of responding to a changing industry.[92] More specifically, most of these tools were based upon volumetric sales, and to the extent that DER customers could avail themselves of net metering, cross-subsidization and equity issues became apparent.

In response, the e21 Initiative first examined regulatory reforms and business model initiatives being undertaken in other jurisdictions. It is noteworthy that the e21 initiative is considering regulatory and business reforms; however, it is doing so in the context of maintaining the status of Minnesota IOUs. Minnesota envisions continued operation of IOU-dominated electricity markets in the state. At the conclusion of its comparative analysis, e21 noted that utility compensation needed to be aligned with broader policy goals and customer interests. One way of achieving that alignment would be to move away from volumetric sales incentives to providing revenue based upon a utility's performance relative to stated public policy goals and values rather than based upon historic costs. Additionally, and consistent with the aim of being more consumer responsive, e21 acknowledged the importance of developing new technologies to increase operational efficiency as well as provide enhanced consumer services.[93]

At the conclusion of initial evaluation, a Phase I report was issued that addressed two fundamental issues. First, e21 looked at ways to shift away from the traditional business practices that provided consumers with little choice toward a model that provided more options regarding how energy was produced and how and when it was consumed and at what price. Second, the report examined ways to shift regulation away from volumetric sales of electricity and away from building large capital-intensive facilities to a regulatory regime based upon performance standards that included energy efficiency, reliability, affordability, and emissions reductions among other public policy goals.[94]

The e21 Initiative was well aware of the complexity of the task facing it. The report was forthcoming in recognizing that the electric system of the future needed to become "cleaner, more flexible, secure and resilient against attack and natural disaster, and able to empower customers to manage and reduce their energy costs ... [and] become more distributed, flexible, intelligent, efficient, real-time controlled, and open to more participants."[95] In order to accomplish all of these objectives, e21 had to account for technological, market, economic, legal, and policy issues. To that end, e21 made a series of consensus recommendations that fell into four categories: (1) performance-based ratemaking, (2) customer options and rate designs, (3) regulatory process reforms, and (4) planning reforms.

Performance-Based Ratemaking. Because the e21 Initiative was sensitive to the needs of Minnesota IOUs, the first recommendation regarding performance-based ratemaking would be available to those utilities that voluntarily opted in to the program. One key design feature of the performance-based recommendation is more comprehensive planning, so that utilities choosing to participate had more time to plan to meet policy goals and that additional time would provide more predictable rates for consumers. Under this scheme, a utility's revenue would be based upon meeting performance metrics instead of being based solely on the volume of electricity sales.

In order to qualify for performance-based rates, a utility would be required to provide two primary documents. First, it must submit a business plan that provides a comprehensive picture of a utility's expected investments and expenditures including how it intends to invest in a more distributed system as well as investments in grid modernization. Additionally, the business plan must specify how the utility would satisfy the stated public policy goals and objectives as set out in the performance metrics. The business plan would stand in for the traditionally adversarial rate case. Nevertheless, the plan would contain sufficient information so that rates could be set. The Initiative was aware that even though there are benefits to a longer rate-making time frame, there are also costs. More specifically, rate adjustment mechanisms are likely necessary particularly for exogenous events such as natural disasters or changes in policy and law. As part of the rate scheme, ratepayers could be protected from costly rate increases through earnings-sharing mechanisms that allow utilities to recoup investments but would require them to share savings with customers.

The second requirement is that the utility must file an integrated resource analysis (IRA). Currently, Minnesota law requires utilities to file an integrated resources plan (IRP) that provides a 15-year, or more, forecast of a utility's expected load and identifies the resources and plans that satisfy that load. Two problems arose with the existing IRP process. First, it was lengthy, and second, many of the issues that were contained in the plan could be relitigated and changed in rate cases. In both instances, efficiency suffered and IRPs were not faithfully followed.

The IRA, by contrast, is intended to provide the same types of information while changing the way information is gathered and used. Instead of relying only on a utility's inputs for the IRP, the IRA would be drafted after gathering information from a broad group of stakeholders with the intent of making the information more useful for regulators, utilities, consumers, and other intervenors. In this way, the IRA is intended to reduce conflicts while more broadly satisfying the business goals of the utility and the public policy goals of regulators.

Customer Options and Rate Designs. The e21 Initiative also focuses on the customer side of electric service. As technology enables customers to acquire power from other sources including self-generation, customer options increase. Utilities must navigate a world that they no longer dominate and one that affects the traditional business model. Regulators have historically balanced customer and utility interests and are now called upon to rebalance that relationship. Through innovative rate designs, utilities can be encouraged to provide new services; customers can be made more aware of the real-time costs of electricity, thus controlling their demand; utilities are able to tailor rates and services based upon unique customer needs; and rates can be designed to enable utilities to engage in pilot projects that allow them to test and evaluate new services, products, and technologies and, eventually, share savings with customers.[96]

By approving pilot projects in advance, regulators can provide assurances to utilities that they can experiment with new technologies and innovative business models without significant financial risks attached. As examples, e21 suggests that a utility might invest in technologies such as LED street lighting, DER services such as modular solar technologies, renewable electricity sales for customers who prefer that option, and energy storage opportunities. Under this proposal, the utility will be afforded some protection in its rates. The Initiative noted that DER services and storage options also provide value to the grid, and, therefore, those services, including such values as grid stability, reliability, and backup power, need to be monetized so that customers who provide them are compensated for the benefits conferred on the grid, and, therefore, benefits conferred upon utilities.

One way to accommodate the use of new technologies and the ability of consumers to also act as energy producers is to design rates that provide accurate and as close to real-time information as possible so that consumers can adjust demand. One method for more accurately providing price signals is through time-varying rates. As the report notes, "time-varying rates can alert customers to opportunities for lowering their current cost of power or signal when is the best time to plug in electric vehicle or sell electricity or other ancillary services back to the grid in order to fetch the best price."[97]

This rate formula can facilitate the adoption of smart appliances and thermostats on the consumer side and the adoption of advanced metering on the utility side. The report also notes that different customer groups, such as trade-sensitive industries and new areas of economic development, may have special energy needs. To serve those needs, e21 recommends that the legislature consider allowing utilities to negotiate rates for such special cases. Additionally, utility–customer partnerships for new sources of on-site generation should be encouraged as should new markets for the electrification of transportation for passenger vehicles, light rail, and municipal fleets. In these ways, the utility becomes an active participant in the design and operation of new electricity markets.

Regulatory Process Reforms. Since the beginning, the regulation of the electric industry has been subject to an adversarial process in which a utility would propose a rate and the utility commission would approve a rate that was just and reasonable. For most of the last century, as utilities enjoyed economies of scale, consumer rates did not increase precipitously. Often they would stay flat and, on occasion, decline. As electricity prices began to rise in the latter third of the last century, consumer advocates became concerned that regulators were too comfortable with utilities, and, therefore, rate review needed more scrutiny. As a consequence of increased rates and increased consumer participation, rate cases became more contentious and controversial. They also became longer and more expensive.

The e21 report recommends a series of regulatory reforms intended to address the complex issues facing the industry, reduce the adversarial nature of rate cases, and reduce the amount of time it takes to put rates into effect. PUCs exercise both judicial and legislative functions. Although they are creatures of statute and, therefore, must comply with statutory mandates, the issues that now confront PUCs are increasingly novel and increasingly complex. Adversarial, winner-takes-all decision-making processes do not lend themselves to problems that affect a multiplicity of actors with a multiplicity of different needs and objectives. PUCs should have the authority to fashion compromise solutions that balance the interests of all parties and that are responsive to public policy goals and the needs of the system to the benefit of all of its participants.

Instead of formal adversarial hearings, for example, the PUC could take a more active role in understanding the interests of the parties and the range of possible solutions. Informal hearings with stakeholders can provide the PUC with information with which to identify common interests and pathways to resolution. Similarly, non-adversarial processes can be adopted to facilitate settlement discussions and propose creative solutions through bilateral or multilateral agreements. Two regulatory reforms can be used more creatively. First is an expanded use of generic dockets instead of waiting for a controversy to arise in a more specific rate case. By way of example, instead of contesting distributed generation or a net metering rate between a utility and a specific customer, the PUC can examine the issues surrounding distributed generation more generally. Second, PUCs must be more forward looking and must anticipate problems through better planning rather than try to solve them after costs have been incurred.

Planning Reforms. The traditional one-way transmission system that relied on large central power stations must adapt to smaller-scale power, two-way communications and sales, demand response, and energy storage. The multiplicity of actors will converge on the distribution segment of the electricity system and a modernized grid will be the point at which that multiplicity of providers and consumers meet. In order to enable that convergence and to experience a smooth transition, planning is necessary.[98] As stated in the report, "[p]roactivley planning for an intelligent, flexible, nimble, efficient, open, and secure distribution system over the next several decades that can handle new distributed energy technologies and the complexity of many more actors in the system will require a coherent strategy."[99]

The most significant planning reform recommendation is that instead of relying on a century-old adversarial rate-making process, ratemaking and planning should go through a broader and more inclusive stakeholder process similar to the one used by e21. Bringing together producers, consumers, utilities, nonutility power providers, academicians, regulators, businesses, and other interested parties should enable industry and regulatory planners to more fully understand the needs and interests of these various stakeholders as the electric industry is being transformed, and, then, plans can be generated to assess and meet those needs.

Future iterations of the e21 Initiative will consider in more detail how the distribution system can integrate demand- and supply-side distributed resources; accommodate more active participation by consumers; better manage two-way flows of information and electricity; and provide efficient, seamless integration and interoperability for the entire system.[100] In short, the primary goal of better planning is to improve the design of the system with the specific intent of improving grid efficiency. For example, the report noted that, in Minnesota, the grid operates at 55 percent efficiency and that improvements can reduce system cost and operate more efficiently. There is, then, room for efficiency improvements with a redesigned grid.

The e21 approach is designed to operate within the existing regulatory and industry framework while adapting that framework to modern needs. IOUs will continue to play a central role and they will continue to be rewarded. However, their rewards will be based upon a set of performance goals that go beyond satisfying an IOU's revenue requirement based upon electricity sales alone. Moreover, IOUs will have to satisfy public policy objectives including the provision of reliable, affordable electricity together with environmental improvements.

Maryland Utility 2.0.

On July 25, 2012, then Maryland governor Martin O'Malley directed his energy advisory, in collaboration with the Maryland Energy Administration, to gather information about improving the resilience and reliability of Maryland's electric distribution system. Of specific concern was the potential of prolonged power outages due to natural disasters attendant to climate change. The task force that was convened conducted a series of roundtable discussions with various stakeholders, and it generated a set of recommendations including: improving reliability reporting, allowing cost trackers to support utility investments, undertaking pilot projects, and increasing citizen participation among others. The task force also recommended that the Energy Future Coalition (EFC) be assigned the task of developing a pilot proposal for the utility of the future.[101]

EFC issued its report entitled *Utility 2.0* in March 2013. The report addressed issues consistent with those discussed in this chapter and made five recommendations regarding: (1) utility revenue, (2) programmable power, (3) utility financing of the smart grid and efficiency, (4) microgrids, and (5) electric vehicle charging. The report envisioned that its recommendations would be tested through voluntary opt-in pilot projects under the operation of Maryland's two leading IOUs – Potomac Electric Power, Inc. and Baltimore Gas & Electric Co. At the heart of the analysis was the importance of aligning utility revenues with customer needs and of adopting cost recovery mechanisms for utility investments in new energy services, including efficiency, and in smart grid technologies.[102]

In order to accomplish both of those goals, the report emphasized the need for changes in utility business models and supporting regulations.[103]

Utility Revenue. The Utility 2.0 proposal promotes performance-based revenue mechanisms because, as the report notes, COS ratemaking "tied to volume of power sales is no longer appropriate."[104] The report recommended that performance should be based upon five metrics that would have the effect of changing a utility's rate of return on equity, or a customer's bill, either positively or negatively, based upon a utility's satisfaction of those metrics. The metrics would include cost, reliability, customer service, and the adoption of new technologies and would support alternative energy resources. The unique aspect of this recommendation is that those factors would be weighted based upon customer evaluation of their importance. In this way, utilities would have information about customer choices and priorities and could plan accordingly with a better understanding of possible profitable revenue streams available for them. Some customers, for example, may value reliability more than other metrics while other customers may more highly value the ability to install rooftop solar-generated electricity. This project is intended to help utilities understand different needs while also gathering information about their own future investments and making utilities more responsive to their consumers.[105]

This recommendation would bifurcate a utility's revenue stream through decoupling volumetric sales and rates. Part of each customer's rate would include the utility's cost of capital such as recovery of debt and interest and repayment of equity. A customer's cost of energy would be based on how well the utility satisfies the performance criteria as established by the customers rather than based upon a utility's assessment of its own revenue requirement. Customers would then have an opportunity to negotiate for the services they prefer to receive from the utility. Customers that are highly satisfied pay somewhat more for those services than customers who do not receive the service that they specify in their individual performance criteria. The report observes that "few changes would be as likely to align utility actions with customer values, requirements and preferences as to adopt such a customer-driven prioritization of performance standards, at the same time providing detailed information that would allow utilities to meet its customers' expressed preferences with precision."[106] As such, an entirely new utility–customer relationship would be established to improve the delivery of energy services through a two-way system of communications.

Programmable Power. As defined in the report, a programmable power pilot project would move toward a "fully integrated and interoperable system of utility customer digital information, controls and communications from the central utility and from energy markets to individual customers and to their separate programmable appliances."[107] This project is specifically intended to integrate into the electric system and into markets a variety of energy resources, efficiency, and storage capabilities through the use of ICT. Through better transparency and interoperability rules, market signals should be more accurate for producers and consumers alike.

Devices such as smart meters and appliances, as well as home energy management systems, will facilitate that integration. Maryland has already been engaged in installing smart meters in homes, and technologies exist to provide these information and market signals although more consumer education is needed. Additionally, variable pricing must be available from and supported by regulators. In order to fully take advantage of those technologies, a pilot project in this area would assist regulators and utilities to design the necessary standards and rules and information architecture needed to maximize ICT efficiency.

One advantage to the emerging electricity industry is increased competition. That advantage, however, presents a difficult choice for regulators. On the one hand, utilities have market experience and they have contacts with customers. To the extent that utilities may compete with third-party providers, they may enjoy a competitive advantage based on past business experience and relationships with customers. On the other hand, to prohibit utilities from engaging in new services may stifle competition and limit efficiency gains. Consequently, in order to determine which path is more productive, two pilot projects are recommended – one that allows a utility to act as a provider of new services and one that prohibits them from doing so.

Utility Financing. In order to implement goals of programmable power, a local utility must be in a position to finance customers who choose to adopt smart grid and efficiency measures. The utility should be able to make capital investments in customer-oriented services, and regulators must be prepared to allow them to earn a return on those investments. As customers install smart devices, the cost of those installations and devices can be paid for through monthly utility bills. Regulators will be required to monitor such financing to ensure customers that interest rates charged by utilities are at market levels at most. More to the point, regulators can require low interest rates so that these markets can become established and utilities do not abuse their already preferred position as long-time providers.

Microgrids. According to the EFC report, a microgrid is defined as: "an integrated energy system consisting of distributed energy generating resources, both conventional ... and renewable generation such as solar roof panels, multiple electrical loads are meters ... and energy storage, operating as a single, autonomous grid either in parallel to or islanded from the existing utility power grid."[108] Microgrids can be constructed on their own and away from the existing utility system or they can be connected to it. In either case, this configuration reduces the load on the grid and can provide more grid stability. The recommendation is to assemble customers in a neighborhood, office park, or residential subdivision to join with a local utility. The microgrid can operate as a mini-distribution system while the utility provides backup power.

The pilot project could start as a customer–utility partnership and test the possibility that the microgrid can become fully functional and operational away from the utility. Such a pilot project can also serve as a testing ground for the advanced ICT systems necessary for the full deployment of the next-generation electric system. Another pilot can also test storage technologies that can provide voltage regulation and frequency controls necessary for microgrid operations. At the same time, storage technologies may contribute value to the utility for which microgrid owners should be compensated. To the extent that customers will need backup power, microgrid customers will be charged for that service.

Electric Vehicle Charging. Clearly, the most significant and most disruptive technology to the electric system will be electric vehicle penetration into the marketplace. The challenge to the electric industry and its regulators is to construct the infrastructure and charging facilities necessary for greater EV deployment. Another challenge is to ensure that the grid stays in balance. EVs can help balance the system. On the one hand, EVs consume power and increase electricity sales; on the other hand, they can provide stabilization services to the grid, particularly to the extent that EVs are charged at off-peak times. Utilities can provide a range of services to facilitate expansion of the EV market. They can provide charging technology to homeowners, provide batteries to EV owners, and purchase electricity to balance load from EV owners when necessary; and, with the ability to draw on EV power, utilities can accommodate more variable power from solar and wind.

The EFC recommendations do not come in a vacuum. Maryland has undertaken a series of innovative energy programs that are consistent with the recommendations and are consistent with the evolving electric industry. The state is already experimenting with alternative vehicle refueling stations, microgrids, photovoltaic solar parking lots, and demand reduction.[109] Similarly, Maryland IOUs are also active in helping customers reduce demand, increasing energy efficiency, promoting safety and reliability, adopting a plug-in recharging pilot, and developing the smart grid.[110]

Maryland's Utility 2.0 provides a nice complement to the Minnesota plan by integrating existing IOUs into a modern grid and by its willingness to undertake a series of pilot projects to test ideas, bring innovations online, and incorporate expressed consumer needs in future planning.

New York REV

The Minnesota and Maryland projects are largely designed around their existing electricity systems including the central importance of IOUs. New York's Reforming the Energy Vision (REV) project, by contrast, is notably and importantly more ambitious. Announced in a Framework Order of the New York Public Service Commission (PSC) in February 2015, REV proposes to dramatically restructure the electric industry in the state[111] and serve as a model for the nation.[112] More specifically the order states that the purpose of the REV is to:

> reorient both the electric industry and the ratemaking paradigm toward a consumer-centered approach that harnesses technology and markets. Distributed energy resources (DER) will be integrated into the planning and operation of electric distribution systems, to achieve optimal system efficiencies, secure universal, affordable service, and enable the development of a resilient, climate-friendly energy system.[113]

This statement of purpose echoes themes in the Maryland and Minnesota approaches that the electric system must be more consumer friendly, incorporate new technologies, and integrate new resources. The REV program, however, goes beyond both of those states by proposing to transform the distribution system through a partnership with major IOUs and two large municipal utilities. More specifically, the REV vision is to establish markets in which customers and nonutility third parties are active participants in system design and operation together with IOUs who will retain their obligation to provide reliable service.[114] Additionally, the REV has set ambitious goals: By 2030, a 40 percent reduction in greenhouse gas emissions from 1990 levels is to be achieved; 50 percent of the state's energy should come from renewable resources; and there should be a 23 percent reduction in energy consumption by buildings from 2012 levels. Further still, the REV is coordinated with a more ambitious state energy plan designed to serve as a "comprehensive roadmap to build a clean, resilient, and affordable energy system" throughout the state.[115]

The Framework Order was based upon an earlier staff report that undertook a fundamental reconsideration of the existing regulatory structure, distribution utilities, emerging energy markets, and clean energy policy goals. The staff report adopted objectives similar to those adopted in Minnesota and Maryland such as customer participation, the need for resource diversity, and system reliability and resilience among other objectives. Additionally, the report acknowledged the drivers that were changing the electricity system such as an aging infrastructure, the need for modernization and the incorporation of new technologies, greater consumer participation, and the need to reduce carbon emissions.[116] In adopting the REV report, the PSC also emphasized the growing importance of ICT to provide more accurate data, enhance cybersecurity, expand customer choice, and improve reliability, power quality, and resilience.[117] Most significantly, the report recognized that the traditional COS paradigm was inadequate to efficiently address the expansion of clean energy, energy efficiency, and new technologies that were not integrated into new utility business models. Consequently, at the heart of the REV project is regulatory and business model innovation on a broader scale than seen before. In addition to smooth interoperability of distribution systems and wholesale markets, the REV report concentrates on three areas: (1) the distribution system, (2) customer participation, and (3) regulatory reform.

Distribution System. The central actor in the REV's future power system is the Distributed System Platform Provider (DSP) that will be designated to coordinate a multiplicity of power providers, consumer activities, and DER within a particular service area. While the DSP will most likely operate under the management of existing utilities, the traditional IOU structure will be radically redesigned. Like many other states, New York has adopted measures to achieve clean power goals including performance-based rates, decoupling, energy efficiency programs, innovative R&D programs, and other activities including a Green Bank[118] to help finance alternative energy projects. Although these various tools are uncoordinated and efficiencies remain to be gained, they position the state well for more comprehensive programming.[119]

The DSP is intended to modernize, plan, design, and operate the state's distribution system,[120] and, in effect, it becomes the utility of the future. In large part, the DSP serves as a platform for bringing together the growing number of participants in the electric system on both sides of the meter. Proper planning should lead to intelligent integration of all actors, operational efficiencies, the adaptation of technological innovations, and the development of ICT, as well as the satisfaction of public policy goals of expanding the use of DER and clean power reliably and affordably.

As an initial matter, a choice must be made between incumbent utilities and independent entities as the DSP operator. REV recognizes that incumbent distribution utilities have decades of experience in planning, construction, monitoring, and balancing the electric system. Consequently, a DSP that operates independently from established IOUs may incur wasteful and redundant learning curve costs and may operate inefficiently. Incumbent utilities regularly interact with the bulk power market as regulated by the New York ISO and, therefore, can more efficiently coordinate and integrate T&D services. Additionally, incumbents have an array of resources that can be deployed to meet the goals of REV. The PSC adopted the REV recommendation that incumbents should serve as DSPs to enhance the "opportunity for integrated operation of the distribution system and for realizing the economic value DER investment."[121] The PSC added the caveat that incumbents will be monitored regarding the exercise of market power particularly with DSP provision of DER services that are also provided by third parties.[122]

Although incumbent IOUs will be situated in a preferred position, they will not be doing business as usual. Instead of focusing on electricity sales, their main task will be to operate a transactional energy platform and deliver and maintain a wider variety of energy products. More notably, the DSP will operate in both regulated and unregulated markets and, therefore, face greater competition than IOUs have experienced before.

Customer Participation. The traditional one-way system in which IOUs sold electricity to consumers must be abandoned in favor of the two-way system discussed throughout this chapter that involves the flow of energy and information between producers and consumers. Consumers must be active participants in the design and operation of New York's new distribution system. More particularly, the REV report focuses on the products, information and communications systems, and enabling technologies available in the new electricity market that will enable traditional consumers to take on a new role as prosumers of energy and ancillary services.[123] In order to effectively enhance consumer participation, the new framework will require more intelligent use of consumer and system data, particularly concerning price and product transparency and consistency.[124]

To make consumer participation more effective, public education will be necessary for the effective functioning of an integrated grid.[125] In order to act effectively, consumers must have information about their energy options and about the costs of exercising them. It is not too much to claim that consumers, even large users, do not fully understand various elements of their monthly bills. At the very least, consumers must understand the costs of their own usage and how to better manage it. In many instances, a simple technological fix, such as smart and programmable thermostats, can provide such information. Consumers must also understand the investments required to adopt new technologies and they will need information about the payback period needed to recoup those investments. The current proliferation of new technologies only exacerbates the information problem. Nevertheless, easy availability of information is necessary for new markets to operate efficiently. In addition to information, consumer participation will be enhanced through other techniques such as aggregation that increases consumer bargaining power and can enhance the adoption of new technologies.

All consumers are not alike. The needs and resources of small residential consumers are significantly different than those of large industrial, commercial, and manufacturing concerns. Large consumers, for example, currently avail themselves of products offered by energy services companies. Such companies can conduct audits, can provide a portfolio of services and technologies, and can help those consumers realize efficiencies. Small consumers should also have access to affordable energy services and resources. By way of examples, an energy service company could provide small consumers with metering retrofit services, wireless HVAC controls, diagnostic sensors, controllable Wi-Fi thermostats, desktop dashboard alerts, and financial business incentives. Under the New York plan, as well as the plans in Minnesota and Maryland, consumer input is a necessary element in constructing the new electricity system.

Regulatory Reform. In addressing regulatory reforms, the REV report first recognized the inadequacy of traditional COS ratemaking specifically, because it incentivized electricity sales and not utility performance. Further, the COS method is inconsistent with utilities acting as platform providers serving multiparticipant markets as intended by the DSP model that is intended to capture network benefits.[126] The report then goes on to recognize that New York had shifted to negotiated multiyear rate cases with the goal of providing opportunities for utilities to improve performance and, on occasion, provide for sharing earnings from efficiency gains with customers.[127] The New York PSC has also employed other mechanisms to adjust rates when necessary and decouple rates under specific circumstances together with the use of other performance measures. New York, like Maryland, found that these ad hoc techniques did not satisfy new and broader objectives designed to transform the entire system.[128]

The report recommended consideration of several changes to traditional ratemaking including long-term rate plans, up to eight years, that would allow utilities more planning time and should reduce the number of contentious rate cases.[129] With a longer-term plan, utilities should be able to take greater advantage of innovations, and managers should be able to concentrate on performance and customers rather than on cost savings from internal operations.

Ratemaking should focus on performance rather than on a utility's internal costs. Even under some performance-based rates,[130] a utility can increase profits by performing better on internal budgets than the rate allows. While such a performance measure improves a utility's efficiency, gains do not necessarily flow to customers because utilities keep the profits made through better business practices. Therefore, rather than basing rates on the utility's costs, rates should be based upon how well a utility satisfies new functions such as improving customer information, operational resilience, integration of renewable resources, and carbon reduction. The idea behind such performance measures is to add value to customers as well as to the utility. Such a rate-making focus, in effect, asks utilities to operate more like competitive firms rather than profit-protected firms. The need for better performance rather than for more sales is especially necessary in DER markets.[131] It should be noted that the recommendation does acknowledge that the utility service obligation will necessitate some financial protection through rates.

The REV report recognized that undergirding the adoption of any new rate-making mechanism will be a set of principles to guide regulators in choosing the proper tool and matching it with an articulated public policy. Above all, the system will be required to provide affordable universal energy service. That service will come from a mix of central and bulk power facilities as well as from consumer generation and energy efficiency measures. As a direct result of encouraging consumer generation and efficiency, rates may need to include standby tariffs so that a utility's fixed costs can be covered by all consumers whether they generate their own electricity or not.

Subsequent to the Framework Order, PSC staff issued a detailed White Paper that addressed regulatory reforms and changes in utility business models. Specifically, the staff found that hardware and software innovations could provide utilities with flexibility that could reduce their costs as well as increase the value of DER. These cost savings and increased values could improve how utilities meet their service obligations while capturing the value of third-party and customer-generated energy resources. Further, these innovations could lead to the development of the smart grid and improve reliability, resiliency, and total system value[132] including value to IOUs.[133] Thus, in order to gain these efficiencies, the staff recommended a comprehensive rate-making reform, which, in turn, would lead to the new utility business models. Regarding ratemaking, the White Paper recommended dramatic change. Traditional ratemaking was simply about allocating historic costs to customer classes. Under REV, however, rate designs should work to lower total cost through more accurate price signals.[134] The paper recognizes that there is no single formula to achieve that end. Instead, a variety of tools including net metering, distributed resources tariffs, market-based mechanisms, standby rates, demand charges,[135] smart home rates, and time-of-use rates, among others will be necessary in order to assess and value an electric system that effectively incorporates DER.[136]

The comprehensive reforms envisioned by the staff would be based upon two ideas. First, ratemaking must allow utilities to earn a fair return on investments and must encourage the integration and deployment of DER. Suggested business model reforms are intended to encourage traditional IOUs to become utilities of the future whose business is the delivery of energy and efficiency through DER, not only the sale of electricity.[137] Second, the utility of the future will operate in a more competitive environment as, "third-party and customer capital and market risk [become] added dimensions to how utilities meet their monopoly service functions."[138]

To facilitate that transition, ratemaking must employ market-based earnings opportunities together with methods to share earnings between utilities and customers through performance-based, not cost-based, rate formula. As stated in the White Paper: "The eventual shift in balance from traditional regulatory incentives to [market-based] opportunities will complete the transition to a business and regulatory model where utility profits are directly aligned with market activities that increase value to customers."[139] As examples, utilities might offer communications as well as energy services; help finance, construct, and operate microgrids; or conduct data analysis to enhance new and developing markets that utilities can benefit from and will be compensated with market-based incentives.[140]

Together with increased competition, new classes of electricity customers are also developing. By way of example, customers with and without DER will require different rate structures. In order to accommodate a variety of customers, rate-making principles are necessary and the White Paper addresses several of them including cost causation, transparency, increased granularity (i.e., serving specific groups of customers), fair value, customer orientation, and rate stability similar to the principles discussed earlier.[141]

These various customer classes can be accommodated through more sophisticated rate structures that unbundle rates to satisfy individual customer needs, that move away from volumetric block rates closer to real-time pricing, and that price electricity based upon consumers' location rather than their membership in traditional customer classes.[142]

In reviewing the staff report, the PSC concluded that the REV would put New York's electric industry "on a sustainable path to controlling customer bills and increasing system efficiency."[143] Further, the PSC recognize that BAU was not sustainable; rather BAU presented greater costs and uncertainties than the REV precisely because current market and technological trends have changed the electricity world. The PSC found that the REV recommendations were "more than sufficient, indeed they are compelling."[144] Still, the REV is seen as a starting point for the regulatory and market transformation of electric distribution in the state. Consequently, a detailed cost-benefit analysis remains to be developed and implemented through additional processes that included the input from various stakeholders. The PSC adopted the recommendation to perform further cost-benefit analysis with specific attention to be paid to utility investments in DSP and energy efficiency as well as utility costs of procuring DER services.

CONCLUSION

Throughout this discussion of new regulatory regimes, several themes emerge. First, changes in the electric industry, most notably increased competition from a multiplicity of providers, including consumers themselves, and changes in public policy, most notably in environmental regulations, are driving regulators and utilities to innovate. Second, regulators are focusing on consumer needs in order to provide more choice and capture efficiencies while diversifying energy resources. Third, the electricity market is becoming more competitive and traditional utilities must necessarily adapt. In response to all of these themes, a new regulatory compact, with a new form of ratemaking, is necessary.

The traditional regulatory compact particularly through its use of COS ratemaking sustained vertically integrated IOUs and encouraged them to expand their operations by constructing larger centralized power plants and selling more electricity. That model, based on the concept of natural monopoly, served the country well most of the century but is ill-equipped to serve the electricity future that is developing. Instead, a new regulatory compact that acknowledges increasing diversity in electricity markets is necessary, and the outlines of that compact have been explained throughout this chapter and the last one.[145] The reality of that compact is becoming more apparent as IOUs experiment with business models and as regulators attempt to support them.

The new regulatory compact, then, is based upon four principles. First, it recommends rewarding power providers for *performance and protecting public goals* such as clean air rather than applying specific regulatory tools with the primary intention of sustaining IOUs.[146] Second, the new regulatory regime moves away from *ex post* decision making such as that applied historically to rate cases and incorporates *ex ante planning* designed to be forward looking and to anticipate future challenges. Third, much of the decision making regarding electricity regulation will involve *multiple stakeholders* and will not be limited to rate contests between PUCs and individual utilities. Instead, multiple power providers as well as consumers will have increased participation in the decision-making process. The final characteristic of new regulatory scheme is that regulators will now consider a *clean power system* rather than the welfare of any individual IOU. In total, these innovative regulatory approaches are intended to treat clean power, rather than cheap electricity, as a public good that must be made readily available and affordable.

PART III

THE DEMOCRATIZATION OF ENERGY

7

Energy and Democracy

Natural disasters such as Hurricane Katrina,[1] Superstorm Sandy,[2] and the typhoon that devastated Fukushima,[3] as well as technical weaknesses that caused the Northeast blackout in October 2003[4] and regulatory failures such as that which ended California electric restructuring efforts[5] share one commonality – they all affect the energy system at enormous costs in economic losses and in disrupted lives.[6] The principal reason for high economic and social costs is that the centralized structure of electricity generation and distribution guarantees concentrated losses when these events occur. Consequently, "[e]lectricity systems are increasingly expected to be prepared for more frequent and intense storms, to rapidly respond to any disruptions, and to minimize all kinds of environmental impacts of their operations."[7] One response to these risks is to restructure the electric system through greater diversity and decentralization. Decentralization, in turn, will democratize energy through increased competition and greater consumer participation. Indeed, such restructuring was in evidence during Superstorm Sandy as microgrids and backup generators remained online and provided electricity to those displaced by the storm.[8]

In an article titled *The Politics of Nature*, Duke law professor Jedediah Purdy begins by noting that "[e]nvironmental crises are defining challenges for the next few decades and probably well beyond."[9] Climate change, of course, is the primary concern of our environmental future. And as importantly, such natural and human-caused disasters raise a large number and variety of concerns about our energy future. The energy sector constitutes approximately 8–9 percent of our country's GDP.[10] Additionally, the United States has developed an approach to the production, distribution, and consumption of energy that has lasted well over a century and is in the midst of an historic transformation.[11] Our energy history leaves a significant legacy and one that constitutes a barrier to the short-term adoption of a cleaner energy portfolio because significant financial and legal resources have been dedicated to designing and sustaining our current energy system. It has been estimated, for example, that $364 billion is spent annually on energy from centralized utilities.[12]

The direct connection between the energy industry and its regulators cannot be overstated because government regulators have supported the development of the traditional energy model. Consequently, any attempt to change a century-old system entails myriad political, policy, legal, and economic issues. Now, regulators must also actively participate in shaping, developing, and supporting a clean power transition. With the changes discussed already, the market is shifting some of that economic value away from investor-owned utilities (IOUs) to their customers and with that shift a new industry–regulator partnership is being fashioned. The reality is that changed energy and environmental circumstances and policies demand our attention and demand new policies and a new politics.

Throughout this book, the transformation of our energy economy has been examined in terms of reversing the traditional hard path of large-scale, centralized power stations toward a decentralized system in which energy, including efficiency, is produced more locally even to the point of being produced by consumers themselves. These changes were driven by technology, new market configurations, and regulatory reforms. The business initiatives discussed in Chapter 5 and the regulatory initiatives discussed in Chapter 6 indicate that both the public and private sectors are not only aware of this transition but are active participants in it. Several components are at the heart of the transformation, including reducing the scale of power production, increasing competition, reducing the dominance of vertically integrated IOUs, and increasing consumer choice. Each of those elements is consistent with the democratization of energy. To more clearly understand the changes in the industry, this chapter begins with an example of a new clean power system and then explains in more detail the democratic consequences of a new energy politics and the clean power transformation.

CLEAN POWER SYSTEM: A SIMULATION

The Massachusetts Institute of Technology's (MIT) *Utility of the Future Study*,[13] discussed in Chapter 5, engages economists, scholars, and industry experts in developing models to assess energy pricing and test accompanying economic regulations for new configurations of electricity distribution. As the distribution system becomes more localized and, more importantly, employs increasing amounts of distributed energy resources (DER), it is necessary to assess the efficiency of the new system, the types of regulations necessary to avoid economic waste, and the types of regulations that match a clean power future. One way to make that assessment is to simulate an urban distribution system, which operates largely independently of centralized power and which deploys significant amounts of DER.[14]

The MIT conducted such a simulation based on the actual characteristics of a 100 square mile section of Denver, Colorado, which allowed the simulation to test the replacement of energy facilities. The simulation relied on street maps that showed the actual topography of Denver in which approximately 190,000 people live and have various energy demands. Roughly 22 percent of the area comprises residential users using low voltage, 45 percent commercial users using medium voltage, and the remaining, industrial users using high voltage. These consumers, naturally, place different demands on the system and consume varying amounts of electricity depending upon the time of day, day of the week, and season of the year. The simulation also accounted for the use of photovoltaic solar generation and, therefore was able to test DER penetration in a dynamic energy environment.

The simulation was based upon a regulatory model that examined system costs relative to load and investments. The simulation also tests the capacity of the system operator to plan for future investments and needs. The central idea is to sharpen planning and investment decisions before the costs are incurred rather than assessing and then imposing the utility's historic costs on consumers. The model was designed to test three regulatory tools: (1) a forward-looking benchmarking of efficient network expenditures, (2) the use of incentives to generate accurate forecasts and encourage cost savings, and (3) an *ex post* adjustment mechanism. The simulation ran two basic scenarios – one that studied the system as if built from scratch and one that took an established network and anticipated changes in energy usage. Additionally, simulations were run for expansions of each basic model particularly for variations in load growth and further DER penetration.

This simulation employs the type of two-stage prudence review discussed in the last chapter. In the first *ex ante* stage, a utility submits a forecast of network uses that are subject to stakeholder and regulator comments. After receiving comments, revisions are made, a final forecast is submitted, and the regulator estimates total expenditures. The utility, then, examines the regulator's estimate and submits an investment plan for operating and capital expenditures. The regulator, in turn, establishes a revenue baseline of costs together with sharing mechanisms, accounting for total expenditures. At this time, an automatic adjustment factor becomes part of the rate to accommodate a certain degree of forecasting uncertainty. Then the final regulatory contract is published. At the end of the year, the utility reports expenditures and the regulator performs the second *ex post* review – an audit of the total expenditures together with any automatic adjustments that were made under the approved plan. At that point, efficiency incentives are computed and final revenue adjustments are calculated and published.

The *ex ante* stage of this regulatory process is crucial. At this stage, forecasting techniques are applied to set a utility's anticipated total expenditures, including operating, maintenance, and replacement costs including cost adjustments and incentives. These anticipated expenditures constitute the utility's revenue requirement. The technique is intended to estimate efficient expenditures, anticipate expansion and quality of service, and generate incentives to reduce network losses. This forecasting also includes a discussion of DER penetration as well as the likely geographic changes in load. Forecasting models "can be designed to accommodate expected changes in network use, technology performance and cost, and network management practices, these models equip the regulator with a forward-looking method to benchmark efficient total network expenditures . . . reducing the uncertainty and information asymmetry is facing the regulator."[15]

In conjunction with this *ex ante* analysis, the regulator must also specify the types of incentives that reward a utility for its efficiency gains and will then share those gains with customers. The incentives identify the *ex ante* regulatory allowances available to utilities for unanticipated costs and provides clear rules for the *ex post* evaluation of both expenditures and adjustments during the regulated period.

The final step of this model is an *ex post* review to calculate the agreed-upon adjustments for the purpose of reducing uncertainty and for providing revenue stability. Depending on the length of the regulatory period, technological and economic changes can occur that can affect the business of utility and the stability of the distribution system. Uncertainty can be reduced by allowing for *ex post* application of revenue adjustments within specified limits to avoid imposing excessive, imprudently incurred costs on customers. A range of tools exist to make these adjustments. The operative regulations can include indexing mechanisms, full or partial cost pass-throughs, revenue triggers, mid-period reviews, and contract reopeners, all of which are designed to ameliorate uncertainty costs while providing notice of possible cost adjustments to consumers.

The advantages of this model are as significant as the challenges. First, the simulated utility can be used to assess operations of actual utilities within a particular geographic service area. Next, the model is decidedly forward looking and, therefore, is an improvement of the method of the retrospective analysis of expenditures that compensates utilities based on their historic costs. Further, the model injects profit sharing into the regulatory relationship between the utility and its customers. Finally, because of the analyses made before and after expenditures, flexibility is introduced into the regulatory process, adjustments can be made more easily, and the knowledge gained by learning-as-doing can be put into use during the next iteration of the simulation.

There are, however, certain drawbacks. Most particularly, even though the model uses both cost-of-service and incentive ratemaking, such as performance-based rates, it focuses on the revenue requirements of the distribution system. Therefore, it will require other incentives for efficiency gains, for the adoption of new technologies, and for the improvement of the quality of service. In other words, regulators will need to consider additional charges to serve as incentives for those purposes.

Challenges from the model result from the granularity that the model can produce. Within a service area there will be customers with and without photovoltaic and customers with and without various sorts of DER; and, the service area can also contain microgrids, particularly with battery storage, that may operate largely or completely independently of the distribution system itself.[16]

Consequently, the difficulty comes in setting rates that fairly charge the various customer classes without burdening others. As a fundamental matter, the cost causation principle should be applied. Customers should only pay for the costs caused by their usage.[17] With advanced information and communication technologies (ICT), it should be possible to either identify customer profiles and assess costs accordingly or go further and set rates for individual customers much like rates for cellphone and Internet services. These individual rates may include a basic service charge and then a menu of customer options that are individually priced. Regardless, pricing in the telecommunications industry functions well and should serve as a model for energy producers and regulators.

THE NO UTILITY FUTURE: A THOUGHT EXPERIMENT

The simulation is intended to demonstrate the possibility that a significantly sized clean power system can operate at the local level and operate largely independently from the power grid. That simulation can be taken a step further as we consider a no-utility future. Throughout much of this book, the utility of the future has been discussed. The utility of the future has generally taken on certain characteristics as described by the business models in Chapter 5 and by the regulatory reforms examined in Chapter 6. Most often, the electricity future centered on an integrated grid that was managed by a distributed system operator (DSO) and the DSO was an incumbent IOU. In the New York, Minnesota, and Maryland plans, those states' existing IOUs played prominent roles.

It is certainly understandable that IOUs would be considered to serve as central actors in a new system because of their technical knowledge and management experience. Further, because of their sunk costs, regulators are reluctant to ignore incumbent utilities; instead, they view them as central to a successful transition. An IOU-dominated electricity future is not the only one that can be imagined. Instead of the utility of the future, consider a future with no utility in which the electricity system is locally owned and operated and serves the citizens and consumers in that area as municipally owned systems have always done.

People can live off the grid. Although the numbers are now small, "grid defection" is becoming an increasing reality for many customers and promises to increase further as consumers adopt alternative energy sources, most notably solar, and combine them with energy storage.[18] One could build an earth home that incorporates active and passive solar applications, a geothermal heat pump, a generator, and energy storage capacities and live completely unconnected to the local distribution network. The cost of living off the grid, however, is prohibitively high for most people. Further, there are network and efficiency gains to be made by living arrangements that connect people, businesses, and production facilities together. Still, the thought that even a small group of various consumer groups can exist unconnected to the local IOU is a thought experiment worth undertaking because it reveals an alternative energy policy and an alternative energy politics that generate a set of new principles that can be drawn upon to design the clean power future.

Technological advances make this thought experiment more of a reality than just an imaginative exercise. It is easier to think of living off the grid in a small community than living off of it as an individual homeowner. Still, individual homeowners who can make use of electric vehicles, solar applications, and energy storage can realize cost savings and can add real value to the local system. Through the use of storage, in particular, an individual homeowner or business owner can provide balancing services for the electricity distribution system and can, in effect, "arbitrage" energy. In other words, they can store energy when it is cheap and sell it when demand increases, thus becoming active energy market players.[19]

Home energy management systems are becoming a regular staple of television commercials. The iconic example is the commercial in which consumers sit on the porch of their vacation home and through the use of their cellphone can control the heating, cooling, home security, and other appliances in their first home. In this way, consumers are empowered by handheld devices that provide immediate access to cost information and provide immediate control over consumption choices.

Expanded opportunities for customized consumer choice are available through a range of products and services. An individual's ability to customize their use of the Internet, telephone service, entertainment services, and shopping is now ubiquitous. New business configurations accompany these changes in the way individuals shop and pay for products and services. In addition to television and cable Internet subscriptions, consider, as further examples, Uber, Airbnb, and Spotify, as well as Amazon, Dell, and eBay. The value of each of those businesses lies in connectivity, the ability to capture network effects from a great multiplicity of users, and the fact that these services can be customized to the individual consumer and priced accordingly. These businesses have created new supply chains and new value propositions and they provide models for the delivery of electricity as well. Yet, the traditional IOU does not now comfortably fit such configurations although experiments are occurring. Navigant research, for example, suggests that the electricity industry can adopt such a format, and instead of a grid controlled by traditional IOUs, the electric system would operate in an "energy cloud."[20]

The cloud can exercise a variety of functions. It can serve as a microgrid operator or a DSO, a virtual power plant, or any combination. The cloud can provide service to an individual end user, an incumbent utility, or a grid operator. In each case, the cloud, as Navigant describes it, is to serve as an "orchestrator," bringing together a wide variety of energy and service providers for the purpose of incorporating DER into the system and creating new value opportunities in the electric industry. Through aggregating consumers and providers and by coordinating transactions between and among them, the cloud creates a more open market for the purchase or sale of energy products and services. Within the energy cloud configuration, a college campus, an industrial park, a residential development, and even an entire city or part of one can operate independently of the traditional grid while having a contractual arrangement for backup power or ancillary energy services such as black start capability within the energy cloud. Another way of conceptualizing a no-utility future is through the greater penetration of microgrids. The Department of Energy defines a microgrid as a "localized grid that can disconnect from the traditional grid to operate autonomously to help mitigate grid disturbances and strengthen grid resilience."[21] Microgrids can operate completely independently from the grid or can stay connected for reserve power and other services. In either case, microgrids replace IOUs as the primary electricity providers and, in effect, reverse the assumptions about economies of scale. In an IOU-dominated electricity world, economies of scale meant that bigger was better. In a microgrid world, however, bigger is not necessarily better as microgrids are able to realize efficiencies by combining distributed generation, demand management, efficiency products and services, and storage at smaller scales to serve more local customer bases.[22]

COMPARING THE UTILITY OF THE FUTURE WITH THE NO-UTILITY FUTURE

The simulation favoring the utility of the future and the thought experiment favoring a no-utility future outline two possibilities for a clean power system. In one respect, both point in the same direction of a more decentralized energy sector that is open to more consumer input. In other respects, however, they are distinguishable regarding the role that IOUs play. Regardless, whether the energy future relies on some form of IOU or dispenses with utilities entirely, the traditional model is past its prime. More importantly, the relationship between energy producers and consumers, the competitiveness of electricity markets, and core idea that energy and economic growth are inextricably linked have changed now and for the foreseeable future.

The assumptions behind the simulation include: the necessity of disaggregating vertically integrated IOUs into independent generation and distribution management operations, the accompanying disaggregation of volumetric sales and performance, the value of using experienced IOUs to reduce learning curve costs of the transition, constructing a distribution system that links local and regional grids, and the belief that a new set of scale economies can be realized.[23] The core problem with the simulation model, and the assumptions behind it, is the commitment to a still largely centralized energy system. Indeed, the three models discussed in Chapter 5 are explicit about maintaining this commitment to incumbents.

The simulation is intended to stimulate traditionally structured IOUs into rethinking their business models. In other words, the simulation anticipates that the utility of the future will be IOU-centric and will remain revenue-based. The premise behind the simulation, then, is that the reconfigured IOU will be the utility of the future and is the preferred method for incorporating new energy and efficiency technologies, for making electricity readily available, for keeping it affordably priced, and for responding to climate change. At the heart of the simulation is an enhanced two-way smart grid that can manage all of these technological changes and, most notably, incorporate significant quantities of variable power. Although current market signals and regulatory constraints may not provide sufficient incentives for a utility to adopt this model, the simulation is also intended to demonstrate the regulatory reforms needed to provide the necessary incentives to do so. In a sense, then, the utility of the future, while not exactly business as usual, is not far from it.

With the exception of the role that IOUs will play, the no-utility thought experiment shares many of the assumptions of the simulation. Electricity should be affordable, reliable, and clean. The electric system should comprise diverse energy resources including efficiency. However, the management of the system will be independent of an IOU and will be managed both locally and equitably, which is to say that communities will have more authority over their energy economy and will be in a position to gain economic benefits that once flowed to IOUs.[24] In addition to the economic returns once captured by IOUs, the no-utility future allows customers to capture those returns and will also create jobs for the local community that it serves. The grid manager will have no ownership interest in the grid and, therefore, will have no incentive to build unnecessary facilities including generation or connections to transmission networks or distribution lines.[25]

By freeing the grid operator from a bias in favor of building physical facilities as they would under the simulation, the thought experiment enables the no-utility grid operator to promote behind-the-meter appliances and software adoptions as well as energy savings and conservation more generally. Energy savings become an asset and not a liability in the no-utility future. With a more open architecture and with a greater variety of energy services, not only will consumers have greater control over their own consumption choices but also they can be active participants in these new energy markets. With better cost information and temperature controls, for example, consumers can opt for intermittent power rather than firm power, knowing that alternatives are available when needed. Similarly, consumers can run their appliances off-peak more easily and simply use less energy rather than construct new facilities. By plugging EVs into the grid, homeowners can provide balancing, ramping, and storage services for the community. In the no-utility future, the grid is not a remote physical facility operated by a remote owner and untouched by consumer needs; rather, the localized grid is a part of the consumer community and will necessarily be more responsive to their needs.

There still remains a significant degree of utility pushback on each of these innovations and regulations. Net metering, as a prime example, has been criticized for its cross-subsidization effects. This criticism often ignores the benefits that consumers can contribute to the electric system and the argument against net metering is more of a political argument favoring incumbents than one that will improve the delivery of electricity. The argument against net metering, as well as arguments against other innovations, often focuses on lost revenue to incumbent utilities rather than on policy propositions to enhance consumer surplus.[26]

The no-utility thought experiment raises precisely the issue of where the regulatory focus should lie. Should system reforms continue to support incumbent utilities or should reforms be aimed at improving the energy system with the objective of increasing not only provider value but customer value as well? Additionally, should our energy system continue to rely on dirty fuels or should it contribute to a clean power future? The answer to both questions is that we must adopt a new energy politics, a more decentralized and democratized politics that lead to a clean future.

ENERGY DEMOCRACY

The essence of the argument that a clean power politics is needed is based on the idea that our traditional energy path (as well as its underlying assumptions) has outlived its useful life. Cheap, but dirty, fossil fuel energy has played a significant role in contributing to economic growth and to the political authority of the United States for most of the twentieth century. By the end of the century, however, the fundamental economic assumptions of traditional energy policy have proven to be seriously flawed.

As noted, technological, business, market, and regulatory changes are also driving the push for a new energy model. Simply, "[e]nergy is becoming 'personal' again in the sense that one type of service doesn't fit all."[27] Instead, because of the needs of a growingly diverse set of customer classes, even down to the individual consumer level, energy will be delivered and priced much differently than in the past. As a result of advanced ICT, emerging energy actors, new utility business models, rising consumer expectations, and regulatory initiatives, the energy landscape is transforming from a century-old centralized fossil fuel model to a decentralized clean power system.

The notion of utility service is changing radically. Historically, utility service simply meant the sale and delivery of electricity to end users. Today, utility service must be reconfigured in two ways. The first shift is from *utility* to *multiple providers*. The second shift is from *electricity* to *energy* (including efficiency). More particularly, "the next-generation definition … of *service* will involve intelligent, sustained support for customers as they make their energy choices and investments. This new definition will also involve support for energy markets as they respond to customer needs and market opportunities."[28] Instead of a large, centralized, interstate fossil-fuel IOU electricity system, the electricity system of the future can be decarbonized, decentralized, and democratized through such configurations as new publicly owned electric utilities, community choice aggregations, or community renewable projects.[29]

The new approach to energy service is customer-centric. In the words of Larry Kellerman, former president of Goldman Sachs' electric power business and now managing partner of Twenty First Century Utilities, the new approach is democratizing.[30] Customers will no longer remain passive consumers of IOU electricity; instead, they will be active participants in new energy markets. Not only may customers reduce consumption, but also they can actually provide energy into the system and provide energy services such as off-peak storage. Although the threat of going off the grid is only nascent, it is a real one nonetheless as these developments show the "increasing recognition of both the potentially disruptive nature of distributed resources and the potential benefits that they might bring."[31]

The clean power future is daunting, particularly if one thinks about the energy future strictly in terms of combating climate change. It is complex, uncertain, and fraught with challenges, not the least of which implicates individual and social psychology that little, if anything, can be or should be done to stand global climate threats. Given the magnitude of the problem, individual or local action may appear futile. Yet, such a pessimistic view is not the case. Instead, a new narrative about the energy/environmental future can be constructed that draws on historic democratic values and can empower us to critically assess traditional policies as well as reevaluate existing legal and political structures.

A new clean power narrative generates an important array of democratic values. Local control imparts a sense of community and responsibility not only for the land on which we live but also for future generations. Also, local arrangements can be more easily made to address regional energy and environmental needs including conservation, species protection, waste disposal, and sustainable agricultural practices among others that are responsive to a warming Earth.[32] This new narrative is more than an exercise of political imagination, it is a road map for a better and more vibrant political economy, a political economy that brings with it new arrangements of political institutions and new political commitments dedicated not only to the needs of the present but also to the needs of the future. It is a political economy of collective engagement and the exercise of an active citizen voice, not the passive actions of the energy consumers of the past.[33]

Local, democratic actions have a vital role to play in developing a forward-thinking clean power ethic. Such energy/environmental action is directly linked with democracy as people who engage in those activities say that they do so because of "the importance of building community; doing the 'right thing' irrespective of outcome; leaving a legacy of trying to avert tragedy for future generations, even if tragedy ensues; and establishing habits and patterns that will equip us and future generations to live in a very different world."[34]

Local energy/environmental action is a reality, not only a possibility. By engaging in activities such as 350.org,[35] voluntary carbon action reduction groups,[36] or the Solutions Project that aims to achieve 100 percent clean energy,[37] individual behavior is changing as consumers reorient their political lives from energy consumerism to democratic energy participation. Proactive involvement with the energy/environmental complex at the local and individual levels is a significant change in thinking about the energy future. Individual action does lead to behavioral change to the good. Just in the category of efficiency improvements, individuals report switching from incandescent to compact fluorescent and LED light bulbs and purchasing more efficient water heaters, furnaces, and toilets, as well as installing programmable thermostats, ceiling fans, and better insulation, all to the end of smarter and more controlled electricity consumption.[38]

It is important to acknowledge that local political actions should not be seen as short-term activities in which participants accept economic losses through reduced consumption; nor must they be seen as activities in which participants absorb the costs of environmental adaptation or mitigation. Instead, political participation should be viewed as a gain in greater democracy and consumer control.[39] Moreover, political participation can also sustain efficient and clean energy markets.

How, though, does an emerging clean power politics connect with democracy? The central democratic principle is to promote greater participation and voice in political and economic institutions. Increased participation, in turn, can generate consensus about public policy among different stakeholders and can generate a greater variety of approaches, solutions, options, and alternatives during the period of transition.[40] A more democratic clean power paradigm affects the production and delivery of energy, its consumption and control, its regulation and enforcement, and energy planning and governance.

Production and Delivery of Clean Power

Significant changes in the production and delivery of electricity are well under way. Today's electricity providers no longer resemble their historic counterparts as the provision and delivery of electricity has become more complex. Although vertically integrated IOUs still supply over half of the nation's electricity, the business structure of electric power providers now assumes multiple forms. Merchant generators, independent system operators, and independent or merchant transmission companies are remaking the electric industry and its regulation. Similarly, "[a]ncillary services such as voltage support, black-start capability, and system balancing can be provided by regulated entities or independent parties competitively bidding for the work."[41] There is an upside to this complexity. As more actors enter the market, competition for production, delivery, and ancillary services increases and consumers should enjoy lower prices and more options.

More importantly, fossil fuel electricity is slowly being replaced. Renewable power generation has, for over 50 years, played a marginal role in power generation.[42] Today, although the contributions of renewable resources, including hydropower, constitute about 12 percent of the US energy profile, their role is growing and is projected to grow significantly in the future, covering up to 80 percent of our electricity needs, as costs of nonfossil fuel resources continue to decline.[43] Indeed, solar power is becoming increasingly affordable as prices have declined by 80 percent in recent years. Similarly, wind power costs have likewise declined over 30 percent as both technologies gain market share.[44] And, demand-side management programs, which treat energy efficiency as an energy resource, help stimulate demand for and local use of smart appliances and controls.[45] Rooftop solar, energy efficiency standards, efficient appliances, heat pumps, and a large array of consumer-friendly technologies produce energy or energy savings right in the backyard or right in the home. Energy production and delivery, through these small-scale technologies, is thus decentralized and is consistent with the alternative soft energy path.[46]

Decentralized power generation can increase grid reliability, improve cybersecurity, reduce congestion, reduce the costs of long-distance transmission, reduce the need for more centralized transmission and distribution facilities, increase efficiency, and expand the number of energy resources used to produce electricity. By way of example, it has been estimated that 80–90 percent of all grid failures begin at the distribution stage. Consequently smaller-scale distribution systems can enhance reliability from the bottom-up rather than from the top-down.[47] Additionally, the smart grid, with its two-way information, as well as energy flows, can improve signals to consumers and can improve forecasting and load balancing.[48] Further, individual consumers can serve as generators by selling electricity back to the grid from the electricity that they generate and they can help improve reliability, particularly as they adopt demand response strategies and expand their storage capacities such as home batteries, solar-plus-storage, and EVs.[49]

As local and state governments expand opportunities for clean energy technologies, especially distributed generation and DER, these experiments will have a direct effect on the entire electric sector. "By any account, decarbonizing the U.S. electric power sector will require large new investments (at multiple scales), sustained technological innovation, extensive reformer regulatory and market structures, and the development of new business models."[50] Fortunately, utilities are experimenting with innovative business models; regulators are experimenting with innovative rate reforms and redesigning whole systems; and consumers have available a wider array of energy products and services to meet energy needs as well as environmental goals in affordable and reliable ways.[51]

Consumption and Control of Clean Power

Consider, next, the consumption and control of energy. As noted earlier, power providers are offering a greater range of services as they participate in regulated and unregulated markets. IOUs no longer monopolize the power production market; instead, they must compete with nonutility providers of various configurations. On the demand side, opportunities to increase market competition are also available. Local governments or private firms can form entities known as power aggregators that can reduce collective action problems by grouping together a large number of small consumers and serve as buying agents to negotiate contract terms and rates for them.[52] Even more substantially, aggregations can form to operate and even own distribution systems as described in the no-utility future scenario.

Smart electricity meters, programmable appliances and thermostats, a variety of energy apps, combined heat and power systems, microgrids, and virtual power plants[53] all provide consumers with the power to control consumption at prices they prefer.[54] In this way, consumer choice is expanded and participation in and control of energy markets expand as more "household and businesses [become] more active participants in [the electricity] infrastructure."[55] Customer choice at the retail level can outperform traditional IOU service, enable consumer control, and provide energy savings for customers.[56] More notably, even, is the rise of the prosumer that both produces and consumes power and can actively participate in energy markets.[57] In short, decision making about energy consumption (and sales) moves from producers to consumers and nowhere is this more apparent than through the increasingly widespread use of DER.

DER generally and microgrids particularly "offer a bottom-up solution platform, often tailored to the specific needs of an end-use customer."[58]

Additionally, small-scale energy facilities can avoid difficult siting issues, can minimize or avoid NIMBY problems such as those posed by larger-scale installations, and can provide energy savings to adopters.[59] Further, efficient use of the smart grid can "empower citizens to more actively engaged in the generation and management of the electricity system at multiple levels"[60] and "in making important decisions about how they will interact with the electricity system"[61] because more information will be available to them with which to make choices. DER "can enable customers and communities to invest much more directly in the transition to a renewable energy future."[62]

Additionally, smart utilities will take advantage of these technological and market changes and serve as managers of reconfigured distribution systems that have the potential of becoming the "vehicles that maximize the value of investments in smart grid infrastructure, and can leverage these utility-owned assets with customer-owned assets."[63]

The concept of bringing together multiple energy producers and consumers is simply an extension of the type of network actors now delivering a wide variety of shopping and telecommunication services. Actors such as Google, Amazon, and eBay, or even social sites such as Facebook, become the central nodes in a network that aggregates information about products and services and makes that information available to billions of customers. The future electric industry can adopt this type of platform. Most importantly, as the number of providers and services increases and as access to those providers and services is facilitated, competition and consumer choice expand.

Regulation and Enforcement of Clean Power

Similarly, the regulation and enforcement of a clean power regime moves from IOUs to additional producers and to consumers. In a clean power economy, there are more producers, more and varied technologies, and increased consumer choice, resulting in greater market discipline thus reducing the need for central government enforcement. At the federal level, for example, actors in wholesale electricity markets have the opportunity for market-based rates that are monitored but not set by the Federal Energy Regulatory Commission. And, at the state level, while retail deregulation has not taken hold to any significant degree, consumer choice of providers is a reality in many jurisdictions. In both instances, the hand of regulation has been lessened. Further, regulation and enforcement at the local level means greater access to the energy system as well as to the political system by citizens/consumers, which should lead to more responsive government behavior.[64]

From the supply side, given the radical changes necessary to move to clean power and away from fossil fuels, new electricity markets are being developed and shaped with an eye on better, more efficient, and cleaner electricity. It is quite likely "that as the electric power system becomes more participatory, the importance of a broad public utility framework to support planning, coordination, and innovation only increases."[65] In other words, a broader energy system framework will require regulators to monitor non-IOU as well as IOU service providers, assess and advance the public policies surrounding an energy transition, and listen to the voices of consumers. In turn, innovative utility business models and innovative regulations will be measured, in large part, on how consumer responsive those innovations actually are.

The regulatory and other legal institutions surrounding a clean power economy shift, at least in part, from the federal to the local level. Citizen participation in energy and climate actions can take place more easily at the local level whether it is a movement to ban or allow fracking in the community,[66] to construct or reject windmill sites, to adopt local energy efficiency standards, or to implement energy-efficient and clean energy-based building codes.[67] Local governments can become active participants in the new energy economy as they make decisions about how their buildings are constructed such as whether they should be certified by Leadership in Energy and Environmental Design or how much efficiency and clean energy should be used to power them. Local governments can also make decisions about the fuels to be used in, and the vehicle efficiency standards of, their fleets.

Additionally, local regulation of diverse energy resources can enhance protection for those local natural resources as well as facilitate energy development planning.[68] Well thought-out energy, environmental, and land-use planning for a community can help either avoid or defer the need for costly expansions of transmission, can distribute savings benefits to both utilities and consumers, and can reduce the costs caused by carbon emissions as examples.[69] Further, energy self-sufficiency for a community can be planned for on a more localized and less expensive basis. In this way, planning goes contrary to traditional utility regulation that rewarded the utility for its capital investments as decisions are transferred from producers to consumers and to their local governments.

While numerous benefits accrue to decentralized energy, conflicts also attend the energy sector and those conflicts are often costly. The proper choice of governance level is not easy for any number of reasons including the fact that different energy resources are located in different geographic areas and have different consequences throughout their fuel cycles. Therefore, energy conflicts abound. Conflicts occur between different energy resources. Wind and solar installations, for example, which may be installed on the surface may also sit over oil and gas reserves that likewise contribute to the energy sector. Consequently, there are property ownership conflicts that must be resolved and that have an effect on the energy future. Additionally, energy resources are found on public and private lands, introducing conflicts among various interested parties. Conflicts, then, occur between different mineral estates; they occur between state and local governments as well as between state and federal regulators.[70] Still, many of these conflicts will be pushed down to the local level rather than determined in the hearing rooms of federal agencies in Washington, DC. Regardless of an increase in possible conflicts among energy producers and consumers, the conflicts can be mediated by improved and more democratic planning and governance mechanisms.

Planning and Governance

Because the electric system must be in balance, planning is always necessary. Today, planning is gaining importance for a variety of reasons including the multiplicity of providers and services, the rise of prosumers, new utility business models and regulatory requirements, and the increased use of variable resources and DER. As a result of these drivers, there is also increased need for resource planning, transparency, and coordination among all of these market actors.

In different degrees, the regulatory models proposed for Minnesota, Maryland, and New York all provide for greater citizen participation in planning for the energy future. Most notably, under Maryland's proposal, citizen evaluation of a utility's energy services will be used to design the metrics against which the utility will be assessed and compensated. Even greater citizen participation is available with the no-utility future thought experiment. As a new, more responsive and resilient grid develops, stakeholder engagement will be central to its success. More notably, the no-utility future essentially means that customers own and operate the distribution system that serves them. Energy governance under this scenario rests in the hands of consumers, not IOUs. This radical change in governance will require a significant amount of public education.

In order to attain effective governance, stakeholder education will be necessary for consumers and it will be necessary for industry and regulators. All of these actors will need to know the types of products and services that will be available, their costs and economic values, the terms and conditions of service, and the contours and limits of governance rules. Precisely because of differing producer and consumer expectations and needs, bringing together various stakeholders in the planning process can enhance the understanding of the new electricity system, the available economic gains, and their changing roles.

At the federal level, the Clean Power Plan (CPP) also recognized that a "robust and meaningful public participation process during state plan development is critical."[71] While public participation regulations for plan implementation have been in place,[72] the final CPP rule specified minimum compliance requirements including the necessity for a public hearing on the final plan before that plan is adopted by the state and submitted to the Environmental Protection Agency. Regulators are also encouraged to engage other state government agencies such as utility regulators and state energy offices and to engage localities and community-based organizations. Further, states are encouraged to conduct outreach meetings particularly to vulnerable communities. In order to satisfy requirements, states must provide "meaningful engagement" as defined by the CPP and states must provide certification that the plan was made available to the public with reasonable notice and an opportunity to be heard before final comments are made.[73]

Utilities must understand that their customers not only can, but are, exercising more choice than in the past, sometimes to the point of defecting the grid entirely. Even those customers who generate their own electricity may need ancillary services such as voltage control and frequency regulation as well as emergency power from the utilities and, therefore, they stay connected. Notwithstanding the degree of grid defection, accurate information about the cost and value of energy products and services is essential for the efficient operation of these new markets.[74] Future regulation must necessarily play a more active role in consumer engagement and better understand customer needs, the challenges faced by consumers and producers and the availability of a panoply of energy services and products for a more efficient system irrespective of whether a state adopts a utility of the future model or the model of a no-utility future.[75]

A substantial literature exists exploring the problem of what level of government is optimal for energy and environmental regulation. Optimality may well be a goal to be pursued, yet existing legal institutions present obstacles to a smooth transition from one regulatory regime to another. Regardless, a case can be made for at least a set of local energy regulations from two perspectives. First, local regulators enjoy certain advantages over other levels of government. Second, citizens, too, enjoy certain advantages in dealing with local governments.

The literature that discusses the level of governance, particularly with reference to environmental regulation, encounters a prisoner's dilemma problem, sometimes referred to as a race-to-the-bottom.[76] The core idea behind this dilemma is that competing regulatory entities, whether they are states or local governments, are reluctant to engage in aggressive environmental regulations for fear of losing a competitive advantage against other communities. Consequently, often it is not in anyone's best economic interests to aggressively regulate the environment. As a direct consequence of this disincentive to enact environmental regulation, society sustains pollution costs that should have been avoided. The CPP provided an incentive for regulators to address both energy and the environment more comprehensively.

Clean technologies enable regulators to offer a different power paradigm than environmental regulations alone. Decentralized, small-scale, labor-intensive clean energy industries and activities should offer a locality a competitive advantage by stimulating jobs,[77] innovations,[78] and investments.[79] Further, local and state governments can serve as "policy laboratories" that engage in regulatory experimentation, which should promote efficiency gains through competition; develop best practices for the local use and distribution of energy; engage in public education through the accumulation and dissemination of local knowledge; enable localities to scale energy activities to the tasks most suitable to them; and search for cooperative solutions with and among other layers of government.[80]

While state governments were required by the CPP to reimagine their energy and environmental policies, local governments can also participate in this energy transition. Local governments have decided advantages for the implementation of clean power technologies and regulations. Land-use decisions, for example, have been traditionally delegated to local governments. Consequently, local governments have knowledge about local conditions that can determine which technologies will be most effective and where.[81] "Variables including the nature of city's primary energy sources, local climate and weather patterns, the nature of the built environment, zoning plans, growth plans, population, and local economic conditions are all directly relevant to the choice of one or more distributed renewable technologies and the means of deployment."[82] Indeed, municipal initiatives now under way involve hundreds of cities engaged in addressing issues including climate change, green job creation, energy efficiency, and alternative fuels.[83]

Local governments have a shared interest with their citizens in promoting local economic development and encouraging clean energy innovators. Through such a shared approach, energy goals and priorities should be more clearly defined; regulatory risks should also be more clearly defined and monetized and, in fact, considerably reduced; and planning and investment should be more reliable and stable.[84] In other words, clean energy planning policies can avoid the race-to-the-bottom problem encountered with environmental regulation.

Small-scale energy technologies deployed at the local level will have shorter time horizons for investment, will require less capital per project, and can rely on arrangements with local government. Community solar projects, for example, involve aggregations of end users who buy at least a portion of their electricity from a decentralized, local solar facility. Because these projects are at a scale larger than individual rooftop solar installations, community solar captures the benefits of both while achieving greater efficiencies than either rooftop or utility-scale can deliver.[85] This investment scenario differs markedly from large-scale projects particularly for nuclear power or clean coal projects that rely on carbon capture and sequestration. Regulatory uncertainties as well as longer time horizons make the cost of capital for those large-scale projects increasingly prohibitive.[86]

From the citizen side of the equation, local energy regulation has the advantage of reducing collective action problems as described in the public choice literature. Local political action (1) will be less costly in terms of organizing, lobbying, preparing for and attending hearings; (2) will also reduce the number of free-riders, thus encouraging participation; (3) should galvanize interest and sharpen the focus on the specific issues to be addressed; (4) should be able to clarify policy initiatives and goals; and (5) should help local businesses deploy energy innovations.[87] Consequently, local government officials are more responsive to citizen concerns while issues are aired, debated, and modified more readily at the local than at either the state or national levels.[88]

Through all of these processes, citizen participation is heightened as citizens choose new political ends, in this case, an integrated clean power future.[89] Such is the democratic impulse. As distributed generation, decentralization and small-scale energy technologies expand, utilities will rethink their business models; consumers will play a more participatory role in energy planning and consumption; and regulators will be called upon to better manage the energy system by balancing new consumer demands with new electric systems. A new and more democratic regulatory framework will develop "to support planning, coordination and innovation"[90] for the clean power transition.

Finally, there is one other dimension of energy democracy that must be considered. The transition to a new energy economy can only be successfully achieved through well thought-out and considered public–private partnerships where government is not the problem, but is part of the solution. Markets are not eschewed in favor of government control. Nor is government regulation eschewed in a bow to market fundamentalism. Instead, government regulation, especially in the development of innovative energy technologies, serves as a stimulant and partner to the private sector.

CONCLUSION

The CPP was intentionally designed to respond to the challenges of climate change such as those suggested by the natural disasters recently encountered. It does so by aligning energy and environmental regulation. Therefore, the CPP, whether it withstands judicial review or not, stands as a significant marker in the US transition to a clean energy economy. The CPP, however, is not the only driver of change in the power sector and in our energy economy more generally. Changes in technology, markets, business practices, and regulations are all driving the transition to clean power. Because of the prominence of energy incumbents, there is resistance to this change and it is a resistance that may not benefit our economic future. Climate change is a paradigmatic example of either paying now or paying later, and later payments will be more costly.

In order to facilitate the transition, a new energy politics is necessary for a more comprehensive understanding of the needs and promises of that future. The drivers already mentioned have provided an important opportunity to change the energy/environmental conversation, identify new political and community values, and explore a new narrative and identity through an active democratic politics.

As an energy society, we can continue discussing a nuclear renaissance, increases in domestic oil and gas production, and/or the potential for clean coal, or we can abandon this old conversation and develop a new set of energy and environmental commitments – a set of commitments that advance the interests of citizens/consumers in the emerging economy. The choice seems obvious as we continue to develop an energy transition away from a traditional fossil fuel economy to one in which environmental concerns are treated together with our energy demands. Incumbent firms, existing institutions and regulations, and the old energy narrative will continue to influence public discussion. A new narrative is developing that is attentive to emerging energy technologies, cognizant of environmental consequences of the fuel cycle, and committed to developing a wider range of energy resources, markets, and participants on both the supply and demand sides of the meter not only to meet but also to actively pursue a more democratic clean power future.

Notes

INTRODUCTION

1. Coral Davenport, *Nations Approve Landmark Climate Accord in Paris*, N.Y. Times (December 12, 2015).
2. White House, Remarks by President Obama at the First Session of COP21 (November 30, 2015) available at www.whitehouse.gov/the-press-office/2015/11/30/remarks-president-obama-first-session-cop21.
3. *United Nations Framework Convention on Climate Change, Paris Agreement*, FCCC/CP/2015/L.9/Rev.1 (December 12, 2015) available at http://unfccc.int/resource/docs/2015/cop21/eng/l09r01.pdf.
4. Bill McKibben, *Falling Short on Climate in Paris*, N.Y. Times (December 13, 2015).
5. Bruce Jones & Adele Morris, *Beyond the Paris Agreement: COP21 Shouldn't Be a Milestone, but Rather a Launching Pad for a New Phase of Climate Action*, Planetpolicy (December 14, 2015); Justin Gillis, *Climate Accord Is a Healing Step, if Not a Cures*, N.Y. Times (December 12, 2015).
6. Julie Hirschfeld Davis, *Obama, Once a Guest, Is Now a Leader in World Talks*, N.Y. Times (December 12, 2015).
7. Editorial, *Silence on the Climate Pact from the Republican Candidates*, N.Y. Times (December 14, 2015); Coral Davenport, *Nations Approve Landmark Climate Accord in Paris*, N.Y. Times (December 12, 2015).
8. Clifford Krauss & Keith Bradsher, *Climate Deal Is Signal to Industry: The Era of Carbon Reduction Is Here*, N.Y. Times (December 13, 2015); Andrew C. Revkin, *The Climate Path Ahead*, Sunday Review: N.Y. Times (December 12, 2015).
9. Breakthrough Energy Coalition homepage at www.breakthroughenergycoalition.com/en/index.html.
10. Mission Initiative homepage at http://mission-innovation.net/.
11. Babara Grady, *Banks Shift Billions and Billions into Clean Energy*, GreenBiz (November 19, 2015).
12. Goldman Sachs GS Sustain, *The Low Carbon Economy: Key Takeaways from the Paris Agreement* (December 14, 2015).
13. Justin Gillis & Clifford Krauss, *Inquiry Weighs Whether Exxon Lied on Climate*, N.Y. Times A1 (November 6, 2015); Timothy Egan, *Exxon Mobil and the G.O.P.: Fossil Fools*, N.Y. Times (November 5, 2015), www.nytimes.com/2015/11/06/opinion/fossil-fools.html.

1 THE CLEAN POWER PLAN AND CLEAN POWER POLITICS

1. Coral Davenport & Gardiner Harris, *Obama to Unveil Tougher Climate Plan With His Legacy in Mind*, N.Y. TIMES 1 (August 2, 2015).
2. Environmental Protection Agency, *Carbon Pollution Emission Guidelines for Existing Stationary Sources: Electric Generating Units; Final Rule*, 80 FED. REG. 64661(2015) (FINAL RULE).
3. WILLIAM W. BUZBEE ET AL., THE CLEAN POWER PLAN: ISSUES TO WATCH (2015) (a report for the Center for Progressive Reform); Emily Hammond & Richard J. Pierce, Jr., *The Clean Power Plan: Testing the Limits of Administrative Law and the Electric Grid*, 7 GEO. WASH. J ENERGY & ENVT L. 1 (2016).
4. *Chamber of Commerce v. EPA*, 577 U.S. (February 9, 2016) available at www.supremecourt.gov/orders/courtorders/020916zr3_hf5m.pdf.
5. US ENERGY INFORMATION ADMINISTRATION, MONTHLY ENERGY REVIEW 16 (June 2015).
6. CENTER FOR THE NEW ENERGY ECONOMY, POWERING FORWARD: PRESIDENTIAL AND EXECUTIVE AGENCY ACTIONS TO DRIVE CLEAN ENERGY IN AMERICA 1 (2014).
7. ALISON CASSADY, THE CLEAN POWER PLAN: A CRITICAL STEP TOWARDS DECARBONIZING AMERICA'S ENERGY SYSTEM (APRIL 15, 2015) (a report for the Center for American Progress).
8. In the case of *In Re: Murray Energy Corp. v. EPA*, Docket No. 14–1112 (D.C. Cir. June 9, 2015), the court rejected the legal challenge to the CPP on the basis that the rule was only proposed and was not "final." This decision leaves open the question of EPA's authority to issue the CPP, and lawsuits challenging the final rule have been filed. *State of West Virginia, et al. v. EPA*, Case No. 15–1363 (United States Circuit Court of Appeals for the District of Columbia Circuit October 23, 2015).
9. Tina Calilung, *The Clean Power Plan: An Introduction to Cooperative Federalism in Energy Regulation*, 4 AMERICAN U. BUS. L. REV. 323 (2015).
10. Environmental Protection Agency, *Carbon Pollution Emission Guidelines for Existing Stationary Sources: Electric Generating Units*, 79 FED. REG. 34830 (June 18, 2014). This rule for existing power plants follows previous rules addressed at curbing emissions reductions from new electric generating facilities and from modified and reconstructed plants. *See* Environmental Protection Agency, *Standards for Performance for Greenhouse Gas Emissions from New Stationary Sources: Electric Utility Generating Units*, 79 FED. REG. 10750 (February 26, 2014); Environmental Protection Agency, *Carbon Pollution Standards for Modified and Reconstructed Stationary Sources: Electric Utility Generating Units*, 79 FED. REG. 34960 (June 18, 2014).
11. FINAL RULE at 64,704–07.
12. 79 FED. REG. at 34,856.
13. FINAL RULE at 64,665. In the CPP, the EPA also envisions emissions reductions of sulfur dioxide, nitrogen oxides, and fine particulate matter. 79 FED. REG. at 34,839.
14. National Conference of State Legislatures, *State Renewable Portfolio Standards and Goal* (January 1, 2014) available at www.ncsl.org/research/energy/renewable-

portfolio-standards.aspx; DSIRE & NC Clean Energy Technology Center, *Database of State Incentives for Renewables & Efficiency* available at www.dsireusa.org/.

15. 79 FED. REG. at 34,846–57.
16. US EPA, *Regulatory Impact Analysis for the Low Carbon Pollution Guidelines for Existing Power Plants and Emission Standards for Modified and Reconstructed Power Plants* (June 2, 2014) available at www2.epa.gov/carbon-pollution-standards/clean-power-plan-proposed-rule-regulatory-impact-analysis.
17. FINAL RULE at 64,679–82. 79 FED. REG. at 34,936; *see also* ENVIRONMENTAL PROTECTION AGENCY, CLIMATE CHANGE IN THE UNITED STATES: BENEFITS GLOBAL ACTION (2015).
18. Energy Innovation Policy and Technology LLC, *Energy Policy Solutions: The Clean Power Plan Is within Reach* (October 2015).
19. FINAL RULE at 64,679–82. *See also* David B. Spence & David E. Adelman, *Cost-Benefit Politics in U.S. Energy Policy* (August 11, 2015) available at http://papers.ssrn.com/sol3/papers.cfm?abstract_id=2642459.
20. *Michigan v. EPA*, 135 S. Ct. 2699, 576 U.S. (2015).
21. *Michigan v. EPA*, 135 S. Ct. 2699, 2715, 576 U.S. (2015) (Slip Op. at 14). Note that the dissent argues that the EPA, on numerous occasions, in fact, considered the costs and benefits of the rule.
22. FINAL RULE at 64,682.
23. FINAL RULE at 64,745.
24. Inara Scott, *Teaching an Old Dog New Tricks: Adapting Public Utility Commissions to Meet Twenty-First Century Climate Challenges*, 38 HARV. ENVT. L. REV. 371 (2014).
25. FINAL RULE at 64,795.
26. FINAL RULE at 64,803–04.
27. FINAL RULE at 64,804.
28. FINAL RULE at 64,809.
29. John Hargrove, *Life without Building Block 4: Energy Efficiency under EPA's Clean Power Plan*, 153 PUB. UTIL. FORT. 20 (October 2015).
30. 79 FED. REG. at 34,871.
31. The proposed rule cited the following: Electric Power Research Institute, *U.S. Energy Efficiency Potential Through 2035* (April 2014); Want Yu & Marilyn A. Brown, *Policy Drivers for Improving Electricity End-Use Efficiency in the U.S.: An Economic-Engineering Analysis* (2014). *See also* MCKINSEY GLOBAL ENERGY AND MATERIAL, UNLOCKING ENERGY EFFICIENCY IN THE U.S. ECONOMY (July 2009); NATIONAL ACADEMY OF SCIENCES, NATIONAL ACADEMY OF ENGINEERING & NATIONAL RESEARCH COUNCIL, AMERICA'S ENERGY FUTURE: TECHNOLOGY AND TRANSFORMATION, ch. 4 (2009); MICHAEL B. GERRARD (ed.), THE LAW OF CLEAN ENERGY: EFFICIENCY AND RENEWABLES (2011); AMERICAN COUNCIL FOR AN ENERGY-EFFICIENT ECONOMY, ENERGY EFFICIENCY IN THE UNITED STATES: 35 YEARS AND COUNTING (June 30, 2015).
32. MAGGIE MOLINA, THE BEST VALUE FOR AMERICA'S ENERGY DOLLAR: A NATIONAL REVIEW OF THE COST OF UTILITY ENERGY EFFICIENCY

PROGRAMS (March 2014) (a report for the American Council for an Energy-Efficient Economy).

33. Charles T. Driscoll et al., *US Power Plant Carbon Standards and Clean Air and Health Co-Benefits*, NATURE CLIMATE CHANGE (May 4, 2015).
34. Energy Efficiency Improvement Act of 2015, S.535, 114th Cong 1st Sess. (2015); David Jackson, *Obama Signs Energy Efficiency Bill*, USA TODAY (April 30, 2015); White House, *Remarks by President before Signing the Energy Efficiency Improvement Act of 2015* (April 30, 2015); Coral Davenport, *Congress Passes Bipartisan Bill to Improve Energy Efficiency*, N.Y. TIMES (April 21, 2015). In addition, Congress is considering legislation to extend production tax credits for energy-efficient investments as well as provide financial supports for efficient building codes, energy-saving technologies, and other efficiency measures. Linda Hardesty, *Energy Legislation Moves in Congress*, ENERGY MANAGER TODAY (July 24, 2015).
35. Alliance to Save Energy, *Fact Sheet: Energy Efficiency Improvement Act of 2015* (March 30, 2015).
36. Susan F. Tierney & Paul J. Hibbard, *Carbon Control and Competitive Wholesale Electricity Markets: Compliance Paths for Efficient Market Outcomes* (May 2015).
37. Executive Office of the President, *The President's Climate Action Plan* (June 2013).
38. Coral Davenport & Julie Hirschfield Davis, *Move to Fight Obama's Climate Plan Started Early*, N.Y. TIMES A1 (August 4, 2015).
39. Clean Air Act, §111(d); 42 U.S.C. §7411(d). *See also* 79 FED. REG. at 34,851–55.
40. *Massachusetts v. EPA*, 549 U.S. 497 (2007); *American Elec. Power Co. v. Connecticut*, 564 U.S.410 (2011).
41. *Utility Air Regulation Group v. EPA*, 134 S. Ct. 2427, 2446, 573 U.S. (June 23, 2014).
42. *Mississippi Comm'n on Envt. Quality v. EPA*, 2015 WL 3461262 (D.C. Cir. 2015).
43. *Whitman v. Am. Trucking Ass'n*, 531 U.S. 457 (2001).
44. 42 U.S.C. § 111(d)(2); *Texas v. EPA*, 726 F. 3d 180 (D.C. Cir. 2013); *see also* Daniel P. Selmi, *Federal Implementation Plans for Controlling Carbon Emission from Existing Power Plants: A Primer for Exploring the Issue* (May 2015).
45. For contrasting positions on the legal arguments, *compare* Testimony of Laurence H. Tribe, Before the House Committee on Energy and Commerce, Subcommittee on Energy and Power, EPA's Proposed 111 (D) Rule for Existing Power Plants: Legal Costs and Issues (March 17, 2015) (opposing EPA authority); *In Re Murray Energy Corp.*, Final Opening Brief of Petitioner, United States District Court, District Of Columbia, Dkt. No, 14–1112 (March 9, 2015) (same) with Testimony of Richard Revesz, Before the House Committee on Energy and Commerce, Subcommittee on Energy and Power (March 17, 2015) (supporting EPA jurisdiction); *In Re Murray Energy Corp.*, Amicus Curiae Brief of Law Professors in support of Respondents, United States District Court, District Of Columbia, Dkt. No, 14–1112 (February 19, 2015) (same).
46. Spence & Adelman.

47. Philip Wallach & Curtlyn Kramer, *State Environmental Agencies Comments on the Clean Power Plan* (May 2015).
48. League of Conservation Voters, *National Environmental Scorecard* available at http://scorecard.lcv.org/.
49. Rebecca Kaplan & Ellen Uchimiya, *Where the 2016 Republican Candidates Stand on Climate Change* (September 1, 2015) (blog post for CBS News); Chris Mooney, Amid Record Global Temperatures, Senate Votes to Block Obama's Clean Power Plan, WASH. POST (November 17, 2015).
50. David M. Herszenhorn, *Votes in Congress Move to Undercut Climate Pledge*, N.Y. TIMES (December 1, 2015); John Schwartz, *Chief of House Science Panel Picks Battle Over Climate Paper*, N.Y. TIMES (December 4, 2015).
51. Jeremy Richardson et al., *States of Progress: Existing Commitments to Clean Energy but Most States on Track to Meet Clean Power Plan's 2020 Benchmarks* (June 3, 2015) (a PowerPoint report for the Union of Concerned Scientists).
52. OnPoint, *Clean Power Plan: NARUC's Kavulla Says Federal Compliance Plan Not Acceptable to States* (December 7, 2015). *See also* Martin T. Ross, David Hoppock & Brian C. Murray, *Ongoing Evolution of the Electricity Industry: Effects of Market Conditions and the Clean Power Plan on States* (July 2016) (CPP compliance costs "relatively inexpensive").
53. FINAL RULE at 64,674–75.
54. FINAL RULE at 64,675.
55. FINAL RULE at 64,675–76.
56. William S. Scherman & Jason J. Fleischer, *The Environmental Protection Agency and the Clean Power Plan: A Paradigm Shift in Energy Regulation Away from Energy Regulators*, 36 ENERGY L. J. 355 (2015).
57. SUSAN TIERNEY, ERIC SVENSON & BRIAN PARSONS, ENSURING ELECTRIC GRID RELIABILITY UNDER THE CLEAN POWER PLAN: ADDRESSING KEY THEMES FROM THE FERC TECHNICAL CONFERENCES 2 (April 2015).
58. Duke Nicholas Institute, *Enhancing Compliance Flexibility under the Clean Power Plan: A Common Elements Approach to Capturing Low-Carbon Emissions Reductions* (March 2015).
59. INTERNATIONAL ENERGY AGENCY, THE POWER OF TRANSFORMATION: WIND, SUN AND THE ECONOMICS OF FLEXIBLE POWER SYSTEMS (February 2014); SECURE AND EFFICIENT ELECTRICITY SUPPLY: DURING THE TRANSITION TO LOW CARBON POWER SYSTEMS (2013); Amory Lovins, *Ramping Up Renewable Electricity*, 7 SOLUTIONS J. 6 (Winter 2014); AMELIA REIVER SCHLUSSER, RENEWABLE, RELIABLE, RESILIENT: POLICY APPROACHES FOR MAINTAINING RELIABILITY IN THE WESTERN GRID UNDER THE CLEAN POWER PLAN (October 2015) (a report for the Green Energy Institute at Lewis & Clark Law School).
60. GENERAL ELECTRIC INTERNATIONAL, INC., PJM RENEWABLE INTEGRATION STUDY: EXECUTIVE SUMMARY REPORT: REVISION 03 6–7 (February 28, 2014).
61. TIERNEY, SVENSON & PARSONS at 15–17 (April 2015); Tierney & Hibbard, *Carbon Control and Competitive Wholesale Electricity Markets*.
62. NERC is a nongovernmental regulatory authority established to evaluate and to improve the reliability of the electric system in North America. Pursuant to the Energy Policy Act of 2005, Congress created an entity known as an electric

reliability organization (ERO) to conduct periodic assessments of reliability and to assess the adequacy of the bulk power system in the country. Further, NERC has been designated by FERC as the ERO for North America. *See also* Steven A. Weiler, *EPA's Clean Power Plan: Charting a Path Forward*, 153 PUB. UTIL. FORT. 18 (July 2015).

63. NORTH AMERICAN ELECTRIC RELIABILITY CORPORATION, POTENTIAL RELIABILITY IMPACTS OF EPA'S PROPOSED CLEAN POWER PLAN: INITIAL RELIABILITY REVIEW (November 2014).
64. Electric Power Research Institute, *Comments of the Electric Power Research Institute on Environmental Protection Agency 40 CFR Par 60* (October 20, 2014).
65. Bloomberg New Energy Finance, *Medium-Term Outlook for US Power: 2015 = Deepest De-carbonization Ever* (April 8, 2015).
66. U.S. Energy Information Administration, *Scheduled 2015 Capacity Additions Mostly Wind and Natural Gas; Retirements Mostly Coal* (March 10, 2015).
67. Jurgen Weiss et al., *EPA's Clean Power Plan and Reliability: Assessing NERC's Initial Reliability Review* v, 14–17 (February 2015) (a Brattle Group report prepared for the Advanced Energy Economy Institute).
68. Alexandra B. Klass, *The Electric Grid at a Crossroads: A Regional Approach to Siting Transmission Lines*, 48 U.C. DAVIS L. REV. 1895 (2015).
69. Martin T. Ross, Brian C. Murray & David Hoppock, *The Clean Power Plan: Implications of Three Compliance Decisions for U.S. States* (May 2015); THE CADAMUS GROUP, INC., EXPLORING AND EVALUATING MODULAR APPROACHES TO MULTI-STATE COMPLIANCE WITH THE EPA'S CLEAN POWER PLAN IN THE WEST (April 29, 2015) (a report for the Western Interstate Energy Board).
70. David Farnsworth, *Navigating EPA's Clean Power Plan for Compliance with Renewable Energy* (February 11, 2015).
71. U.S. ENERGY INFORMATION ADMINISTRATION, ANNUAL ENERGY OUTLOOK 2015 WITH PROJECTIONS TO 2040 ES-6 (April 2015).
72. ELECTRIC POWER RESEARCH INSTITUTE, THE INTEGRATED GRID: REALIZING THE FULL VALUE OF CENTRAL AND DISTRIBUTED ENERGY RESOURCES (2014) and THE INTEGRATED GRID: A BENEFIT-COST FRAMEWORK (February 2015); BRANDON OWENS, THE RISE OF DISTRIBUTED POWER (2014) (a report for General Electric).
73. Susan F. Tierney, *The Value of "DER" to "D": The Role of Distributed Energy Resources in Supporting Local Electric Distribution System Reliability* (March 31, 2016).
74. U.S. ENERGY INFORMATION ADMINISTRATION, ANNUAL ENERGY OUTLOOK 2015 WITH PROJECTIONS TO 2040 ES-5 (April 2015).
75. Steven Nadel, Neal Elliott & Therese Langer, *Energy Efficiency in the United States: 35 Years and Counting* (June 2015).
76. Mark Chediak & Dana Hull, *Musk Plots Energy Storage Fix Where Utility Industry Failed*, BLOOMBERG NEWS (April 28, 2015); Rocky Mountain Institute, *The Economics of Battery Energy Storage: How Multi-Use, Customer-Sited Batteries Deliver the Most Services and Value to Customers and the Grid* (October 2015); Richard Fioravanti, *Storage Grows Up: More Than Just Energy, It's Becoming Part of the Grid*, 153 PUB. UTIL. FORT. 48 (September 2015).

77. Weiss at 39–50.
78. FINAL RULE at 64,671.
79. Gerry Anderson (chair and CEO of DTE Energy), *Written Opening Statement*, Federal Energy Regulatory Commission: Technical Conference On Environmental Regulations and Electric Reliability, Wholesale Electricity Markets, and Energy Infrastructure, Docket No. AD15-4–000; *see also Supplemental Comments of the Edison Electric Institute*, Federal Energy Regulatory Commission: Technical Conference on Environmental Regulations and Electric Reliability, Wholesale Electricity Markets, and Energy Infrastructure, Docket No. AD15-4–000.
80. FINAL RULE at 64,671.
81. Weiss at v, 14–50.
82. TIERNEY, SVENSON & PARSONS at 3.
83. TIERNEY, SVENSON & PARSONS at 14.
84. TIERNEY, SVENSON & PARSONS at 15.
85. Jonas Monast et al., *Enhancing Compliance Flexibility under the Clean Power Plan: A Common Elements Approach to Capturing Low-Cost Emissions Reductions* (March 2015); CADMUS; National Association of Clean Air Agencies, *Implementing EPA's Clean Power Plan: Menu of Options* (May 2015); FRANZ T. LITZ & JENNIFER MACEDONIA, CHOOSING A POLICY PATHWAY TO STATE 111(D) PLANS TO MEET STATE OBJECTIVES (April 2015) (a report for the Great Plains Institute and the Bipartisan Policy Center).
86. TIERNEY, SVENSON & PARSONS at 6.
87. Weiss at v, 14–52, 59.
88. TIERNEY, SVENSON & PARSONS at 11–12.
89. Brian Parsons & John Jimison, *Comments and Written Statement* (by a coalition of public interest organizations), Federal Energy Regulatory Commission, *Denver Regional Technical Conference on Environmental Regulations and Electric Reliability, Wholesale Electricity Markets, and Energy Infrastructure*, Docket No. AD15-4-000 (February 25, 2015) (for the Western Electricity Coordinating Council which promotes system reliability for a region that extends from Canada to Mexico and includes all portions in 14 states); *see also* Susan Tierney, Paul Hibbard & Craig Aubuchon, *Electric System Reliability and EPA's Clean Power Plan: The Case of PJM* (March 16, 2015).
90. Tierney, Hibbard & Aubuchon.
91. Tommy Vitolo et al., *Lower Electric Costs in a Low-Emission Future* (July 2015) (a report for Synapse Energy Economics, Inc.) (also citing other studies that reach a similar conclusion).
92. BLOOMBERG NEW ENERGY FINANCE, 2015 FACTBOOK: SUSTAINABLE ENERGY IN AMERICA (February 2015).
93. US DOE, ENERGY INFORMATION ADMINISTRATION, ANALYSIS OF THE IMPACTS OF THE CLEAN POWER PLAN (MAY 2015); Steve Clemmer, *EIA Analysis Shows the EPA's Clean Power Plan Is Affordable, Renewable Energy Makes a Key Contribution* (June 3, 2015).
94. CITI, RISING SUN: IMPLICATIONS FOR US UTILITIES, 22, 26 (2013); PETER KIND, ENERGY INFRASTRUCTURE ADVOCATES, DISRUPTIVE CHALLENGES:

FINANCIAL IMPLICATIONS AND STRATEGIC RESPONSES TO A CHANGING RETAIL ELECTRIC BUSINESS 1 (2013) (both reports discuss the "death spiral" for electric utilities). For an analysis of the death spiral discussion, *compare* Elisabeth Graffy & Steven Kihm, *Does Disruptive Competition Mean a Death Spiral for Electric Utilities?*, 35 ENERGY L. J. 1 (2014) *with* David Raskin, *Getting Distributed Generation Right: A Response to "Does Disruptive Competition Mean a Death Spiral for Electric Utilities?,"* 35 ENERGY L.J. 262 (2014). *See also* Joseph P. Tomain, *Traditionally-Structured Electric Utilities in a Distributed Generation World*, 38 NOVA L. REV. 473 (2014).

95. Robert J. Brulle, *Institutionalizing the Way: Foundation Funding in the Creation of U.S. Climate Change Counter-Movement Organizations*, 122 CLIMATE CHANGE 681 (2014).
96. Gwynne Taraska & Alison Cassady, *Fact Sheet: Efforts to Repeal or Weaken Renewable Energy Schedules in the States* (March 10, 2015).
97. North American Reliability Corporation, *Potential Reliability Impacts of EPA's Proposed Clean Power Plan* (November 2014).
98. INSTITUTE FOR 21ST CENTURY ENERGY, U. S. CHAMBER OF COMMERCE, ASSESSING THE IMPACT OF POTENTIAL NEW CARBON REGULATIONS IN THE UNITED STATES 2 (2014).
99. Matt Lee-Ashley & Claire Moser, *With Fossil Fuels the Focus of Its First 100 Days, the New Congress Has No Results to Show* (April 15, 2015) (a report for the Center for American Progress).
100. Greg Dotson, *Appropriations Showdown on Climate Change* (September 15, 2015) (a blog for the Center for American Progress).
101. Union of Concerned Scientists, *Strengthening EPA's Clean Power Plan* 1 (October 2014).
102. Alison Cassady, *Mitigating Natural Gas Use in the Electricity Sector: Renewable Energy, Energy Efficiency, and the Role of States in Implementing Clean Power Plan* (December 2014); *States Have a Responsibility to Support and Implement the Clean Power Plan* (March 9, 2015) (both reports are for the Center for American Progress).
103. INSTITUTE FOR 21ST CENTURY ENERGY at 10–11.
104. Coral Davenport & Marjorie Connelly, *Most in G.O.P. Say They Back Climate Action*, N.Y. TIMES 1 (January 31, 2015).
105. Pew Research Center, *What the World Thinks about Climate Change in 7 Charts* (November 5, 2015); YALE PROJECT ON CLIMATE CHANGE COMMUNICATION, 4C & GEORGE MASON UNIVERSITY CENTER FOR CLIMATE CHANGE COMMUNICATION, CLIMATE CHANGE IN THE AMERICAN MIND (October 2014).
106. Jim Rossi, *"Mal-Adaptive" Federalism: Addressing the Structural Barriers to Interstate Coordination in Sustainability Initiatives*, 64 CASE WESTERN L. REV. 1759 (2014); Alexandra B. Klass & Jim Rossi, *Revitalizing Dormant Commerce Clause Review for Interstate Coordination*, 100 MINN. L. REV. 129 (2015); David B. Spence, *Federalism, Regulatory Lags, and the Political Economy of Energy Production*, 161 U. PENN. L. REV. 431 (2013); Hari M. Osofsky & Hannah J. Wiseman, *Dynamic Energy Federalism*, 72 MARYLAND L. REV. 773 (2013); *Hybrid Energy Governance*, 2014 ILL. L. REV. 1 (2014).

107. Alexandra B. Klass & Elizabeth Wilson, *Interstate Transmission Challenges for Renewable Energy: Federalism Mismatch*, 65 VAND. L. REV. 1801 (2012); Alexandra B. Klass, *Takings and Transmission*, NORTH CAROLINA L. REV. 1079 (2013).
108. *Piedmont Envt. Council v. FERC*, 558 F.3d 304 (4th Cir. 2009).
109. William Boyd & Ann E. Carlson, *Accidents of Federalism: Rate Design and Policy Innovation in Public Utility Law*, 63 U.C.L.A. L. REV. (2016); J. Kevin Hardy & L. Margaret Barry, *Local Initiatives* in MICHAEL B. GERRARD & JODY FREEMAN (eds.), GLOBAL CLIMATE CHANGE AND U.S. LAW (2nd ed. 2014).
110. Hari M. Osofsky & Hannah J. Wiseman, *Regional Energy Governance under the Clean Power Plan*, 43 ECOLOGY L. Q. 143 (2016).
111. Nuclear Energy Institute, *American Voice Strong Support for Nuclear Energy* (2014); MASSACHUSETTS INSTITUTE FOR TECHNOLOGY, THE FUTURE OF NUCLEAR POWER: AN INTERDISCIPLINARY MIT STUDY ch. 9 (2003); YALE PROJECT ON CLIMATE CHANGE COMMUNICATION, *Nuclear Power in the American Mind*.
112. Dennis Jacobe, *Americans Want More Emphasis on Solar, Wind, Natural Gas: Oil, Nuclear, and Coal Are More Popular with Republicans in the South* (March 27, 2013); Tom Caiazza, *CAP Poll Finds Fossil-Fuel Interests Dominate Agenda of New Congress, but Americans Favor Renewable Energy, Environmental Protections* (January 15, 2015).
113. The New York Times/Stanford University/Resources for the Future, *Poll on Global Warming* (January 7–22, 2015).
114. Daniel Yergin, *America's New Energy Reality*, N.Y. TIMES SUNDAY REVIEW 9 (June 10, 2012); see also Daniel Yergin, *Who Will Rule the Oil Market?*, N.Y. TIMES SUNDAY REVIEW (January 23, 2015).
115. JAMES GUSTAVE SPETH, AMERICA THE POSSIBLE: MANIFESTO FOR A NEW ECONOMY 97 (2012).
116. Jedediah Purdy, *The Politics of Nature: Climate Change, Environmental Law, and Democracy*, 119 YALE L. J. 1122, 1189 (2010).
117. FRANK ACKERMAN & LISA HEINZERLING, PRICELESS: ON KNOWING THE PRICE OF EVERYTHING AND THE VALUE OF NOTHING (2004).
118. Justin Gillis & John Schwartz, *Deeper Ties to Corporate Case for Doubtful Climate Researcher*, N.Y. TIMES (February 21, 2015); Terrence McCoy, *Florida Scientist Told to Remove Words "Climate Change" from Study on Climate Change*, WASH. POST (March 10, 2015).
119. TED NORDHAUS & MICHAEL SHELLENBERGER, THE END OF ENVIRONMENTALISM: FROM THE DEATH OF ENVIRONMENTALISM TO THE POLITICS OF POSSIBILITY 15 (2007).
120. Sarah Krakoff, *Parenting the Planet* in DENIS G. ARNOLD (ed.), THE ETHICS OF GLOBAL CLIMATE CHANGE 145 (2014).
121. ANTHONY GIDDENS, THE POLITICS OF CLIMATE CHANGE 4 (2009) (emphasis added).
122. *Id.* at 8.
123. *Id.* at 8 and chs. 3–9.
124. *Id.* at 9 and chs. 3–9.
125. William Boyd, *Public Utility and the Low-Carbon Future*, 61 U.C.L.A. L. REV. 1614 (2014).

126. ARTHUR OKUN, EQUALITY AND EFFICIENCY: THE BIG TRADE-OFF (1975).
127. Kelly Levin et al., *Overcoming the Tragedy of Super Wicked: Constraining Our Future Selves to Ameliorate Global Climate Change*, 45 POLICY SCI. 123 (2012); Richard J. Lazarus, *Super Wicked Problems and Climate Change: Restraining the Present to Liberate the Future*, 94 CORNELL L. REV. 1153 (2009).
128. 21 U.S.C. §§601 et seq.
129. SIDNEY A. SHAPIRO & JOSEPH P. TOMAIN, ACHIEVING DEMOCRACY: THE FUTURE OF PROGRESSIVE REGULATION ch. 8 (2014).
130. Elizabeth Fisher, *Environmental Law as "Hot" Law*, 25 J. ENVT. L. 347 (2013).
131. Levin, *Overcoming the Tragedy of Super Wicked.*
132. Energy Innovation Policy and Technology LLC, *The Costs of Delay: Waiting Until 2020 Could Cost Nearly $400 Billion* (October 2015).
133. Lincoln L. Davies, *Alternative Energy and the Energy-Environment Disconnect*, 46 IDAHO L. REV. 473 (2010); Alexandra Klass, *Climate Change and the Convergence of Environmental and Energy Law*, 24 FORDHAM ENVT. L. REV. 180 (2013); Amy Wildermuth, *The Next Step: The Integration of Energy Law and Environmental Law*, 31 UTAH ENVT. L. REV. 369 (2011); Uma Outka, *Environmental Law and Fossil Fuels: Barriers to Renewable Energy*, 65 VANDERBILT LAW REVIEW 1679 (2012); TOMAIN, ENDING DIRTY ENERGY POLICY at ch. 9.
134. LINCOLN DAVIES ET AL., ENERGY LAW AND POLICY 8–11 (2015).

2 DEFINING AND MEASURING CLEAN POWER

1. Matt Richtel, *San Diego Vows to Move Entirely to Renewable Energy in 20 Years*, N.Y. TIMES A19 (December 16, 2015).
2. NATIONAL RENEWABLE ENERGY LABORATORY, RENEWABLE ELECTRICITY FUTURES STUDY (2012) (4 vols.).
3. Mark Z. Jacobson et al., *100% Clean and Renewable, Wind, Water, and Sunlight (WWS) All-Sector Energy Roadmaps for the 50 United States*, 8 ENERGY ENVIRON. SCI. 2093 (2015).
4. AMORY LOVINS, MARVIN ODUM & JOHN ROWE, REINVENTING FIRE: BOLD SOLUTIONS FOR THE NEW ENERGY ERA (2011); DAN YORK ET AL., MAKING THE BUSINESS CASE FOR ENERGY EFFICIENCY: CASE STUDIES OF SUPPORTIVE UTILITY REGULATION (December 2013) (a report for the American Council for an Energy Efficient Economy); Robert H. Socolow, *Truths We Must Tell Ourselves to Manage Climate Change*, 65 VAND. L. REV. 1455 (2012).
5. There are those that argue that the United States lacks a clean energy policy. *Compare* Lincoln Davies, *Tracing U.S. Renewable Energy Policy*, 43 ENVT. L. REPTR. 10220 (2013) with E. Donald Elliott, *Why the United States Does Not Have a Renewable Energy Policy*, 43 ENVT. L. RPTR. 10095 (2013); *see also* Magali Delmas & Maria J. Montes-Sancho, *US Policies for Renewable Energy: Context and Effectiveness*, 39 ENERGY POLICY 2273 (2011).
6. *See* DANIEL YERGIN, THE QUEST: ENERGY, SECURITY, AND THE REMAKING OF THE MODERN WORLD 4 (2011); JEFFREY D. SACHS, THE PRICE OF CIVILIZATION: REAWAKENING AMERICAN VIRTUE AND PROSPERITY 201–04 (2011); THOMAS

L. FRIEDMAN & MICHAEL MANDELBAUM, THAT USED TO BE US: HOW AMERICA FELL BEHIND IN THE WORLD IT INVENTED AND HOW WE CAN COME BACK (2011).

7. Another way of conceiving of a clean power economy has been characterized as "sustainable capitalism" defined as "reforming markets to address real needs while integrating environmental, social and governance (ESG) metrics throughout the decision-making process." Al Gore & David Blood, A *Manifesto for Sustainable Capitalism*, WALL ST. J. A21 (December 14, 2011).
8. Regulatory Assistance Project & Center for Climate and Energy Solutions, *Clean Energy Standards: State and Federal Policy Options and Implications* (November 2011).
9. *See* RICHARD K. LESTER & DAVID M. HART, UNLOCKING ENERGY INNOVATION: HOW AMERICA CAN BUILD A LOW-COST, LOW-CARBON ENERGY SYSTEM 3 (2012).
10. *Compare* Lincoln Davies, *Power Forward: The Argument for a National RPS*, 42 CONN. L. REV. 1339 (2010) (favoring national standards) *with* Jim Rossi, *The Limits of a National Renewable Portfolio Standard*, 2011 U. ILL. L. REV. 361 (2011) (disfavoring a national RPS).
11. Sonia Aggarwal & Hal Harvey, *Rethinking Policy to Deliver a Clean Energy Future*, 26 ELECTRICITY J. 7, 8 (October 2013); Bob Wallace & Zachary Shahan, Solar & Wind Power Prices Often Lower Than Fossil Fuel Power Prices (April 13, 2015) available at http://cleantechnica.com/2015/04/13/solar-wind-power-prices-often-lower-fossil-fuel-power-prices/. For future growth in renewable generated electricity, see DOE ENERGY INFORMATION ADMINISTRATION, ANNUAL ENERGY OUTLOOK 2015 WITH PROJECTIONS TO 2040 ES-6 to ES-7 and 24–25 (April 2015).
12. QUADRENNIAL ENERGY REVIEW: ENERGY TRANSMISSION, STORAGE, AND DISTRIBUTION INFRASTRUCTURE S-1 (April 2015).
13. In the first quarter for 2015, for example, renewable electricity outpaced natural gas for new electricity generation. Zachary Shahan, *Renewable = 84% of New Electricity Generation Capacity in 1st Quarter of 2015* (May 10, 2015); Federal Energy Regulatory Commission, *Office of Energy Infrastructure Update for April 2015* (April 2015). Regarding the declining cost of wind power, *see* American Wind Association, *Get the Facts* (2015).
14. RPSs and alternative energy portfolio standards operate in similar ways and have different titles.
15. Center for Climate and Energy Solutions, *Renewable and Alternative Energy Portfolio Standards* available at www.c2es.org/node/9340; DSIRE & NC Clean Energy Technology Center, *Database of State Incentives for Renewables & Efficiency* available at www.dsireusa.org/.
16. Union of Concerned Scientists, *How Renewable Electricity Standards Deliver Economic Benefits* 3 (May 2013).
17. National Renewable Energy Laboratory, *Technology Deployment: State & Local Governments: Renewable Portfolio Standards* available at www.nrel.gov/tech_deployment/state_local_governments/basics_portfolio_standards.html.
18. Joseph P. Tomain, *"Steel in the Ground": Greening the Grid with the iUtility*, 39 ENVT'L L. 931, 956–57 (2009).

19. Joshua P. Fershee, *Renewable Mandates and Goals* in MICHAEL B. GERRARD (ed.), THE LAW OF CLEAN ENERGY 77 (2011).
20. Fershee at 80.
21. Jim Rossi, *The Limits of a National Renewable Portfolio Standard*, 42 CONN. L. REV. 1425, 1431 (2010).
22. Alexandra B. Klass & Jim Rossi, *Revitalizing Dormant Commerce Clause Review for Interstate Coordination*, 100 MINN. L. REV. 129 (2015).
23. Lincoln L. Davies, *Power Forward: The Argument for a National RPS*, 42 CONN L. REV. 1339 (2010). See also Fershee at 84–86.
24. David B. Spence, *The Political Barriers to a National RPS*, 42 CONN. L. REV. 1451 (2010).
25. Rossi at 1433–36.
26. Rossi at 1434.
27. National Renewable Energy Laboratory, *Technology Deployment: State & Local Governments: Feed-In Tariffs* available at www.nrel.gov/tech_deployment/state_local_governments/basics_tariffs.html.
28. JURGEN WEISS, SOLAR ENERGY SUPPORT IN GERMANY: A CLOSER LOOK (July 2014) (a report from the Brattle Group prepared for Solar Energy Industries Association).
29. Craig Morris, *Spanish Feed-In Tariffs – A Wrapup* (July 22, 2013) available at www.renewablesinternational.net/spanish-feed-in-tariffs-a-wrapup/150/537/71424/.
30. TOBY D. COUTURE ET AL., A POLICYMAKER'S GUIDE TO FEED-IN TARIFF POLICY DESIGN (July 2010) (a report for the National Renewable Energy laboratory).
31. U.S. Energy Information Administration, *Feed-in Tariff: A Policy Tool Encouraging Deployment of Renewable Electricity Technologies* (May 30, 2013) available at www.eia.gov/todayinenergy/detail.cfm?id=11471 and *Electricity Feed-In Tariffs and Similar Programs* (June 4, 2013) available at www.eia.gov/electricity/policies/provider_programs.cfm.
32. Felix Mormann, *Clean Energy Federalism*, 67 FLA. L. REV. 1621 (2015).
33. Lincoln L, Davies, *Reconciling Renewable Portfolio Standards and Feed-In Tariffs*, 32 UTAH ENVT. L. REV. 311 (2012).
34. Davies, *Reconciling* at 314.
35. Jedediah Purdy, *The Politics of Nature: Climate Change, Environmental Law, and Democracy*, 119 YALE L. J. 1122 (2010).
36. *Yellowstone Act of 1872*, 17 Stat. 32.
37. *See e.g.* JAMES RASBAND, JAMES SALZMAN & MARK SQUILLACE, NATURAL RESOURCES LAW AND POLICY ch. 6 (2d ed. 2009); SANDRA B. ZELLMER & JAN LAITOS, PRINCIPLES OF NATURAL RESOURCES LAW 168–84 (2014).
38. John C. Dernbach & Marianne Tyrrell, *Federal Energy Efficiency and Conservation Laws* in MICHAEL B. GERRARD (ed.), THE LAW OF CLEAN ENERGY 25, 26 (2011).
39. *See e.g.* Breakthrough Staff, *The Year of Our High-Energy Planet* (2014) available at http://thebreakthrough.org/index.php/issues/ecomodernism/2014-the-year-of-our-high-energy-planet; Michael Shellenberger & Ted Nordhaus, *Why Having a Realistic View of Energy Efficiency Matters to Climate Change* (October 24, 2014) available at http://thebreakthrough.org/index.php/voices/michael-

shellenberger-and-ted-nordhaus/why-having-a-realistic-view-of-energy-efficiency-matters-to-climate-change; JESSE JENKINS, TED NORDHAUS & MICHAEL SHELLENBERGER, ENERGY EMERGENCE, REBOUND & BACKFIRE S EMERGENT PHENOMENA (February 2011).

40. MAX LUKE ET AL., LIGHTING, ELECTRICITY, STEEL: ENERGY EFFICIENCY BACKFIRE IN EMERGING ECONOMIES (September 2014) (a report for the Breakthrough Institute).
41. Energy Policy and Conservation Act, Pub. L. No. 94–163 (1975).
42. John A. Hodges, *Appliances, Lighting, Computers, Data Centers, and Computer Servers*, in MICHAEL B. GERRARD (ed.), THE LAW OF CLEAN ENERGY ch. 12 (2011).
43. Energy Conservation and Production Act, Pub. L. No. 94–385 (1976).
44. National Energy Conservation Policy Act, Pub. L. No. 95–619 (1978).
45. Dernbach & Tyrrell at 27.
46. National Appliance Energy Conservation Policy Act of 1987, Pub. L. No. 100–12 (1987).
47. *Id.*
48. Energy Policy Act of 1992, Pub. No. L. 102–486 (1992).
49. Energy Policy Act of 2005, 109–58 (2005).
50. Energy Independence and Security Act of 2007, Pub. L. No. 110–40 (2007).
51. J. Cullen Howe, *Buildings* in MICHAEL B. GERRARD (ed.), THE LAW OF CLEAN ENERGY ch. 13 (2011).
52. *Id.* at 27–28.
53. American Recovery and Reinvestment Act of 2009, Pub. L. No. 111–5 (2009).
54. *Id.* and 30–32. *See also* LINCOLN DAVIES ET AL., ENERGY LAW AND POLICY 546–564 (2014).
55. Energy Future Coalition, *Comments by the Energy Future Coalition: Key Elements for Clean Energy Standard Proposals* 5 (2011).
56. *Clean Energy Standard Act of 2012*, S. 2146, 112th Cong. 2d Sess.
57. US Energy Information Administration, *Analysis & Projections: Analysis of the Clean Energy Standard Act of 2012* 2 (May 2, 2012).
58. US Energy Information Administration, *Analysis & Projections* at 3–4. *See also* Anthony Paul, Karen Palmer & Matt Woerman, *Designing by Degrees: Flexibility and Cost-Effectiveness in Climate Policy* (February 2014) (arguing that the CES should be recalibrated to achieve higher efficiencies than as designed in the proposed legislation).
59. Energy Future Coalition at 2.
60. US ENERGY INFORMATION ADMINISTRATION, ANNUAL ENERGY REVIEW 2011 12 (September 2012); Monthly Energy Review 16 (December 2014).
61. NATIONAL ACADEMY OF SCIENCES, NATIONAL ACADEMY OF ENGENDERING & NATIONAL RESEARCH COUNCIL, REAL PROSPECTS FOR ENERGY EFFICIENCY IN THE UNITED STATES (2010) and MCKINSEY GLOBAL ENERGY AND MATERIALS, UN LOCKING ENERGY EFFICIENCY IN THE U.S. ECONOMY (July 2009). *But see* Hunt Allcott & Michael Greenstone, *Is There an Efficiency Gap?* (July 19, 2012) (arguing that market failures do exist, and while there is an energy efficiency gap, it is smaller than anticipated by McKinsey). *See also* publications of the American Council for an Energy-Efficient Economy at www.aceee.org/publications.

62. Energy Future Coalition at 2–4.
63. White House, *Obama Administration Finalizes Historic 54.5 MPG Fuel Efficiency Standards* (August 28, 2012).
64. Dernbach & Tyrrell at 34.
65. Noah M. Sachs, *Can We Regulate Our Way to Energy Efficiency? Product Standards as Climate Policy*, 65 VAND. L. REV. 1631, 1637–39 (2012).
66. Alexandra B. Klass, *State Standards for Nationwide Products, Revisited: Federalism, Green Building Codes, and Appliance Efficiency Standards*, 34 HARV. ENVT. L. REV. 335, 40 (2010).
67. Edna Sussman, *Reshaping Municipal and County Laws to Foster Green Building, Energy Efficiency, and Renewable Energy*, 16 N.Y.U. ENVTL. L. J. 1, 8 (2008).
68. Klass at 344 (footnotes omitted).
69. Klass at 343–44.
70. Dernbach & Tyrrell at 38.
71. Klass at 344–45.
72. For CO_2 reductions and energy cost savings, *see* Appliance Standards Awareness Project, CO_2 Tracker, and $$ Tracker available at www.appliance-standards.org/ estimating cumulative electricity savings through 2030.
73. Energy Star, *Overview of 2013 Achievements* available at www.energystar.gov/.
74. Hepburn Act of 1906, 49 U.S.C. §§1 et seq.
75. Federal Power Act, 16 U.S.C. §§824-791a.
76. The Natural Gas Act of 1937, 15 U.S.C. §§717 et seq.
77. JOHN CLARK, ENERGY AND THE FEDERAL GOVERNMENT: FOSSIL FUEL POLICIES, 1900–1946 (1987).
78. Atomic Energy Act of 1954, 42 U.S.C. §§2001 et seq. (putting commercial nuclear power under civilian control); the Price-Anderson Act, 42 U.S.C. §§2210 et seq. (establishing a compensation scheme and limiting liability in the case of a nuclear accident).
79. Mona L. Hymel, *The United States' Experience with Energy-Based Tax Incentives: The Evidence Supporting Tax Incentives for Renewable Energy*, 38 LOYOLA U. CHI. L. J. 43 (2006).
80. Richard Rubin, *Bill Would Revive Dozens of Tax Breaks*, WALL ST. J. (December 16, 2015); Chris Mooney, *The Budget Bill Will Unleash Wind and Solar*, WASH. POST (December 17, 2015).
81. Scudder Parker & Frances Huessy, *What's a Utility to Do: Next-Generation Energy Services and a New Partnership to Serve Customers* 24 (November 2013).
82. *See SZ Enterprises, LLC d/b/a Eagle Point Solar v. Iowa Utilities Board*, 850 N.W.2d 441 (Iowa 2014); Elisabeth Gaffey & Steven Kihm, *Does Disruptive Competition Mean a Death Spiral for Electric Utilities?*, 35 ENERGY L. J. 1 (2014) (no); David Raskin, *Getting Distributed Generation Right: A Response to "Does Disruptive Competition Mean a Death Spiral for Electric Utilities?,"* 35 ENERGY L. J. 263 (2014) (maybe); Joseph P. Tomain, *Traditionally-Structured Electric Utilities in a Distributed Generation World*, 38 NOVA L. REV. 473 (2014) (no); Charles E. Bayless, *The Death of the Grid?*, 152 PUB. UTIL. FORT. 24 (December 2014) (no).
83. William Boyd, *Public Utility and the Low Carbon Future*, 61 U.C.L.A. L. REV. 1614, 1633 (2014).

84. Union of Concerned Scientists, Policy Context of Geologic Carbon Storage (July 7, 2001).
85. MASSACHUSETTS INSTITUTE OF TECHNOLOGY, THE FUTURE OF COAL: OPTIONS FOR A CARBON-CONSTRAINED WORLD ch. 4 (2007).
86. John G. Reed & Helena M. Tavares, *Government Financing, Loans, and Guarantees* in DAVID J. MUCHOW & WILLIAM A. MOGEL (eds.), 2 ENERGY LAW AND TRANSACTIONS §31003[1] (April 1997).
87. DAVID J. MUCHOW & WILLIAM A. MOGEL (eds.), 2 ENERGY LAW AND TRANSACTIONS §59.04 (September 2006).
88. DOE, Office of Fossil Energy, *Clean Power Initiative* available at http://energy.gov/fe/science-innovation/clean-coal-research/major-demonstrations/clean-coal-power-initiative.
89. Energy.gov, Office of Fossil Energy, *Carbon Capture and Storage from Industrial Sources* available at http://energy.gov/fe/science-innovation/carbon-capture-and-storage-research/carbon-capture-and-storage-industrial (last visited December 29, 2015).
90. Energy.gov, Office of Fossil Energy, *Clean Coal Research* available at http://energy.gov/fe/science-innovation/clean-coal-research (last visited July 28, 2015).
91. Jeffrey Tomich, *DOE Pulls Plug on FutureGen Coal Project*, ENERGYWIRE (February 4, 2015).
92. Wendy B. Jacobs, *Trends, Challenges and Next Steps in CCS Regulation* Slide 6 (May 27–28, 2014) (PowerPoint presentation at the 6th Annual International Energy Agency CCS Regulatory Network Meeting).
93. REPORT OF THE INTERAGENCY TASK FORCE ON CARBON CAPTURE AND STORAGE 7–8 (August 2010) available at http://energy.gov/fe/services/advisory-committees/interagency-task-force-carbon-capture-and-storage (last visited July 28, 2015).
94. Howard Herzog & Jan Eide, *Rethinking CCS – Moving Forward in Times of Uncertainty*, CORNERSTONE: THE OFFICIAL JOURNAL OF THE WORLD COAL ASSOCIATION (June 2013).
95. Union of Concerned Scientists, *Policy Context*; Environmental Defense Fund, *Carbon Capture and Sequestration: Storing Carbon to Reduce Emissions* available at www.edf.org/energy/carbon-storage; DAN LASHOF & STARLA YEH, CLEANER AND CHEAPER: USING THE CLEAN AIR ACT TO SHARPLY REDUCE CARBON POLLUTION FROM EXISTING POWER PLANTS, DELIVERING HEALTH, ENVIRONMENTAL, AND ECONOMIC BENEFITS (March 2014) (a report for NRDC); *see also* Alexandra B. Klass & Elizabeth J. Wilson, *Climate Change and Carbon Sequestration: Assessing a Liability Regime for Long-Term Storage of Carbon Dioxide*, 58 EMORY L. J. 103 (2008).
96. Lincoln L. Davies, Kirsten Uchitel & John Ruple, *Understanding Barriers to Commercial-Scale Carbon Capture and Sequester in the United States: An Empirical Assessment*, 59 ENERGY POLICY 745, 748 (August 2013).
97. JAN EIDE, RETHINKING CCS – STRATEGIES FOR TECHNOLOGY DEVELOPMENT IN TIMES OF UNCERTAINTY ch. 2 (2013) (PhD thesis) available at http://sequestration.mit.edu/bibliography/index.html.

98. Wendy B. Jacobs, *Carbon Capture and Sequestration* in MICHAEL GERRARD & JODY FREEMAN (eds.), GLOBAL CLIMATE CHANGE AND U.S. LAW ch. 17 (2d ed. April 2014).
99. Union of Concerned Scientists, *Policy Context* at 3–4.
100. Jacobs at Slides 8 & 9.
101. U.S. Congressional Budget Office, Federal Efforts to Reduce the Cost of Capturing and Storing Carbon Dioxide 2 (2012); Wendy B. Jacobs, *Carbon Capture and Sequestration* in MICHAEL GERRARD & JODY FREEMAN (eds.), GLOBAL CLIMATE CHANGE AND U.S. LAW ch. 17 (2d ed. April 2014).
102. Arnold W. Reitze, Jr., *Carbon Capture and Storage (Sequestration)*, 43 ENVTL. L. REPT. 10414 (May 2013).
103. *Energy Security Act of 1980*, 42 U.S.C. §8802. *See generally* Gary E. Guy, *Biomass* in DAVID J. MUCHOW & WILLIAM A. MOGEL (eds.), 3 ENERGY LAW AND TRANSACTIONS ch. 72 (May 2013).
104. Union of Concerned Scientists, *The Promise of Biomass: Clean Power and Fuel – If Handled Right* 2 (September 2012).
105. Union of Concerned Scientists, *The Promise of Biomass* at 1.
106. James M. Van Nostrand & Anne Marie Hirschberger, *Biofuels* in MICHAEL B. GERRARD (ed.), THE LAW OF CLEAN ENERGY 445, 448–49 (2011); Union of Concerned Scientists, *The Energy-Water Collision: Corn Ethanol's Threat to Water Resources* (October 2011).
107. JOSEPH P. TOMAIN & RICHARD D. CUDAHY, ENERGY LAW IN A NUTSHELL 524–27 (2d ed. 2011).
108. JAMES H. WILLIAMS ET AL., POLICY IMPLICATIONS OF DEEP DECARBONIZATION IN THE UNITED STATES 87–88 (2015) (a report for the Sustainable Development Solutions Network).
109. Tim Searchinger & Ralph Heimlich, *Avoiding Bioenergy Competition for Food Crops and Land* 12 (January 2015) (a working paper for the World Resources Institute).
110. Renewable Fuels Association, Advanced Ethanol (March 2014) available at www .ethanolrfa.org/pages/advanced-ethanol.
111. James H. Stock, *The Renewable Fuel Standard: A Path Forward* 3 (April 2015).
112. BIPARTISAN POLICY CENTER, OPTION FOR REFORMING THE RENEWABLE FUEL STANDARD: A REPORT FROM THE STAFF OF THE BIPARTISAN POLICY CENTER (DECEMBER 2014).
113. Stock at 23–27.
114. Van Nostrand & Hirschberger at 449.
115. Union of Concerned Scientists, *The Promise of Biomass* at 4.
116. Environmental Defense Fund, *Biodiesel in California: Companies Fueling Positive Change* available at www.fuelinggrowth.org/biodiesel-in-california-companies-fueling-positive-change/.
117. World Nuclear Association, *Comparative Carbon Dioxide Emissions from Power Generation* available at www.world-nuclear.org/education/comparati veco2.html (nuclear power trade association); *see also* Jim Rossi & Emily Hammond, *Electric Power Generation Fuels* in MICHAEL B. GERRARD & JODY FREEMAN (eds.), GLOBAL CLIMATE CHANGE AND U.S.

LAW (2d ed. 2014). *But see* Amory B. Lovins, Imran Sheikh & Alex Markevich, *Nuclear Power: Climate Fix or Folly?* (December 2008); *Editorial, Nuclear Energy and Sustainable Development*, 74S1 ENERGY POL. S1 (December 2014); Peter Theil, *The New Atomic Age We Need*, N.Y. TIMES A19 (November 28, 2015).

118. Amory B. Lovins, *Renewable Energy's "Footprint" Myth*, ELECTRICITY J. 24 (July 2011).
119. DOUG VINE & TIMOTHY JULIANI, CLIMATE SOLUTIONS: THE ROLE OF NUCLEAR POWER (April 2014) (a report for the Center for Climate and Energy); John R. Norris, *Nuclear at a Crossroads*, 152 PUB. UTIL. FORT. 18 (July 2014).
120. Ann Stouffer, *Nuclear Energy: Upward Trends in U.S. Leadership, Innovative Reactors* (November 2012) (prepared for the Nuclear Energy Institute a nuclear trade association).
121. Michael Cooper & Dalia Sussman, *Nuclear Power Loses Support in New Pool*, N.Y. TIMES (March 22, 2011). *See also* Lincoln L. Davies, *Beyond Fukushima: Disasters, Nuclear Energy, and Energy Law*, 2011 BRIGHAM YOUNG L. REV. 1937 (2011).
122. Nuclear Energy Institute, *New Nuclear Energy Facilities* available at www.nei.org/keyissues/newnuclearplants/.
123. *Energy Policy Act of 2005*, Pub. L. 109–58 (2005). Regarding subsidies, *see* Public Citizen, *Nuclear Giveaways in the Energy Policy Act of 2005* (2005).
124. Ellen Reinhardt & Sean Powers, *Plant Vogtle Nuclear Power Plant Price Tag Soars, Construction Delayed* (December 16, 2014); Ray Henry, *1-Year Delay Possible at Plant Vogtle, Watchdog Says*, AUGUSTA CHRONICLE (December 16, 2014); Rob Pavey, *Georgia Power Reports Costs, Challenges of Vogtle Expansion*, AUGUSTA CHRONICLE (August 31, 2012); Walter C. Jones, *Westinghouse Electrical Co. Will Complete the Contract, Taking Over for CB&I, the Original Contractor*, FLORIDA TIMES UNION (October 28, 2015).
125. Kristi E. Swartz, *Timeline for U.S.'s Newest Reactor Stretched into 2019*, ENERGYWIRE (January 30, 2015).
126. Kristi E. Swartz, *Fla. Utility See Nuclear Delays as Generation Needs Increase*, ENERGYWIRE (January 27, 2015).
127. U.S. Energy Information Administration, *Levelized Cost and Levelized Avoided Cost of New Generation Resources in the Annual Energy Outlook 2015* (June 2015) (wind cheaper than nuclear power).
128. Norris at 20.
129. DOE Energy Information Administration, *Levelized Cost and Levelized Avoided Cost of New Generation Resources in the Annual Energy Outlook 2015* (June 2015); THOMAS F. STACY & GEORGE S. TAYLOR, LEVELIZED COST OF NEW ELECTRICITY GENERATING TECHNOLOGIES (June 2015) (a report for the Institute for Energy Research) (nuclear LCOE favorable against wind and solar); JOEL B. EISEN ET AL., ENERGY, ECONOMICS AND THE ENVIRONMENT 428–30 (2015); LINCOLN DAVIES ET AL., ENERGY LAW AND POLICY 305 (2015). *See also* Jessica R. Lovering, Arthur Yip & Ted Nordhaus, *Historical Construction Costs of Global Nuclear Power Reactors*, 91 ENERGY POL. 371 2016) (construction costs for nuclear power plants are higher in the United States than in other countries around the world.)

130. JOHN M. DEUTCH & ERNEST J. MONIZ, THE FUTURE OF NUCLEAR POWER: AN MIT INTERDISCIPLINARY STUDY (2003); JOHN M. DEUTCH ET AL., UPDATE OF THE MIT 2003 FUTURE OF NUCLEAR POWER (2009). *But see* Thomas B. Cochran, *Critique of "The Future of Nuclear Power: An Interdisciplinary Study"* (from NRDC) available at www.c2es.org/events/2004/10-50-workshop-proceedings.
131. TED NORDHAUS, JESSICA LOVERING & MICHAEL SHELLENBERGER, HOW TO MAKE NUCLEAR CHEAP: SAFETY, READINESS, MODULARITY, AND EFFICIENCY 19–22 (June 2014).
132. NORDHAUS, LOVERING & SHELLENBERGER at 11 and 15–17.
133. Josh Freed, *Back to the Future: Advanced Nuclear Energy and the Battle against Climate Change* (December 12, 2014).
134. Energy.Gov, *Small Modular Nuclear Reactors* available at www.energy.gov/ne/nuclear-reactor-technologies/small-modular-nuclear-reactors.
135. NORDHAUS, LOVERING & SHELLENBERGER at 25 and 31.
136. EETV, *Third Way's Freed Says Government Support Essential to Commercializing Advanced Nuclear Technology* (December 16, 2014) available at www.eenews.net/tv/videos/1912/transcript; Josh Freed & Ingrid Akerlind, *Nuclear Energy Renaissance Set to Move Ahead without U.S.* (August 8, 2014); NORDHAUS, LOVERING & SHELLENBERGER at 62–66; EDWIN LYMAN, SMALL ISN'T ALWAYS BEAUTIFUL: SAFETY, SECURITY, AND COST CONCERNS ABOUT SMALL MODULAR REACTORS 5 (September 2013) (a report for the Union of Concerned Scientists).
137. Energy.Gov, *Small Modular Nuclear Reactors* available at www.energy.gov/ne/nuclear-reactor-technologies/small-modular-nuclear-reactors.
138. Lyman at 4–6.
139. *Id.*
140. US ENERGY INFORMATION ADMINISTRATION, ANNUAL ENERGY OUTLOOK 2014 LR-9 to LR-10 (April 2014).
141. U.S. NRC, *Japan Lessons Learned* available at www.nrc.gov/reactors/operating/ops-experience/japan-dashboard.html.
142. Lincoln L. Davies, *Beyond Fukushima: Disasters, Nuclear Energy, and Energy Law*, 2011 B.Y.U L. REV. 1937, 1952–56 (2011).
143. Environmental Protection Agency, *Carbon Pollution Emission Guidelines for Existing Stationary Sources: Electric Generating Units; Final Rule*, 80 FED. REG. 64737–738(2015) (FINAL RULE).
144. Kurt Kleiner, *Nuclear Energy: Assessing Emissions, Nature Reports: Climate Change* (September 24, 2008); *see also* Benjamin K. Sovacool, *Valuing the Greenhouse Gas Emissions from Nuclear Power: A Critical Survey*, 36 ENERGY POLICY 2940 (June 2008).
145. Eric Lipton & Clifford Krauss, *Giving Reins to the States over Drilling*, N.Y. TIMES (August 23, 2012).
146. Clifford Krauss & Ashley Parker, *Romney Energy Plan Would Expand Oil Drilling on U.S. Land and Offshore*, N.Y. TIMES (August 22, 2012).
147. Joseph P. Tomain, Shale Gas and Clean Energy Policy, 63 CASE WESTERN L. REV. 1187 (2013).

148. US Energy Information Administration, *Monthly Energy Review* 37 (January 2015).
149. US Energy Information Administration, *Monthly Energy Review* 71 (January 2015).
150. U.S. ENERGY INFORMATION ADMINISTRATION, ANNUAL ENERGY OUTLOOK 2014 WITH PROJECTIONS TO 2040 MR-23 (April 2014).
151. Energy.gov, Office of Fossil Energy, *Why Is Shale Gas Important?* available at http://energy.gov/fe/downloads/why-shale-gas-important (last viewed February 28, 2015) (relying on: National Petroleum Council, *Prudent Development: Realizing the Potential of North America's Abundant Natural Gas and Oil Resources* (2011) (Executive Summary at 7 and 16); and Staff, *Surprise Side Effect of Shale Gas Boom: A Plunge in U.S. Greenhouse Emissions*, FORBES (December 7, 2012)).
152. INTERNATIONAL ENERGY AGENCY, WORLD ENERGY OUTLOOK 2012: EXECUTIVE SUMMARY 1 (2912)
153. Richard J. Pierce, Jr., *Natural Gas Fracking Addresses All of Our Major Problems*, 4 J. ENERGY & ENVTL. L. 22 (Summer 2013).
154. John D. Podesta & Timothy E. Wirth, *Natural Gas: A Bridge Fuel for the 21st Century* (August 10, 2009) (on behalf of the Center for American Progress); Stephen P.A. Brown, Alan J. Krupnick & Margaret A. Wells, *Natural Gas: A Bridge to a Low-Carbon Future* (December 2009) (on behalf of Resources for the Future and the National Energy Policy Institute).
155. The White House, *Remarks by the President in State of the Union Address* (January 24, 2012) available at www.whitehouse.gov/the-press-office/2012/01/24/remarks-president-state-union-address.
156. IEA WORLD ENERGY OUTLOOK 2012 1–2 (November 2012) available at www.worldenergyoutlook.org/; *see also* Michael Levi, *Think Again: The American Energy Boom*, FOREIGN AFFAIRS (June 18, 2012) available at www.foreignpolicy.com/articles/2012/06/18/think_again_the_american_energy_boom.
157. ALAN J. KRUPNICK ET AL., THE NATURAL GAS REVOLUTION: CRITICAL QUESTIONS FOR A SUSTAINABLE ENERGY FUTURE 1 (March 2014) (a report for Resources for the Future).
158. Stephen P.A. Brown, Steven A. Gabriel & Ruud Egging, *Abundant Shale Gas Resources: Some Implications for Energy Policy* (April 2012) (for Resources for the Future and the National Energy policy Institute) available at www.rff.org/Publications/Pages/PublicationDetails.aspx?PublicationID=21098.
159. Pierce at 5.
160. John Corrigan & Jim Hendrickson, *Shale vs. Coal*, 150 PUB. UTIL. FORT. 20 (May 2012).
161. Christopher Goncalves, *Breaking Rules and Changing the Game: Will Shale Gas Rock the World?*, 35 ENERGY L. J. 225 (2014) (arguing that mid-term prospects for LNG exports are positive through 2020 but uncertain after that because of questions about the ability of importing countries to make use of LNG.)
162. Peter R. Orszag, *Natural-Gas Can Drive Us Toward a Better Future* (June 12, 2012) available at www.cfr.org/economics/natural-gas-cars-can-drive-us-toward-better-economy/p28625; Floyd Norris, *Natural Gas for Vehicles Could Use U.S. Support*, N.Y. TIMES (June 21, 2012).

163. U.S. Energy Information Administration, *Natural Gas: U.S. Natural Gas Wellhead Price* available at www.eia.gov/dnav/ng/hist/n9190us3m.htm.
164. WILLIAMS at 14.
165. *See e.g.* Norimitsu Onishi, *Vast Oil Reserve May Now Be Within Reach, and Battle Heats Up*, N.Y. TIMES (February 4, 2012); Chip Brown, *North Dakota Went Boom*, N.Y. TIMES MAGAZINE 22 (February 3, 2012).
166. NATIONAL PETROLEUM COUNCIL, PRUDENT DEVELOPMENT: REALIZING THE POTENTIAL OF NORTH AMERICA'S ABUNDANT NATURAL GAS AND OIL RESOURCES 21 (2011).
167. ALISON CASSDAY, THE CLEAN POWER PLAN: A CRITICAL STEP TOWARD DECARBONIZING AMERICA'S ENERGY SYSTEM (April 15, 2015) (a report for the Center for American Progress).
168. Union of Concerned Scientists, *Gas Ceiling: Assessing the Climate Risks of an Overreliance on Natural Gas for Electricity* 5 (September 2013).
169. Beren Argetsinger, *The Marcellus Shale: Bridge to a Clean Energy Future of Bridge to Nowhere?: Environmental, Energy and Climate Policy Considerations for Shale Gas Development in New York State*, 29 PACE ENVTL. L. REV. 321, 336 (2011).
170. U.S. DEPARTMENT OF ENERGY, QUADRENNIAL ENERGY REVIEW: ENERGY TRANSMISSION, STORAGE, AND DISTRIBUTION S-6 (April 2015).
171. Environmental Defense Fund, *Natural Gas – A Briefing Paper for Candidates* 16 (August 10, 2012) available at http://blogs.edf.org/energyexchange/2012/08/10/natural-gas-a-briefing-paper-for-candidates/.
172. US Environmental Protection Agency, *Carbon Pollution Emission Guidelines for Existing Stationary Sources: Electric Utility Generating Units; Proposed Rule*, 79 FED. REG. 34830, 34862 (June 18, 2014).
173. Haewon McJeon et al., *Limited Impact on Decadel-Scale Climate Change from Increased Use of Natural Gas*, 514 NATURE 482 (October 23, 2014); Robert W. Howarth, Renee Santoro & Anthony Ingraffea, *Methane and the Greenhouse-Gas Footprint of Natural Gas from Shale Formations*, 106 CLIMATE CHANGE 679 (2011) (this study, often referred to as the Cornell Study, has been criticized, and in some instances refuted. However, other studies such as McJeon's suggest that emissions are greater than those estimated by the EPA. Krupnick et al. at 24. *See also* Claire Moser, Nidhi Thakar & Matt Lee-Ashley, *Reducing Methane Pollution from Fossil-Fuel Production on America's Public Lands: A Needed Step to Combat Climate Change* (October 6, 2014) (an issue brief for the Center for American Progress).
174. A.R. Brandt et al., *Methane Leaks from North American Gas Systems*, 343 SCIENCE 733 (February 13, 2014).
175. U.S. EPA Office of Air Quality Planning and Standards, *Oil and Natural Gas Compressors* (April 2014).
176. U.S. EPA Office of Air Quality Planning and Standards, *Oil and Natural Gas Sector Hydraulically Fractured Oil Well Completions and Associated Gas during Ongoing Production* (April 2014).
177. U.S. EPA Office of Air Quality Planning and Standards, *Oil and Natural Gas Sector Leaks* (April 2014).

178. U.S. EPA Office of Air Quality Planning and Standards, *Oil and Natural Gas Sector Liquids Unloading Processes* (April 2014); *Oil and Natural Gas Sector Pneumatic Devices* (2014).
179. White House, *Climate Action Plan: Strategy to Reduce Methane Emissions* (March 2014).
180. Coral Davenport, *Obama Is Planning New Rules on Oil and Gas Industry's Methane Emissions*, N.Y. Times (January 13, 2015).
181. Alison Cassady, *Cutting Methane Pollution from Oil and Gas Industry to Meet U.S. Climate Commitments* (December 4, 2015) (a blogpost for the Center for American Progress).
182. Thomas W. Merrill & David M. Schizer, *The Shale Oil and Gas Revolution, Hydraulic Fracturing, and Water Contamination: A Regulatory Strategy*, 98 Minn. L. Rev. 145 (2013).
183. U.S. Environmental Protections Agency, Study of the Potential Impacts of Hydraulic Fracturing on Drinking Water Resources: Progress Report (December 2012).
184. Jamison Cocklin, *EPA Expects to Publish Long-Awaited Draft Fracking Report in March* (October 21, 2014).
185. US Environmental Protection Agency, EPA's Study of How Drawled Fracturing and Its Potential Impact on Drinking Water Resources available at www2.epa.gov/hfstudy/published-scientific-papers.
186. Francis O'Sullivan & Sergey Paltsev, *Shale Gas Production: Potential versus Actual Greenhouse Gas Emissions*, 7 Envt. Res. Lett. 1, 2 (2012).
187. Ohio EPA, *Drilling for Natural Gas in the Marcellus and Utica Shales: Environmental Regulatory Basics* (November 2012).
188. Hannah J. Wiseman, *Risk and Response in Fracturing Policy*, 84 U. Colo L. Rev. 729 (2013).
189. Francis O'Sullivan & Sergey Paltsev at 2.
190. Argetsinger at 332–336.
191. 42 U.S.C. §300h(d)(1)(2006).
192. Jeffrey Dintzer & Elizabeth Burnside, *Law360, Take It Easy on Fracking* (March 15, 2011); Amy Teimann, *Why You Need to Know about Fracking – It May Be Coming to a Field or Neighborhood Near You* (October 8, 2011); Earthworks, *The Halliburton Loophole* available at www.earthworksaction.org/issues/detail/inadequate_regulation_of_hydraulic_fracturing.
193. Mike Soraghan, *Senate Votes to Keep "Halliburton Loophole"; Regulation Stays with States*, Energywire (January 29, 2015).
194. U.S. Envtl. Prot. Agency, *EPA Initiates Rulemaking to Set Discharge Standards for Wastewater from Shale Gas Extraction* (October 2011).
195. Stronger is the State Review of Oil & Gas Environmental Regulations initiated by the US EPA. *See Regulatory Determination for Oil and Gas and Geothermal Exploration, Development and Production Wastes*, 53 Fed. Reg. at 25, 447 (July 6, 1988).
196. Editorial, *The Danger of Urban Drilling*, N.Y. Times A18 (November 28, 2015).
197. David B. Spence, *The Political Economy of Local Vetoes*, 93 Tex. L. Rev. 351 (2014); *see also* John R. Nolan & Steven E. Gavin, *Hydrofracking: State*

Preemption, Local Power, and Cooperative Governance, 63 CASE WESTERN L. REV. 995 (2013).

198. Nicholas St. Fleur, *The Alarming Research behind New York's Fracking Ban*, THE ATLANTIC (December 14, 2014).
199. Jack Healy, Heavyweight Response to Local Fracking Bans, N.Y. TIMES (January 3, 2015); Jack Healy *After Citizen-Led Action, Cities Face Costly Fights with Oil and Gas Industry*, N.Y. TIMES 11 (January 5, 2015).
200. Jack Healy, *Colorado Communities Take on Fight against Energy Land Leases*, N.Y. TIMES 15 (February 3, 2012).
201. Department of the Interior, Bureau of Land Management, *Oil and Gas; Hydraulic Fracturing on Federal and Indian Lands*, 80 FED. REG. 16,128 (March 26, 2015) (to be codified at 43 CFR Part 3160).
202. In *Wyoming v. Department of Interior*, Case No. 2:15-CV-043-SWS (September 30, 2015), The US District Court for the District of Wyoming ruled that the Bureau of Land Management lacked authority to bring the rule and that matter is on appeal. *But see* Hannah J. Wiseman, *Written Testimony for "The Future of Hydraulic Fracturing on Federally Managed Lands,"* U.S. House of Representatives, Committee and Natural Resources, Subcommittee on Energy and Mineral Resources (July 15) (testimony asserting the legality of the Bureau of Land Management rule).
203. David Spence, *Fracking Regulations: Is Federal Hydraulic Fracturing Regulation Around the Corner* (2013).
204. Jody Freeman, *The Wise Way to Regulate Gas Drilling*, N.Y. TIMES (July 5, 2012).
205. Dana R. Caulton et al., *Toward a Better Understanding and Quantification of Methane Emissions from Shale Gas Development*, PNAS EARLY EDITION (August 2014).
206. Hannah J. Wiseman, *Risk and Response in Fracturing Policy*, 84 COLO. L. REV. 729 (2013).
207. David A. Dana & Hannah J. Wiseman, *A Market Approach to Regulating the Energy Revolution: Assurance Bonds, Insurance, and the Certain and Uncertain Risks of Hydraulic Fracturing*, 99 IOWA L. REV. 1523 (2014); SHEILA OLMSTEAD & NATHAN RICHARDSON, MANAGING THE RISKS OF SHALE GAS DEVELOPMENT USING INNOVATIVE LEGAL AND REGULATORY APPROACHES (June 2014) (a report for Resources for the Future).
208. Brian G. Rahm et al., *Shale Gas Operator Violations in the Marcellus and What They Tell Us About Water Resource Risks*, 82 ENERGY POLICY 1 (2015).
209. ALLISON CASSADY, MITIGATING NATURAL GAS USE IN THE ELECTRICITY SECTOR (December 2014) (a report for the Center for American Progress).
210. Justin Gillis, *Paris Climate Talks Avoid Scientists' Idea of "Carbon Budget,"* N.Y. TIMES (November 28, 2015).
211. Energy Future Coalition et al., *Three Pillars: A Comprehensive Approach to Setting Clean Energy Standards for the Electricity Sector* 2–3 (April 2009).
212. INTERNATIONAL PANEL ON CLIMATE CHANGE, CLIMATE CHANGE 2014: SYNTHESIS REPORT 2 (2014).
213. David Biello, *Record Levels of CO_2 Herald the Future of Climate Change*, SCIENTIFIC AMERICAN (November 10, 2015).
214. *Id.*

215. PriceWaterhouseCoopers, *Two Degrees of Separation: Ambition and Reality: Low Carbon Economy Index 2014* (September 2014).
216. International Panel on Climate Change At 20.
217. Ted Parson, *Emmett Institute Updates from the Climate Conference: UCLA Faculty and Students Participating in COP21/CMP11*, Legal Planet (November 30, 2015).
218. James Hansen et al., *Target Atmospheric CO_2: Where Should Humanity Aim?* (2008); Jams Hansen et al., *Assessing "Dangerous Climate Change": Required Reduction of Carbon Emissions to Protect Young People, Future Generations and Nature*, PLOS ONE (December 2013).
219. Michael P. Vandenbergh & Jonathan M. Gilligan, *Beyond Gridlock: The Private Governance Response to Climate Change*, 40 Colum. Envtl. L. J. 217 (2015).
220. Vandenbergh & Gilligan.
221. Mara Prentiss, Energy Revolution: The Physics and the Promise of Efficient Technology 296 (2015).
222. Lester & Hart at 16; *see also* Robert Pollin et al., Green Growth: A U.S. Program for Controlling Climate Change and Expanding Job Opportunities ch. 7 (September 2014).
223. Lester & Hart at 17.
224. Williams et al. at 9.
225. James H. Williams et al., Pathways to Deep Decarbonization in the United States 87–88 (November 2015) (a report for the Sustainable Development Solutions Network).
226. Jason S. Johnson, *The False Federalism of EPA's Clean Power Plan* (May 2015) (arguing that CPP costs exceed economic benefits but does not discuss health and environmental benefits).

3 THE POLITICAL ECONOMY OF CLEAN POWER

1. Jedediah Prudy, After Nature: A Politics for the Anthropocene 258 (2015).
2. Paul Sabin, The Bet: Paul Ehrlich, Julian Simon, and Our Gamble over Earth's Future (2013); *see also* Cass R. Sunstein, *The Battle of Two Hedgehogs*, 60 N.Y.Rev. Books 21 (December 5, 2013).
3. Bill Mckibben, Eaarth: Making a Life on a Tough New Planet (2010).
4. Emily Hammond & David Spencer, *The Regulatory Contract in the Marketplace*, 69 Vand. L. Rev. 141 (2015).
5. Ted Nordhaus & Michael Shellenberger, Break Through: From the Death of Environmentalism to the Politics of Possibility (2007).
6. The Intergovernmental Panel on Climate Change offers a useful definition: "Climate change refers to a change in the state of the climate that can be identified (e.g., by using statistical tests) by changes in the mean and/or the variability of its properties, and that persists for an extended period, typically decades or longer." Intergovernmental Panel on Climate Change, *Climate Change 2014: Impacts, Adaptation and Vulnerability* 4 (2014) also referred to as the Fifth Assessment report or AR5 and can be found at www.ipcc.ch/.

7. Sidney A. Shapiro & Joseph P. Tomain, Achieving Democracy: The Future of Progressive Regulation (2014).
8. Elizabeth Bast et al., Empty Promises: G20 Subsidies to Oil, Gas and Coal Production (November 2015); John Schwartz, Global Fossil Fuel Subsidies Dwarf Funding Commitment to Climate Change, N.Y. Times 9 (December 6, 2015).
9. Nancy Pfund & Ben Healy, *What Would Jefferson Do? The Historical Role of Federal Subsidies in Shaping America's Energy Future* (September 2011) (a report for Double Bottom Line Venture Capital).
10. Joseph P. Tomain, Ending Dirty Energy Policy: Prelude to Climate Change (2011).
11. Jim Manzi, *The New American System*, National Affairs 3 (Spring 2014).
12. Written Testimony of Robert Weissman, *Before the Senate Judiciary Committee on "Examining the Federal Regulatory System to Improve Accountability, Transparency and Integrity"* (June 10, 2015) (on behalf of Public Citizen of which Mr. Weissman serves as president).
13. Center for the New Energy Economy, Colorado State University, Powering Forward: Presidential and Executive Agency Actions to Drive Clean Energy in America (2014); American Energy Innovation Council, *Restoring American Energy Innovation Leadership: Report Card, Challenges, and Opportunities* (February 2015); *Catalyzing American Ingenuity: The Role of Government in Energy Innovation* (2011).
14. Mariana Mazzucuto, The Entrepreneurial State: Debunking Public vs. Private Myths chs. 4 and 5 (2014).
15. Bloomberg New Energy Finance & Business Council for Sustainable Energy, 2015 Factbook: Sustainable Energy in America (February 2015).
16. Institute for 21st Century Energy, *Energy Works for US: Solutions for Securing America's Future* (2013).
17. Business Roundtable, Taking Action on Energy: A CEO Vision for America's Energy Future (February 2013).
18. Stanley Reed & Sara Hamdan, *Life after Oil in the Mideast*, N.Y. Times B1 (December 5, 2015); Clifford Krauss, *Oil Prices: What's Behind the Drop? Simple Economics*, N.Y. Times (October 5, 2015); Jeremy Ashkenas, Alicia Parlapiano & Hannah Fairfield, *How the U.S. and OPEC Drive Oil Prices*, N.Y. Times (October 5, 2015).
19. Joseph Tomain, *The Romney-Ryan Energy Plan" Back to States' Rights* (August 23, 2012) available at www.progressivereform.org/CPRBlog.cfm?idBlog=5555E3AE-B09D-063C-3AAA0AD358F3CB84.
20. Business Roundtable at 2.
21. Institute for 21st Century Energy, *Energy Works* at 3.
22. *Id.*
23. Business Roundtable at 2 and 4–5.
24. Institute for 21st Century Energy, *Energy Works* at 4.
25. Business Roundtable at 7.
26. Institute for 21st Century Energy, *Energy Works* at 5.
27. *Id.*

28. Matthew L. Wald, *New Energy Struggles on Its Way to Markets*, N.Y. Times A11 (December 28, 2013); *see also* Center for Climate and Energy Solutions, *Climate Solutions: The Role of Nuclear Power* (April 2014) available at www.c2es.org/publications/climate-solutions-role-nuclear-power.
29. Richard A. Muller, Energy for Future Presidents 3 (2012).
30. William Nordhaus, The Climate Casino: Risk, Uncertainty, and Economics for a Warming World 3 (2013).
31. Nicholas Stern, A Blueprint for a Safer Planet: How to Manage Climate Change and Create A New Era of Progress and Prosperity 7 (2009).
32. Massachusetts Institute of Technology, The Future of Coal: Options for a Carbon-Constrained World (2007); Alexandra B. Klass, *CPR Perspective: Carbon Capture and Geologic Sequestration* (July 2009) available at www.progressivereform.org/perspCarbonCapture.cfm.
33. Governor's Independent Investigation Panel, Upper Big Branch: The April 5, 2010 Explosion: A Failure of Basic Coal Mine Safety Practices (May 2011); U.S. Department of Labor, *Performance Coal Company, Upper Big Branch Mine-South, Massey Energy Company, Mine ID: 46–08436, Single Source Page* available at www.msha.gov/PerformanceCoal/PerformanceCoal.asp.
34. Trip Gabriel, Michael Wines, & Coral Davenport, *Chemical Spill Muddies Picture in a State Wary of Regulations*, N.Y. Times 1 (January 19, 2014).
35. Center for Public Integrity, *Breathless and Burdened* (2014) available at www.publicintegrity.org/environment/breathless-and-burdened.
36. Thomas W. Merrill & David M. Schizer, *The Shale Oil and Gas Revolution, Hydraulic Fracturing, Water Contamination: A Regulatory Strategy*, 98 Minn. L. Rev. 145 (2013).
37. Kansas City Star, *House Panel to Review Kansas Fracking Industry, Earthquakes* (January 21, 2014); State Impact, *How Oil and Gas Disposal Wells Can Cause Earthquakes* (January 2014); Mike Soraghan, *Earthquakes: Okla. Oil and Gas Activity "Likely" Linked to Record-setting Seismic Surge*, EnergyWire (May 6, 2014).
38. Center for Climate and Energy Solutions.
39. Energy Policy Act 2005, Pub. L. No. 109–58 (August 8, 2005).
40. Nuclear Energy Institute, *DOE Finalizes Vogtle Loan Guarantees* (February 20, 2014).
41. Doug Kaplow, Nuclear Power: Still Not Viable without Subsidies (2011) (a report for the Union of Concerned Scientists); *see also* Amory B. Lovins, *The Economics of a US Civilian Nuclear Phase-Out*, 69 Bulletin of the Atomic Scientists (March 2013).
42. Institute for 21st Century Energy, *Energy Works* at 29.
43. Business Roundtable at chs. VI and VII.
44. Heritage Foundation, Twelve Principles to Guide U.S, Energy Policy (June 26, 2007).
45. AR5 at 3.
46. National Climate Assessment (May 2014).

47. Encyclical Letter, Laudato Si' *of the Holy Father Francis on Care for Our Common Home* (2015). *See also* Bill McKibben, *The Pope and the Planet*, N.Y. REV. BOOKS 40 (August 13, 2015).
48. United Nations Framework Convention on Climate Change, Paris Agreement, FCCC/CP/2015/L.9/Rev.1 at 20 (December 12, 2015) available at unfccc.int/resource/docs/2015/cop21/eng/l09r01.pdf.
49. ELIZABETH KOLBERT, FIELD NOTES FROM A CATASTROPHE: MAN, NATURE, AND CLIMATE CHANGE (2006); PADDY WOODWORTH, OUR ONCE AND FUTURE PLANET: RESTORING THE WORLD IN THE CLIMATE CHANGE CENTURY (2013); ELIZABETH KOLBERT, THE SIXTH EXTINCTION: AN UNNATURAL HISTORY (2014); NORDHAUS, THE CLIMATE CASINO.
50. US Government Accountability Office, *Climate Change: Energy Infrastructure Risks and Adaptation Efforts* (January 2014).
51. AR5 at 6–8.
52. AR5 at 11–21.
53. Justin Gillis, *Panel's Warning on Climate Risk: Worst Is Yet to Come*, N.Y. TIMES (March 31, 2014); Alexander Martin, *Climate Change Impact Is Wide, U.N. Says*, WALL ST. J. (March 31, 2014).
54. *Rio Declaration on Environment and Development*, Annex 1, Principle 15, U.N. Doc. A/CONF. 151/26 (Vol. 1) (August 12, 1992).
55. John S. Applegate, *Embracing a Precautionary Approach to Climate Change* in DAVID M. DRIESEN (ed.), ECONOMIC THOUGHT AND U.S. CLIMATE POLICY 173–81 (2010).
56. Applegate at 181–189.
57. Lisa Heinzerling, *Climate Change, Human Health, and the Post-Cautionary Principle* in DAVID M. DRIESEN (ed.), ECONOMIC THOUGHT AND U.S. CLIMATE POLICY 173–81 (2010).
58. Applegate at 185–86.
59. CASS R. SUNSTEIN, WORST-CASE SCENARIOS ch. 3 (2007).
60. E.F. SCHUMACHER, SMALL IS BEAUTIFUL: ECONOMICS AS IF PEOPLE MATTERED (1973).
61. DONELLA H. MEADOWS ET AL., THE LIMITS TO GROWTH: A REPORT OF THE CLUB OF ROME'S PROJECT ON THE PREDICAMENT OF MANKIND (1972).
62. JEDEDIAH PURDY, AFTER NATURE: A POLITICS FOR THE ANTHROPOCENE ch.8 (2015).
63. MARK SAGOFF, THE ECONOMY OF THE EARTH: PHILOSOPHY, LAW AND THE ENVIRONMENT (1988).
64. AMARTYA SEN, THE IDEA OF JUSTICE (2009); *see also* Stanford Encyclopedia of Philosophy, *The Capability Approach* (April 14, 2011) available at plato.stanford.edu/entries/capability-approach/. This entry provides a good description of the concept of capabilities together with a useful bibliography of Sen's work in this area.
65. MARTHA NUSSBAUM, CREATING CAPABILITIES: THE HUMAN DEVELOPMENT APPROACH (2011); *see also, id.* Stanford Encyclopedia also for a short bibliography of Nussbaum's work in the field.
66. DIANE COYLE, THE ECONOMICS OF ENOUGH: HOW TO RUN THE ECONOMY AS IF THE FUTURE MATTERS 26 (2011).

67. Diane Coyle, GDP: A Brief but Affectionate History 122 (2014).
68. Coyle, GDP at 137 (2014).
69. Coyle, GDP at 139 (2014).
70. Joseph E. Stiglitz, Amartya Sen & Jean-Paul Fitoussi, *Report by the Commission on the Measurement of Economic Performance and Social Progress* 11–15 (September 14, 2009).
71. Rob Dietz & Dan O'Neill, Enough Is Enough: Building a Sustainable Economy in a World of Finite Resources 25–29 (2013).
72. International Energy Agency, World Energy Outlook 2004 334 (2004).
73. James H. Williams et al., Policy Implications of Deep Decarbonization in the United States 24–25 (2015) (a report for the Sustainable Development Solutions Network).
74. Jeffrey D. Sachs, Common Wealth: Economics for a Crowded Planet 57 (2008) (emphasis in original); *see also* Gro Harlem Brundtland et al., *Environment and Development Challenges: The Imperative to Act* (2012).
75. Neva Goodwin, *Prices and Work in the New Economy* (April 2014). Several organizations and think tanks are undertaking this work under the banner of the new economics movement. *See e.g. Center for the Advancement of a Steady State Economy* homepage at http://steadystate.org/; *Tellus Institute* homepage at www.tellus.org/; *New Economics Institute* homepage at www.neweconomics.org/; *New Economy Coalition* homepage at http://neweconomy.net/; *Institute for New Economic Thinking* homepage at http://ineteconomics.org/; and, *Institute for Policy Studies* homepage at www.ips-dc.org/.
76. James Gustave Speth, The Bridge at the End of the World: Capitalism, The Environment, and Crossing from Crisis to Sustainability 116 (2008).
77. Dietz & O'Neill at 18–19.
78. McKibben, *The Pope and the Planet* at 41–42.
79. Speth, Bridge at 113.
80. James Gustave Speth, America the Possible: Manifesto for a New Economy ch. 1 (2012).
81. Speth, Bridge at 124.
82. *Id. See also* Speth, America the Possible at 98; Naomi Klein, This Changes Everything: Capitalism vs. the Climate (2014).
83. Sidney A. Shapiro & Joseph P. Tomain, Achieving Democracy: The Future of Progressive Regulation (2014).
84. Hannah Fairfield, *The Best of Both Worlds in Cutting Emissions?*, N.Y. Times Sunday Review 3 (June 8, 2014); *see also* Tom Dutzik & Elizabeth Ridlington, A *Double Success: Tackling Global Warming while Growing the Economy with an Improved Regional Greenhouse Gas Initiative* (2013); *Environment Northeast, Economy-Wide Benefits of RGGI: Economic Growth through Energy Efficiency* (June 2011).
85. Jeffrrey D. Sachs, Common Wealth: Economics for a Crowded Planet (2008). *See also* Jeffrey D. Sachs, The Price of Civilization: Reawakening American Virtue and Prosperity (2011).
86. The White House, *President Barack Obama's State of the Union Address* (January 28, 2014).

87. Executive Office of the President, *The President's Climate Action Plan* 19 (June 2013).
88. *See* Environmental and Energy Study Institute, *Obama Administration FY 2015 Budget Proposal: Sustainable Energy, Buildings, Transportation and Climate* (March 2014).
89. Climate Action Plan.
90. Associated Press, *Obama Administration Halts New Coal Leases on Federal Lands*, N.Y. TIMES (January 15, 2016).
91. *Climate Action Plan* at 6–14, 17–19.
92. NATIONAL CLIMATE ASSESSMENT at ch. 4 at 114.
93. TOMAIN, ENDING DIRTY ENERGY POLICY at chs. 3 and 4.
94. WORLD COMMISSION ON ENVIRONMENT AND DEVELOPMENT, OUR COMMON FUTURE 8 (1987).
95. THE PRESIDENT'S COUNCIL ON SUSTAINABLE DEVELOPMENT, TOWARDS A SUSTAINABLE AMERICA: ADVANCING PROSPERITY, OPPORTUNITY AND A HEALTHY ENVIRONMENT FOR THE 21ST CENTURY 21–24 (May 1999) (recognizing the need for cleaner electricity and transportation); THE PRESIDENT'S COUNCIL ON SUSTAINABLE DEVELOPMENT, SUSTAINABLE AMERICA: A NEW CONSENSUS FOR THE PROSPERITY, OPPORTUNITY AND A HEALTHY ENVIRONMENT FOR THE FUTURE (1996); THE PRESIDENT'S COUNCIL ON SUSTAINABLE DEVELOPMENT, BUILDING CONSENSUS: A PROGRESS REPORT ON SUSTAINABLE AMERICA (1997); THE PRESIDENT'S COUNCIL ON SUSTAINABLE DEVELOPMENT, THE ROAD TO SUSTAINABLE DEVELOPMENT: A SNAPSHOT OF ACTIVITIES IN THE UNITED STATES (March 1997). These reports are available at http://clinton4.nara.gov/PCSD/Publications/index.html.
96. NATIONAL ENERGY POLICY DEVELOPMENT GROUP, NATIONAL ENERGY POLICY (May 2001).
97. U.S. Department of Energy, 2013 *Strategic Sustainability Performance Plan* (June 2013) available at http://energy.gov/eere/spo/downloads/2013-strategic-sustainability-performance-plan.
98. Rosina M. Bierman & Pamela A. Matson, *Energy in the Context of Sustainability*, DAEDALUS 146, 147 (Winter 2013).
99. The United Nations adopted eight millennium development goals with the aim of reducing poverty. Goal seven addresses environmental sustainability. The goals and related information can be found at www.un.org/millenniumgoals/.
100. United Nations Framework Convention on Climate Change, Paris Agreement 21.
101. THE SECRETARY GENERAL'S HIGH–LEVEL GROUP ON SUSTAINABLE ENERGY FOR ALL, SUSTAINABLE ENERGY FOR ALL: A FRAMEWORK FOR ACTION 5 (January 2012) (ENERGY FOR ALL). *See also* BAN KI-MOON, SUSTAINABLE ENERGY FOR ALL (November 2011).
102. ENERGY FOR ALL at 5.
103. CLEANEDGE, A STATUS REPORT ON RISING COMMITMENTS AMONG CORPORATIONS AND GOVERNMENTS TO REACH 100% RENEWABLES (2015).
104. CERES & SUSTAINALYTICS, GAINING GROUND: CORPORATE PROGRESS ON THE CERES ROADMAP FOR SUSTAINABILITY (2014) available at www.ceres.org/roadmap-assessment/progress-report/progress-report.

105. World Economic Forum, Insight Report: Global Risks 2014 (9th ed. 2014) available at www.weforum.org/reports/global-risks-2014-report.
106. The idea of natural monopoly is that there are certain characteristics of an industry such that a single firm is superior to multiple firms. First, a single firm can continue to realize economies of scale over a long-range production. Second, a multiplicity of firms would make wastefully duplicative capital investments. Consumers, for example, do not need a multiplicity of TV cable lines, telephone lines, and gas or electricity lines to their homes. Thus utility regulation is intended to correct that market failure and to provide a good deemed to be in the public interest. Joseph P. Tomain & Richard D. Cudahy, Energy Law in a Nutshell 39–42 (2nd ed. 2011); Joseph P. Tomain, *Whither Natural Monopoly?* in Peter Z. Grossman & Daniel H. Cole (eds.), The End of a Natural Monopoly: Deregulation and Competition in the Electric Power Industry 111 (2003).
107. Ann E. Carlson & Robert W. Fri, *Designing a Durable Energy Policy*, Daedalus 119 (Winter 2013).
108. REN21, Renewables 2013 Global Status Report 13 (2013). The figures for electricity generation also include hydropower.
109. *American Recovery and Reinvestment Act of 2009*, Pub. L. No. 111–15 (2009).
110. Peter Ogden, Mari Hernandez & Ben Bovanick, *Galvanizing Clean Energy Investment in the United States* (April 3, 2014) available at www.americanprogress.org/issues/green/report/2014/04/03/87092/galvanizing-clean-energy-investment-in-the-united-states/.
111. Ogden, Hernandez & Bovarnick at 2.
112. Ecova, Inc, *How to Capitalize on Billions in Available Energy Incentives: 4 Types of Qualifying Energy Efficiency Investments* (June 2013) available at www.ecova.com/news-media/whitepapers/billions-in-available-incentives-whitepaper.aspx.
113. Jaclyn Trop & Diane Cardwell, *Tesla Plans $5 Billion Battery Factory for Mass-Market Electric Car*, N.Y. Times (February 26, 2014); *see also Energy Manager Today Staff, Energy Storage Market Sees Funding Boom* (March 6, 2014) available at www.energymanagertoday.com/energy-storage-market-sees-funding-boom-099254/; Erica Gies, *Lithium Producer Chases Tesla's Bold Battery Plan*, N.Y. Times B3 (March 17, 2014).
114. Tesla Powerwall: Tesla Home Batter homepage at www.teslamotors.com/powerwall; Diane Cardwell, *Tesla Ventures into Solar Power Storage for Home and Business*, N.Y. Times (May 1, 2015).
115. Daimler, *Sales Launch of Private Energy Storage Plants* (June 9, 2015) available at http://media.daimler.com/dcmedia/0-921-614316-1-1820346-1-0-1-0-0-0-0-0-0-1-@aj.a1.s177018-0-0-0-0.html.
116. Bloomberg New Energy Finance, *Clean Energy Defies Fossil Fuel Price Crash to Attract Record $329Bn Global Investment in 2015*, (January 14, 2016).
117. CDP, *Lower Emissions, Higher ROI: The Rewards of Low Carbon Investment* (January 15, 2014) available at www.cdp.net/en-US/Results/Pages/Carbon-Action-Reports.aspx.
118. PEW Charitable Trust at 1; REN21, Global Futures Report 2103 at 32–35.
119. Williams et al. at 38–48.

120. Public Broadcasting System, *American Experience: Energy Crisis* available at www.pbs.org/wgbh/americanexperience/features/bonus-video/presidents-economy-carter/.
121. Jon A. Krosnick & Bo MacInnis, *Does the American Public Support Legislation to Reduce Greenhouse Gas Emissions?*, DAEDALUS 27–28 (Winter 2013); Roger E. Kasperson & Bonnie J. Ram, *The Public Acceptance of New Energy Technologies*, DAEDALUS 90 (Winter 2013).
122. Krosnick & MacInnis at 26, 33–34 (Winter 2013); Kasperson & Ram at 90.
123. Krosnick & MacInnis at 35–36.
124. Dietz, Stern & Weber at 81–84.
125. RICHARD H. THALER & CASS R. SUNSTEIN, NUDGE: IMPROVING DECISIONS ABOUT HEALTH, WEALTH, AND HAPPINESS 193–96 (2008); CASS R. SUNSTEIN, SIMPLER: THE FUTURE OF GOVERNMENT 134–36 (2013).
126. Thomas Dietz, Paul C. Stern & Elke U. Weber, *Reducing Carbon-Based Consumption through Changes in Household Behavior*, DAEDALUS 78, 79–80 (Winter 2013).
127. Christina Hood, Managing Interactions between Carbon Pricing and Existing Energy Policies 4 (2013) (a report for the International Energy Agency).
128. Hood at 4.
129. Patrick Luckow et al., *2013 Carbon Dioxide Price Forecast* 5–7 (November 2013) (a report for Synapse Energy).
130. Luckow.
131. Luckow at 5.
132. Lawrence H. Goulder & Andrew R. Schein, *Carbon Taxes vs. Cap and Trade: A Critical Review* (August 2013) available at www.nber.org/papers/w19338.
133. Goulder & Schein at 1–3.
134. Rena Steinzor, Michael Patoka & James Goodwin, *Behind Closed Doors at the White House: How Politics Trumps Protection of Public Health, Worker Safety and the Environment* (November 2011) (a report for the Center for Progressive Reform); Simon Haeder & Susan Webb Yackee, *Influence and the Administrative Process: Lobbying the U.S. President's Office of Management and Budget*, 109 AM POL. SCI. REV. 507 (August 2015).
135. Brookings: Planet Policy, *Why the Federal Government Should Shadow Price Carbon* (July 13, 2015): Joseph P. Tomain, *Shadow Rates: Financing Clean Energy*, 51 INFRASTRUCTURE 1 (Spring 2012).
136. US Environmental Protection Administration, *Fact Sheet: The Social Cost of Carbon* (2013) available at www.epa.gov/climatechange/EPAactivities/economics/scc.html.
137. *Id.*
138. David P, Littell, *Putting a Price on Carbon: How EPA Can Establish a U.S. GHG Program for the Electricity Sector*, 152 PUB. UTIL. FORT. 16, 17 (February 2014).
139. Luckow at 3–4.
140. Daniel A. Farber, *Modeling Climate Change and Its Impacts: Law, Policy, and Science*, 86 TEX. L. REV. 16545 (2008).
141. Luckow at 15.
142. CDP North America, *Use of Internal Carbon Price by Companies as Incentive and Strategic Planning Tool: A Review of Findings from CDP 2013 Disclosure*

(December 2013). *See* CDP homepage at www.cdp.net/en-US/Pages/HomePage .aspx.

143. Encyclical Letter of the Supreme Pontiff Francis, Laudato Si': On Care for Our Common Home 70–91(2015).
144. Sarah Krakoff, *Parenting the Planet* in Denis G. Arnold (ed.), The Ethics of Global Climate Change 145 (2014); World Commission on Environment and Development, Our Common Future (1987).
145. Donella Meadows et al., The Limits to Growth: A Report for the Club of Rome's Project on the Predicament of Mankind (1974).
146. The report and its critical reception are discussed in Joseph P. Tomain, Ending Dirty Energy Policy: Prelude to Climate Change ch. 2 (2011).
147. Shapiro & Tomain, Achieving Democracy at ch. 6.
148. Sarah Krakoff, *Planetarian Identity Formation and the Relocalization of Environmental Law*, 64 Florida L. Rev. 87, 98–99 (2012).
149. William Boyd, Douglas Kysar & Jeffrey J. Rachlinski, *Law, Environment, and the "Non-Dismal" Social Sciences*, 8 Ann. Rev. of L. and Soc. Sci. 183 (2012).
150. Purdy at 1185.
151. Purdy at 1196.
152. Purdy at 1202.
153. Tomain, Ending Dirty Energy Policy at chs. 1 and 2; *The Dominant Model of United States Energy Policy*, 61 U. Colo. L. Rev. 355 (1990).
154. Charles E. Bayless, *The End of an Age: Survival in the New Market Requires Embracing New Technologies and Practices*, 152 Pub. Util. Fort. 20 (April 2014).
155. Rosina M. Bierman & Pamela A. Matson, *Energy in the Context of Sustainability*, Daedalus at 153–55 (Winter 2013).
156. Bierman & Matson at 146, 153 (Winter 2013); Michael Hayden, Curt Hebert & Susan Tierney, Cyber Security and the North American Electric Grid: New Policy Approaches to Address an Evolving Threat 1 (February 2014) (a report from the Bipartisan Policy Center).
157. Sara Hastings-Simon, Dickon Pinner & Martin Stuchey, *Myths and Realities of Clean Technologies* (April 2014) (a white paper for McKinsey & Company).
158. Business Roundtable at 9, 42.

4 INNOVATION POLICY AND INSTITUTIONS

1. Arnulf Grübler, Nebojša Nakićenović & David G. Victor, *Dynamics of Energy Technologies and Global Change*, 27 Energy Policy 247, 248 (1999); *see also* Neil E. Harrison & John Mikler, *An Introduction to Climate Innovation* in Neil E. Harrison & John Mikler (eds.), Climate Innovation: Liberal Capitalism and Climate Change 1, 3 (2014).
2. William J. Baumol, The Free-Market Innovation Machine: Analyzing the Growth Miracle of Capitalism (2002); William J. Baumol, Robert E. Litan & Carl J. Schramm, Good Capitalism, Bad Capitalism, and the Economics of Growth and Prosperity (2007); William H. Janeway, Doing Capitalism in the Innovation Economy: Markets, Speculation and the State (2012).

3. Jim Manzi, *The New American System*, NATIONAL AFFAIRS 3 (Spring 2014).
4. Manzi at 6–7; SIDNEY A. SHAPIRO & JOSEPH P. TOMAIN, ACHIEVING DEMOCRACY: THE FUTURE OF PROGRESSIVE REGULATION ch. 2 (2014).
5. Manzi at 9–12; MARIANA MAZZACUTO, THE ENTREPRENEURIAL STATE: DEBUNKING PUBLIC VS. PRIVATE MYTHS chs. 4–5(2014).
6. Ernest J. Moniz, *Stimulating Energy Technology Innovation*, 141 DAEDALUS 81 (Spring 2012).
7. *See generally* CHARLES W. WESSNER & ALAN WM. WOLFF (eds.), RISING TO THE CHALLENGE: U.S. INNOVATION POLICY FOR THE GLOBAL ECONOMY (2012).
8. Richard K. Lester & David M. Hart, UNLOCKING ENERGY INNOVATION: HOW AMERICA CAN BUILD A LOW-COST, LOW-CARBON ENERGY SYSTEM 38 (2012).
9. AMERICAN ENERGY INNOVATION COUNCIL, CATALYZING AMERICAN INGENUITY: THE ROLE OF GOVERNMENT IN ENERGY INNOVATION 11–13 (2011) (AEIC, CATALYZING AMERICAN INGENUITY).
10. LESTER & HART at x, 3–4, 30–31.
11. Bill Gates, *We Need Clean-Energy Innovation, and Lots of It*, GATES NOTES (July 29, 2015); *see also* Bipartisan Policy Center, *Restoring American Energy Innovation Leadership: Report Card, Challenges, and Opportunities* (February 2015).
12. Breakthrough Energy Coalition homepage at www.breakthroughenergycoalition .com/en/news.html.
13. Robert MacNeil, *Climate Policy, Energy Technologies, and the American Developmental State* in NEIL E. HARRISON & JOHN MIKLER (eds.), CLIMATE INNOVATION: LIBERAL CAPITALISM AND CLIMATE CHANGE 45 (2014); LESTER & HART at 31.
14. JAMES H. WILLIAMS ET AL., POLICY IMPLICATIONS OF DEEP DECARBONIZATION IN THE UNITED STATES 13 (2015) (a report for the Sustainable Development Solutions Network).
15. Kelly Sims Gallagher et al., *The Energy Technology Innovation System*, 37 ANNU. REV. ENVIRON. RESOUR. 137 (2012); *see also* MAZZACUTO at 34–41 (2014); HARRISON & MIKLER at 12; LESTER & HART at 3.
16. JANEWAY at 1–10 and ch. 10; MAZZACUTO at 47–48 (2014).
17. Gallagher et al. at 150.
18. Jim Manzi & Peter Wehner, *Conservatives and Climate Change*, 24 NATIONAL AFFAIRS 17 (Summer 2015).
19. Office of the President, *The Cost of Delaying Action to Stem Climate Change* (June 2014).
20. Jason S. Johnston, The False Federalism of EPA's Clean Power Plan, Virginia Law and Economics Research Paper No. 16 available at http://papers.ssrn.com /sol3/papers.cfm?abstract_id=2604308## (May 2015); Manzi & Wehner, *Conservatives and Climate Change*.
21. Stefan Ambec et al., *The Porter Hypothesis at 20: Can Environmental Regulation Enhance Innovation and Competitiveness?*, 7 REV. ENVTL ECON. AND POL. 2 (January 2013).
22. Paul Sullivan, *The Investment Impact of Climate Change*, N.Y. TIMES B4 (December 5, 2015).

23. David Frankel & Humayun Tai, *Giving US Energy Efficiency a Jolt* (December 2013) (a report for McKinsey & Company).
24. Janeway at ch. 11 (2012); Shapiro & Tomain at ch. 4 (2014).
25. Laura Diaz et al., Transforming U.S. Energy Innovation 59 (November 2011).
26. American Energy Innovation Council (AEIC), Catalyzing American Ingenuity; American Energy Innovation Council a Business Plan for America's Energy Future (2010) (AEIC, a Business Plan).
27. AEIC, Catalyzing American Ingenuity at 5 and ch. 1.
28. Lester & Hart at 26.
29. Gallagher et al. at 140; Lester & Hart at 26–27.
30. Lester & Hart at 60.
31. Lester & Hart at 36.
32. Mazzacuto at 57–62.
33. Gallagher et al. at 149–50.
34. Editorial, *Challenges for R&D and Innovation in Energy*, 83 Energy Pol. 193 (August 2015).
35. Jesse Jenkins & Sara Mansur, *Bridging the Clean Energy Valleys of Death: Helping American Entrepreneurs Meet the Nation's Energy Innovation Imperative*, The Breakthrough 9 (November 2011).
36. Bipartisan Policy Center, America's Energy Resurgence: Sustaining Success, Confronting Challenges 99 (February 2013).
37. Lester & Hart at 67.
38. Hal Harvey, Jeffrey Rissman & Sonia Aggarwal, *Energy Technology Innovation Leadership in the 21st Century* 3–4 (January 2013).
39. Gallagher et al. at 146–47.
40. James H. Williams et al., Policy Implications of Deep Decarbonization in the United States (2015) (a report for the Deep Decarbonization Pathways Project); Ann E. Carlson & Robert W. Fri, *Designing a Durable Energy Policy*, 142 Daedalus 119, 121–22 (Winter 2013).
41. Joseph P. Tomain, Ending Dirty Energy Policy: Prelude to Climate Change chs. 3 & 4 (2011); Harvey, Rissman & Aggarwal, *Energy Technology Innovation Leadership in the 21st Century* 3; *see also* Robert W. Fri & Stephen Ansolabehere, *The Alternative Energy Future: Challenges for Technological Change*, 141 Daedalus 5, 7 (Spring 2012).
42. Manzi at 18–25.
43. Ambec at 12.
44. Grübler et al. at 249; Harvey et al. at 4; Harrison & Mikler at 7; Nicolson & Stepp at 15; Diaz et al. at 65; and, Mazzacuto at 48.
45. Mazzacuto at ch. 9.
46. Albert C. Lin, *Lessons from the Past for Accessing Energy Technologies for the Future*, 61 UCLA L. Rev. 1814, 1819 (2014).
47. See Laura Diaz Anadon et al., *The Pressing Energy Innovation Challenge of the US National Laboratories*, Nature Energy (September 2016); T.J. Glauthier et al., Securing America's Future: Realizing the Potential of DOE National Laboratories: Final Report of the Commission to Review the Effectiveness of the National Energy Laboratories (2015); Report of

THE SECRETARY OF ENERGY TASK FORCE ON DOE NATIONAL LABORATORIES (2015).

48. NATIONAL RENEWABLE ENERGY LABORATORY, RENEWABLE ELECTRICITY FUTURES REPORT (2012) is a four-volume study that examines penetration of renewable electricity resources, generation and storage technologies, end-use demand, and the operation and planning for bulk power systems. See also *National Renewable Energy Laboratory, Transportation Energy Futures Project* available at www.nrel.gov/analysis/re_futures/.
49. Scott Andes, Mark Muro & Matthew Stepp, *Going Local: Connecting National Labs to Their Regions to Maximize Innovation and Growth* (September 2014) (a report for the Brookings Institution).
50. Andes, Muro & Stepp at 4–12.
51. MAZZUCATO at 105–10.
52. MAZZUCATO at 78.
53. COMMITTEE ON PROSPERING IN THE GLOBAL ECONOMY OF THE 21ST CENTURY: AN AGENDA FOR AMERICAN SCIENCE AND TECHNOLOGY, RISING ABOVE THE GATHERING STORM: ENERGIZING AND EMPLOYING AMERICA FOR BRIGHTER ECONOMIC FUTURE (2007); *see also* NATIONAL ACADEMY OF SCIENCES, NATIONAL ACADEMY OF ENGINEERING, & NATIONAL RESEARCH COUNCIL, AMERICA'S ENERGY FUTURE (2009); ELECTRICITY FROM RENEWABLE RESOURCES: STATUS, PROSPECTS, AND IMPEDIMENTS (2010).
54. MAZZUCATO at 78–79.
55. RISING ABOVE THE GATHERING STORM.
56. *America Creating Opportunities to Meaningfully Promote Excellence in Technology, Education, and Sciences Act of 2007*, Pub. L. No. 110–69.
57. *American Recovery and Reinvestment Act*, Pub. L. No. 111–5.
58. FY 2015 Congressional Budget, Advanced Research Projects Agency-Energy (ARPA-E) at 349.
59. FY 2015 Congressional Budget, Advanced Research Projects Agency-Energy (ARPA-E) at 354.
60. MAZZUCATO at 132–35.
61. FY 2015 Congressional Budget, Advanced Research Projects Agency-Energy (ARPA-E) at 355.
62. ADVANCED RESEARCH PROJECTS AGENCY-ENERGY, STRATEGIC VISION 2013 (2013).
63. *See generally* DEPARTMENT OF ENERGY, OFFICE OF SCIENCE, ENERGY FRONTIER RESEARCH CENTERS: TECHNICAL SUMMARIES (August 2014).
64. BIPARTISAN POLICY CENTER at 103–07.
65. See Robert Atkinson et al., *Strengthening Clean Energy Competitiveness: Opportunities for America COMPETES Reauthorization* (June 2010) (a report for the Information and Technology Foundation, the Breakthrough Institute and the Brookings Institution); AMERICAN ENERGY INNOVATION COUNCIL.
66. JENKINS & MANSUR at 7.
67. Editorial, *Challenges for R&D and Innovation in Energy*, 83 ENERGY POL. 193 (August 2015).
68. *See e.g.* Kassia Yanosek, *Policies for Financing the Energy Transition*, 141 DAEDALUS 94, 96 (Spring 2012).

69. Bipartisan Policy Center at 98.
70. MIT, *Carbon Capture & Storage: Cancelled and Inactive Projects* available at https://sequestration.mit.edu/tools/projects/index_cancelled.html.
71. *See* Energy.gov, Office of Energy Efficiency & Renewable Energy, *Offshore Wind Advanced Technology Demonstration Projects* available at http://energy.gov/eere/wind/offshore-wind-advanced-technology-demonstration-projects.
72. *See e.g.* Energy.gov, Office of Energy Efficiency & Renewable Energy, *Solar* available at http://energy.gov/eere/renewables/solar.
73. Jenkins & Mansur, *Bridging the Clean Energy Valleys of Death* at 13.
74. Bipartisan Policy Center at 109–11.
75. Harrison & Mikler at 25–28.
76. Mazzucato at 127–29.
77. Harrison & Mikler at 19, 36.
78. Frankfurt School-UNEP Collaborating Centre for Climate & Sustainable Energy Finance & Bloomberg New Energy Finance, Global Trends in Renewable Energy Investment 2014 17 and ch. 8 (2014).
79. Hiroko Tabuchi, *Venture Capitalists Return to Backing Science Start-Ups*, N.Y. Times (October 12, 2014) (reporting VC investments of $1.24 billion for industrial and energy start-ups in the first half of 2014, which was below the 2008 peak of $4.46 billion for those two sectors).
80. Bipartisan Policy Center at 101; Jenkins & Mansur, *Bridging the Clean Energy Valleys of Death* at 7; Yanosek at 99.
81. Mazzucato at 48.
82. *See generally* Jeffrey Rissman, Hallie Kennan & Maxine Savitz, Unleashing Private-Sector Energy R&D: Insights from Interviews with 17 R&D Leaders (January 2013) (a report for the American Energy Innovation Council).
83. Robert Pollin et al., Green Growth: A U.S. Program for Controlling Climate Change and Expanding Job Opportunities 242 (September 2014) (a report for the Center for American Progress and the Political Economy Research institute at the University of Massachusetts Amherst).
84. *Id.*
85. Luke Mills, *Global Trends in Clean Energy Investment*, Bloomberg New Energy Finance 5 (July 2014); Frankfurt School-UNEP at 23.
86. REN21 Renewable: Global Futures Report 2013 32 (2013).
87. Bloomberg New Energy Finance, *Stronger First Quarter for Global Investment in Clean Energy* (April 16, 2014).
88. Bloomberg New Energy Finance, *The Americas Stand Out in Solid Q3 for Clean Energy Investment* (October 7, 2015).
89. Frankfurt School-UNEP at 31–34.
90. REN21, Renewables 2014: Global Status Report 103 (2014).
91. REN21, Renewables 2013: Global Status Report 13 (2013). The figures for electricity generation also include hydropower.
92. Justin Doom, *Clean-Energy Spending at $175 Billion on Chinese Rise* (October 2, 2104) available at www.bloomberg.com/news/2014-10-02/clean-energy-spending-at-175-billion-on-chinese-rise.html.

93. Bloomberg New Energy Finance, *Clean Energy Defies Fossil Fuel Price Crash to Attract Record $329Bn Global Investment in 2015* (January 14, 2016).
94. Luke Mills at 10.
95. Deutsche Bank, *Energy and Climate Strategy: Supporting the Transition to Sustainable Growth* available at www.db.com/cr/en/environment/energy-and-climate-strategy.htm.
96. Citi, *Citi Climate Change Universe* 1 (March 2013).
97. Citi at 9.
98. JP Morgan Chase & Co., *Environmental and Social Policy Framework* (April 2014) available at www.jpmorganchase.com/corporate/Corporate-Responsibility/driving_sustainability_through_business.htm.
99. Lin at 1823; Stefan Heck & Matt Rogers, Resource Revolution: How to Capture the Biggest Business Opportunity in a Century 228 (2014).
100. Lin at 1823.
101. Pollin at 31. *See also* Daniel Gross, *The Real Solyndra Scandal: It's That No One Noticed the Enormous Success of the Government Program behind It,* Slate (June 12, 2015) available at http://www.slate.com/articles/business/the_juice/2015/06/peter_davidson_steps_down_from_energy_department_his_loan_program_was_responsible.html.
102. Mazzucato at 129–32.
103. Pollin at 262.
104. Moniz.
105. Arnulf Grübler at 260–63; 267–69.
106. Arnulf Grübler at 252–55.
107. Lin at 1832.
108. OnPoint, *DOE: ARPA-E Director Martin Discusses Ambitious Process for Jump-starting Energy Technologies* (March 4, 2014) available at www.eenews.net/videos/1793.
109. President's Council of Advisors on Science and Technology, Report to the President on Accelerating the Pace of Change in Energy Technologies through an Integrated Federal Energy Policy (November 2010). *See also* AEIC, Catalyzing American Ingenuity, *supra* note.
110. U.S. Department of Energy, QTR: Report on the First Quadrennial Technology Review (September 2011).
111. Quadrennial Energy Review: Energy Transmission, Storage, and Distribution S-4 (April 2015).
112. U.S. Department of Energy, QTR at 1–4.
113. *Interim Report of Technology Transition Task Force to the Secretary of Energy Advisory Board* (July 20, 2011) available at http://energy.gov/downloads/doetechnologytffinal-junpdf.
114. The White House, *Presidential Memorandum – Establishing a Quadrennial Energy Review* (January 9, 2014).
115. Office of Energy Policy and Systems Analysis, *The Quadrennial Energy Review (QER)* available at http://energy.gov/epsa/quadrennial-energy-review-qer.
116. U.S. Department of Energy, *Quadrennial Energy Review: Scope, Goal, Vision, Approach, Outreach: QER Slideshow* 6 (May 15, 2014).

117. *Id.* at 26.
118. QUADRENNIAL ENERGY REVIEW: ENERGY TRANSMISSION, STORAGE, AND DISTRIBUTION S-4 (April 2015).
119. IEEE Joint Task Force on Quadrennial Energy Review, *IEEE Report to DOE QER on Priority Issues* (September 5, 2014).
120. ADVANCED ENERGY ECONOMY INSTITUTE, MARKETS DRIVE INNOVATION: WHY HISTORY SHOWS THAT THE CLEAN POWER PLAN WILL STIMULATE A ROBUST INDUSTRY RESPONSE (July 2015).

5 CLEAN POWER SYSTEMS

1. John Slocum, *Threat from Behind the Meter: The Case for Utilities to Compete Directly with Distributed Resources*, 151 PUB. UTIL. FORT. 46, 50 (July 2013); *Fereidoon P. Sioshansi, Why the Time Has Come to Rethink the Utility Business Model*, 25 ELECTRICITY J. 65 (August–September 2012).
2. Jon Wellinghoff & Steven Weissman, *The Right to Self-Generate as a Grid Connected Customer*, 36 ENERGY L. J. 101 (2015).
3. The difference between DG and DER is that DG focuses on nonutility electricity generation while DER includes those providers as well as energy efficiency.
4. ELECTRICITY INNOVATION LAB ROCKY MOUNTAIN INSTITUTE, RATE DESIGNED FOR THE DISTRIBUTION EDGE: ELECTRICITY PRICING FOR A DISTRIBUTED RESOURCE FUTURE 11 (August 2014).
5. Joseph Wiedman & Tom Beach, *Distributed Generation Policy: Encouraging Generation on Both Sides of the Meter*, 26 ELECTRICITY J. 88 (October 2013).
6. *Id.* at 11.
7. Rick Fioravanti & Nicholas Abi-Samra, *Working at the Edge of the Grid: How to Find Value in Distributed Energy Resources*, 152 PUB. UTIL. FORT. 32 (May 2014).
8. Electric Power Research Institute, *The Integrated Grid: Realizing the Full Value of Central and Distributed Energy Resources* 10 (2014). *See generally* Peter Kind, *Disruptive Challenges: Financial Implication and Strategic Responses to a Changing Retail Electric Business* 1 (January 2013) (report prepared for the Edison Electric Institute). *See also* Citi Research, *Rising Sun: Implications for US Utilities* 22, 26 (August 8, 2013).
9. Midwest Publishing Company, *Electric Utility Industry Overview* available at w ww.midwestpub.com/electricutility_overview.php.
10. Charles K. Ebinger & John P. Banks, *The Electricity Revolution* (November 8, 2013).
11. Charles E. Bayless, *The End of an Age: Survival in the New Market Requires Embracing New Technologies and Practices*, 152 PUB. UTIL. FORT. 21 (April 2014).
12. Kind at 3. *See also* JOHN STERLING ET AL., TREATMENT OF SOLAR GENERATION IN ELECTRIC UTILITY RESOURCE PLANNING (October 2013) (a report for the National Renewable Energy Laboratory).
13. Michael T. Burr, *Turning Energy Inside Out: Amory Lovins on Negawatts, Renewables, and Neoclassical Markets*, 151 PUB. UTIL. FORT. 29, 31 (March 2013); Amory B. Lovins, *Saving Gigabucks with Negawatts*, 115 PUB. UTIL. FORT. 19 (March 21, 1985). Not surprisingly, the first instinct of incumbents is

to fight. *See e.g.* Fereidoon P. Sioshansi, *Utility of the Future, or Future of the Utility?* Breaking Energy (November 13, 2013).

14. James H. Williams et al., Policy Implications of Deep Decarbonization in the United States 59 (2015) (a report for the Sustainable Development Solutions Network); Joseph P. Tomain, *Building the iUtility*, 146 Pub. Util Fort. 28 (August 2008).
15. Electricity Innovation Lab Rocky Mountain Institute, *New Business Models for the Distribution Edge: The Transition from Value Chain to Value Constellation* 13 (April 2013).
16. Special Report, *Experts Weigh Impact of Distributed Generation on Utility Business Model*, Grid (January 28, 2014).
17. Bloomberg New Energy Finance, 2014 Sustainable Energy in America: Factbook (February 2014).
18. Joseph P. Tomain, Ending Dirty Energy Policy: Prelude to Climate Change ch. 4 (2011).
19. Joel Makower, State of Green Business 2014 (January 21, 2014).
20. Citi Research at 6.
21. Owen Zinaman et al., Power Systems of the Future: the 21st Century Power Partnership Thought Leadership Report 19 (February 2015).
22. Richard K. Lester & David M. Hart, Unlocking Energy Innovation: How America Can Build a Low-cost, Low-Carbon Energy System 19–22 (2012).
23. Bayless at 24.
24. David Malkin & Paul A. Centolella, Results-Based Regulation: A Modern Approach to Modernize the Grid 7 (2013); *Jersey Central Power & Light Co. v. FERC*, 810 F.2d 1168, 1189 (D.C. Cir. 1987) (Starr, J. concurring).
25. Leonard S Hyman, Andrew S. Hyman & Robert C. Hyman, America's Electric Utilities: Past, Present and Future 152 (Table 18–1) and 158 (Table 18–8) (8th ed. 2005).
26. Karl Mcdermott, Edison Elec. Inst., Cost of Service Regulation in the Investor-Owned Electric Utility Industry: A History of Adaptation 17 (2012); Peter Kind, Energy Infrastructure Advocates, Disruptive Challenges: Financial Implications and Strategic Responses to a Changing Retail Electric Business 1 (2013).
27. Harvey Averch & Leland L. Johnson, *Behavior of the Firm under Regulatory Constraint*, 52 Am. Econ. Rev. 1052 (1962); Joseph P. Tomain & Richard D. Cudahy, Energy Law in a Nutshell ch. 4 (2d ed. 2011).
28. Hyman at 164 (Table 19–1) 170 (Table 19–6) and 188 (Table 20–7).
29. Lincoln Davies et al., Energy Law and Policy chs. 4 & 5 (2014).
30. Joseph P. Tomain, Nuclear Power Transformation (1987); Richard J. Pierce, Jr., *The Regulatory Treatment of Mistakes in Retrospect: Cancelled Plants and Excess Capacity*, 132 U. Pa. L. Rev. 497 (1984).
31. *See Jersey Central power & Light, Co. v. FERC*, 810 F.2d 1168 (D.C. Cir 1987). In this case, an en banc panel of the United States Court of Appeals for the District of Columbia upheld a FERC ruling that allowed Jersey Central to recover its investments in a failed nuclear power plant over a 15-year period. Jersey Central

sought to recover a $397 million investment over a 15-year period. Jersey Central wanted to place the unamortized portion that remained each year into the rate base. FERC allowed the 15-year amortization (i.e., allowed the utility to recover $26.4 million as an expense for 15 years) but disallowed including the unamortized portion in the rate base and that ruling was upheld by the Circuit Court.

Regulators applied other rules as well. Some regulators, for example, applied the prudent investment test which held that investments that were prudent when made should be recovered from ratepayers. *See e.g. In re Rochester Gas & Elec. Corp.*, 45 P.U.R. 4th 386 (N.Y. P.S.C. January 13, 1982); *In re United Illuminating Co.*, 55 P.U.R. 4th 252 (Conn. Dept. Pub. Util. Control August 22, 1984). And other regulators applied a used and useful test that held that ratepayers were not to be saddled with the cost of an investment that produced no electricity. See *Duquesne Light Co. v. Barasch*, 488 U.S. 299 (1989). In this case, the Supreme Court upheld a Pennsylvania state statute that mandated that only capital investments that were used and useful could be recovered through rates.

32. Joseph P. Tomain, *Whither Natural Monopoly?: The Case of Electricity* in Peter Z. Grossman & Daniel H. Cole (eds.), The End of a Natural Monopoly: Deregulation and Competition in the Electric Power Industry 111 (2003).
33. Laura M. Holson, *California's Largest Utility Files for Bankruptcy*, N.Y. Times (April 7, 2001).
34. Sidney A. Shapiro & Joseph P. Tomain, *Rethinking Reform of Electricity Markets*, 40 Wake Forest L. Rev. 497 (2005); Joseph P. Tomain & Richard D. Cudahy, Energy Law in a Nutshell 408–22 (2d ed. 2011).
35. Lincoln Davies et al., Energy Law and Policy.
36. *See e.g.* McDermott at viii–x and 17–40 (June 2012). In addition to nuclear power and restructuring, McDermott notes other periods of stress including the rise of inflation during the 1970s, excess capacity in the 1980s, and a current challenge to restore customer and investor confidence in the industry.
37. Joseph P. Tomain, Nuclear Power Transformation (1987).
38. Tomain & Cudahy at 198–201.
39. Severin Borenstein & James Bushnell, *The U.S. Electricity Industry after 20 Years of Restructuring*, 7 Annu. Rev. Econ. 437, 443–45 (May 2015).
40. Ronald Lehr, America's Power Plan: New Utility Business Models: Utility and Regulatory Models for the Modern Era 4 (2013).
41. Hyman at 157(Table 18–7) (8th ed. 2005).
42. U.S. Energy Information Administration, *Electric Power Industry Overview 2007* available at www.eia.gov/electricity/archive/primer/; Hyman at 217 (Table 21–7).
43. Massachusetts Institute of Technology, The Future of the Electric Grid: An Interdisciplinary Study 4 (2011).
44. Ceres, Inc. & Clean Edge, Inc., Benchmarking Utility Clean Energy Deployment: 2014 (July 2014).
45. Navigant Consulting, The 21st Century Electric Utility: Positioning for a Low-Carbon Future (July 2010).
46. Rocky Mountain Institute et al., *The Economics of Grid Defection: When and Where Distributed Solar Generation Plus Storage Competes with Traditional Utility Service* 6 (February 2014).

47. Scott Burger & Max Luke, *Business Models for Distributed Energy Resources: A Review and Empirical Analysis* (April 2016).
48. Edison Electric Institute, *New Regulatory Frameworks for Electric Infrastructure Investment* (May 2011) available at www.eei.org/issuesandpolicy/stateregulation/Pages/RegulatoryFrameworks.aspx.
49. *See e.g. Piedmont Environmental Council v. FERC*, 558 F.3d 304 (4th Cir. 2009).
50. *Transmission Planning and Cost Allocation by Transmission Owning and Operating Public Utilities*, 136 FERC ¶61,051 (July 21, 2011).
51. *See Illinois Commerce Commission v. FERC*, 576 F.3d 470 (7th Cir. 2009); *Illinois Commerce Commission v. FERC*, 756 F.3d 556 (7th Cir. 2014).
52. William Boyd & Ann Carlson, *Accidents of Federalism: Rate Design and Policy Innovation in Public Utility Law*, 63 U.C.L.A. L. Rev. (2016).
53. U.S. Energy Information Agency, Annual Energy Outlook 2015 with Projections To 2040 ES-6, 16–17, 24–26 (April 2015).
54. Hyman at ch. 6.
55. Amory Lovins, *Three Major Energy Trends to Watch*, 6 Solutions J. 6, 7 (Summer 2013).
56. Federal Energy Regulatory Commission, State of the Markets Report 2012 43 (2012).
57. CBS News, *Home Electricity Use in US Falling to 2001 Levels* (December 30, 2013) available at www.cbsnews.com/news/home-electricity-use-in-us-falling-to-2001-levels/.
58. U.S. Department of Energy, Annual Energy Outlook 2013 with Projections to 2040 71 (April 2013).
59. Energy consumption per capita has been relatively flat or declining since roughly 1990. *See* U.S. Energy Information Administration, Annual Energy Review 2011 12 (September 2012).
60. Jason Channel et al., Energy Darwinism: the Evolution of the Energy Industry 75 (October 2013) (a report for Citi GPS).
61. U.S. Department of Energy, Annual Energy Outlook 2013 with Projections to 2040 71 (April 2013).
62. Appliance Standards Awareness Project (ASAP) homepage at www.appliance-standards.org/. The ASAP tracks appliance standards and reports on how state and federal standards reduce carbon emissions and produce energy savings.
63. Rocky Mountain Institute, The Economics Of Grid Defection; Net Energy Metering, Zero Net Energy and the Distributed Energy Resource Future: Adapting Electric Utility Business Models for the 21st Century (2012).
64. Ann Carlson, *Industry Will Try to Keep the Clean Power Plan from Taking Effect Pending Court Decision on Its Legality*, Legal Planet (July 7, 2015) (blog post).
65. Ebinger & Banks.
66. Kind at 3. *See also* John Sterling et al., *Treatment of Solar Generation in Electric Utility Resource Planning* (October 2013) (a National Renewable Energy Laboratory report).
67. Borenstein & Bushnell at 454–55.
68. Bloomberg New Energy Finance, 2014 Sustainable Energy in America: Factbook (February 2014); Makower, State of Green Business.

69. Burr at 31; Amory B. Lovins, *Saving Gigabucks with Negawatts*, 115 Pub. Util. Fort. 19 (March 21, 1985). Not surprisingly, incumbents tend to fight. *See e.g.* Perry Sioshansi, *Utility of the Future, or Future of the Utility?* Breaking Energy (November 13, 2013).
70. Joseph P. Tomain, *Building the iUtility*, 146 Pub. Util. Fort. 28 (August 2008).
71. Massachusetts Institute Of Technology & ITT Comillas, The MIT Utility Of the Future Study: White Paper 22 (December 2013).
72. MIT, *Utility of the Future Study* homepage at https://mitei.mit.edu/research/utility-future-study.
73. *Id.*
74. Massachusetts Institute Of Technology & ITT Comillas at 22.
75. Steven Nadel & Garrett Herndon, The Future of the Utility Industry and the Role of Energy Efficiency viii (June 2104); Electricity Innovation Lab at 12–13.
76. UtilityDive Brand Studio, *2015 State of the Electric Utility: Survey Results* 9 (2015).
77. Richard Fioravanti, *Energy Storage: Out of the Lab and Onto the Grid*, 153 Pub. Util. Fort. 30 (April 2015).
78. Massachusetts Institute Of Technology & ITT Comillas, The MIT Utility of the Future Study 1 (2014). *See also* Massachusetts Institute of Technology & ITT Comillas, The MIT Utility of the Future Study: White Paper (December 2013); Dave Grossman, *Advancing Smart Electricity Networks: A Report of the First Aspen Institute Initiative on Smart Energy and Network Technologies* (2013).
79. Massachusetts Institute Of Technology at 7–10.
80. Joseph Scalise, *California Public Utilities Commission: The Business Model for the Electric Utility of the Future* (October 8, 2013).
81. Ahmad Faruqui & Eric Shultz, *Demand Growth and the New Normal*, 150 Pub. Util. Fort. 22 (December 2012); Bayless at 23.
82. Paul Woods, *The Social Utility*, 150 Pub. Util. Fort. 40 (December 2012).
83. Massachusetts Institute Of Technology at 13.
84. Peter Fox-Penner, Smart Power: Climate Change, the Smart Grid and the Future of Electric Utilities ch. 11 (2010); Hal Harvey, *The Great Reinvention of the Electric Utility* (2015) available at http://americaspowerplan.com/2014/09/the-great-reinvention-of-the-electric-utility/.
85. Navigant at 23–26.
86. Ronald J. Binz et al., Practicing Risk-Aware Electricity Regulation: 2014 Update (November 2014) (a report for Ceres) ("This report, authored by utility industry and finance experts, concludes that almost without exception the riskiest investments for utilities – ones that could cause the most financial harm for utilities, ratepayers and investors – are large base load fossil fuel and nuclear plants. In contrast, energy efficiency, distributed energy and renewable energy . . . are seen as more attractive investments that have lower risks and costs." at 3).
87. Nadel & Herndon at x.
88. Ronald L, Lehr, *New Utility Business Models: Utility and Regulatory Models for the Modern Era*, 26 Electricity J. 35, 42 (October 2013).
89. William Boyd, *Public Utility and the Low-Carbon Future*, 61 U.C.L.A. L. Rev. 1614 (2014).

90. Steve Kihm, Jim Barrett & Casey J. Bell, *Designing a New Utility Business Model? Better Understand the Traditional One First* 1 (2014) (reference omitted).
91. Zinaman at 3.
92. Lehr at 44; Ronald L, Lehr, America's Power Plan: New Utility Business Models: Utility and Regulatory Models for the Modern Era 14 available at http://americaspowerplan.com/wp-content/uploads/2013/10/APP-UTILITIES.pdf.
93. Lehr at 44.
94. Harvey at 1.
95. Zinaman at 4.
96. Jenny Roehm, *Electrifying Your Customer: Five Steps to Better Relations with Your Most Important Client*, 153 PUB. UTIL. FORT. 44 (April 2015).
97. Zinaman at 5.
98. NADEL & HERNDON at x.
99. SCUDDER PARKER & FRANCES HUESSY, WHAT'S A UTILITY TO DO? NEXT GENERATION ENERGY SERVICES AND A NEW PARTNERSHIP TO SERVE CUSTOMERS (2013) (a report for Vermont Energy Investment Corporation).
100. NADEL & HERNDON at viii.
101. PARKER & HUESSY at 8.
102. NADEL & HERNDON at 47–48.
103. Ignacio J. Pérez-Arriage, Scott Burger & Tomás Gómez, *Electricity Services in a More Distributed Energy System* 3 (March 2016).
104. Burger & Luke at 6.
105. Harvey at 3.
106. UtilityDive at 5–6; Tom King, *New Grids Now: Connecting America's Energy Network to the 21st Century* available at http://us.nationalgridconnecting.com/wp-content/uploads/2014/02/Connect21_WhitePaper_high-res.pdf.
107. Amy L. Stein, *Distributed Reliability*, 87 U. COLO. L. REV. 887(2016).
108. IGNACIO PÉREZ-ARRIAGA ET AL., FROM DISTRIBUTION NETWORKS SMART DISTRIBUTION SYSTEMS: RETHINKING THE REGULATION OF EUROPEAN DSOS: FINAL REPORT 41–45 (June 2013).
109. MASSACHUSETTS INSTITUTE OF TECHNOLOGY at 31.
110. Zinaman at 27.
111. PÉREZ-ARRIAGA ET AL. *See also* Burger & Luke at 17–27.
112. PARKER & HUESSY at 3.
113. MASSACHUSETTS INSTITUTE OF TECHNOLOGY at 32 MASSACHUSETTS INSTITUTE OF TECHNOLOGY at 31.
114. Zinaman at 27–29; Sonia Aggarwal & Robbie Orvis, *Distribution Optimization: Ready for Takeoff*, 153 PUB. UTIL. FORT. 32 (June 2015).
115. MASSACHUSETTS INSTITUTE OF TECHNOLOGY at 37.
116. MASSACHUSETTS INSTITUTE OF TECHNOLOGY at 37.
117. UtilityDive at 10.
118. NADEL & HERNDON at 57.
119. Lehr at 43.
120. Electricity Innovation Lab Rocky Mountain Institute at 4.
121. Lehr at 43.
122. LEHR, AMERICA'S POWER PLAN at 16–17.
123. Zinaman at iv.

124. *Id.* at 175–76.
125. Zinaman at 31–37.
126. Fox-Penner at 175.
127. *Id.* at 179–80.
128. Electricity Innovation Lab at 1.
129. Nadel & Herndon at 48–50.
130. Massachusetts Institute Of Technology at 35.
131. Fox-Penner at 189.
132. Electricity Innovation at 13.
133. Zinaman at 22.
134. Zinaman at 22.
135. Lehr at 44.
136. Burger & Luke at 15–16.
137. Zinaman at 22.
138. Ronald Lehr, America's Power Plan at 18–19.
139. Electricity Innovation at 15.
140. Fox-Penner at 198.
141. *Id.* 198–202.
142. Nadel & Herndon at 51.
143. UtilityDive at 7.
144. UtilityDive at 10.
145. UtilityDive at 10.
146. UtilityDive at 17–18; Zinaman at 23.
147. Zinaman at 23; Burger & Luke at 10–15.
148. Fox-Penner at 192–98.
149. UtilityDive at 13.
150. Electricity Innovation at 7.
151. Electricity Innovation at 9.
152. Kind at 14–17.
153. Edison Electric Institute & Natural Resources Defense Council, *EEI/NRDC Joint Statement to State Utility Regulators* (February 12, 2014); *see also* Joseph P. Tomain, *Building the iUtility*, 146 Pub. Util. Fort. 28 (August 2008); *Steel in the Ground: Greening the Grid with the iUtility*, 39 Envt. L. 931 (2009).
154. NRG, *News Release: World's Largest Solar Thermal Power Project at Ivanpah Achieves Commercial Operation* (February 13, 2014).
155. Next Era Energy, *Our Company* available at www.nexteraenergy.com/company/our_company.shtml.
156. Eric Wesoff, *SolarCity and Direct Energy Form $124M Fund for Commercial and Industrial Solar* (September 10, 2013).
157. SolarCity, *SolarCity and Viridian Team to Provide Clean Energy Day and Night* (September 23, 2013).
158. Martin LaMonica, *Inside the Utility-Renewable Power Play* (November 25, 2013).
159. *See* Solar City homepage at www.solarcity.com/residential/. *See also* Sungevity homepage at www.sungevity.com/.
160. Burr at 31 (March 2013) (quoting Amory Lovins).
161. *See* Rocky Mountain Report, *Net Energy Metering* at 47.
162. Burr at 33.

163. Robert Uluski, *Modernization Foundation: Near-Term Vision for Advanced Distribution Management*, 152 PUB. UTIL. FORT. 45 (January 2014).
164. Sara C. Brown & Paul R. McCary, *Peaceful Coexistence: Independent Microgrids Are Coming. Will Franchised Utilities Fight Them or Foster Them?*, 151 PUB UTIL. FORT. 38, 39 (March 2013).
165. As defined by the vendor, Fuel Cell Energy, fuel cells "are electrochemical devices that combine fuel with oxygen from the ambient air to produce electricity and heat, as well as water. The non-combustion, electrochemical process is a direct form of fuel-to-energy conversion, and is much more efficient than conventional heat engine approaches. CO_2 is reduced, due to the high efficiency of the fuel cell, and the absence of combustion avoids the production of NO_x and particulate pollutants." Anthony Leo, *Stationary Fuel Cell Power Systems with Direct FuelCell Technology Tackle Growing Distributed Baseload Power Challenge* available at www.fuelcellenergy.com/products-services/products/.
166. Bloom Energy homepage at www.bloomenergy.com/.
167. Fuel Cell Energy homepage at www.fuelcellenergy.com/.
168. Scott Hempling, *Protecting Innovation during Consolidation: The Advantages of Alertness* (February 2104).
169. Electricity Innovation Lab Rocky Mountain Institute at 9.
170. *Id.*
171. Andrew Kosnaski & Ramesh Shankar, *Embracing Disruption: Developing a Leadership Role for Utilities in Alternative Technologies*, 152 PUB. UTIL. FORT. 16 (January 2014).
172. Electricity Innovation Lab Rocky Mountain Institute at 14–15; *see also* Rocky Mountain Institute Report, *Net Metering Report* at 46.
173. *Id.* at 16; Margaret Jolly, David Logsdon & Christopher Raup, *Capturing Distributed Benefits: Factoring Customer-Owned Generation into Forecasting, Planning, and Operations*, 150 PUB. UTIL. FORT. 32 (August 2012).

6 REGULATORY INNOVATION

1. Jesse D. Jenkins & Ignacio Pérez-Arriaga, *The Remuneration Challenge: New Solutions for the Regulation of Electricity Distribution Utilities under High Penetrations of Distributed Energy Resources and Smart Grid Technologies* 8–9 (September 2014).
2. Ahmad Faruqui & Eric Shultz, *Demand Growth and the New Normal*, 150 PUB. UTIL. FORT. 22 (December 2012); Peter Kind, *Disruptive Challenges: Financial Implications and Strategic Responses to a Changing Retail Electric Business* (January 2013).
3. Jim Pierobon, *Don't Hold Your Breath for Any Progress Stemming from the Joint Statement by NRDC and EEI* (February 17, 2014).
4. GE Digital & Analysis Group, *Results-Based Regulation: A Modern Approach to Modernize the Grid* 7 (2013).
5. *Jersey Central Power & Light, Co. v. FERC*, 810 F.2d 1168, 1189 (D.C. Cir 1987).
6. WILLIAM T. GORMELY JR., THE POLITICS OF PUBLIC UTILITY REGULATIONS (1983); KARL MCDERMOTT, EDISON ELEC. INST., COST OF SERVICE

REGULATION IN THE INVESTOR-OWNED ELECTRIC UTILITY INDUSTRY: A HISTORY OF ADAPTATION 25 (2012).

7. MCDERMOTT at ix.
8. MCDERMOTT at 41.
9. Joseph P. Tomain, *The Dominant Model of United States Energy Policy*, 61 U. COL. L. REV. 355 (1990).
10. National Energy Act of 1978 comprised five major pieces of energy legislation: the Public Utilities Regulatory Policies Act of 1978, Pub. L. No. 95–617, 92 Stat 3117; the Energy Tax Act of 1978, Pub. L. No. 95–618, 92 Stat. 3174; the National Energy Conservation Policy Act of 1978, Pub. L. No. 95–619, 92 Stat. 3206; the Power Plant and Industrial Fuel Use Act of 1978, Pub. L. No. 95–620, 92 Stat. 3289; and, the National Gas Policy Act of 1978, Pub. L. No. 95–621.
11. *Public Utility Regulatory Policies Act* of 1978, Pub. L. No. 95–617.
12. Federal Energy Regulatory Commission, *What Is a Qualifying Facility?* Available at www.ferc.gov/industries/electric/gen-info/qual-fac/what-is.asp.
13. *American Paper Inst., Inc. v. American Elec. Power Serv. Corp.* 461 U.S. 402 (1983).
14. U.S. ENERGY INFORMATION ADMINISTRATION, ELECTRIC POWER MONTHLY WITH DATA FOR OCTOBER 2013 Table ES1.B (December 2013).
15. Michael J. Zimmer, *Cogeneration and Independent Power Production* in DAVID J. MUCHOW & WILLIAM A. MOGEL (eds.), III ENERGY LAW AND TRANSACTIONS ch. 70 at §70.14 (March 2013).
16. Energy Policy Act of 2005, §1251 (16 U.S.C. §2621(d)).
17. U.S. Department of Energy, *Green Power Markets: Net Metering*.
18. Mona L. Hymel, *The United States' Experience with Energy-Based Tax Incentives: The Evidence Supporting Tax Incentives for Renewable Energy*, 38 LOY. U. CHI. L. J. 43 (2006); *Environmental Tax Policy in the United States: A "Bit" of History*, 3 ARIZ. J. ENVTL. L. POL'Y 157 (2013).
19. *Massachusetts v. EPA*, 549 U.S. 497(2007).
20. U.S. Energy Information Administration, *Most States Have Renewable Portfolio Standards* (February 2, 2012) available at www.eia.gov/todayinenergy/detail.cfm?id=4850; *see also* U.S. Department of Energy, *Database of State Incentives for Renewable and Efficiency* (DSIRE) available at www.dsireusa.org/.
21. Richard D. Cudahy, *PURPA: The Intersection of Competition and Regulatory Policy*, 16 ENERGY L. J. 419 (1995).
22. Kind at 4.
23. SIDNEY A. SHAPIRO & JOSEPH P. TOMAIN, ACHIEVING DEMOCRACY: THE FUTURE OF PROGRESSIVE REGULATION (2014).
24. JOSEPH P. TOMAIN, ENDING DIRTY ENERGY POLICY: PRELUDE TO CLIMATE CHANGE ch. 6 (2011); *The iUtility* in ALYSON C. FLOURNOY & DAVID M. DREISEN (eds.), BEYOND ENVIRONMENTAL LAW : POLICY PROPOSALS FOR A BETTER ENVIRONMENTAL FUTURE ch. 10 (2010); *"Steel in the Ground": Greening the Grid with the iUtility*, 39 ENVTL. L. 931 (2009).
25. ENERGY FUTURE COALITION. UTILITY 2.0 9–13 (March 15, 2013); Massachusetts Institute of Technology and IIT-Commillas, *The MIT Utility of the Future Study* 13–14 (2014); JAMES H. WILLIAMS ET AL., POLICY IMPLICATIONS OF DEEP DECARBONIZATION IN THE UNITED STATES 66–71 (2015) (a report for the Sustainable Development Solutions Network).

26. J. Gregory Sidak & Daniel F. Spulber, Deregulatory Takings and the Regulatory Contract: The Competitive Transformation of Network Industries in the United States 29 (1997).
27. David B. Raskin, *The Regulatory Challenge of Distributed Generation*, 4 Harv. Bus. Rev. Online 38, 47 (2013).
28. Kind at 18.
29. Andrew Kosnaski & Ramesh Shankar, *Embracing Disruption: Developing a Leadership Role for Utilities in Alternative Technologies*, 152 Pub. Util. Fort. 16 (January 2014); Raskin at 48.
30. *Compare* Sidak & Spulber *with* Susan Rose-Ackerman & Jim Rossi, *Disentangling Deregulatory Takings*, 71 N.Y.U. L. Rev. 851 (1996).
31. Kind at 10.
32. Robert E. Curry, Jr., *The Law of Unintended Consequences: The Transition to Distributed Generation Calls for a New Regulatory Model*, 151 Pub. Util. Fort. 44, 147 (March 2013).
33. *Market Street Railway Co. v. Railroad Commission of California*, 324 U.S. 548 (1945).
34. Jason Channel et al., Energy Darwinism: The Evolution of The Energy Industry 73 (October 2013) (a report for Citi GPS).
35. Electricity Innovation Lab Rocky Mountain Institute, New Business Models for the Distribution Edge: The Transition From Value Chain To Value Constellation 8 (April 2013).
36. Owen Zinaman et al., *Power Systems of the Future: A 21st Century Power Partnership Thought Leadership Report* 3 (February 2015).
37. Joel Makower, State of Green Business 2014 (January 21, 2014); Citi Research, *Citi Climate Change Universe* (March 5, 2013) (projecting the need for $37 trillion in energy transformation over the next 50 years with $24 trillion of that amount devoted to clean energy including gas and $6 trillion in renewable power generation).
38. Ashley Brown & Jillian Bunyan, *Valuation of Distributed Solar: A Qualitative View*, 27 Electricity J. 27 (December 2014).
39. R. Thomas Beach & Patrick G. McGuire, *Evaluating the Benefits and Costs of Net Energy Metering in California* (January 2013).
40. Brad Copithorne, *Four Utilities Thinking Beyond "Wires and Poles"* (October 9, 2013).
41. Amory Lovins, *Don't Cry for the Electric Utilities*, Rocky Mountain Institute (February 12, 2014).
42. *In Re Restructuring New Hampshire's Electric Utility Industry*, 171 P.U.R.4th 564 (N.H. P.U.C. 1996) (footnotes omitted).
43. James C. Bonbright, Principles of Public Utility Rates (1961).
44. James C. Bonbright, Albert L. Danielsen & David R. Kamerschen, Principles of Public Utility Rates ch. 4 (2d ed. 1988); Charles F. Phillips, Jr., The Regulation of Public Utilities: Theory And Practice Part II (2d ed. 1988); Joseph P. Tomain & Richard D. Cudahy, Energy Law in a Nutshell ch. 4 (2d ed. 2011).
45. McDermott at 18–23 (fuel adjustment mechanisms); Mark Newton Lowry, Matthew Makos & Gretchen Waschbusch, *Alternative Regulation for Evolving Utility challenges: An Updated Survey* 5–13 (January 2013) (a report for the Edison

Electric institute) (on cost trackers); another mechanism, known as construction work in progress, recovers costs during construction periods.

46. *Id.*
47. Lowry at 31–36.
48. This tendency to invest and expand is also known as the A-J effect, or the Averch-Johnson effect, based upon the seminal paper Harvey Averch & Leland L. Johnson, *Behavior of the Firm under Regulatory Constraint*, 52 AM. ECON. REV. 1052 (1962).
49. GE Digital at 3.
50. Kind at 1.
51. Michael T. Burr, *Turning Energy Inside Out: Amory Lovins on Negawatts, Renewables, and Neoclassical Markets*, 151 PUB. UTIL FORT. 29, 30 (March 2013) (quoting Amory Lovins).
52. Jesse D. Jenkins & Ignacio J. Pérez-Arriaga, *Improved Regulatory Approaches for the Remuneration of Electricity Distribution Utilities with High Penetrations of Distributed Energy Resources*, 38 ENERGY J. ___ (forthcoming 2017).
53. TOMAIN, ENDING DIRTY ENERGY POLICY at 174–79.
54. MICHAEL R. SCHMIDT, PERFORMANCE-BASED RATEMAKING: THEORY AND PRACTICE (2000).
55. Scott H. Strauss & Jeffrey A. Schwarz, *Transmission Incentive Overhaul: FERC's ROE Incentive Adder Policy Sends the Wrong Signals*, 149 PUB. UTIL. FORT. 32 (February 2009).
56. Lowry.
57. SCOTT HEMPLING, REGULATING PUBLIC UTILITY PERFORMANCE: THE LAW OF MARKET STRUCTURE AND JURISDICTION ch. 7 (2013).
58. Regulatory Assistance Project, *Revenue Regulations and Decoupling: A Guide to Theory and Application* (August 2011); *see also* Lowry at 15–21.
59. U.S. Energy Information Administration, *Feed-in Tariff: A Policy Tool Encouraging Deployment of Renewable Electricity Technologies* (May 30, 2013).
60. David Malkin & Paul A. Centolella, *Results-Based Regulation: A More Dynamic Approach to Grid Modernization*, 152 PUB. UTIL. FORT. 28 (March 2014).
61. SOLAR ELECTRIC POWER ASSOCIATION, RATEMAKING, SOLAR VALUE AND SOLAR NET ENERGY METERING – A PRIMER 14 (2013).
62. Philip Q. Hanser, *Rate Design by Objective*, 150 PUB. UTIL. FORT. 48, 49 (September 2012).
63. GE Digital at 14.
64. PAMELA MORGAN, A DECADE OF DECOUPLING FOR US ENERGY UTILITIES: RATE IMPACTS, DESIGNS, AND OBSERVATIONS (rev. February 2013).
65. Edison Electric Institute & Natural Resources Defense Council, *EEI/NRDC Joint Statement to State Utility Regulators* 2 (February 12, 2014).
66. John Sterling, *Getting Past New Metering: A Forward-Looking Solution to Rate Reform, for When Solar Costs Hit Bottom*, 153 PUB. UTIL. FORT. 38 (December 2015).
67. GE Digital at 14–16.
68. Rocky Mountain Institute, *Net Energy Metering, Zero Net Energy and the Distributed Energy Resource Future: Adapting Electric Utility Business Models for the 21st Century* 46 (March 2012).

69. Electricity Innovation Lab at 14.
70. Rocky Mountain Report, *Net Energy Metering* at 43.
71. Electricity Innovation Lab at 13–14.
72. Electricity Innovation Lab at 10.
73. *Id.* at 10.
74. Rocky Mountain Report, *Net Energy Metering* at 41.
75. Rocky Mountain Report, *Net Energy Metering* at 36–47.
76. Jesse D. Jenkins & Ignacio J. Pérez-Arriaga, *Improved Regulatory Approaches for the Remuneration of Electricity Distribution Utilities with High Penetrations of Distributed Energy Resources*, 38 Energy J. (forthcoming 2017).
77. *Utility Reform Network v. California PUC*, 2014 Cal. App. LEXIS 119 (February 5, 2014); *In Re Petition of Northern States Power Co. to Initiate a Competitive Resource Acquisition Process*, MPUC Docket No. E-002/CN-12-1240 (March 5, 2013).
78. Joseph Hall & Thomas Gorman, Market Manipulation: The Business Questions, 153 Pub. Util. Fort. 52 (November 2015).
79. Douglas Canter, Ronald H. Levine & Abraham J. Rein, *Market Manipulation: Staying a Step Ahead*, 153 Pub. Util. Fort. 22 (April 2015).
80. New York Public Service Commission, *Order Adopting Regulatory Policy Framework and Implementation Plan* 62–72 (February 26, 2015) (Framework Order).
81. MIT Energy Initiative, The MIT Utility of The Future Study: White Paper (December 2013).
82. Electric Power Research Institute, The Integrated Grid: Realizing The Full Value of Central And Distributed Energy Sources (2014) (EPRI).
83. Gridwise Alliance, *The Future of the Grid: Evolving to Meet America's Needs* (December 2014) (a report for the U.S. Department of Energy).
84. Electric Power Research Institute, The Integrated Grid: A Benefit-Cost Framework (February 2015) (EPRI: Benefit-Cost).
85. Ken Silverstein, *Diversifying Utility Regulation: State Regulators Voice Opinions as Mixed as the Nation's Geography*, 152 Pub. Util. Fort. 24 (November 2014); William C. Miller, Roland J. Risser & Steven Kline, *Regulatory Policies for the Transition to the New Business Paradigm* in Fereidoon P. Sioshansi (ed.), Distributed Generation and Its Implications for the Utility Industry 321 (2014).
86. EPRI at 36; *see also* Electricity Innovation Lab at 13.
87. Advanced Energy Economy Institute, Toward A 21st Century Electricity System In California (August 11, 2015); Rocky Mountain Institute, Net Energy Metering.
88. John Farrell, *Beyond Utility 2.0 to Energy Democracy* 33–36 (December 2014) (a report for the Institute for Self Reliance).
89. E21 Initiative, Phase I Report: Charting A Path To A 21st Century Energy System In Minnesota (December 2014).
90. e21 Initiative, *Working Paper: Overview of the Current Utility Business Model in Minnesota* 2 (February 2014).
91. *Id.*

92. *Id.*
93. e21 Initiative, *Working Paper: Summary of Complementary Utility Regulatory Reform and Business Model Initiatives* 7–8 (February 2014).
94. E21 INITIATIVE, PHASE I REPORT at 1; *see also* John P. Banks, *Why Performance-Based Regulation Is Important for the Electric Utility Transformation*, BROOKINGS: PLANETPOLICY (December 3, 2015) (blogpost).
95. *Id.*
96. New York State Department of Public Service, *Staff White Paper on Ratemaking and Utility Business Models* 33–37 (July 28, 2015) (*White Paper*).
97. E21 INITIATIVE, PHASE I REPORT at 17.
98. E21 INITIATIVE, PHASE I REPORT at 20–21.
99. E21 INITIATIVE, PHASE I REPORT at 4.
100. E21 INITIATIVE, PHASE I REPORT at 21.
101. GRID RESILIENCY TASK FORCE, WEATHERING THE STORM (September 24, 2012).
102. ENERGY FUTURE COALITION. UTILITY 2.0 1–4 (March 15, 2013).
103. ENERGY FUTURE COALITION at 6.
104. ENERGY FUTURE COALITION at 20.
105. ENERGY FUTURE COALITION at 20–25.
106. ENERGY FUTURE COALITION at 24.
107. ENERGY FUTURE COALITION at 25.
108. ENERGY FUTURE COALITION at 32.
109. Maryland Energy Administration homepage at http://energy.maryland.gov/.
110. Baltimore Gas & Electric Co. homepage at www.bge.com/; Pepco home page at www.pepco.com/.
111. New York Public Service Commission, *Order Adopting Regulatory Policy Framework and Implementation Plan* (February 26, 2015) (Framework Order).
112. Andrew O. Kaplan, *REV'ed and Ready to Go*, 153 PUB. UTIL. FORT. 16, 17 (May 2015).
113. Framework Order at 3.
114. Framework Order at 12.
115. NEW YORK STATE ENERGY PLANNING BOARD, THE ENERGY TO LEAD: 2015 NEW YORK STATE ENERGY PLAN VOL. 1 (2015).
116. New York State Department of Public Service Staff, *Reforming the Energy Vision* 1–2; 6–7 (April 24, 2014) (REV); *see also* Framework Order at 16–30.
117. Framework Order at 22–23.
118. KEN BERLIN ET AL., STATE CLEAN ENERGY FINANCE BANKS: NEW INVESTMENT FACILITIES FOR CLEAN ENERGY DEPLOYMENT (September 2012); Hallie Kennan, *Working Paper: State Green Banks for Clean Energy* (January 2014) (report for Energy Innovation Policy and Technology, LLC).
119. REV at 9–10.
120. Framework Order at 31–45.
121. Framework Order at 49.
122. Framework Order at 51–53; 62–72.
123. REV at 30–43.
124. Framework Order at 53–61.
125. REV at 33–35.

126. *See also* New York State Department of Public Service, *Staff White Paper on Ratemaking and Utility Business Models* 23–27 (July 28, 2015) (*White Paper*).
127. *White Paper* at 18–21.
128. REV at 46–50.
129. *White Paper* at 70–73.
130. Benjamin Mandel, *Toward Policy-Responsive Performance-Based Regulation in New York State* (March 2015) (a report for Guarini Center: Environment, Energy and Land Use Law – NYU Law School); Sonia Aggarwal & Eddie Burgess, *New Regulatory Models* (March 2014).
131. Guarini Center: Environment, Energy and Land Use Law – NYU Law School, *Building New York's Future Electricity Markets: Identifying Policy Prerequisites and Market Relationships* 6–7 (July 2015).
132. *White Paper; see also* CARL LINVILL, JOHN SHENOT & JIM LAZAR, DESIGNING DISTRIBUTED GENERATION TARIFFS WELL: ENSURING FAIR COMPENSATION IN A TIME OF TRANSITION (November 2013) (a report for Regulatory Assistance Project).
133. Steve Kihm et al., *You Get What You Pay For: Moving Toward Value in Utility Compensation: Part One – Revenue and Profit* (June 2015).
134. *White Paper* at 73–74.
135. *Compare* Ahmad Faruqui, *The Case for Introducing Demand Charges in Residential Tariffs* (June 25, 2015) (in favor of demand charges) *with* Barbara R. Alexander, *Residential Demand Charges: A Consumer Perspective* (June 2015) (opposed).
136. *White Paper* at 73–76; 95–106.
137. *White Paper* at 9–11.
138. *White Paper* at 22.
139. *White Paper* at 10.
140. *White Paper* at 31–33.
141. *White Paper* at 95.
142. ELECTRICITY INNOVATION LAB at 21–29.
143. Framework Order at 118.
144. Framework Order at 119.
145. Guarini Center: Environment, Energy and Land Use Law – NYU Law School, *Building New York's Future Electricity Markets* at 2–4.
146. David J. O'Brien, *Searching for Equilibrium: How to Achieve It in the Era of Distributed Energy*, 153 PUB. UTIL. FORT. 20, 26 (August 2015).

7 ENERGY AND DEMOCRACY

1. Joseph P. Tomain, *Katrina Consequences: What Has Government Learned?: To a Point*, 52 LOYOLA L. REV. 1201 (2006); *Lost in the Flood*, 23 PACE ENVT. L. REV. 219 (2005–2006) (review of ADRIAN J. BRADBROOK ET AL., EDS., THE LAW OF ENERGY FOR SUSTAINABLE DEVELOPMENT (2005)).
2. LINCOLN L. DAVIES ET AL., ENERGY LAW AND POLICY 19–22 (2014).
3. Lincoln L. Davies, *Beyond Fukushima: Disasters, Nuclear Energy, and Energy Law*, 2011 BRIGHAM YOUNG L. REV. 1937 (2011).

4. U.S.-Canada Power System Outage Task Force, Final Report on the August 14, 2003 Blackout in the United States and Canada: Causes and Recommendations (April 2004).
5. Joseph P. Tomain, *The Past and Future of Electricity Regulation*, 32 Envt. L. 435 (2002); Severin Borenstein, *The Trouble with Electricity Markets: Understanding California's Restructuring Disaster*, 16 J. Econ. Persp. 191, 198–200 (2002).
6. Total costs of the 2003 U.S.-Canadian blackout, as an example, were estimated between $4 billion and $10 billion. U.S.-Canada Power System Outage Task Force at 1.
7. Jennie C. Stephens, Elizabeth J. Wilson & Tarla Rai Peterson, Smart Grid (R)evolution 15 (2015).
8. John Farrell, *Beyond Utility 2.0 to Energy Democracy* 29 (December 2014) (a report for the Institute for Self Reliance).
9. Jedediah Purdy, *The Politics of Nature: Climate Change, Environmental Law, and Democracy*, 119 Yale L. J. 1122, 1125 (2010).
10. Institute for Energy Research, *A Primer on Energy and the Economy: Energy's Large Share of the Economy Requires Caution in Determining Policies That Affect It* (February 16, 2010); Gregor MacDonald, *Here's What Happens When US Energy Spending Passes 9% of GDP*, Business Insider (June 11, 2011).
11. Joseph P. Tomain, *The Dominant Model of United States Energy Policy*, 61 Univ. Colorado L. Rev. 355 (1990).
12. Farrell at 2–3.
13. MIT, *Utility of the Future Study* at https://mitei.mit.edu/research/utility-future-study.
14. Jesse D. Jenkins & Ignacio Pérez-Arriaga, *The Remuneration Challenge: New Solutions for the Regulation of Electricity Distribution Utilities Under High Penetrations of Distributed Energy Resources and Smart Grid Technologies* 8–9 (September 2014).
15. Jenkins & Pérez-Arriaga at 25.
16. Massoud Amin, *Microgrids and Battery Storage: In Search of Enlightened Policy to Build a Solid Business Case*, 154 Pub. Util. Fort. 28 (January 2016).
17. Ignacia Pérez-Arriaga & Ashwini Bharatkumar, *A Framework for Redesigning Distribution Network Use of System Charges under High Penetration of Distributed Energy Resources: Principles for New Problems* (October 2014).
18. Peter Bronski et al., *The Economics of Load Defection: How Grid-Connected Solar-Plus-Battery Systems Will Compete with Traditional Electric Service, Why It Matters, and Possible Paths Forward* (April 2015) (a report for Rocky Mountain Institute & Homer Energy).
19. Farrell at 29–30.
20. Jan Vrins et al., *From Grid to Cloud: A Network of Networks – In Search of an Orchestrator*, 153 Pub. Util. Fort. 50 (October 2015).
21. Energy.Gov: Office of Electricity Delivery & Energy Reliability, *The Role of Microgrids in Helping to Advance the Nation's Energy System* at http://energy.gov/oe/services/technology-development/smart-grid/role-microgrids- helping-advance-nation-s-energy-system.
22. Michael T. Burr, *Economy of Small: How DG and Microgrids Change the Game for Utilities*, 151 Pub. Util. Fort. 20 (May 2013).

23. Farrell at 30–31.
24. JOHN FARRELL, ADVANTAGE LOCAL – WHY LOCAL ENERGY OWNERSHIP MATTERS (September 2014) (a report for the Institute for Self Reliance).
25. Farrell at 39.
26. Ashley Brown & Jillian Bunyan, *Valuation of Distributed Solar: A Quantitative View*, 27 ELECTRICITY J. 27 (December 2014); Robert L. Borick, *An Empirical Analysis of New Metering* (February 28, 2014) (PowerPoint presentation to the Harvard Electricity Policy Group).
27. Sunil Cherian, Integrated Energy: *Distributed Energy + Distributed Controls = Distributed Benefits*, 152 PUB. UTIL. FORT. 18 (December 2014).
28. Scudder Parker & Frances Huessy, *What's a Utility to Do: Next-Generation Energy Services and a New Partnership to Serve Customers* 3 (November 2013).
29. Uma Outka, *Cities and the Low-Carbon Grid*, 46 ENVT. L. 105 (2016).
30. E&ETV, *TFC Utilities' Kellerman Says Power Plan, Paris Agreement Catalysts for Transforming Electric Power Sector* (January 12, 2016) available at www.eenews.net/videos/2073.
31. Black & Veatch Insights Group, 2015 *Strategic Directions: U.S. Electric Industry Report* 28 (2105).
32. ENCYCLICAL LETTER at ¶¶ 179–80.
33. PURDY, AFTER NATURE at ch. 8.
34. Sarah Krakoff, *Planetarian Identity Formation and the Relocalization of Environmental Law*, 64 FLORIDA L. REV. 87, 90 (2012).
35. 350.org is a grassroots organization that coordinates a global network of public actions. Its homepage can be found at http://350.org/about/what-we-do/.
36. Krakoff at 107–33.
37. The Solutions Project homepage at http://thesolutionsproject.org/.
38. Krakoff at 118–20.
39. Krakoff at 91.
40. ENCYCLICAL LETTER at ¶183.
41. Sonia Aggarwal & Hal Harvey, *Rethinking Policy to Deliver a Clean Energy Future*, 26 ELECTRICITY J. 7, 12 (October 2013).
42. US DEPARTMENT OF ENERGY, MONTHLY ENERGY REVIEW 4–6 (February 2015).
43. NATIONAL RENEWABLE ENERGY LABORATORY, RENEWABLE ELECTRICITY FUTURES STUDY: EXECUTIVE SUMMARY iii (2012).
44. Aggarwal & Harvey at 8.
45. Aggarwal & Harvey at 11.
46. William Boyd, *Public Utility and the Low-Carbon Future*, 61 U.C.L.A. L. REV. 1614, 1634 (2014).
47. Peter Asmus, *Microgrids: Friend or Foe for Utilities?*, 153 PUB. UTIL. FORT. 19, 20 (February 2015).
48. Joseph P. Tomain, *Smart Grid, Clean Energy and US Policy*, 13 J. COMPETITION AND REG. IN NETWORK INDUSTRIES 187 (2012).
49. Hannah J. Wiseman, *Urban Energy*, 40 FORDHAM URB. L. J. 1793 (2013); Amy L. Stein, *Distributed Reliability*, 87 U. COLO. L. REV. (forthcoming 2016).
50. Boyd at 1682; ADRENE BRIONES ET AL., VEHICLE-TO-GRID (V2G) POWER FLOW REGULATIONS AND BUILDING CODES REVIEW BY THE AVTA (September 2012);

Willett Kempton, Yannick Perez & Marc Petit, *Public Policy for Electric Vehicles and for Vehicle to Grid Power* (2014).

51. TOMAIN, ENDING DIRTY ENERGY POLICY at ch. 6; Joseph P. Tomain, *Traditionally-Structured Electric Utilities in a Distributed Generation World*, 38 NOVA L. REV. 473 (2014); American Council on Renewable Energy, *Evolving Business Models for Renewable Energy: 2014 Industry Review* 5–10 (June 2014).
52. Office of Ohio Consumers' Council, *The Basics of Governmental Energy Aggregation* (2011).
53. "A micro grid is a group of interconnected loads and distributed energy resources within clearly defined electrical boundaries that acts as a single controllable entity with respect to the grid." "Virtual power plants are groups of distributed generation assets managed by one entity." James Newcomb et al., *Distributed Energy Resources: Policy Implications of Decentralization* 46 notes 36 and 87, 26 ELECTRICITY J. 65 (October 2013).
54. American Council on Renewable Energy, *Evolving Business Models for Renewable Energy: 2014 Industry Review* 5 (June 2014).
55. Boyd at 1628; *Local Energy* at 897.
56. Philip R. O'Connor & Erin M. O'Connell-Diaz, *Evolution of the Revolution: The Sustained Success of Retail Electricity Competition* (July 2015).
57. Farrokh Rahimi & Sasan Mokhtari, *From ISO to DSO: Imagining a New Construct – An Independent System Operator for the Distribution Network*, 152 PUB. UTIL. FORT. 42 (June 2014).
58. Asmus at 20.
59. *Local Energy* at 897–99.
60. STEPHENS, WILSON & PETERSON at 28.
61. *Id.* at 29.
62. Joseph Wiedman & Tom Beach, *Distributed Generation Policy: Encouraging Generation on Both Sides of the Meter*, 26 ELECTRICITY J. 88, 89 (October 2013).
63. Asmus at 19.
64. *Local Energy* at 947–48. See also Uma Outka, *Intrastate Preemption in the Shifting Energy Sector*, 86 COLORADO L. REV. 927 (2015).
65. Boyd at 1682.
66. David B. Spence, *The Political Economy of Local Vetoes*, 93 TEXAS L. REV. 351 (2014); Hannah J. Wiseman, *Governing Fracking from the Ground Up*, 93 TEXAS L. REV. 29 (2015).
67. NAOMI KLEIN, THIS CHANGES EVERYTHING: CAPITALISM VS. CLIMATE 10 (2014); Purdy at 1193–99.
68. Uma Outka, *Intrastate Preemption in the Shifting Energy Sector*, 86 COLORADO L. REV. 927 (2015).
69. Weidman & Beach at 101–03.
70. Hannah J. Wiseman, *Urban Energy*, 40 FORDHAM URB. L. J. 1793 (2013).
71. Environmental Protection Agency, *Carbon Pollution Emission Guidelines for Existing Stationary Sources: Electric Generating Units* [EPA-HQ-OAR-2013–0602; FRL-XXXX-XX-OAR] RIN 2060-AR33 963 (August 4, 2015) (FINAL RULE).
72. 40 C.F.R. §60.23 (2014).
73. FINAL RULE at 963–67.

74. GRIDWISE ALLIANCE, THE FUTURE OF THE GRID: EVOLVING TO MEET AMERICA'S NEEDS 21–22 (December 2014) (a report for the U.S. Department of Energy).
75. Parker & Huessy at 18–19.
76. *Local Energy* at 916–17.
77. E2 ENVIRONMENTAL ENTREPRENEURS, CLEAN ENERGY WORKS FOR US: 2013 YEAR-IN-REVIEW AND Q4 REPORT (February 2014); AMERICAN COUNCIL FOR AN ENERGY-EFFICIENT ECONOMY, HOW DOES ENERGY EFFICIENCY CREATE JOBS? (undated); RACHEL GOLD, STATE BY STATE, APPLIANCE STANDARDS SAVE MONEY, CREATE JOBS, AND PROTECT THE ENVIRONMENT (May 25, 2011) (a report for the American Council for an Energy-Efficient Economy); CASEY BELL, PROVING ENERGY EFFICIENCY CREATES JOBS: SEEKING A NEW STANDARD MODEL (January 22, 2014) (a report for the American Council for an Energy-Efficient Economy); ACORE, CALCEF & CLIMATE POLICY INITIATIVE, STRATEGIES TO SCALE-UP U.S. RENEWABLE ENERGY INVESTMENT (2013); ENVIRONMENTAL AND ENERGY STUDY INSTITUTE, FACT SHEET: JOBS IN RENEWABLE ENERGY AND ENERGY EFFICIENCY (2014) MCKINSEY GLOBAL ENERGY AND MATERIALS, UNLOCKING ENERGY EFFICIENCY IN THE U.S. ECONOMY (July 2009).
78. SARA HASTINGS-SIMON, DICKON PINNER & MARTIN STUCHTEY, MYTHS AND REALITIES OF CLEAN TECHNOLOGIES (April 2014) (a report for McKinsey & Company).
79. REN21, RENEWABLES 2014 GLOBAL STATUS REPORT 72 (2014).
80. *Local Energy* at 881–82, 933–34.
81. *Id.* at 883–84 and 936–40.
82. *Local Energy* at 936–37.
83. Mayors Climate Protection Center, *About the Mayors Climate Protection Center* available at www.usmayors.org/climateprotection/about.asp; C40Cities, *Climate Leadership Group* available at http://www.c40.org/; UN Sustainable Development Knowledge Platform, *Cities for Climate Protection Campaign* available at https://sustainabledevelopment.un.org/index.php?page=view&type=1006&menu=1348&nr=1498 (sites last visited March 10, 2015).
84. Aggarwal & Harvey at 10.
85. Chris Vlahoplus et al., *Community Solar: Answers to Questions You Were Afraid to Ask*, 153 PUB. UTIL. FORT. 32 (December 2015).
86. Boyd at 1683–93.
87. *Local Energy* at 922–31.
88. *Local Energy* at 940–48.
89. Purdy at 1138.
90. Boyd at 1682.

Index